MULTINATIONAL ENTERPRISES IN LESS DEVELOPED COUNTRIES

Multinational Enterprises in Less Developed Countries

Edited by

Peter J. Buckley
Professor of Managerial Economics
University of Bradford Management Centre

and

Jeremy Clegg
Lecturer in Business Economics
University of Bath

MACMILLAN

First published 1991

Published by
MACMILLAN ACADEMIC AND PROFESSIONAL LTD
Houndmills, Basingstoke, Hampshire RG21 2XS
and London
Companies and representatives
throughout the world

Printed in Great Britain by
WBC Ltd, Bridgend

British Library Cataloguing in Publication Data
Multinational enterprise in less developed countries.
1. Developing countries. Multinational companies
I. Buckley, Peter J. (Peter Jennings), 1949– II. Clegg, Jeremy
338.8881724
ISBN 0–333–52688– 0

For Alice and Alicia

Contents

List of Tables   ix

List of Figures   xii

Preface and Acknowledgements   xiii

List of Contributors   xv

PART I   INTRODUCTION   1

1   Introduction and Statement of the Issues
    Peter J. Buckley and Jeremy Clegg   3

PART II   THEORY   25

2   Multinational Enterprises in Less Developed
    Countries: Cultural and Economic Interactions
    Peter J. Buckley and Mark Casson   27
3   On the Transferability of Management Systems: The
    Case of Japan
    Klaus Weiermair   56

PART III   MARKET STRUCTURE AND WELFARE
           EFFECTS   77

4   Strategic Trade Policy and the Multinational
    Enterprise in Developing Countries
    Edward M. Graham   79
5   Market Rivalry, Government Policies and
    Multinational Enterprise in Developing Countries
    Homi Katrak   92
6   The Impact of Foreign Investment on Less Developed
    Countries: Cross-Section Analysis versus Industry
    Studies
    Rhys Jenkins   111

PART IV   TRADE AND INVESTMENT   131

7   Countertrade: Theory and Evidence
    Mark Casson and Francis Chukujama   133
8   Factors Influencing Foreign Direct Investment by

Transnational Corporations in Host Developing
Countries: A Preliminary Report
Donald J. Lecraw 163

PART V EMPIRICAL STUDIES OF FOREIGN
DIRECT INVESTMENT IN LESS
DEVELOPED COUNTRIES 181

9 Foreign Multinationals and Industrial Development in
Africa
John Cantwell 183
10 Yugoslav Foreign Direct Investment in Less
Developed Countries
Patrick Artisien, Matija Rojec and Marjan Svetlicic 225
11 The Evolution of Multinationals from a Small
Economy: A Study of Swedish Firms in Asia
Raj Aggarwal and Pervez N. Ghauri 248
12 Multinational Activity in the Mediterranean Rim
Textile and Clothing Industry
Jim Hamill 270
13 Service Sector Multinationals and Developing
Countries
Peter Enderwick 292

PART VI SUMMARY AND CONCLUSION 311

14 Some Concluding Remarks
John H. Dunning 313

Bibliography 322

Index 343

List of Tables

2.1 Factors in the Long-run Economic Success of a
    Nation   33
6.1 Choice of Technique – Results of Studies using
    Samples of Firms (Excluding Matched Pairs)   115
6.2 Choice of Technique – Results of Studies Using
    Matched Pairs   117
6.3 Results of Studies of Research and Development   119
6.4 Results of Studies of Export Performance   121
6.5 Results of Studies of Import Propensities   122
6.6 Results of Studies Comparing Wages   124
7.1 Regression Analysis of the Propensity to Engage in
    Counterpurchase in a Cross Section Sample of 35
    Countries   153
7.2 Regression Analysis Disaggregated by Type of
    Country   154
7.3 Regression Analysis of the Propensity to Engage in
    Buy-Back   158
8.1 Variable Definition and Sign   175
8.2 Statistical Results   178
9.1 Average Annual Flow of Inward Foreign Direct
    Investment, 1974–85   185
9.2 Sectoral Distribution of Foreign Direct Capital
    Stock, 1975   187
9.3 Percentage Distribution of Foreign Direct Capital
    Stock, 1975   188
9.4 Sectoral Distribution of Foreign Direct Capital
    Stock, 1982   188
9.5 Percentage Distribution of Foreign Direct Capital
    Stock, 1982   190
9.6 The Sectoral Distribution of Foreign Direct Capital
    Stock in 16 Non-African Developing Countries in
    1982 (%), for Comparative Purposes   192
9.7 The Sectoral Distribution of Numbers of Foreign
    Affiliates in Africa Based on Counts for 1982–83   200
9.8 A List of some of the Most Historically Significant
    Investors in Africa   206
9.9 The Revealed Comparative Advantage of

Developing Africa in Total Developing Country
Exports   213
9.10 The Revealed Comparative Disadvantage of
Developing Africa in Total Developing Country
Imports   214
9.11 A Typology of Foreign Multinationals with Interests
in Africa, and the Industrial and Geographical
Characteristics of their Investments   219
10.1 Number of Yugoslav Economic Entities Abroad,
end of 1986   227
10.2 Sectoral Distribution of Yugoslav Enterprises in
LDCs, mid-1987   230
10.3 Ownership Structure of Yugoslav FDI in LDCs, 1986   231
10.4 Motives of Yugoslav Investors in LDCs   234
10.5 Reasons for Preferring a Minority-Owned Joint
Venture   237
10.6 Impact of Legal Constraints in 15 Host Countries
(LDCs) on % Share of Equity in Yugoslav
Minority-Owned Joint Ventures   239
10.7 Major Problems of Yugoslav Enterprises in
Developing Countries   243
11.1 The Seven Phases of the Product Life Cycle Theory   254
11.2 Swedish Foreign Direct Investment   258
11.3 Swedish Foreign Direct Investment by Areas of the
World   259
11.4 Largest Swedish Firms in Terms of 1986 Sales   260
11.5 Employment Abroad in Foreign Subsidiaries of
Swedish Firms   261
11.6 Reinvested Profits in Swedish Foreign Direct
Investments   262
11.7 Acquisitions of Foreign Production Companies by
Swedish Companies   262
12.1 Growth and Characteristics of Mediterranean Rim
Textiles: Summary Table by Country   274
12.2 Textile Exports of Selected Mediterranean Rim
Countries to the OECD 1974–86   276
12.3 Textile Exports from Selected Mediterranean Rim
Countries by Destination (1986)   276
12.4 Distribution of Mediterranean Textile Exports
within EC (1986)   277

12.5   Foreign Participation in the Maltese Textile Industry
       (1985)   281
12.6   Stock of Foreign Direct Investment in the Maltese
       Textile Industry by Country of Origin (1985)   282
12.7   Foreign Investment in Morocco: 1985 and 1986   283
12.8   Foreign Investment in Turkey's Textile Industry   285
12.9   Factors Influencing the Future Competitiveness of
       Mediterranean Rim Textile Producers   287
12.10 Mediterranean Rim Textiles and Clothing: Industry
       Restructuring and Future Prospects   290
13.1   Analysis of Service Exports for Selected Countries
       1981   294
13.2   Service Sector Direct Investment Abroad as a
       Percentage of Total Stock of Direct Investment   297
13.3   Service Sector Growth Rates 1965–82 and Level of
       Economic Development   298
13.4   Technology Receipts in Relation to Direct
       Investment Income from Affiliates for US Parents by
       Industry 1977   300

List of Figures

2.1 The Development of International Trade between
    Developed Countries   46
2.2 The Role of Developed Countries in the
    Development of LDCs   48
3.1 Management System and Environmental Influence   61
3.2 Japanese Production System and 'Humanware'   71
5.1a The Fixed and Variable Costs of Employing the Old
    and New Machines in the Parent Country   96
5.1b The Fixed and Variable Costs of Employing the Old
    and New Machines in the LDC Host   97
5.2 The MNE Subsidiary's Marginal Cost and Revenue
    Curves with and without Rivalry   99
5.3 Barriers to Entry and MNEs' Choice of Technique   103
7.1 Scatter Diagram of Commodity Concentration and
    Propensity to Engage in Counterpurchase   155

Preface and Acknowledgements

The time for a reappraisal of the role of multinational enterprises in less developed countries is overdue. There have been significant changes in the attitudes of both multinational enterprises and policy-makers in less developed countries. This opportunity was seized by the UK Region of the Academy of International Business (AIB) in devoting its 1989 Annual Conference to examining modern perspectives on these issues.

A total of 32 articles were submitted in response to the call for papers. Each was subjected to a blind refereeing process, each paper being reviewed by three members of the Editorial Board, including the editors. We would like to place on record our thanks for the dedicated efforts of the Board which ensured that the final selection of papers are contributions of high quality.

Membership of the Board comprised:

Dr Michael Z. Brooke, Brooke Associates and formerly Director of the International Business Unit, UMIST

Professor Mark Casson, University of Reading

Professor Edward (Monty) Graham, Institute for International Economics, Washington, DC

Professor Colin Kirkpatrick, Department of Project Planning, University of Bradford

Professor Bruce Kogut, Wharton School, University of Pennsylvania and Stockholm School of Economics

Sanjaya Lall, Institute of Economics and Statistics, University of Oxford

Professor Donald Lecraw, University of Western Ontario

Robert D. Pearce, Senior Research Fellow, University of Reading

Professor Edith T. Penrose, Emeritus Professor, INSEAD, Visiting Senior Research Fellow, University of Bradford Management Centre

Professor Louis T. Wells, Graduate School of Business Administration, Harvard University

The Conference was held at the University of Bath, 7–8 April 1989. Each paper had an appointed discussant who later commented on the paper as presented, also acting as discussion summarisers. In this capacity we would like to thank Danny Van den Bulcke, Hafiz Mirza, Jim Hamill, Mark Casson, Homi Katrak, John Crosbie, Don Lecraw, Brian Dawes, Fred Burton, Mo Yamin, John Cantwell and Colin Kirkpatrick. A number of the above also chaired sessions. Comments from the floor were informative and challenging and many excellent discussions took place. We would like to thank all the conference participants for their enthusiastic responses.

The editors would like to thank Mrs Sylvia Ashdown for her speedy and efficient word processing of drafts of this book and in liaising with the contributors, and Mrs Elizabeth Cridford for her help in organising the Conference.

It is hoped that the outcome of this process is a volume which represents a major and timely contribution to the literature. It covers: the process of development, welfare effects, trade and foreign investment, the pattern of foreign direct investment, technology transfer and policy issues.

Special thanks are due to John Dunning for his support and invaluable contribution to the Conference.

Peter J. Buckley
Jeremy Clegg
Bradford and Bath

List of Contributors

Raj Aggarwal, Edward J. and Louise E. Mellen Chair in Finance, John Carroll University, USA.

Patrick Artisien, Lecturer in Business and Economics, Cardiff Business School, UK.

John Cantwell, Lecturer in Economics, University of Reading, UK.

Mark Casson, Professor of Economics, University of Reading, UK.

Francis Chukujama, Researcher, Department of Economics, University of Reading, UK.

John H. Dunning, ICI Research Professor in International Business, University of Reading, UK.

Peter Enderwick, Professor of Management, University of Waikato, New Zealand.

Pervez N. Ghauri, Chair, Department of Marketing, Oslo Business School, Norway.

Edward M. Graham, Research Fellow, Institute for International Economics, Washington, DC.

Jim Hamill, Senior Lecturer in International Business, University of Strathclyde International Business Unit, UK.

Rhys Jenkins, Lecturer in Development Studies, University of East Anglia, UK.

Homi Katrak, Reader in Economics, University of Surrey, UK.

Donald J. Lecraw, Professor, School of Business Administration, University of Western Ontario, Canada.

Matija Rojec, Research Associate, Centre for International Cooperation and Development, Ljubljana, Yugoslavia.

Marjan Svetlicic, Director, Centre for International Cooperation and Development, Ljubljana, Yugoslavia.

Klaus Weiermair, Professor of Economics, Faculty of Administrative Studies, York University, Canada.

Part I
Introduction

1 Introduction and Statement of the Issues

Peter J. Buckley and Jeremy Clegg

1.1 CONTEXT

In the last 20 years the attitudes of policy-makers towards multinational enterprises (MNEs), together with the issues preoccupying researchers, have undergone profound shifts. Development policy in the 1960s and 1970s were frequently predicated upon the notion that international trade inevitably brought dependence on foreign (developed) economies. Accordingly the trade policy of many less developed countries (LDCs) was designed to close off their economies, typically employing tariff protection. One result of this was that MNEs were induced to set up local production within these LDC markets to substitute for the exports they had lost.

There are many problems to be found with such import-substituting foreign direct investment (FDI), not least on efficiency grounds. However, the perverse consequence of protectionist trade policy was that it brought forth an even more marked dependence on developed country firms, concentrated within the LDC economy itself following an apparent invasion of international capital. It was then small wonder that LDCs, and the United Nations on their behalf, perceived MNEs primarily as a threat. Such developed country firms easily dwarfed the indigenous enterprises of these often fragile economies, and were sometimes seen as posing no less a threat to LDC governments themselves. Calls for international measures to restrain the behaviour of MNEs in LDCs encapsulated the mood of the time. A leading example of this is the United Nations 'Code of Conduct' begun in the 1970s but which still only exists in draft form.

The influential writings of economists such as Hymer had much to do with fashioning these perspectives on MNEs (Lecraw 1985a). A further outgrowth was the interest of LDC host countries in alternative forms of involvement to FDI in the local economy (Buckley, 1985). These include licensing and other types of contractual arrangements which were seen as methods of unbundling the FDI package,

3

enabling the host country to benefit from technology transfer without the ancillary foreign control, and with an accompanying reduction both in the rent component paid to the foreign firm and in possible adverse business practices. Natural resource-oriented FDI was also linked by some to exploitation of weak host countries.

Despite certain lasting influences, the isolationist ethos has now largely waned. A number of factors are recognised to have contributed to this, including the world recession and unemployment, which drove home the conclusion that LDC growth prospects depend intimately on those in the developed countries. In fact, following the resurgence of growth in the developed economies in the 1980s, the proportion of FDI directed towards developing countries has declined, partly due to technological changes favouring production in developed host countries and coupled with the greater attraction of high income markets.

The deflationary consequences of the international debt crisis, in the form of the debt repayment burdens and servicing difficulties of a number of LDCs, have contributed greatly to their adverse growth prospects. For development to proceed LDCs are in urgent need not only of technology, managerial and entrepreneurial expertise, but also of foreign exchange, both to service debt and to enable the import of essential goods and equipment. Therefore the renewed interest in the MNEs has much to do with their role as suppliers of capital and scarce foreign exchange. As opposed to the structuralist school of economic development which emphasised the failures of the price system as an allocator of resources in LDCs, much contemporary development policy embraces deregulation and economic liberalisation and the value of adhering to comparative advantage in leading development (see, for example, Cook and Kirkpatrick, 1988). It follows that the measures employed to attract MNEs must be consistent with underlying comparative advantage in order to generate export-oriented domestic activity – a theme of a number of papers in this volume.

It is also true that multinational enterprises are no longer identified so strongly with the traditional source countries. Enterprises from the newly industrialising countries (NICs) and the centrally planned socialist economies have significant participation in a number of LDCs, and often appear more ready to form collaborative ventures with local firms to complement their own resources. These enterprises may be particularly attractive to LDCs, and are not so associated with unfavourable business practices as are the largest MNEs from the developed market economies.

Naturally many controversies remain in the study of MNEs in LDCs. How far is it true that MNEs crowd out local enterprise? What type and level of surveillance should the host government exercise over foreign firms, which still retain the capability to remit earnings and foreign exchange out of the host country? It is not possible to address all such issues fully in a book of selected papers. What is intended, however, is that key issues are investigated in depth and new insights and perspectives gained.

The above arguments emphasise how important perceptions have been in the formulation of policy stances. This volume intends to deepen the understanding of the critical issues as a stimulus to the formulation of policy. The papers in this volume not only pursue the interaction of MNEs and LDCs using rigorous economic analysis but also introduce and develop new perspectives on this relationship which lie outside conventional economic analysis, and which employ unorthodox concepts, such as notions of culture. The progress which MNEs have made in assisting development in key regions and sectors is also covered and the scope for further progress is assessed.

1.2 THE PROCESS OF DEVELOPMENT

There is no such thing as the 'average' or representative less developed country. The concept of the LDC is an unwieldy one, often poorly defined, or defined tautologously for the specific purpose of the researcher concerned. The term is frequently applied loosely to cover a range of economies from the poorest in terms of income per capita (as are found, for example, in Africa) to the newly industrialising countries of South East Asia, with their dynamic growth profiles.

However, on statistical grounds alone it is hazardous to take measures of income as definitive of the level of economic development, even with knowledge about its distribution. This is true for any country but is especially so for LDCs, where the informal sector can dominate the formal sector. Measures of income fail to account for wealth, especially that in non-financial assets. In fact any one-dimensional measure of development is unsatisfactory and in conceptual terms the structure of industry and infrastructural development (especially transport systems, communications, public amenities and utilities), should be included in measures of social wealth.

It is evident therefore that the sectoral and industrial distribution of FDI into an LDC is itself indicative of the state of economic development. Development also has implications for the structure of society. In fact the causality is two-way, and recognition of this in the theory of international business heralds an interdisciplinary approach to deeper understanding of the relationship between MNEs and LDCs.

A holistic grasp of the determinants of international business competition has long been hamstrung by the abstraction of models of international economics (epitomised by the Hecksher-Ohlin-Samuelson model). Such models explain inter-industry economic structure, but ignore issues such as foreign economic participation by firms. Theories of the economics of international business address the causes of foreign participation directly, but in a static or at best, comparative static setting. These approaches fashion international business as logical responses to firm-specific and location-specific economic assets. The role of institutional and social artefacts, such as the legal system, is largely seen as indirect and exogenous. A more significant omission is the role of cultural incentives to enterprise. Social and cultural factors are recognised as crucial to the formation of domestic enterprise, but have not yet been assimilated into international business theory. This is a flaw in our understanding of the process of international business.

Comparative studies of international business continually reveal the significance of differences between source countries. National characteristics must in some way be pertinent, as suggested by Linder (1960) and Vernon (1966). Ultimately the growth of economic activity and competitiveness depends on entrepreneurial drive. The paper by Buckley and Casson makes a first and crucial step in uniting this concept with the development and internationalisation process.

Buckley and Casson invoke cultural factors to explain the persistence of underdevelopment, as found in many of the poorest of the LDCs, and explore the role played by MNEs in transmitting certain cultural attitudes to host countries. Their approach eschews a simplistic definition of development, and instead details development as a progression in the structure of national economic activity between the industrial sectors of agriculture, manufacturing and services. Harnessing the concept of entrepreneurship as a culture-specific feature helps explain why competitive risk-taking often varies systematically between countries. It also provides a reason why countries which are otherwise abundant in resources by the customary economic measures fail to make progress in economic development.

Entrepreneurship is not a quality identified solely with a managerial and professional élite; it can also apply to middle and lower level management and to labour. In its constructive form as attention to detail and quality of manufacture, it is equally required at the production level. This pervasive ethos is embodied in attitudes such as a scientific outlook and commitment to voluntary methods of social and economic coordination. The origin of entrepreneurial culture, under autarky, is attributed to the internal topography of a country – whether and how far it promotes internal trade. If internal trade is favoured this engenders profitable risk-taking which is then assimilated into the domestic culture. To this extent it can be endogenously created. The key factor which is a necessary stimulus to international competition via trade is a further geographic feature – the potential to develop entrepôt facilities.

Conventional economic resources (such as raw materials) are therefore necessary but not sufficient for development. Thus a clear opportunity is opened up for developed countries to assist in the development process of LDCs. Historically much participation by developed countries in LDCs has been accompanied by colonialism. However, Buckley and Casson show that the MNE may perform the mediation of entrepreneurial culture from source to host nation at the same time as engaging in foreign direct investment. This approach furnishes some answers to problems which have occurred in empirical testing, such as explaining the direction of FDI between countries which might otherwise appear indistinguishable in their complement of non-human economic resources. Almost invariably in empirical testing economic variables alone are employed to predict the flow of trade and investment, in accordance with conventional international economic and business theory. However, this new perspective has profound implications for the way we see the relationship between MNEs and LDCs. It introduces social and cultural factors as explanations of competitiveness, and also affords an alternative explanation for the conflicts often reported between MNEs and LDC host countries. Such conflicts may to some extent have their roots in cultural differences rather than in issues of political sovereignty.

The significance of cultural differences is scrutinised by Weiermair who focuses on Japanese management practices. Weiermair argues that Japanese culture and Japanese management practices are distinct, and that while the former is uniquely Japanese the latter is in fact accessible to managements of all nationalities. The role of Japanese culture, however, has worked to promote the adoption of best practice management techniques at a faster rate than has occurred in the West, despite the fact that these techniques are universally taught. Culture in this sense amounts to a competitive weapon, corroborating Buckley and Casson's view that cultural attributes can explain systematic differences in competitiveness between firms drawing on different cultural backgrounds.

This provides a valuable test case and insight into the role of culture in fostering development. It is, however, important to note that the cultivation of managerial prowess in Japan since the Second World War has not been through inward FDI into Japan. Rather it has arisen through export competition in the West and from a synergy between the native culture and the special conditions obtaining following the US occupation, stimulating the indigenous generation of management practices (Buckley and Mirza, 1985). In the NICs of South East Asia, however, transfers have more commonly occurred through FDI. It is evident, therefore, that management practice can be disassociated from the indigenous aspects of culture, as elsewhere demonstrated by the use of international management contracts.

Undoubtedly the bulk of management-related transfers occur through FDI, although FDI cannot be considered a panacea for problems in the dissemination of management expertise. Underlying differences in cultural attitudes can cause conflicts within MNEs in terms of their headquarter-subsidiary relationships. Weiermair points out that this schism interferes also with the integration of MNEs into the host economy, creating problems with local suppliers and contractors and with training institutions and government bodies. In the Japanese case this explains their firms' tendency to export their domestic industrial linkages following the establishment of foreign affiliates.

These observations agree with Buckley and Casson's view that informal education, to prime LDC workforces to assimilate formal scientific outlook, is a crucial substrate for the stimulation of the development process. In view of the compelling nature of these ideas it seems likely that future research will include an appraisal of these key aspects of culture and the impact of MNEs on cultural attitudes in the host, rather than being restricted to conventional issues alone.

1.3 WELFARE, DISTRIBUTION AND MARKET POWER

Unlike cultural issues, those of the economic impacts of MNEs have been the subject of extensive research. A strong understanding of these influences has long been considered essential for the formulation of policy. For the reasons noted at the beginning of this chapter, the character of much of the debate over MNEs in LDCs was formed in the context of inefficient import-substituting and raw materials-oriented extractive FDI. LDCs' experiences of both types have greatly coloured their perspectives on MNEs. It was argued earlier that much import-substituting FDI was not based on genuine comparative advantage; as a consequence the gains, in terms of value added, from such FDI would be at best modest. In such circumstances MNE-LDC relations are in the form of a zero-sum game, so issues of bargaining over the distribution of the gains, together with those of market power, assume a disproportionate importance. These invidious overtones of FDI are also present in natural resources extraction, arising not from comparative disadvantage but from problems over the distribution of income between MNE and host, given that the MNE has inherent discretion over the pricing of intra-firm trade. In this case the problem comes to a head over the use of transfer price manipulation, although there is often no less of an incentive for MNEs engaged in import-substituting FDI to employ this.

The scope for the LDC host to both maximise local value added, and the share of this retained in the domestic economy, forms the focus of Graham's chapter exploring optimal host strategic trade policy. Building on the infant industry argument for trade protection, Graham shows that even if a concentrated host industry is composed of competing firms, including an MNE subsidiary able to produce at efficient scale and matching the landed price of imported substitutes, then the net benefits from protection will nevertheless be negative. From this it is clear that a developing country need never grant import protection to an MNE on the grounds that this assists domestic development and welfare.

Economies of learning are then introduced by Graham. This is a crucial step strongly supported by theory, especially that expressed in this volume. Dynamic scale economies result from experience effects usually associated with routine production alone; however in the context of the multinational enterprise they can also arise from the inculcation of source-country cultural attitudes. Under these circumstances it is especially important to model trade policy accurately. Graham's analysis reveals that, where learning takes place, the granting of trade protection by host governments actually retards the learning process and therefore the reduction in average costs, as the MNE strives to curtail output to obtain monopoly profits.

Graham's chapter therefore exposes the nature of past flaws in LDCs' trade policy towards MNEs, which has resulted in distortions in their economies. To the long established criticism that infant industry protection was frequently maintained too long by LDCs, we can add that the rate of development is also likely to have been compromised by the very use of tariff protection. It transpires in chapter 4 that the only grounds for tariff protection are when it performs the role of compensation, by way of a risk premium, to investors in exceptionally risky LDCs. However, this implies a minimal use of protection as compared to its widespread adoption as an instrument of development policy.

The chapter by Katrak is targeted on the analysis of the industrial consequences of import-substituting FDI, and draws some contrasts between alternate market structures in LDC hosts. In particular this chapter throws new light on the debate over the capital intensity of MNE production in LDCs. This is widely recognised as a crucial issue both because of its impact on foreign exchange reserves (when capital goods are imported) and because of its possible implications for host employment. Serious methodological obstacles render this issue notoriously resistant to clarification by empirical testing alone.

Katrak examines the conditions under which MNEs would choose to transfer capital-intensive versus labour-intensive production techniques to their LDC subsidiaries. With the assumption of a homogeneous product it is shown that the capital intensity of least cost production is positively related to the volume of output and, by extension, to market share. Accordingly, monopoly in an LDC host economy promotes the adoption of capital-intensive production methods. It follows that the use of import restrictions is likely to encourage both monopoly and the choice of capital intensity in production. The situation may also arise where tariff protection stimulates both market sharing arrangements and capital-intensive production, causing future new entry to be blocked.

The dire nature of Katrak's findings reinforces the censure of much former LDC trade policy. However, he notes that these conclusions on capital intensity relate only to import-substituting MNE production and not to export-oriented FDI; here capital intensity may

actually enhance international competitiveness. The distinction between these two types of FDI is critical and is revisited in chapter 8 in
the appraisal of appropriate policy formulation in a world where
export promotion is of prime importance.

A final section of Katrak's chapter argues that there are strong
reasons for believing that MNEs operate in differentiated final product markets, not least because the theory of FDI is founded on the
existence of firm-specific advantages. The implication of this for
MNE-LDC interaction is that indigenous firms are disposed to behave less aggressively towards MNEs, as their products are likely to
be differentiated. Accordingly, a lone MNE subsidiary competing
against indigenous firms may employ the more capital-intensive
technique. However, in a situation of oligopoly in the host LDC and
where there are subsidiaries of more than one MNE, all producers
may be forced to adopt labour-intensive techniques. Katrak's analysis
therefore reveals a serious omission found in much empirical work,
which largely fails to account for market structure, rivalry and the
involvement of more than one MNE. This insight may help to explain
the lack of consensus in the empirical literature, reviewed in the
chapter by Jenkins, over the factors determining capital intensity,
and in particular that of foreign versus indigenous firms. In operational terms many studies may have omitted to test for the effects of
such variables, resulting in a plethora of conflicting findings. The value
of a sound theoretical approach therefore cannot be overstated.

Despite the confusions in the existing literature, Jenkins concludes
that where MNEs and local firms are in direct competition with each
other, within the same market segment, they will both adopt the
same degree of capital intensity. An earlier survey of the literature by
Casson and Pearce (1987) concluded that indigenous firms' production was more labour-intensive than that of the MNEs operating
within the same industries. At first sight these conclusions appear in
contradiction. However, the survival strategy of LDC firms is frequently based on following the behaviour of their incoming MNE
rivals. This points to the existence of a disequilibrium in local firms'
choice of production methods. Because of the technology gap, MNE
capital intensity characteristically exceeds that of locally-owned
firms; however, in the steady state such differences may evaporate as
firms come to compete directly. Therefore the closer one defines the
degree of product rivalry between MNE and native firms, the greater
is the degree of similarity which is likely to be found between the two
in terms of production methods.

This adoption of MNE practices in production techniques extends to further aspects of conduct, notably marketing. These are just some of the complications which confound researchers who seek to identify the true impact of MNEs on LDC hosts using comparisons between foreign subsidiaries and local firms. These problems are most acute in cross-industry regressions, and consequently Jenkins advocates the use of case studies on firms and industries over time. The only consensus reached by the current literature is that foreign affiliates have generally higher import propensities than indigenous firms. The absence of a matching consensus on export propensities precludes any generalisations on balance of payments effects. Nevertheless, this alone implies that MNEs are associated with some curtailment of local linkage effects, the causes of which may be those argued by Buckley and Casson, and by Weiermair in this volume.

It must remain at present a matter for speculation whether the adoption of MNEs' advertising strategies by local firms serves to amplify any adverse social and cultural impacts of FDI. Nevertheless, one thing is clear: the nature and course of indigenous enterprise is permanently altered once a foreign affiliate is present.

1.4　TRADE AND INVESTMENT

Less developed economies as a group do tend to have one particular external economic feature in common: they typically face problems of export promotion and of foreign exchange scarcity. In this connection Casson and Chukujama investigate the factors promoting the use of countertrade arrangements. These are defined as contractual arrangements under which the export of a good is linked to the import of other goods. According to some commentators, countertrade could already account for as much as one third of all trade, perhaps even rising to one half by the turn of the century. However, any estimates are hazardous because so much countertrade is cloaked in secrecy.

Countertrade arrangements are often seen as 'new forms' of international economic involvement; however, in certain respects they are regressive. Casson and Chukujama emphasise the defects of countertrade as compared with the advantages of multilateral trade using hard currencies. Other writers on the same topic are less critical of countertrade, pointing instead to the income generated under these arrangements which might never have arisen in their absence. The benefits or otherwise of countertrade will remain a matter of controversy, depending on the alternate situation hypothesised by the researcher. However, it is generally accepted that countertrade is second best in theoretical terms compared to multilateral trade, and to the equity-based international arrangements whose functions they partially perform. It is on this basis, the authors argue, that the value added sacrificed by adopting countertrade is in effect the price which countries are prepared to pay to preserve the status quo. As a result political motives are often involved where countertrade is chosen.

A number of general factors are thought to stimulate countertrade, such as world-wide deflation and government constraints on foreign equity involvement. Following a discussion of four types of countertrade arrangements (counterpurchase, barter, buy-back and production sharing) counterpurchase and buy-back are subjected to empirical investigation. The former was found to increase with commodity concentration of exports, country indebtedness (linked to domestic price distortions) and policy stance on countertrade. Buy-back arrangements are associated with restrictions on foreign equity ownership, a reputation for poor export quality and with low indigenous technological capacity.

The policies pursued by countries engaged in countertrade could not contrast more markedly with those investigated by Lecraw, yet they are directed at addressing substantially the same problems – export promotion and foreign exchange scarcity. Lecraw's research is driven by the current interest in formulating LDC policy so as to maximise inward FDI to provide a source of long-term capital and foreign exchange, without which LDC development is severely hampered. The most pressing difficulty facing many LDCs remains their high debt burdens. Despite the plethora of proposals to alleviate this, the scope for inward FDI appears of especial interest. This is because LDC real income per capita is generally below that of ten years ago, with commensurately lower rates of domestic investment. Growth prospects, including those for exports, are not generally favourable.

Against this austere background, inward FDI has much to commend it, especially that of an export-oriented nature. Other forms of long-term capital provide exchange but do not have the same power to direct LDC investment into activities of potential comparative advantage, because they do not confer new technology and entrepreneurship. This can be very important, not only because of the much documented imperfections in international technology markets (and particularly those relating to LDCs) but also because LDC capital markets are often poorly developed and inefficient. FDI can place LDC activity directly into its appropriate position in international competition, so enhancing both output and exports. Moreover, apart from conveying marketing advantages, it is thought that MNEs help LDC exports to bypass developed country protection, and perhaps also to reduce the likelihood of its imposition (see chapter 12).

Lecraw starts with the premise that LDCs should wish to encourage export and natural resource-oriented FDI in particular. From the empirical work his foremost conclusions are that LDC policy can do much to promote such inward FDI, despite being constrained in crucial respects. Policy variables under the complete direction of governments, such as tariffs and tax rates, have certain drawbacks. Tariffs necessarily favour import-substituting FDI, while the value of tax concessions is the subject of continued debate. It is widely thought that tax concessions do not substantially alter international investment decisions and therefore that they needlessly relinquish valuable tax revenue (Casson and Pearce, 1987). Here it is found that tax concessions favour natural resource- and export-oriented FDI, but not import-substituting FDI. This suggests that tax concessions are most effective when they enhance an existing or potential comparative advantage.

Other policy variables under the complete or partial discretion of governments, such as the real exchange rate and the openness of the economy to FDI (by which is meant high incentives or low barriers, or both) share further practical limitations. Lecraw finds that the effect of a once and for all change in these variables is exhausted after two to three years, implying that, to maintain a policy stance to encourage a continuous inflow of FDI, incentives would need to be regularly adjusted. This is clearly not feasible for some policy variables. It is also found that natural resource prices exert the strongest influence on resources-oriented inward investment, but these clearly lie outside the control of the host country. Lecraw's other findings suggest that hosts should pursue policies to stabilise their country risks in order to maximise FDI inflows, while it transpires that the importance of host infrastructure is inadequately captured by the transportation variable.

In the long term inward FDI is probably best promoted by factors which governments are able to influence relatively indirectly (such as the skill-adjusted wage rate and domestic demand, in the cases of export-oriented and local market-seeking FDI respectively). It is therefore desirable to foster an intrinsically attractive locational base, which will be conducive not only to inward FDI but also to domestically owned enterprise and investment. Accordingly, the priority of host governments should be to employ these longer-term positive, rather than short-term negative inducements to inward FDI. These are most likely to maximise local value added and the bargaining power of LDC governments over the distribution of this income.

1.5 DISTRIBUTION OF FDI WITHIN AND BETWEEN COUNTRIES AND INDUSTRIES

Four chapters focus on FDI either from particular source countries or in particular host regions, or both. It is apposite to mention here that statistics on the book value of FDI, the accepted measure according to the IMF (IMF, 1977; Billerbeck and Yasugi, 1979) have serious flaws as a proxy for productive activity by MNEs. One illustration is the negative FDI stocks recorded not infrequently in Middle Eastern host countries. This arises because of extensive local borrowing, rendering FDI meaningless as a measure of local activity by subsidiaries. It is evident from this alone that FDI values are universally distorted to varying and unknown degrees. The merits of the chapters in this section are that they do not rely on FDI values alone to appraise MNE activity, often employing carefully prepared alternate measures. This is crucial when the distribution of FDI is being examined.

In the decade 1975–85 the share of US multinationals in world outward FDI declined from 44 per cent to 35 per cent. At the same time that of West Germany rose from 6 to 8 per cent, while Japan's share increased from 6 to 12 per cent. Against the downward trend normally assumed for a mature foreign investing nation, the share of the UK in world outward FDI rose from 13 to 15 per cent. These facts demonstrate a simple point – that the role of the US in world FDI is now a relatively lesser one, and that FDI has become characteristically less of a US phenomenon. To this trend we can add the rise of the newly outward investing countries, with their contrasting outward investment patterns. These countries include the centrally planned socialist economies and the newly industrialising countries, both of which have a greater proclivity to participate, via FDI and other forms, in the economies of LDCs.

It is still the case that the bulk of outward FDI remains in the hands of the developed countries and so their outward investment patterns largely determine the access of LDCs to FDI. In fact the shares of LDCs in the outward FDI of the four developed countries, mentioned above, have experienced significant reductions, though infrequently in absolute values. In aggregate, these shares fell most between 1980–85, from 25 to 23 per cent (USA), 22 to 18 per cent (UK), 18 to 15 per cent (West Germany) and from 55 to 52 per cent (Japan). The causes of this apparent retrenchment are believed to include the increased tendency for MNEs to seek locations within the major developed country markets, and secondly the decline in domestic demand in those LDCs bearing high international debt burdens. It is evident that there will be profound variations in fortunes between LDCs, and in their prospects for inward FDI.

The thrust of Cantwell's research is that, as suggested by the Buckley and Casson approach, African developing countries need to encourage inward FDI in target industries able to generate downstream processing activities in which host countries have a potential comparative advantage. Using revealed comparative advantage trade indices, Africa's comparative advantage is found to lie increasingly in the exports of extractive industries, which already characterise its trade. If coupled with further inward FDI into the processing of especially metal products, wood and paper, textiles and clothing and food, Cantwell foresees scope for export-led growth. FDI is the form of foreign involvement recommended by Cantwell, especially joint ventures, on the grounds that this is more efficient than contractual arrangements when so many smaller African firms lack the complementary resources of production experience and finance. Source country MNEs with much to offer include experienced ones from Canada and Sweden, but also those seeking resources for home import, from Japan, the Federal Republic of Germany and the newly industrialising countries, of which the last may be particularly adept at small-scale activities.

At present, African inward FDI in textiles is concentrated in North Africa, originating mainly from the Federal Republic of Germany, Italy and Hong Kong, and has been spurred by quota restrictions on South East Asian textile exports. The revealed comparative advantage of Africa therefore results at least partly from government-induced distortions as well as from African low-wage labour. In any event, the priority of African host governments should be to develop indigenous infrastructures and export orientation in order to reduce the current dependence on inefficient import-substituting manufacturing FDI.

Africa is the premier location for Yugoslav FDI in developing countries, albeit boosted by capital invested in Liberian shipping companies. Artisien, Rojec and Svetlicic survey Yugoslav FDI and report that, by the end of 1986, 19 per cent of Yugoslav FDI was located in developing countries. Of this figure, 54 per cent were in the form of the minority-owned joint ventures characteristic of Yugoslav FDI in LDCs. While affiliates in developed countries are principally engaged in marketing Yugoslav exports, in developing countries they are found to be concentrated in production.

The chapter by Artisien, Rojec and Svetlicic furnishes a clear illustration of the road to outward FDI which centrally planned economies can take, following the appropriate reforms to reduce centralisation. While these policy changes were crucial, much of the character of Yugoslav FDI derives from domestic constraints and exigencies. The authors' survey finds that Yugoslav firms were typically capital-scarce and therefore favoured minority joint ventures in manufacturing, with the added spur that Yugoslav FDI is low in technological sophistication. They find that host investment incentives are unimportant for location decisions (perhaps due to the market-seeking nature of Yugoslav FDI), and moreover that joint ventures responding to these tend to be the least successful. In respect of policy, one avenue for developing countries to pursue is suggested by the estimate that the cost of information accounts for up to 70 per cent of production costs. Yugoslav firms' pre-investment strategies are thought to be very weak, in which respect they are probably not alone amongst existing and future MNEs from centrally planned economies and newly industrialising countries. Host governments might therefore usefully consider subsidising the collation of basic information for these firms, preparatory to any investments.

The novel hypothesis that the product life-cycle model applies to, and has special implications for, FDI from small countries is investigated by Aggarwal and Ghauri. Focusing on Swedish FDI in Asia, they argue that subsequent to the initial expansion abroad, these foreign subsidiaries evolve to challenge the parent firm, at an earlier stage than would be the case for larger MNEs with more extensive home markets. Were this generally the case, the implication for developing countries is that such FDI would integrate locally and form host linkages more readily. According to this controversial hypothesis, developing countries might wish to favour MNEs from smaller developed countries, such as Sweden, the centrally planned socialist economies and NICs, for each of which similar conclusions may be expected to apply.

The chapters by Hamill and Enderwick study selected key industries and sectors relating to development. Hamill focuses on the factors which have made seven Mediterranean rim countries (Algeria, Egypt, Greece, Malta, Morocco, Tunisia and Turkey) leading locations for the production and export of textiles and clothing. The highly tradable output of the textiles industry can play a central role in economic development, as noted earlier. In each of these seven countries, this industry accounts for between 20 and 45 per cent of manufacturing output and employment, and between 1 and 40 per cent of total exports, reflecting the variation in export success between the countries. The contribution of MNEs to this success is also variable, both in extent and form, and encompasses majority-owned FDI, joint ventures, licensing, offshore processing and subcontracting, turnkey arrangements and other forms of technology transfer and assistance.

Despite the export success of the Mediterranean rim countries, they risk two types of over-reliance. Firstly, much of their success arises from locational advantages which are subject to reasonably swift changes: low wage labour, a favourable (labour-intensive) state of technology, developed countries' restrictions on textile imports from countries covered by the Multifibre Arrangement, coupled with certain European Community preferential trade agreements. The only necessarily permanent advantage is found to be that of proximity to the main final market of the European Community.

While protectionism is a possible response to the Mediterranean rim countries' continued export success, only Turkey has so far been affected. Some security is afforded by the specialisation of the region in processing, as it therefore constitutes a major market for intermediate exports of yarns and fabrics from the European Community. The second source of over-reliance is on foreign firms' marketing and branding advantages. At present the leading host policy associated with successful export performance is a liberal attitude towards foreign participation, including the provision of export-processing zones. Hamill advocates a greater degree of balance in the proportion of inward foreign involvement, and argues that indigenous ownership advantages are now required to mitigate the inevitable erosion of locational advantages if competitiveness is to be maintained.

Empirical research on MNEs in developing countries is predominantly concerned with the manufacturing and primary sectors. Enderwick's chapter seeks to redress this balance by arguing that service sector growth constitutes a source of development rather than merely being a consequence of it. *Prima facie*, the low tradability of many services might appear to preclude export-led growth, with only 8 per cent of services' output being traded internationally as compared with 55 per cent for manufacturing and mining. However, technological developments continually render services more tradable, while the services sector is very often complementary to the production of goods for export.

Enderwick argues that there is a particularly valuable role early in development for inward FDI in transport and communications, as supported by Buckley and Casson's chapter. Indeed, a clear message is that host infrastructure and business services are among the most robust long-run determinants of inward FDI in all industries and it is to these that inward FDI can make a direct contribution. FDI in services often conveys a higher proportion of 'soft technology' than manufacturing investment. This involves the know-how of running an enterprise, and equates almost precisely with the cultural transfers already advocated in this volume. It is also believed that the subsidiaries of service sector MNEs are more autonomous than their manufacturing counterparts, which suggests a higher degree of integration with the host economy.

The idea of complementarity between the service and manufacturing sectors can be taken still further, and Enderwick suggests that service sector outward FDI by developing countries can form part of a strategy to promote the export of manufactures. A dual role in the promotion of development is therefore envisaged for FDI by LDCs, both in the source country and in those lower income LDC hosts for which such FDI is thought to be particularly suitable. Enderwick advocates that both inward and outward FDI in services by developing countries be encouraged as it does much more than conventionally supposed to aid host development, while bringing competitive benefits and diversifying LDCs' industrial bases.

1.6 TECHNOLOGY TRANSFER

Technology transfer is an issue which occupies a central position in the literature on LDCs (Buckley, 1985; Casson, 1979). The contributions in the chapters of this volume have provided a number of implications for the way we view technology transfer. Firstly, the definition of technology has been broadened to include the soft technology argued to be conveyed especially by service sector MNEs, although the chapters by Buckley and Casson and Weiermair suggest that the closely related concepts of entrepreneurial culture and management systems are an intrinsic and critical component of FDI in all sectors.

The interplay between these unorthodox cultural and social elements and the transfer of conventional scientific technology is one which has profound consequences for LDCs' development. The empirical literature has extensively documented the failures of technology transfer and notably the low success rates in the formation of backward linkages by MNEs in LDC economies. Despite its drawbacks, analysed extensively in this volume, import-substituting FDI in general creates stronger local linkages than export-oriented (manufacturing and extractive) FDI. Casson and Pearce (1987) argue that this may be because quality control over output is less crucial for products sold locally in LDCs. This may be true, but given the desire of LDCs to reorient their economies towards exports, it is a matter of some urgency to investigate how the required indigenous conditions can be kindled.

It was suggested in these chapters that indigenous firms in LDCs frequently fail to win contracts for the supply of intermediate products to MNE subsidiaries and as a consequence fail to develop as innovators (note the parallels with the analysis of the role of education in chapters 2 and 3). Over the years much blame has been directed towards the multinationals for this state of affairs. However, the evidence of this volume suggests that the LDCs themselves have contributed in no small part, and that conversely there is much they can do to improve the situation. The problems of foreign subsidiaries in finding suitable local suppliers are associated with low quality control in host industry; the underlying problem, however, is likely to be a lack of receptiveness to external ideas. Such receptiveness is founded on early informal and formal education; in this volume a case in point is provided by Japan, analysed in chapter 3.

The most appropriate policies for economic development have been identified as long-term in nature, and should include policy directed towards education. Education, however, is expensive for LDCs, and here the role of services FDI may be crucial in assisting development. Services FDI often involves a higher degree of manpower training and education than manufacturing, and especially raw materials-oriented FDI. This suggests that inward FDI in services has been, and still is, a greatly under-utilised source of development. Because of the long-term nature of education, the use of demonstration plants and other inclusive forms of technology transfer will be invaluable in LDCs for the foreseeable future. The evidence in this volume is that the long-run inflow of FDI into LDCs is best assured by the intrinsic qualities of their economies, and especially of their indigenous manpower. These attributes are also those which promote indigenous enterprise and indigenously based international competition via outward FDI.

1.7 POLICY ISSUES

The policy stances of many LDCs have already changed considerably, as discussed by Dunning in chapter 14. Despite this fact there is much scope for policy reformulation and refinement, as many LDCs are currently only at the exploratory stage in establishing their policy programmes. Dunning overviews the evidence of the chapters contained in this volume and links them to the world-wide changes which have characterised the relationship between MNEs and the developing countries.

The increasing sophistication on the parts of both multinational enterprises and LDCs regarding their approaches to and expectations of foreign direct investment has characterised the 1980s. The management of policy by LDCs to encourage the optimal type of inward investment has accompanied a renewed interest in FDI as a package of resources. Some constituents of FDI have only now begun to be fully appreciated, while others, such as the element of long-term capital, have been rediscovered. To a certain extent, therefore, the attractiveness of FDI has risen relative to the alternative forms of foreign involvement. In spite of this, many LDCs are encountering serious difficulties in securing an increased or even a stable share of global FDI. Dunning points to the current problems of LDCs as adversely affecting their bargaining power relative to MNEs. The best course of action in this case is for LDCs to adopt an integrated approach towards attracting inward FDI.

The clear theoretical and empirical conclusions of this volume are that policies directed specifically at attracting FDI through short-term measures have not met with long-term success. These policies include many which formed the mainstay of LDC policy. Policies which seek to increase inward FDI by restricting imports risk seriously prejudicing domestic efficiency, competition and export competitiveness. Negative policy measures in general, which involve constraining one form of international involvement in an attempt to encourage another, are widely argued to be inferior in terms of economic efficiency and welfare. With respect to countertrade in particular, in chapter 7, Casson and Chukujama advocate the promotion of institutional innovation within the free market system to render countertrade obsolete.

Dunning notes that policy advisers to the LDCs now advocate a global approach to managing their relationships with MNEs. This is essential because LDCs are not only in competition with each other for investment, but also with the developed countries themselves. The intensity of this competition is likely to become more marked as technological developments occur which favour production within the developed countries. The goal of LDCs to attain export-oriented domestic economies carries with it many benefits, but it also has risks firmly attached. Export orientation necessarily means an intensification of international competition, but it is a position which must be based on sound domestic economic foundations.

1.8 PRELUDE TO THIS COLLECTION

This introduction has served to draw out some key findings from the papers in this volume. The editorial role has been facilitated by the magnificent cooperation of the individual authors. We have, in concert with the referees, attempted to select the most stimulating papers and to aid the authors in making the most of their material. However, we have not imposed uniformity of approach or standardisation of expression – for instance, the authors use alternative terms for the multinational enterprise (MNE), most notably TNC (Transnational Corporation, the UN's preferred usage) and MNC (Multinational Corporation). Despite this policy, the volume is coherent and internally consistent.

It is clear that a major reappraisal of the role of the MNE in LDCs is underway. This is reflected not only in changes in attitudes and policies but also in underlying theory. Standard techniques of analysis based on comparative static equilibria are giving way to an approach based on dynamics. This requires attention to foreign direct investment as a process, with a time dimension. Further, it necessitates the introduction of concepts which have lain outside conventional economic analysis such as culture, cooperation, trust, reciprocity and managerial systems. This volume represents a step on the way to a more interdisciplinary study of the process of development and the role of the MNE in that process. Not all our authors will subscribe to such an interpretation; some of them indeed counsel against overstepping traditional disciplinary boundaries. However, it must be clear to all that a widening of usable and tractable concepts is firmly on the agenda. This methodological debate provides a keen edge to the contributions.

The excitement of new theoretical approaches must not detract from the solid empirical contribution made in the pages below. Presentation of new data, new analytical angles and novel types of foreign investment and involvement enliven the subject material. Policy must be based on an understanding of what exists and what the key choices might be. The mix of theory, empirical work and policy conclusions is an intrinsic feature of the contribution made by this volume and the Conference which preceded it.

Part II
Theory

2 Multinational Enterprises in Less Developed Countries: Cultural and Economic Interactions

Peter J. Buckley and Mark Casson

2.1 INTRODUCTION

This paper analyses the operations of multinational enterprises (MNEs) in less developed countries (LDCs) in terms of the interplay between two types of culture. The MNE, it is claimed, personifies the highly entrepreneurial culture of the source country, whilst the LDC personifies the less entrepreneurial culture of the typical social group in the host country. This view places MNE-LDC relations in an appropriate historical perspective. It is the entrepreneurial culture of the source country which explains why in the past that country had the economic dynamism to become a developed country (DC). Conversely, the limited entrepreneurial culture of the host country explains why it has been so economically static that it has remained an LDC. The current problems perceived by MNEs in operating in certain LDCs – and also the problems perceived by these LDCs with the operation of foreign MNEs – reflect the difficulties of attempting to bridge this cultural gap.

The concept of entrepreneurial culture is, of course, related to the concept of 'modernisation' which appears in the sociology of development (Eisenstadt, 1973; Herskovits, 1961; Inkeles and Smith, 1974). There are important differences, however. The concept of entrepreneurial culture derives from economic theories of the entrepreneur (Hayek, 1937; Kirzner, 1973; Knight, 1921; Schumpeter, 1934) which identify specific functions such as arbitrage, risk-bearing and innovation needed for economic development. It describes the cultural values which stimulate the emergence of individual personalities capable of performing these functions competently. Modernisation, on the other hand, typically begins with a wide range of

27

attitudes associated with Western industrial societies, and examines how far these attitudes have permeated LDCs. Entrepreneurial theory suggests that not only are some 'modern' attitudes irrelevant to economic development, but others are actually inimical to it. Emphasis on entrepreneurial culture does not therefore imply a trite endorsement of 'modern' values. Entrepreneurial theory has been applied to development issues by a number of previous writers – Hagen (1962), Hoselitz (1961), Kilby (1971) and McClelland and Winter (1969), for example – but along rather different lines.

Countries classified as LDCs form an extremely heterogeneous group. Indeed, differences between the poorest and the wealthiest LDCs are in some respects greater than between the wealthiest LDCs and many DCs. This paper is concerned principally with the poorest and most persistently underdeveloped LDCs – such as some countries of sub-Saharan Africa. Since these countries are, generally speaking, the ones with the lowest MNE involvement, it may be asked why a focus on these countries is appropriate. One reason is that this low involvement itself merits explanation, since the continuing confinement of these countries to the periphery of the world economy is of considerable policy interest (Wallerstein, 1979). By examining the difficulties encountered by the small number of MNEs that actually invest in these countries, the lack of interest of the majority can be explained in terms of their rational perception of the size of the problem. The second reason is that the starker contrast between wealthy DCs and the poorest LDCs reveals cultural influences in a sharper relief.

Levels of development can vary not only across LDCs but also across regions within any one of them. This point is fully recognised by the analysis in this paper, which emphasises that regional differences in development are endemic in DCs as well (Berger and Piore, 1980). The difference between urban (especially metropolitan) and rural areas is fundamental in this respect. Indeed the analysis below suggests that many international differences in levels of development can be ascribed to differences in the relative influence of urban as opposed to rural culture.

Multinationals differ too; in the present context, differences between source countries are likely to be most significant because these affect the national culture upon which the headquarters of the firm draws. There can also be differences between firms from the same country due, for example, to the religious affiliations of the founders, or the impact of the size of the firm on its organisation and leadership style. Due to limited space, however, this paper abstracts from such considerations by working with the concept of a representative MNE.

Section 2 delineates the main areas in which conventional economic theory appears to be deficient in explaining MNE behaviour in LDCs. The 'residual' phenomena which remain unexplained by economic factors, it is suggested, may be explicable by cultural factors instead. The analytical core of the paper comprises sections 3–7. These sections consider in detail the interaction between geographical and cultural factors in the process of development. Section 3 identifies three conditions for successful economic development; one is geographical – entrepôt potential – and two are cultural – a scientific outlook, and a commitment to voluntary methods of social and economic coordination. Sections 4–6 elaborate on each of these factors in turn, generating a check-list of country characteristics relevant to economic development. Section 7 draws on the core analysis to expound an evolutionary model of world development, which focuses on the dynamics of the linkages between DCs and LDCs, as mediated by MNEs. Section 8 returns to the key issues identified in section 2. It explains how difficulties faced by some LDCs in learning new technologies originate in specific cultural factors, and urges that these same cultural factors explain other phenomena too. Attention is drawn to the weaknesses as well as the strengths of contemporary entrepreneurial cultures, and it is suggested that some of the cultural values transmitted by MNEs to LDCs hinder rather than help the process of development. Section 9 concludes the paper with suggestions for further research.

2.2 KEY ISSUES

Any analysis of multinational operations in LDCs must address a number of key stylised facts. Some of these facts are readily explained by conventional economic theory (see, for example, Casson and Pearce, 1987), but others are not. The facts that conventional theory can explain include:

(1) *The limited scale and disappointing economic performance of import-substituting manufacturing investments in LDCs.* This is partly attributable to inappropriate LDC trade policies. By protecting relatively small domestic markets for finished manufactures, LDC governments have encouraged the proliferation of downstream assembly-type operations of less than efficient scale. It is only the

ability to charge monopoly prices well above world export prices that has encouraged MNEs to continue operating in these protected markets.

(2) *The increase in foreign divestments since the oil price shocks of the mid-1970s* is partly explained by the reduction in real consumer incomes in oil-exporting LDCs, which has reduced local demand for relatively sophisticated MNE-produced goods. The threat of blocked profit repatriations from countries with balance of payments difficulties has also encouraged a pre-emptive liquidation of foreign investments by MNEs.

(3) *The recent poor performance of resource-based investments in Africa and Latin America* is partly explained by another consequence of the oil price shocks – namely the recession in Western heavy industries – and by the continuing protection of domestic agriculture in industrial societies. It is also due partly to the development of new mineral deposits in the Asia-Pacific region. Finally, the emergence of synthetic substitutes has reduced the long-term demand for certain minerals (although the price advantage of oil-based substitutes has declined).

(4) *The use of capital-intensive technologies by MNEs in labour-abundant LDCs* can be explained partly by the cost of adapting to local conditions a technology originally developed for use in Western locations. It can also be explained by the importance of mechanisation in meeting quality standards in export markets – and in home markets dominated by wealthy consumers (in countries with a highly-skewed distribution of income). The distortion of factor prices in LDC markets through minimum wage legislation, capital subsidies, and so on may also be significant.

Some of the salient points which existing theory cannot easily explain are:

(5) *The failure of technology transfer to generate sustained innovative capability in LDC industries.* The much slower rate at which foreign technologies are assimilated by the poorest LDCs compared to newly industrialising countries such as South Korea, or successfully industrialised countries such as Japan, suggests that cultural factors may inhibit the acquisition of scientific ideas and Western working practices.

(6) *The confinement of modern industry to 'enclaves', and in particular the failure of foreign investors to develop backward linkages with indigenous suppliers.* Where resource-based investments are concerned, there may be limited opportunities for backward linkages'

in any case. Even in developed countries, furthermore, large-scale investments often fail to develop a local supply base; the disciplined routine of work in large plants seems to inhibit the 'incubation' of entrepreneurial skills in the local workforce. Nevertheless, the frequent claim by MNE managers of medium-size manufacturing operations that the quality of local supplies is persistently deficient suggests that there may be a systematic failure in LDCs to appreciate the importance of component quality and of precision work in manufacturing industries.

(7) *Poor internal relations, both between headquarters and subsidiary, and between management and labour within the foreign subsidiary.* Conflicts between different groups within the firm over the distribution of profit, the level of investment, and so on, are common in any business activity, and there may be special reasons – such as the high risks perceived by foreign investors and their consequently short-term perspective on cash flow – why these conflicts may be particularly acute in respect of LDC operations. Nevertheless, it is also possible that the failure to resolve these conflicts effectively is due to frequent misunderstandings caused by cross-cultural barriers to communication.

(8) *The tendency for industrialisation through foreign technology to precipitate the disintegration of traditional social groups within the host economy.* All innovation does, of course, involve 'creative destruction', but the social groups of developing countries seem to be much more vulnerable in this respect than do equivalent social groups in the developed world.

It is worth noting that even the 'successful' explanations in (1)–(4) involve only the most proximate causes of the effects involved. Thus in respect of (1), for example, it is possible to ask the more fundamental question of why so many LDC governments opted for protectionism in the first place. Were they susceptible to economic analysis supporting import-substitution because they were predisposed to break economic as well as social and political ties with their colonial powers in order to bolster independence? It seems that – in this case at least – the more fundamental are the questions asked, and the further back the quest for explanation goes, the more likely are cultural factors to become significant.

A good theory often has the capacity to explain more than was originally asked of it, and it is claimed that this is also true of the analysis presented here. The theory can explain not only contemporary differences between DCs and LDCs, but also certain aspects of the historical process of industrialisation in countries which have become DCs. Thus the vulnerability of traditional social groups, for example, noted above, applies also to the social groups which became extinct a century or more ago during the industrialisation of DCs. There is insufficient space in the present paper, however, to document all the relevant facts, let alone substantiate the claim of the theory to explain them.

2.3   THE PROCESS OF DEVELOPMENT

A necessary condition for development in any locality is that there are resources with a potential for exploitation. Conventional economic theory tends to underestimate the obstacles that lie in the path of realising this potential, however. Working with traditional concepts of resource endowment – land, labour and capital – cross-section regressions using the total factor productivity approach have only limited success in explaining international differences in material economic performance (as measured by per capita GNP) (Pack, 1987). Some countries clearly under-perform by failing to realise their potential, and the question is why this should be so (Leibenstein, 1968).

Differences in education and training are commonly cited as a possible explanation, and the analysis presented here is generally consistent with this view. It goes beyond it, however, in recognising that education takes place largely outside formal institutions. Early education, in particular, is effected through family influence, peer group pressure within the local community, and so on. To benefit fully from formal education it may be necessary for people to 'unlearn' beliefs from their informal education. But if the conflict between the two sets of beliefs is acute then psychological obstacles to unlearning may arise. Measures of educational input based on gross expenditure fail to capture these important factors. The analysis in this paper helps to identify those aspects of the formal curriculum which are crucial in supporting economic development. It also identifies those elements of general culture which prepare people to benefit from such education.

Two main obstacles to the efficient use of national resources can be identified. The first is geographical: the inability to effect a division of labour due to obstacles to transportation. In this context, it is argued below that the presence of a potential entrepôt centre is crucial in

TABLE 2.1   *Factors in the long-run economic success of a nation*

I. Geographical factors that influence entrepôt potential.
  A Location near to major long-distance freight transport routes.
  B Natural harbour with inland river system.
  C Extensive coastline.
  D Land and climate suitable for an agriculture with potential for local downstream processing.
  E Mineral deposits and energy resources.

II. Entrepreneurial culture.
  Technical aspects.
  A Scientific attitude, including a systems view.
  B Judgemental skills, including
      (i)   ability to simplify
      (ii) self-confidence
      (iii) detached perception of risk
      (iv) understanding of delegation
  Moral aspects
  C Voluntarism and toleration.
  D Association with trust, including
      (i)   general commitment to principles of honesty, stewardship, and the like
      (ii) sense of corporate mission
      (iii) versatile personal bonding (friendship not confined to kin)
      (iv) weak attachments to specific locations, roles, and so on.
  E High norms in respect of effort, quality of work, accumulation of wealth, social distinction, and so on.

facilitating the development of a region. The second is the absence of an entrepreneurial culture. An entrepreneurial culture provides an economy with flexibility – in particular, the structural flexibility to cope with changes in the division of labour. These changes may be progressive changes stemming from essentially autonomous techno-logical innovations, or defensive changes made in response to resource depletion or various environmental disturbances.

An entrepreneurial culture has two main aspects: the technical and the moral (see Table 2.1). The technical aspect stimulates the study of natural laws through experimentation, and the assimilation of technologies developed by other cultures too. It also develops judge-mental skills in decision-making – skills that are particularly import-ant in simplifying complex situations without unduly distorting perceptions of them (Casson, 1988b).

Entrepreneurial opportunities are usually best exploited through contracts, organisation-building, and other forms of association. The moral aspect involves a grasp of the principles involved in voluntary associations of this kind. These principles include commitments to honesty, stewardship, and other values that underpin contractual arrangements of both a formal and informal nature. They also include a concept of group mission which is needed to mitigate agency problems in large organisations. A willingness to trust people other than kin is also important. Finally, there must be no rigid attachments to specific occupational roles or places of residence which can inhibit social or geographical mobility at times when structural adjustments are required.

It is worth stressing the diversity of the elements embraced by this moral aspect. Some of these elements have recently been eroded within Western industrial societies (Hirsch, 1977). These societies – notably the US – have developed an extreme competitive individualism, in which levels of trust are inefficiently low. The level of trust required for successful voluntary association is more likely to be present in countries with sophisticated traditional cultures that have recently been modernised – such as Japan.

It is useful to distinguish between high-level entrepreneurship, as exemplified by Schumpeter's heroic vision of system-wide innovation, and low-level entrepreneurship of the kind undertaken by petty traders in small market towns, which can be analysed using the Austrian concepts of arbitrage and market process. High-level entrepreneurship generally requires all the elements of entrepreneurial culture itemised in Table 2.1, whilst low-level entrepreneurship requires only some – it depends principally on good judgement, and to some extent on the absence of attachments that impede mobility. It is this contrast between high-level and low-level entrepreneurship – rather than the presence or absence of entrepreneurship – which seems to be important in explaining the difference between DCs and LDCs. In other words, it is a relative and not an absolute difference with which the analysis is concerned.

Geographical and cultural factors are linked because the geography of a territory can influence the kind of culture that emerges within it. This is because geographical impediments to communication reduce personal mobility and partition a country into small isolated social groups. Internal coordination within these groups tends to rely on primitive mechanisms of reciprocity and the like which depend crucially on stability of membership (Casson, 1988a,b). As explained below, the cultures of these groups are likely to emphasise conformity and coercion rather than individuality and choice, and so inhibit spontaneous entrepreneurial activity.

Good communications, on the other hand, provide opportunities for appropriating gains from interregional trade. Groups that inhabit areas with good communications will tend to prosper, provided their leaders adopt a tolerant attitude towards entrepreneurial middlemen who promote trade. Groups which develop an entrepreneurial culture will tend to expand the geographical scope of their operations (through commercially-inspired voyages of discovery, and so on). Technological advances in transportation will be encouraged because their liberal policies permit the appropriation of material rewards by inventors and innovators. Geographical expansion eventually brings these groups into contact with isolated groups who occupy resource-rich locations. These locations would be inaccessible without the transportation technology and logistical skills of the entrepreneurial group. Equipped with superior technology, the entrepreneurial group can, if its leaders wish, subdue the isolated groups by military means. Different entrepreneurial groups may become rivals in pre-empting opportunities for the exploitation of overseas resources. This may lead to military conflict between the groups, or to a compromise solution where each group maintains its own economic empire and political sphere of influence.

The creation of a transport infrastructure within these hitherto isolated territories not only gives access to resources (and incidentally improves imperial defence); it also tends to undermine the viability of indigenous cultures. Ease of transportation promotes personal mobility and so destroys the stability of membership on which the local groups' methods of internal coordination depend. The confrontation between MNEs and LDCs can be understood as one aspect of this final phase in which the technologies of the entrepreneurial societies are transferred to the regions occupied by the hitherto isolated social groups. To fully understand the nature of this confrontation, however, it is necessary to study in detail the various aspects of the process of development outlined above.

2.4 GEOGRAPHICAL DETERMINANTS OF ENTREPÔT POTENTIAL

A division of labour creates a system of functionally specialised elements. The elements which constitute the system have complementary roles. The division of labour is normally effected over space. Different activities are concentrated at different locations and are connected by intermediate product flows. A large system typically comprises interrelated subsystems, and usually the subsystems themselves can be further decomposed.

System operation over space depends on ease of transportation, and in this context the existence of low-cost facilities for the bulk movement of intermediate products is crucial.

Water transport has significant cost advantages for the bulk movement of freight, and this implies that a good river system and a long coastline (in relation to land area) is an advantage. These conditions are most likely to be satisfied by an island or peninsula with low-lying terrain. Water transport is, however, vulnerable through icing, flooding, and the like, and so geological features that facilitate road and rail construction are also useful.

Good transportation expands the area of the market for the final output of each process. It permits a much finer division of labour because economies of scale in individual plants can be exploited more effectively. In general, steady expansion of the market permits the evolution of system structure. The horizontal division of labour expands to proliferate varieties of final product whilst the vertical division of labour extends to generate a larger number of increasingly simple (and hence more easily mechanised and automated) stages of production.

The development of a region depends not only on the progress of its internal division of labour, but also on its ability to participate in a wider division of labour beyond its boundaries. The external division of labour (as traditional trade theory emphasises) allows the region to specialise in those activities which make the most intensive use of the resources with which it is relatively best endowed.

The interface between the internal and external division of labour is typically an entrepôt centre. Whether or not a region includes a location with entrepôt potential will exert a significant influence on its development (Hodges, 1988). The general advantages of water transport, noted earlier, are reflected in the fact that the cost of long-distance bulk transportation is normally lowest by sea. This means that port facilities are normally necessary for successful entrepôt operation. Since ships afford significant economies of scale in their construction and operation a successful port must be designed to handle large sea-going (and ocean-going) vessels.

A port located close to major international and intercontinental shipping routes may become an important node on a global network of trade. Port activities will comprise both the transhipment of bulk consignments on connecting trunk routes and also 'break bulk' and 'make bulk' operations geared to local feeder services. In this context, the location of the port on the estuary of an extensive river system is advantageous. A centre of transhipment and consolidation is, moreover, a natural place at which to carry out processing activities. Handling costs are reduced because goods can be unloaded directly into the processing facility from the feeder systems, and then later loaded directly from the processing facility onto the trunk system (or vice versa).

The need for processing exported goods depends upon the type of agricultural and mineral production undertaken in the hinterland of the port. In the pre-industrial phase of port development, agricultural processing is likely to be particularly significant. Now crops such as corn and barley offer relatively limited opportunities for downstream processing before consumption – baking and brewing being respectively the main activities concerned – whilst rice feeds into even fewer activities. Animal production, by contrast, generates dairy products, meat and hides, while hides, in turn, feed into the leather and clothing sequence. Sheep are particularly prolific in generating forward linkages, as their wool feeds into the textile sequence. The textile sequence is simple to mechanise and has the capacity to produce a wide range of differentiated fashion products. (Cotton feeds into a similar sequence, but unlike sheep does not generate meat and hides as well.) The potential for forward linkages varies dramatically, therefore, from rice growing at one extreme to sheep farming on the other.

The location of the processing at the port depends, of course, on it being cheaper to locate the processing in the exporting rather than the importing country. This requirement is generally satisfied by both agricultural and mineral products. The perishability of agricultural products means that processing is usually done as close to the source as possible. Mineral products, though durable, lose weight during processing, and so to minimise transport costs it is usually efficient to process close to the source as well.

Mineral processing is, however, energy-intensive, and energy sources, such as fossil fuels, are often even more expensive to transport than mineral ores themselves. The absence of local energy resources can therefore lead to the relocation of processing away from the exporting country. Mineral processing can also generate hazardous by-products. Access to a coastline near the port where such by-products can be dumped is important, therefore, if minerals are to be processed before export.

Whilst the processing of imported products is likely to be of much less economic significance, for reasons implicit in the discussion above, there are a few exceptions. Imports from an LDC, for example, may well arrive in a raw state, because of the lack of suitable energy supplies or labour skills in the exporting country. Furthermore, the more sophisticated are consumer tastes in the importing country, the more extensive is the processing that is likely to be required. Thus the greater the gap in development between the exporting and importing country, the more likely it is that the amount of value added in import-processing will be significant.

The agglomeration of activities within a port provides an opportunity for exploiting economies of scale in the provision of defence, law and order, drainage and sewage systems, and so on. It also provides a large local market which promotes the development of highly specialised services – not only commercial services, but also consumer services – of the kind that could never be provided in country areas with dispersed populations. (Such economies of urbanisation can, of course, be provided without a port, and many countries do, in fact, contain inland administrative capitals which support such services. The viability of such capitals often depends, however, on cross-subsidisation from tax revenues generated at an entrepôt centre, and the social benefits derived from them may therefore be imputed to entrepôt activity.)

It is sometimes claimed that, contrary to the argument above, entrepôts devoted to the bulk export of agricultural products and raw materials are inherently enclavistic. The crucial question here is how fast the linkages between the entrepôt and the village communities of the hinterland develop. In the history of Western DCs provincial agricultural marketing and light manufacturing have grown up in medium-sized towns whose merchants intermediate between the village and the entrepôt. Even in LDCs with limited rural transport infrastructure, the tentacles of trade can extend to the village in respect of livestock farming because livestock can be driven to market over distances that are prohibitive so far as the carriage of crops is concerned. It is, therefore, only if rural culture is strongly opposed to merchant activity that the entrepôt is likely to remain an enclave indefinitely.

The conditions most favourable to industrialisation, it may be concluded, are the existence of a natural harbour close to major shipping routes, good internal communications between the port and its hinterland, livestock farming in the hinterland, abundant endowments of both minerals and primary energy sources, and a coastline suitable for the disposal of pollutants. These considerations alone go some way towards explaining both the early industrialisation of temperate-climate, mineral-rich island countries with coastal deposits of fossil fuels, and good inland river systems, such as the United Kingdom, and their relative decline once their minerals and fossil fuels have been depleted and their comparative advantage in livestock farming has been undermined by the development of overseas territories.

2.5 SCIENTIFIC OUTLOOK AND SYSTEMS THINKING

A territory with entrepôt potential can find its development inhibited by an unsuitable culture. Cultural constraints inhibit entrepreneurship both directly, by discouraging individual initiative, and indirectly by encouraging political leaders to distort incentives and over-regulate the economy.

In some societies the absence of a scientific outlook may well be a problem. Western analysts studying LDCs typically perceive this problem as resulting from the absence of any Renaissance or Enlightenment. The society has not gone through an intellectual revolution in which a mystical view of the world gives way to a more realistic one. The society still relies on anthropomorphic explanations of natural processes, interprets unusual but scientifically explicable events as omens and perceives its real-world environment as the centre of a metaphysical cosmos. This emphasis on things as symbols of something beyond inhibits recognition of things as they really are. It discourages the understanding of nature in terms of mechanism and system interdependency.

A realistic systems view of nature does, however, raise philosophical problems of its own, which can be resolved in various ways. A major difficulty is that if man himself, as a part of nature, is pure mechanism, then choice and moral responsibility become simply an illusion caused by lack of self-knowledge. Western liberal thought resolves this problem through Cartesian dualism, in which the moral world of intentional action coexists alongside the physical world of mechanism.

The scientific outlook does not imply, as is sometimes suggested, a completely secular view of the world. Western Christian thought has also embraced dualism by redefining the role of God as the creator and architect of a self-contained universe, rather than as a supernatural force intervening directly through everyday events. The view that man is fashioned in the image of God encourages the idea that man too has creative abilities. Rejection of the view that the Earth is the centre of the universe diminishes man's stature and raises that of nature, encouraging the idea that nature is worthy of serious investigation. Man's contact with God can no longer reasonably be maintained through sacrifices offered in anticipation of favours, but it can be sustained in other ways, such as an appreciation of the elegance and simplicity of physical laws which express this design. Man's creative abilities can be used to explore this design through observation and experiment.

The systems view of nature translates readily into a systems view of production. Production involves a system created by man and superimposed on the system of nature, with which it interacts. A systems view of production involves awareness of the principle of the division of labour – in particular, the importance of decomposing complex tasks into simple ones and allocating resources between these tasks according to comparative advantage. The systems view also emphasises that the strong complementarities between different elements of the system make it vulnerable to the failure of any single element and so create a strong demand for quality control.

The close connection between religious beliefs and attitudes to nature means that in countries where mysticism or superstition prevail, a scientific outlook and systems thinking are unlikely to develop. The concept of harnessing nature to control the future is absolute folly to people who believe that the future is already pre-ordained, or is in the personal hands of powerful and arbitrary gods. As a consequence, their ability to assimilate technological know-how will be very low. Awareness of how local operations fit into a global division of labour will be minimal. For example, the idea that system complementarities necessitate continuity of operation, rigorous punctuality, and so forth, will be quite alien to local operatives. Appreciation of the importance of quality control in the manufacture of components and intermediate products will be missing too.

2.6 COMPETITIVE INDIVIDUALISM VERSUS VOLUNTARY ASSOCIATION

The development of a scientific attitude in the West was associated with the rise of individualism. The idea that people are intelligent and purposeful was applied democratically. Intelligence was not something confined to a traditional élite, but a feature of every mature adult. Emphasis on intelligence led to demands for reasoned argument rather than appeal to traditional authority or divine revelation for the legitimation of moral objectives.

Individualism asserts that each person is the best judge of how his own interests are served. He can deal with other individuals as equals, and use his intelligence to safeguard his own interests in his dealings with them. Interference in other people's affairs on paternalistic grounds is unacceptable. Individualism claims that everyone is capable of forming judgements on wider issues too. Since different people have different experiences, no one can assume that their own opinion is necessarily correct, and so toleration of other people's views is required. Differences of opinion over collective activity need to be resolved peacefully, and so in political life commitment to the democratic process is regarded as more important than approval of the outcome of the process.

Four aspects of individualism are worthy of special mention. The first is the alienability of property, which helps to promote markets in both products and labour. The demystification of the world through the emergence of a scientific outlook undermines the view that people impart something of themselves to the things they produce. It breaks the anthropomorphic link between production and use. As the product of labour becomes depersonalised and objectified, it becomes acceptable to alienate it for use by others. Conversely, it becomes acceptable to claim ownership over things one did not produce. So far as natural resources are concerned, they no longer need to be held in common by the territorial group. They can be privately appropriated, giving the owner an incentive to manage them properly and avoid excessive depletion.

The second aspect is freedom of entry (and of exit) which allows individuals to switch between trading partners and between markets without the permission of established authority. Such freedom also implies freedom from statutory regulation of entry too.

Thirdly, respect for contract, and a right of recourse to an independent judiciary for the resolution of contractual disputes, are aspects of individualism which are important in reducing transaction costs.

Finally, an individualist appreciates that multilateral trade is most easily established through separately negotiated bilateral trades in which goods are bought and sold using a medium of exchange. He recognises that currency is useful as a specialised medium of exchange, and that the most convenient currency is the debt of a reputable debtor such as the sovereign or the state. Individualism is therefore tolerant of debt and of the personality cult that surrounds notes and coin that carry the head of the sovereign. It imposes obligations on the debtor, however, to live up to his reputation through self-restraint: in particular he must not debase the currency through over-issue.

A major cultural weakness of LDCs seems to be a lack of individualistic thinking. In the extreme case of a primitive rural economy, the link between production and consumption remains unbroken: individuals consume what they themselves produce, and thereby forego the gains from trade. In so far as there is a division of labour, it is confined to within a social group. Different activities are coordinated both by relations of reciprocity between individual members and by members' common sense of obligation to the leader. These mechanisms are most effective within small, stable and compact groups, such as the extended family or the village community. In such groups members regularly expect to encounter one another again, offenders quickly acquire a reputation for bad behaviour and can be easily punished by the leader and, indeed, by other members of the group.

A major defect of such coordination mechanisms is they depend crucially on stability of membership. If it becomes easy for members to quit, then reputations become less valuable, and punishment is easier to evade. Moreover, conditions of geographical isolation, which tend to promote stability of membership, also mean that the threat of expulsion from the group can be very severe. This allows a leader to acquire enormous power over individual members, provided he can 'divide' the members against each other or otherwise prevent them joining forces to overthrow him. Thus while isolation may help to promote close emotional ties between the followers, the leader may be feared rather than respected or loved.

Individualism has its own problems, however, in coordinating the activities of groups. Because individualism promotes inter-group mobility, it not only undermines the 'despotic' solution to intra-group coordination but also the internal reputation mechanism too. A purely competitive form of individualism, which encourages individuals to join teams purely for the material benefits, offers no effective substitute for primitive reciprocity.

When followers' efforts can be easily monitored by the leader there is little problem for competitive individualism, because the material rewards of each member can be linked to his individual performance. When effort becomes difficult to monitor, however, material incentives have to be related to team output, and when the team is large a share of the team bonus may be insufficient to prevent team members slacking. Unless there is a shared sense of corporate mission, individuals are likely to put too little effort into team activity. The leader cannot trust his followers not to slacken. If the leader cannot be trusted either then the followers may not respond to his incentives anyway, because they believe he will default on the agreement if he can get away with it.

Another problem of individualism is that the inalienability of the individual's right to quit may induce higher rates of inter-group mobility than are compatible with efficiency. Successful teamwork often requires members to accumulate on-the-job experience in learning to anticipate each other's actions; unrestricted freedom to enter and exit can allow transitory members who lack this experience to profit at the expense of their colleagues.

Widening the range of an individual's legitimate commitments from mere respect for property and contract to generate trust by instilling a sense of corporate mission significantly modifies the moral basis of individualism. The resulting philosophy is essentially one of voluntary association. This philosophy retains many of the attributes of competitive individualism, but emphasises that the contract of group membership involves acceptance of discipline imposed by the leader. Freedom exists principally in choosing between alternative group commitments, rather than in maintaining full discretion within the chosen group. It also emphasises that commitment to a group is a source of emotional satisfaction, and that more commitment rather than less may make people better off. It does not attempt to repudiate the 'minimal commitment' of competitive individualism but rather to augment this commitment with others.

Widening the range of commitments creates the possibility of moral conflicts. To a heavily committed individual, indeed, it is the resolution of moral dilemmas that often appears to be the essence of choice. Experience in coping with moral dilemmas of this kind may well improve general decision-making skills.

The global organisation of production implemented by sophisticated MNEs depends crucially upon such commitments to mitigate what would otherwise be insuperable agency problems. However intense the competition between MNEs, within each MNE cooperation between the parent and each subsidiary needs to be maintained at a high level. A clear group mission, articulated by a charismatic business leader who makes an effective role model, can be crucial in this respect.

It is therefore worth noting that the kind of individualism harnessed by the successful MNE is very different from the culture of unrestrained self-assertion – or even exhibitionism – which can be found in many societies, including LDCs. The extrovert 'individualism' of adolescent males, for example, has little connection with the mature individualism of the successful entrepreneur. People who exhibit no self-restraint cannot normally be trusted, and so make poor business risks for financiers, and bad employees. The observation, often heard, that there is 'too much individualism' rather than too little in LDCs, confuses exhibitionism with the mature individualism described above. It is not too much individualism that is the problem, but too little individualism of the appropriate kind.

2.7 GEOGRAPHICAL AND CULTURAL ASPECTS OF A GLOBAL TRADING SYSTEM

The preceding analysis suggests that the differences between developed countries (DCs) and LDCs lie not only in resource endowments but in the fact that the territories of the former embrace potential entrepôt centres and that cultural obstacles to the realisation of this potential are relatively weak. An LDC is likely to be a country that has no entrepôt potential, and poor internal communications which make it unlikely to develop an indigenous entrepreneurial culture. A DC, on the other hand, is a country with both entrepôt potential and an entrepreneurial culture.

A country that has entrepôt potential but lacks an indigenous entrepreneurial culture is likely to find that, in the course of time, entrepôt operations emerge under the ownership and control of foreign entrepreneurs based in DCs. These entrepreneurs have the system thinking needed to recognise the entrepôt potential, and are likely to control established international transport and distribution systems into which the new operations can be integrated. The external commercial relations of these countries may become heavily dependent upon an international trading system governed by the requirements of DC markets, and controlled by DC interests, whilst profits generated by entrepôt operations may be repatriated too.

Within any given historical epoch, the process of development begins with the countries that later emerge as the DC investors in LDCs. These countries may subsequently go into decline, but this process of decline is not considered here – it is treated as a separate issue, involving the transition from one historical epoch to another (cf. Wiener, 1981).

In modelling the process of development in global terms, the advantages of water transport over land-based transport – emphasised earlier – play an important role. These advantages mean that maritime trade between entrepôt centres in different countries is likely to be of much greater significance for each country than inland trade between the entrepôt and its remoter hinterland. The fortunes of individual countries are therefore closely linked to their place within the world trading system. Another consequence of the dominance of maritime trade is that even DCs may experience a degree of dualism in their development, between the entrepôt centre on the one hand, and the remoter hinterland on the other. A somewhat ironic corollary of this is that the most unfortunate LDCs, which have no valuable resources and no entrepôt potential, may be the only countries not to experience dualism, purely because they have no development either.

A typical sequence of global development is shown in Figures 2.1 and 2.2. There are two phases. The first involves the rise of DCs prompted by the development of trade between them. The second involves the emergence of LDCs and their own subsequent development.

In the first phase (see Figure 2.1) it is assumed that there are two potential DCs, A and B, each of which is initially segmented into isolated social groups which control particular resources (see sector (a)). Resource endowments are denoted by circles, with large endowments that have foreign trade potential (because, for example, the output is non-perishable and has a high value per unit weight) being denoted by two concentric circles. Each square box encloses a group of people who share a common culture and reside close to a given resource endowment.

Both countries have a natural harbour which forms a potential entrepôt centre. The resources all lie in a hinterland which can be accessed given suitable investment in transport infrastructure. The

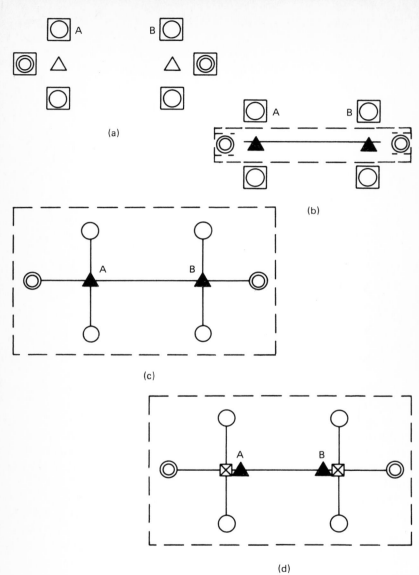

Note: For explanation of symbols, see text.

FIGURE 2.1   *The development of international trade between developed countries*

harbour represents a potential entrepôt centre, and is denoted by a white triangle. It is assumed that in each country the indigenous culture around the major resource is reasonably progressive, so that this potential can be realised. A line of communication is established between the groups controlling the major resource of each country, and two-way trade develops through the entrepôt ports. Realisation of the entrepôt potential is indicated by the switch from the white triangle to the black one in sector (b).

The trade flow intensifies communications between the two countries, leading to cultural homogenisation. This is illustrated by the fact that the two countries now lie within the same box – at least so far as the entrepôt centres and the export-oriented hinterlands are concerned. This culture differs from the cultures of the isolated groups in the less promising hinterlands. The trading system strengthens the progressive element in the indigenous culture of the export-oriented hinterland by giving greater emphasis to the individual's right to hold property and his ability to fend for himself in the negotiation of trades. Competition between the port and the hinterland for employees also stimulates a friendlier and less autocratic style of leadership within social groups. This new commercial culture is distinguished from the culture of the isolated groups by the use of a dashed line in the figure.

As each entrepôt centre develops, the advantages of utilising more fully its indivisible facilities – notably the port – encourage the generation of additional feeder traffic by investment in transport links with the less-promising areas of hinterland (see sector (c)). The entrepôt now handles not only additional export traffic, but also inter-regional traffic between different parts of the hinterland. In other words, the entrepôt becomes a hub for domestic freight transport too. Each country becomes homogenised around the commercial culture as a result. This stage of evolution may well be protracted. Many so-called developed countries still contain isolated rural areas where the commercial culture has made limited inroads.

Before this stage has been completed, the fourth stage may begin. This involves processing exports at the port, in order to reduce the bulk and increase the value of long-distance cargo. Downstream processing of this kind is illustrated in the figure by a cross within a square (see sector (d)). Industrialisation around the port will have further cultural consequences, but these are not considered here.

The second phase of the development sequence begins when one of the developed countries, say A, makes contact with an LDC, C. C

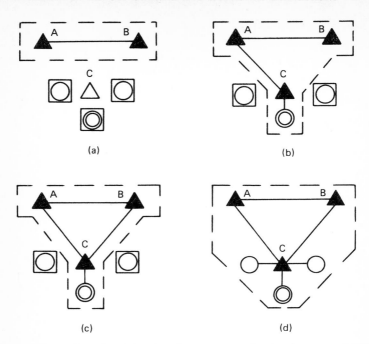

FIGURE 2.2   *The role of developed countries in the development of LDCs*

is still in the situation that A was in at the beginning of the first phase, but with this difference – that C remains undeveloped partly because it has a less progressive culture. Its initial state is illustrated in sector (a) of Figure 2.2. The figure has been simplified by omitting the domestic trade flows within countries A and B.

If A discovered C before B does, A may attempt to monopolise trade with C, so that all trade between B and C has to be routed *via* A. Colonial occupation or control of international shipping lanes may be used to enforce the exclusion of B. So far as C is concerned, it is faced with the impact *via* A, of an established commercial culture which has evolved over a long time from roots which were, in any case, more progressive. This opens up a wide cultural gap within C between the highly commercial imported culture of the entrepôt centre on the one hand and the less-promising areas of hinterland on the other. This is illustrated in sector (c). Cultural dualism impedes the final stage of development, shown in sector (d), where linkages are established with the remaining hinterland. Downstream processing around the entrepôt centre may also develop in this final stage, but this is not shown in the figure.

Two main social groups are available to bridge this cultural gap. One is the resident expatriates, who may have moved abroad originally as employees of the MNE or the DC government. The other is the group of indigenous individuals – merchants and other educated people drawn mainly from the middle and upper ranks of the host society – who are quick to take advantage of the profit opportunities from cultural brokerage. They are willing to learn the language and customs, and adopt the style of dress, of the DC – and perhaps send their children to be educated there as well – in order to consolidate their position. The size of these two groups, and their ability to combine forces where necessary, is crucial in determining the spread of entrepôt influence within the DC.

The analysis suggests that while the process of development in an LDC is similar in outline to that previously followed by an established DC, there are three important differences, which arise chiefly because the LDC is a latecomer to development.

First, the reason why it is a latecomer is partly that it has an unprogressive culture. There may be considerable resistance to the development of entrepôt activity, and indigenous entrepreneurs may be so slow off the mark that foreigners dominate the operations. There may even be political support for a policy of closing the harbour to foreign merchants.

Secondly, if the entrepôt centre is opened up under colonial rule, foreign merchants may enjoy significant market power. Thus few of the gains of trade that accrued to the developed country in the early stages of its own development may accrue to the LDC as it passes through a similar stage itself.

Thirdly, the LDC is confronted with a very sophisticated trading system organised by developed country trade, and with a matching culture very much at variance with its own. Thus, although superficially it might seem that an LDC should be able to catch up quickly with developed countries, its vulnerability to the exercise of market power and the magnitude of the cultural gap may well cause discrepancies in the level of development to persist for a very long time.

2.8   CULTURAL ASPECTS OF MNE OPERATIONS

The MNE is the major institution through which both the technology and the entrepreneurial culture of the DC is transferred to the LDC economy. The largest and most sophisticated MNEs are based in DCs; they utilise advanced technologies to operate internationally rationalised production systems. Systems thinking is highly developed in the headquarters of these firms. Strategic attitudes to competition are also well developed because of continuing oligopolistic rivalry between MNEs in major DC markets.

The analysis in this paper shows that there are substantial cultural barriers to disseminating attitudes of this kind to indigenous managers, and to their subordinates, in LDCs. One obvious way of educating local employees is to send out managers from headquarters on short-term overseas appointments. This may encounter difficulties if the location is sufficiently unattractive to Western eyes that managers resist reassignment to the extent that they prefer to resign instead. In any case, these managers may have difficulties communicating with their subordinates, so while headquarters-subsidiary relations may be good, internal relations within the subsidiary may be poor. In some cases resident expatriates may be employed instead, though there is a risk that they will be out of touch with the more sophisticated ideas developed at headquarters.

An alternative is to hire locally and send recruits to headquarters for extensive training before they return to the subsidiary. Training is, however, likely to be difficult – even at headquarters – unless the local recruits already have some Western-style education, which may well mean that indigenous recruitment is confined to a small social élite. This strategy is inappropriate, moreover, when establishing a new subsidiary; managers will normally have to be sent out from headquarters to organise recruitment, and they can only be replaced when the flow of trained recruits has come on-stream.

Cross-cultural barriers also explain why spill-overs from MNE operations in LDCs are so limited. The capacity of indigenous competitors to imitate – let alone adapt or improve upon – imported technologies is limited by their lack of scientific outlook. Similarly, the inability of local firms to emerge as subcontractors competing against imported component supplies stems from their failure to appreciate the importance of precision and punctuality – an importance that is so transparent once a systems view of production is adopted.

This is not to deny that profit-oriented indigenous innovation will occur. It will proceed slowly, however – because, for example, the nature of the innovation may have to be explained with the aid of an expensive foreign-run 'demonstration' plant, as the basic scientific logic cannot be assimilated. Cautious indigenous businessmen may wait for an indigenous innovator to operate successfully before committing themselves. Unfortunately, if the indigenous innovator does not understand the logic of the situation, he may be unable to improvise solutions to unforeseen difficulties, and so the innovation may gain an undeserved reputation for being unworkable.

When significant spill-overs do occur, and agglomerations of local industries begin to develop, the effect on the cultural life of the indigenous communities can be devastating. The development of urban areas in which MNE activities are concentrated draws labour away from the rural areas. The migration of rural labour is a selective process. Younger and more entrepreneurial workers are attracted to the towns, leaving the least entrepreneurial workers, and the immigrants' aged dependents, behind. Although rural incomes may be partially sustained by intra-family remittances from the towns, the loss of the more productive and entrepreneurial individuals may well harden the conservative and inward-looking attitudes of those who are left behind. Faced with rising out-migration, the reputation mechanisms that coordinate the activities of rural communities are undermined. Rural economic performance declines, and the dualistic structure of the economy is reinforced.

Meanwhile, cut off from their traditional life-style, new urban workers tend to consume a higher proportion of the convenience products and sophisticated durables marketed by the MNEs. Some of these products are promoted using advertising strongly influenced by Western-style competitive individualism. Instead of creating an urban culture based upon voluntary association, which could lead in the long run to a lively entrepreneurial society, commercial media tend to promote attitudes of unrestrained self-assertion which are inimical both to industrial discipline and to honest business practices.

The social disruption caused by MNE activities does not end here, however. The tradition of subservience to despotic authority, sustained in isolated communities, can sometimes be usefully exploited by MNEs searching for cheap unskilled labour that is easily disciplined by intimidation. Women and children accustomed to absolute paternal authority may become useful factory or plantation employees, for example. Once the women acquire a measure of economic independence, however, the economic basis for paternal authority is undermined, and attempts to sustain it through religious teaching may only be able to slow the trend rather than reverse it. As a result, the whole fabric of traditional family organisation may be thrown into disarray.

Another form of disruption is to encourage mass immigration of refugees or landless peasants from other areas in order to depress wages in the locality of the subsidiary. Besides redistributing income away from labour, this strategy carries major problems of cultural integration within the local community, which may spill over into violence, particularly where the immigrants are readily recognised by their language, style of dress, or physical characteristics.

Finally, there is the political disruption which may result from the fragmentation of political alliances which occurs when some local leaders opt for cooperation with foreign interests whilst others oppose it. Both groups may be forced into extreme positions – one as 'lackeys' of the foreign power and the other as intransigent fundamentalists favouring isolation. This fragmentation of the polity may enable the foreign power to 'divide and rule' the country.

This rather negative view of the social consequences of the MNE may be countered by many instances in which MNEs have attempted to become good corporate citizens of the host country. The difficulty here is that many LDCs – particularly former colonies – are in fact agglomerations of different tribes and castes, and that the concept of a good citizen with which the MNE conforms is merely the view held by the social group that is currently in power. Thus in a country with a long history of internal divisions, being officially recognised as a good citizen may require covert discrimination against rival indigenous groups.

Situations of this kind pose various dilemmas for the MNE. In a country, for example, where the religion of the dominant group stresses paternal authority, should contracts for the employment of married women be negotiated through their husbands, so that women in effect become wage-slaves? Is obstructing the economic liberation of women a satisfactory price to pay for being a good corporate citizen and maintaining the economic basis of traditional family life?

In many recently-independent LDCs political power changes frequently, often in response to military initiatives. Should the MNE favour political stability and, if so, use its economic influence on the military to secure the kind of stable regime most acceptable to the

liberal Western conscience? If the MNE remains aloof, and instability continues, it is likely to be confronted with a series of corrupt
demands for payments to government officials, as the holders of
influential offices attempt to make their fortunes before they are
deposed in the next change of government. Should the MNE jeopar-
dise the interests, not only of its shareholders, but also of its indigenous employees by refusing to make payments, or should it respect
'local culture' and support the bribery endorsed by the 'unofficial
constitution'?

The way managers resolve these moral issues will be determined by
the MNE's own corporate culture, which will in turn reflect, at least
in part, the national culture of the DC in which it is headquartered.
In this respect the balance between the philosophies of competitive
individualism and voluntary association in the source country culture
will be a critical factor in determining how far broad moral concerns
dominate the pursuit of shareholders' short-term interests.

2.9 CONCLUSION

Previous economic literature on MNEs in LDCs has tended to
concentrate on issues of market power and the choice of contractual
arrangements (for example, Lall and Streeten, 1977; Calvet and
Naim, 1981). The integration of cultural issues into an economic
analysis of the subject reflects the authors' belief that economic
factors such as these cannot entirely explain the relevant phenomena.
This paper has not proved that cultural factors must be taken into
account. It is always possible that some new and more sophisticated
economic explanation of these phenomena could be contrived instead. Putting this unlikely possibility to one side, however, this
paper has taken a step towards analysing the way that cultural factors
in economic development impact upon, and are modified by, the
MNE.

A great deal of further work needs to be done before the hypotheses advanced in this paper can be properly tested. The full extent of
the cultural differences among LDCs, and among the DC countries in
which MNEs are based, needs to be recognised. The performance of
a given MNE in a given LDC is likely to be governed by (a) the
degree of entrepreneurship in the culture of the firm, (b) the degree
of entrepreneurship in the culture of the host country, and (c) an
'interaction' or 'coupling' term which captures the overall degree of

similarity between the cultures, recognising that culture is a multi-faceted phenomenon.

To apply this method it is necessary to profile the cultures of both the entities involved. It may require in-depth interviews with many people to establish profiles which can make any claim to objectivity. Complete objectivity can never be achieved, of course, in any study of cultural phenomena because of the distortion created by the culture-specific prejudices of the observer. Nevertheless, it is unnecessary to go to the other extreme and adopt an entirely relativistic view. Different observers may still be able to agree on some things, even if they cannot agree on everything.

Cultures contain a certain amount of inertia because of the way they are transmitted between generations through family upbringing. Nevertheless, the advent of public education and mass media communications has the potential to accelerate cultural change. The trend towards greater rapidity of cultural change does, indeed, give a sense of urgency to understanding the mechanisms, and the economic effects, involved.

Economic changes can themselves precipitate cultural change, because they affect the shared experiences of members of a society. The increasing interdependence within the world economy is, in fact, another reason why the process of cultural change may have speeded up. This paper has, unfortunately, treated culture as though it were an exogenous parameter rather than an endogenous variable. A full study of cultural factors would, however, involve a dynamic analysis containing feedback loops of a kind far too complex to be considered here.

Even in its present state, though, the theory provides some simple predictions about comparative economic development. It suggests, for example, that small island economies which enjoy a sophisticated cultural legacy may be better equipped to develop than mainly land-locked countries whose cultural traditions are derived almost exclusively from small isolated rural communities. The entrepôt potential and cultural legacy of Hong Kong, Singapore and Taiwan, say, may therefore explain why they have been able to industrialise and develop indigenous business services so much faster than many sub-Saharan African economies. This is quite consistent with the view that outward-looking trade policies have also promoted their development. It underlines, however, the earlier suggestion that trade policy itself may, in the long run, be culturally specific. Imposing outward-looking trade policies on a less entrepreneurial country in Africa is unlikely to have the same dramatic result as has the voluntary adoption of such policies in South East Asian NICs.

Finally, it should be noted that recognition of cultural factors has significant welfare implications. The emotional benefits that individuals derive from group affiliation are commonly omitted from the preference structures assumed in conventional social cost-benefit analysis of foreign investment. The cultural specificity of the policymaker's own attitudes are also ignored, although these attitudes are crucial in validating the highly materialistic individual preferences assumed in conventional policy analysis. On a more specific level, the failure of conventional analysis to recognise the important economic function of culture in reducing transaction costs, means that conventional analysis has overlooked the significant material as well as emotional costs that cultural disintegration poses on many sectors of the economy. A number of judgements about the net benefits of foreign investment derived from conventional analysis will have to be carefully reconsidered in the light of this cultural analysis.

Acknowledgements

Previous versions of this chapter were given at the EIBA Conference, Antwerp, December 1987, to the Department of Economics seminar at the University of Surrey, October 1988, and to the First Japan AIB Meeting, Waseda University, Tokyo, November 1988. The authors would like to thank the contributors for their comments, and Geoffrey Jones, Matthew McQueen and Hafiz Mirza for comments on an earlier version.

3 On the Transferability of Management Systems: The Case of Japan

Klaus Weiermair

3.1 INTRODUCTION

Over the past decade or so a considerable amount of research regarding the nature and functioning of Japanese firms and Japanese management has been carried out. It resulted in numerous books and an even greater number of articles in professional and academic journals, too numerous indeed to be cited in an introductory paragraph such as this one. Writing yet another essay on Japanese management therefore requires some justification. The present chapter concerning the transferability question of Japanese management has in the main been motivated by the ascendancy and challenge of a 'Japanese-type' system of management among MNEs in general and Pacific Rim MNEs in particular and an associated perceived lack of relevant material in both the economics and management literature. At the same time it was felt that the present discussion on the transferability of organisational structure and/or management styles had been too much steeped in US/Japan comparisons and stereotyping at the expense of a more general/conceptual approach dealing with the applicability of management systems in alternate socio-cultural and economic environments.

The recent rise of interest in the transferability of Japanese management methods has on the Japanese side been associated with the greater appearance of Japanese MNEs on European and American markets. Foreign interest, on the other hand, has been nurtured by hopes to emulate some of the Japanese success stories, thereby stimulating or turning around sagging productivity and industrial performance in a number of mature industries.

The paper is organised as follows: section 3.2 deals with the varying usage and meaning of terms which have been employed in the discussion of management system and know-how transfer; section

3.3 describes the constituent external and internal organisational factors of the system of management, using the example of Japan; section 3.4 shows the interrelationship and interdependence of the aforementioned factors in the evolution and adaptation of Japanese management over time; in section 3.5 an attempt is made to answer the question as to the transferability of the Japanese system of management over time and across different jurisdictions. The final section 3.6 examines the relevance of the approach to less developed countries.

3.2 MANAGEMENT SYSTEM, STRATEGY AND STYLE

As has been mentioned in the introduction, literature surveys in comparative management typically yield the following two observations:

(a) there is an extensive descriptive use of the labels 'Japan and Japanese' and 'US and American' management which often stand as a substitute for a more rigorous comparative analysis of organisational structure, conduct and performance; and,
(b) concepts such as management system, management philosophy, management strategy and/or management practices are being used interchangeably without clearly defining what those terms stand for and how they relate to other key contextual internal and external organisational phenomena.

Management concepts when applied to US/Japan comparisons most frequently refer to human resource management practices, which furthermore are often provided void of any evolutionary and/or environmental context (Nanto, 1982; Bowman, 1986). In the same vein of analysis other treatises have emphasised and contrasted particular comparative aspects of decision-making (Hayashi, 1988), motivation of employees (Amano, 1982; Randsepp, 1986), importance and emphasis of quality and quality control (Jacobs, 1982; Garvin, 1986), strategic management (Digman, 1982) and/or communication techniques and leadership style (Ruch, 1982; Ouchi 1984).

Great care has to be taken in the use of management concepts when analysing international differences regarding the conduct and performance of management in differing environments. In order to distil country-specific conditioning elements of management a concept is needed which should be general enough to allow certain aspects of management (for example, management style) on account of intra- or interorganisational differences to vary but which at the same time is concrete enough to capture country-specific factors of influence. Concepts such as management philosophy, strategy and/or methods may consequently be drawn too narrowly, focusing on aspects which are subject to considerable non-country-specific variation. For example, a great many different leadership styles, management practices and philosophies can be found across European and American firms or industries. Similarly, differences, albeit smaller ones, can be found across organisations in Japan (Nonaka, 1985; Kono, 1988). A more workable and more instructive term, and one which will be used throughout this paper, would be 'Management System'.

As most socio-technical systems, the management system is determined by a multitude of environmental and internal organisational factors which, under stable conditions, are perfectly adjusted to each other and where changes in one factor usually require balancing changes in one or several of the other co-determining forces. Over time and with changes in key environmental conditions management systems evolve different strategies and behaviours. Thus the view of management system entertained here resembles that of the evolutionary perspective of organisation theory (Weick, 1979; Astley 1985). It is also more in tune with recent contributions from the frontiers of microeconomic research (Williamson 1985; Leibenstein 1989; Nelson and Winter, 1982).

Although the next section deals mainly with the Japanese system of management, the discussion could easily be broadened to deal more generally with factors shaping management systems in other jurisdictions.

3.3   INTERNAL AND EXTERNAL ORGANISATIONAL FACTORS

In order to provide a clear frame of reference for the comparative analysis to follow it is first necessary to discuss the key factors of the external context within which the firm and its strategic processes are embedded. Subsequently we will list those internal organisational factors which are among the more prominent in distinguishing the

Japanese management system. In attempting to describe a system of management, particularly its evolution over time, through heuristic methods, great care has to be taken in constructing variables in such a manner as to avoid 'decayed stereotypic or pragmatic' descriptions. As we will argue later that the most distinguishing feature of Japan's management system is its quick adaptability to environmental changes, we cannot but stress the dynamic nature of the relationships discussed below.[1]

The task of comparing differently evolving systems of management across jurisdictions with varying institutional endowments is next to impossible if one were to rely exclusively on orthodox economic theories and/or analyses (Weiermair, 1986). For orthodox formulations foresee 'tight profit maximization' over sharply (market) defined opportunity sets which are taken as given, with firms in the industry and the industry as a whole adjusting to equilibrium size and with innovation being absorbed into the traditional framework rather mechanically. Product markets become in this formulation the almost exclusive motor of managerial strategies. While not denying the role of product markets, notably global product markets, in creating certain convergencies in management strategies across different jurisdictions, the theoretical underpinnings of the present comparative management approach in addition originate in evolutionary theories of economic adjustment (Nelson and Winter, 1982) and relaxation of the profit maximisation postulate (Leibenstein, 1989). Such more generalised theories (with neoclassical propositions forming a special case) are necessary when attempting to explain persistent adjustment pattern differences of firms within and across industries, jurisdictions and/or time under otherwise similar product market conditions. An obvious, and for our purpose instructive case in point has been the differential managerial response to the present restructuring of the international economy among North American, European and Japanese firms, particularly in those industries which could be termed global. Japanese firms generally have been acknowledged to have a superior performance in terms of both size and speed of restructuring (Dore, 1986; Yasumuro, 1988; Pegels, 1984). In order better to delineate the various factors which traditionally impinge on management and to show their interrelatedness we discuss separately external and internal organisational factors as they apply to the Japanese system of management. Schematically the interrelationship between management system and our chosen four external (environmental) factors are depicted in Figure 3.1. Industrial relations and modes of finance constitute both internal and external factors organisational; they will be discussed together with the other internal organisational determinants.

In mechanical terms the four blocks surrounding the system of management in Figure 3.1 could be thought of as cog wheels, which are propelled by the energy in the respective blocks, which in turn is transmitted to the central wheel representing the management system. The process of transmission is determined by both the energy generated in the four outside blocks and the material characteristics of the transmission machine (sharpness and size of teeth in the wheels, material of wheels, for example, steel vs. rubber). Sharp, long and narrowly spaced cogs together with the use of hard materials make for a very precise, mechanical fit (with low levels of tolerance). This produces a micrometer type of adjustment in the central wheel in response to movements in any of the environmental wheels. Given the size of the teeth, it also suggests a slow process of transmission. In contrast to this highly synchronised and tightly fitted system we could devise one which uses cog wheels that are smooth, short and wide and are made of soft material (rubber). In this case opposite results, with respect to the mechanics of transmission will be achieved. The transmission impact will be much stronger (because of the larger width of the teeth) but there will be a much greater level of variance (tolerance) on account of the softer material of the wheels and the wider shape of the teeth. The engineering-minded reader will no doubt discover a large number of possible permutations between material types and various shapes of teeth yielding variations in transmission systems which may or may not have their equivalent in social systems. For the present purpose our 'imagery of mechanics' is to serve as a heuristic device to delineate inter-country differences regarding the fit between environment and management systems.

If we take the two blocks on the right-hand side representing government-business relations and inter-firm relationships, large differences are usually reported to exist between companies in the United States and Japan. Government-business relations are usually depicted as cooperative in Japan, providing large positive externalities to the management system of the large Japanese firm, while being characterised as adversarial with negative externalities in the case of the United States (Pegels, 1984; Toshimasu, 1985). Similarly inter-firm relations follow more the organisation principle in Japan, whereby scale and scope economies in the common pursuit of training, R&D and other information exchange activities among firms

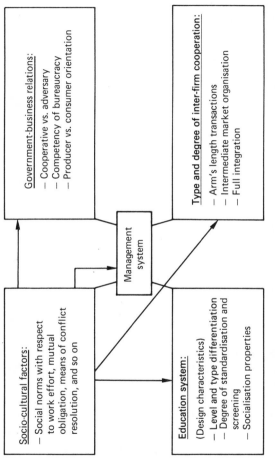

FIGURE 3.1 *Management system and environmental influence*

provide positive externalities, whereas the relationship between firms and between firms and suppliers or contractors in the West have been typified more by arm's length transactions involving the pure market principle (Itami, 1985; Imai and Itami, 1981; Imai, 1988; Yoshino, 1968). Cultural factors or socio-cultural norms, no doubt, have helped, at least in part, to establish and maintain these inter-firm and business-government relations. The perception of the state as a father of the nation supporting and complementing markets wherever necessary certainly differs greatly from Western visions of the role of governments and has deep roots in Japan's history of economic development (Benedict, 1946). Similarly, long-term noncontractual relations between a network of firms can be said to be nurtured by social norms of long-term mutual obligations (Rehder, 1981).[2] The education system affects the system of management first and foremost through the provision of human capital in the form of more or less specialised managerial élites; in the second place it supplies manpower at various levels of skill to be hired by and utilised and further trained in the enterprise. A fair amount of empirical research has shown the education system, through its structural configuration and screening properties, to yield symmetrical consequences in the employment system (Maurice *et al.*, 1980). Again there appears to be a very close match between education and management system in the case of Japan in that great homogeneity of workers at given levels of education provides for a more effective group-oriented organisational style, including consensual decision-making at the managerial level and quality control circles at the operational level (Cole, 1979). Changes such as Japan's much discussed educational reforms in regard to screening (entrance exams) and the planned greater degree of specialisation and occupational preparation are likely to result in transformations of the one-to-one relationship between education and the employment practices of companies.

Finally, the question as to the overall influence of culture on both the management system and the other external environmental factors has to be addressed. A cultural contingency framework in which organisational structures and processes are expressed as a function of the external organisational environment including social, economic and political institutions has been put forward by Child (1981) and several authors have described the impact of Japanese culture on organisational structures and processes through individual needs, values, attitudes and perceptual tendencies (Child, 1981; Yamamura,

1975; Marsh and Mannari, 1976). A number of studies in this vein of analysis have identified the need for vertical social organisation, preference for groupism and the need for dependence and affiliation as individual traits with cultural origin and have found Japanese managers and workers on average to show a higher prevalence of these characteristics (Yamamura, 1975; Sethi, 1975; Cole, 1979). These observations have been confirmed by Ouchi (1981) and Pascale and Athos (1981), who in turn have demonstrated their instrumental value for the Japanese system of Management.[3]

A mushrooming literature has dealt with internal organisational factors said to be linked to or responsible for Japan's unique system of management (Yoshino, 1968; Dore, 1973, Hazama, 1963; Iwata, 1977; Urabe and Ohmura, 1983; Urabe, 1988). Before putting internal organisational factors of Japanese management into a more dynamic and evolutionary framework of analysis at the end of this section, we present below briefly the major determinants as they have appeared in the management literature. Most authors list all or the majority of the following factors as internal conditions of the Japanese system of management:

- separation between capital (ownership) and management
- status equalisation among workers
- stable, seniority-based, pay system
- structuring of internal labour markets and
- consensual management/labour relations and enterprise unionism.

The non-existence of stockholder representatives on the board of directors among Japanese firms and the high proportion of bank financing together with the organisational principles guiding the intra- and inter-firm allocation of financial resources have been well described (Imai, 1980). There is also consensus that this has contributed greatly to the professionalisation of management and to the shift from a short- to a long-run orientation in managerial objectives (Royama, 1985). Status equalisation between white and blue collar workers, which led to the abolishment of previously separated promotion sequences, payment systems and fringe benefit packages, has had the effect of opening up communication between management, staff specialists and workers. This in turn has increased organisational learning through horizontal information flows (Aoki, 1986; Nonaka, 1988) thus supporting and facilitating incremental innovation (Urabe, 1988: p. 13).[4]

When taken together the stable pay system and the career development system (internal labour markets) constitute the cornerstone of employment practices of large Japanese companies. They include the recruitment, promotion and extensive further training of high school and university graduates in long and complex promotion and training ladders, with frequent job rotation across broadly defined job cluster, slow evaluation and promotion and a 'merit and ability' pay system which closely follows the process of skill accumulation within the firm. The description of human resource management practices in Japanese firms has filled entire books and is frequently the subject of articles in management journals (Lee and Schwendiman, 1982; Clark, 1979; Ouchi, 1981, 1984). In many respects the survival of enterprise unionism and the persistence of consensual management labour relations can be viewed as a logical consequence of the other components of the human resource management system, for example, participatory style of management, rich and full exchange of information, long-term mutual trust and obligation relations and relative job security. As has been pointed out elsewhere, the great advantages of cooperative union-management relations lie in the fact that collective bargaining is here limited to narrowly defined distributive issues such as wages, bonus payments or reductions in working hours, while in other jurisdictions, where collective bargaining prevails, it can extend to non-distributive issues such as standards and methods of work, job demarcation, speed of the conveyor, and so on. In turn this makes conflict resolution much more difficult than analytical methods in the setting of joint participation (March and Simon, 1958).

It should be pointed out that the above discussed pillars of the Japanese management and industrial relations system, for instance, life-long employment, the seniority wage system (nenkō), and enterprise unionism, have been given an entirely different interpretation by Japanese Marxists. For they consider the present situation to have evolved from a series of 'reactionary and repressive' measures by the Occupation, the government and managements aimed at controlling and/or purging union militancy and communist infiltration in the period following the Second World War. Thus, according to their view, 'present cooperative enterprise unions came into existence as a result of the defeats of unions that were bold enough to carry out long-term strikes against the discharge of their members. This fact implies that, contrary to common belief, enterprise unions originally were not cooperative in their attitude towards management, but were borne in the course of bitter struggles' (Tokunaga, 1983: pp. 313–29). Another associated and often quoted view is that of differing 'managerial ideologies and methods of worker co-optation' suggesting that industrial paternalism has not only had a long tradition, dating back to the formulation of industrial élites in Meiji Japan, but that variations thereof still cast a long shadow on today's workplace practices and institutions (Karsh, 1983: pp. 81–3). Having briefly sketched out major elements contained in mainstream descriptions and analyses of Japanese management, an attempt is made below to view these elements within a broader theoretical framework of varying patterns of microeconomic adjustment. Of particular interest are the firm's typical decision-making processes *vis-à-vis* different types of environmental change (for instance, contraction, changes in rate, composition and incidence of enterprise growth). According to Nelson and Winter (1982) different stylised response strategies and decision-making processes, such as replication, control, imitation, innovation or contraction, are largely determined by the 'organisational capabilities' of firms. In turn these derive from organisational skills, which, together with the organisation's memory, produce 'organisational routines'. The latter form the core of organisational functioning and are central to the firm's economic selection processes (Nelson and Winter, 1982: pp. 96–136). Using the above framework the previous observations regarding the functioning of the Japanese system of management could be reinterpreted as follows:

(1) Organisations tend to search for new organisational routines when faced with severe adversity. Japanese firms found themselves in such a situation in the period following immediately after the Second World War. As a rule new organisational routines are designed to foster either imitation (or other firms) or innovation. Japanese firms decided initially to opt for imitation and incremental innovation in well focused markets/products.

(2) Given the tight fit between environmental and internal organisational conditions in Japan, which could also be viewed as a constraint, Japanese large business organisations were, from early on, forced to a much greater degree than their counterparts abroad to conceive and design an internally and externally consistent system of management. By necessity this design had to be more holistic in nature; it also meant that it had to be more sensitive (or vulnerable) to changes in the environment.

(3) Conditions in (1) and (2) have had the effect of institutionalising to a much greater degree within Japanese firms a 'permanent'

search for new organisational routines (leading in consequence to imitation or innovation processes). A number of recent studies have emphasised this form of organisational learning as a comparative advantage of the large Japanese business firm (Abegglen and Stalk, 1985; Shimada and MacDuffie, 1987; Tomer, 1987; Imai, 1980, 1988; Kagono, Nonaka, Sakakibara and Okimura, 1983; Nonaka, 1988).

(4) Thus the typical management system of the large Japanese firms, including MNEs, seems to be much more geared towards accepting and living with permanent internal changes, which furthermore call for perpetual adaptations between internal and external organisational forces. Furthermore, this evolutionary process has in the main been conditioned by environmental shocks, which had their main effects at home (due to the global export strategies chosen by Japanese MNEs throughout much of the post-war period).

Typical examples of restructuring and re-adaptation of Japanese firms are provided in the next section.

3.4 ENVIRONMENTAL CHANGE AND THE EVOLUTIONARY ADAPTATIONS OF JAPANESE MANAGEMENT

A useful way to inquire into the adaptability and evolutionary character of the Japanese system is to evaluate historical antecedents in terms of adjustments to major environmental shocks such as the revaluation of the Yen (Yendaka), the oil crisis, or major demographic changes in the market for labour. Following that we may want to speculate on the adjustment of the management system to competition from NIC countries and globalisation, industrial restructuring and new forms of technology-driven competition.

Both the oil crisis and the continuing deterioration of the dollar, which first started in 1971, directly affected the export competitiveness of Japanese companies. Cost price ratios rose anywhere from 40 to 300 per cent depending on the combined effects of higher raw material and energy costs and lower Yen export proceeds, which varied widely across industries. To the surprise of some Western observers, but expectedly for those familiar with Japanese management, companies mastered the various dollar and oil crises of the seventies remarkably well. The reasons for this are associated with the design characteristics of the external and internal organisational factors conditioning the Japanese system of management and their mutual reinforcement. First of all there was the idea of a besieged Japan, which was important before the war and which has re-emerged since the early seventies, especially after the 1972 US embargo on soya exports to Japan ('the food weapon') and after the rise in oil prices in 1973. This vision, which has been used skilfully by the government and management to invigorate and motivate every worker to overcome this 'national crisis' through improved perform-ance and productivity; both a flexible wage and employment system (flexibility through overtime work and pay, temporary workers, subcontractors as partial employment buffers and bonus system) and inflexible markets with respect to finance and supplier relations, provided for a long-term trajectory of adjustment (Wakasugi, 1988). Rationalisation cartels in order to reduce capacity in troubled indus-tries and subsidisation of new technology in such mature industries as textiles were government-induced complements of this process. Finally, cooperative trade unions, who accepted temporary freezes in wages and bonuses and an accelerated employment of new techno-logies enabled management to orchestrate this miraculous adjust-ment in terms of increased productivity and unchanged export prices (Dore, 1986).

It appears that the Japanese system of management was somewhat less capable of coping with the various secular changes of labour markets, notably secular shifts in demographics, work expectations and ethics of young workers (Shinjinrui). A seniority-based wage system for everybody and life-long employment in large firms are highly contingent upon high rates of economic growth, a regular and unchanging supply of fresh university and high school students and an unchanging or incrementally changing technological environment. All of these conditions, however, have undergone considerable change in the seventies and eighties. While economic growth has been halved, a post-war baby-boom generation is now eligible for middle management positions, which have become scarce because of both the slowed rate of economic growth and the recently introduced extension of the legal mandatory retirement age. With a top-heavy population distribution it has become increasingly difficult to con-tinue guaranteeing a steep pay curve with annual rises. The glut of supervisors, caused by these demographic shifts, has been further aggravated by the information revolution which has made much of the information collection, sorting and reporting of middle manage-ment redundant (Nakatani, 1988). Not surprisingly many national employment surveys now find that many more workers want to change jobs and many more companies express concern about a lack of management positions and a consequent erosion of employee morale. The Japanese hiring, training, promotion and wage system, which has been highly effective in distributing rewards in such a way as to maximise skill formation and effort over an employee's working life, appears no longer viable. The problems are further aggravated by value changes noted first among those in the baby-boom generation who are displaying a greater need for self expression and are less 'organisation-directed' (Nemoto, 1987). Given the tight and synchronised fit between education and employment systems it would be necessary simultaneously to adjust external and internal organisational processes of skill formation (for instance, a greater degree of occupational preparation and professionalisation in schools in order to cope with the higher (mobility-induced) costs of on-the-job training). There has been virtually no adjustment in the education system and throughout most of the seventies and eighties companies attempted to cope with demographic shifts and value changes through existing institutional arrangements (for example, increased retirement of executives into subsidiary or subcontracting firms). It was not until the mid-eighties that organisations began considering radical overhauls in their organisational structures as they were beginning to realise limitations to the conscientious diligence that workers have displayed so far (Nakatani, 1988). As is probably typical for adjustments in a tightly synchronised system of management, changes began to occur when possibilities for new synergies through mutual adaptation and reinforcement developed. These were: increased needs to diversify into new products and engage in more intensified research and development, an on-going process of industrial restructuring towards knowledge-intensive and service sector products, rising educational attainment and individuality among new company recruits and a drop in the value of company-specific human capital due to the information processing and standardisation properties of computerisation (Nakatani, 1988). The process in which many large Japanese firms are presently engaged involves a move from vertical to horizontal organisations, an intensified spinning off of companies and increased networking, an emphasis on diversification, creativity and the provision of a fast track for company stars. If completed, these developments would imply the disappearance of the traditional Japanese management system. As some would argue the transition was largely facilitated by the tight fit of the old system and the help of external and internal organisational conditions. An example is the recent targeting of the software industry by MITI and the intensified acquisition of research and knowledge and entrepreneurship through inter-firm networks (Imai, 1988). Another illustration is the rejuvenation of management and engineering teams, for instance, Honda's latest model 'City' was constructed by a team with an average age of 29!

The Japanese business climate has shifted, it seems, from order to chaos, from stability to dynamic flux. Some authors have suggested more or less convincingly that Japanese management, particularly its information-gathering and decision-making processes allowing for more ambiguity, will be predestined to cope with such changes (Nonaka, 1988; Mroczkowski and Hanaoka, 1989). This then leaves us with the final question as to how Japanese management, most notably that which is exercised by MNEs, will cope with globalisation and internationalisation. How much are the Japanese able to cope with changes abroad and how much of their management system is applicable in other jurisdictions?

3.5 TRANSFERABILITY OF THE JAPANESE SYSTEM OF MANAGEMENT

The transferability question is of relevance in two principal areas. First of all, in the West there exists at the present time much talk and a swelling literature on the need for new managerial competencies associated with economic restructuring and the management of change; therefore it should be of some interest to investigate the extent to which the Japanese system may be suited to embrace these new forms of management. Secondly there is the question as to how well Japanese MNEs' system of management has performed in the recent past. We begin with the last point first.

If we discount the presence of Japanese multinationals in the Pacific region it is probably fair to state that the internationalisation and globalisation of Japanese industry and management have been a fairly recent phenomenon. Furthermore, the rush to foreign investment has in some cases, notably with the United States, been much less planned due to the unexpected rise of expected protectionist barriers (Nakatani, 1988). Perceptions of employing a different and not easily transferable system of management may at least in part have explained the reluctance of the Japanese firm to move abroad earlier (Trevor, 1983). Fortunately the rush of Japanese foreign investment in the late seventies and eighties has produced a large and mounting empirical literature on the strategies and adaptation experience of Japanese MNEs (Kujawa, 1986; Dunning, 1985b, 1986; Shimada *et al.*, 1987; Trevor, 1983, 1987; Thurley, 1983; Yoshikara and Bartlett, 1987; Abo, 1987; Park, Juergens and Melz, 1985; Ozawa, 1979). Based on findings in this research the following observations emerge:

- Japanese firms have been relatively successful in wholesale transplants of Japanese style production systems, particularly in such sectors as automobiles, machine building and engineering.
- European and American workers seem to have taken well to the Japanese form of job organisation, production control and labour participation. They have taken well, it appears, to Japanese management's efforts to restructure jobs, careers and pay scales along policies pursued in Japan and have rewarded management with substantial improvements in productivity and participation (Shimada, 1987; Abo, 1987; White and Trevor, 1983; Park *et al.*, 1985).
- Foreign workers have also reported relatively more respect for Japanese managerial competence in comparison with local management (Thurley, 1983; Thurley, Trevor and Worm, 1983).

The Japanese success in transplanting entire manufacturing systems abroad comes as no great surprise. For many years, the West, but notably the United States, has downplayed and/or neglected developments in production management in favour of loftier pursuits in marketing and finance and have held onto outdated 'Taylorism' as a form of shop-floor management (Schonberger, 1986). Nowhere is Japan's supremacy more evident than in the conceptualisation and management of their automobile plants both in Europe and the USA. As shown in Figure 3.2 all aspect of hard, soft and humanware of manufacturing have been integrated into a holistic approach which is transferable across jurisdictions.

Japanese management has been far less successful with white collar workers and hence with service-related businesses. The long-term orientation of Japanese management equally ran into adaptation difficulties in markets with extremely short product cycles, which are also often dominated by service organisations (for instance, financial and business services). Japanese MNEs tried to opt for compromises or two-track systems, which as might have been expected, did not

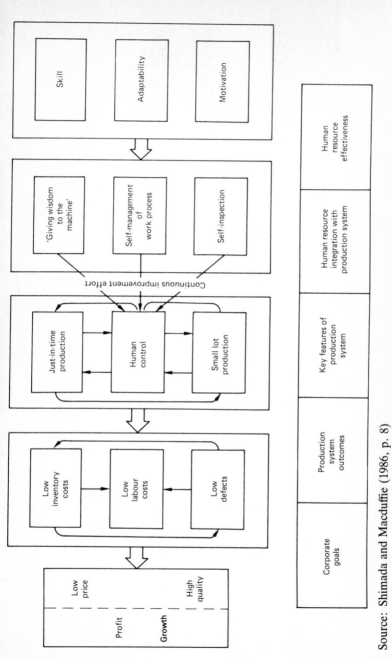

Source: **Shimada and Macduffie (1986, p. 8)**

FIGURE 3.2 *Japanese production system and 'HUMANWARE'*

work well given the highly synchronised nature of the Japanese system of managing (Abo, 1987; Yoshihara and Bartlett, 1987; Yoshida, 1987). Problems were similarly reported with respect to the exchange activities of Japanese firms with their external organisational constituents such as suppliers, subcontractors, education and training institutions and governmental bodies. Although there has been a tendency to induce the export of Japanese infrastructure in order to extend system synergies abroad (for example, Japanese banking, subcontracting through Japanese networks, large Jetro offices abroad, and so on) there are natural limits to such exports. Again, Japanese firms had to resort to compromise policies (Abo, 1987).

Problems of deciding on a suitable blend between Japanese and foreign systems of management have been further aggravated by a lack of experience as well as resistance to change on the part of local management. The latter was particularly true for middle management which frequently felt threatened in its existence from the combined effects of foreign take-overs and introduction of new technologies.

As has been indicated previously, the question as to which system of management may be more transferable is intrinsically related to the needs of future management, thus posing the question as to which system can most easily embrace rapid technological change, operate in turbulent and global markets and manage radically different work forces. A number of social scientists as well as hard-nosed empirical business researchers have probed this question and produced the following consensual list of required changes in management practices/skills:

- improved capabilities in environmental scanning
  (read fracture lines and recognise market opportunities)
- engage in pro-active management
  (opportunity-seeking attitude, manage from the outside in and develop positioning and repositioning skills)
- make improvements in human resource management
  (take people as key resources, who relish change; manage in an environment of equals; improve the balance between generalist and specialist skills)
- promote more creativity, learning and innovation
  (encourage people to learn and be creative, strike a better balance between chaos and control, attempt remote management, make specialists user driven)

- use the transformation impact of new technologies
  (creative use of information, open focused planning with evolution in mind, a new information management mindset, recognise the strategic role of the software industry)
- improve the management of complexity
  (manage multiple stakeholders, manage many things at the same time, manage transition) (Morgan, 1988).

The above-described management recipes for greater customisation and recognition of local customers needs to be carried out with flexible manufacturing systems, greater economies of scale and new forms of remote and network management, facilitated by new information technologies and a greater recognition of human resources as strategic company assets could almost be viewed as a blueprint for the presently evolving system of Japanese management (Nonaka, 1988). Notwithstanding the problems of managing multi-racial work forces, where Japanese MNEs are still involved in a trial and error process, it is probably not too far-fetched to speak of a present 'Japanisation of international business', which is emerging even in those industries and markets which have prevented the Japanese from entering (for example, the automobile industry in France). The transferability question therefore ought to be viewed much more from the vantage point of future management requirements and it is here that the evolution of the global supply model of Japanese MNEs has proven more effective than the traditional European decentralised multi-domestic production structure or the American multinational, centralised mass-production structure (Yasumuro, 1988). It remains to be seen whether this new form of international business organisation and management will drive away older types through international competition analogous to the take-over of American management methods and structures during the period following the Second World War.

3.6 THE JAPANESE MANAGEMENT SYSTEM AND JAPANESE MNEs IN LESS DEVELOPED COUNTRIES

Buckley and Casson's contribution in this volume (chapter 2) has identified entrepreneurial attitudes and geographical/institutional determinants of entrepôt potential as key success factors behind both MNE performance and the general process of economic development in less developed economies. A critical evaluation of Japanese MNEs and their system of management therefore has to address the question as to the performance of Japanese firms with regard to the transfer and transformation of their organisational (entrepreneurial) culture and with respect to the establishment of superior institutional conditions for entrepôt development in comparison to their European and North American counterparts. Fewer studies on Japanese management in LDCs exist, but those which are available, similarly attest to the relatively greater adjustability of Japanese management techniques and to their potential for transfer into foreign LDCs. At the same time there is evidence suggesting that Japanese MNEs in LDCs have been greatly helped by the presence and orchestration of diligent Japanese development aid programmes and by the exportation of unique Japanese institutional/market arrangements, notably the 'sogo shosha' or trading companies. As to the latter a good account regarding the role and functioning of Japanese trading companies in overcoming market failures, institutional rigidities and/or structural deficiencies for trade in LDCs can be found in Kojima and Ozawa (1984).

From an early stage, in addition to their function of multinational intermediation the sogo shoshas have developed extensive expertise and skills as organisers and/or coordinators of large-scale turn-key projects in LDCs providing transaction intermediation, quasi-banking and information gathering (Kojima and Ozawa, 1984; p. 26). In the more recent past they have also entered manufacturing ventures which in the main are centred on technologically standardised, labour-intensive industries; 80 per cent of these are concentrated in developing countries. Through the parcellisation of manufacturing into many separate but closely linked ventures Japanese trading companies were not only able to maximise the span of their trading territory and minimise possible risks associated with it, but thereby have also created what Kojima/Ozawa termed 'infrastructural entrepreneurs' (Kojima and Ozawa, ibid.: p. 40). Finally Japanese MNEs have been able to benefit from the export of favourable government/business relations, which they consumed in the form of lobbying for Japanese foreign aid funds associated with particular manufacturing and/or turnkey projects. Examples such as Mitsubishi's special Yen loan for the Mombasa airport in 1972 or Shimazu's urban renewal project in Baghdad in 1979 abound. While North American and European MNEs have equally engaged and used national and international organisations to overcome structural impediments, the Japanese system of management, it is argued, has been more effective on account of its holistic (environment embracing) approach and its greater abilities to create 'entrepreneurial infrastructures'.

The second observation concerns the relative success of Japanese MNEs in transferring organisational (entrepreneurial) cultures and managerial techniques to operations in LDC countries. Based on survey results the general conclusion with respect to the flexibility of Japanese management is that it has adjusted its practices to the constraints imposed by local conditions but has done so in a way which retains as many features of its domestic operation as possible. Consequently overseas operations in LDCs lie somewhere in between those characterising their home offices and those in the typical company domestic to the country in which the Japanese foreign subsidiaries are operating. A typical example of this is the wide variety of indicators in the field of human resource management: the width and depth of skill development, the ability to retain workers, the extent of rotation, degree of intra-firm information transfer, job security guarantees or levels of participation in decision-making observable among Japanese MNEs in Asia and Latin America (Ishida, 1985; Ishimura and Yoshihara, 1985). What seems to distinguish Japanese MNEs from their European and/or North American counterparts, who share the same local constraints and often pursue similar strategies, is the 'disciplined flexibility' of Japanese management. As has been argued earlier in this paper, this in turn derives largely from a more holistic and/or thorough approach inherent in the Japanese system of management.

Notes

1. On this point we gratefully acknowledge various comments made by the discussant Hafiz Mirza and John Dunning.
2. Another and equally fruitful approach analyses the aforementioned institutional arrangements in terms of either X-efficiency or transaction cost theoretical considerations. Given the nature of the post-war Japanese economy, which has been largely based on focused manufacturing and incremental innovation, it can be shown, for example, that the kind of information sharing and governance of inter-firm and government-business relations have been efficient institutional adaptations under the aspect of transaction cost minimisation. Such an analysis would also allow for some of the key parameters to change in evolutionary fashion, thereby

altering institutional arrangements via transaction cost changes. Future changes, such as increased immigration, greater and more complex linkages to the external economy and the rise of the service economy with attendant changes in the number and size distribution of firms, are all likely to lead to an increase in the degree of social heterogeneity within and across organisations, thus making policing through social norms and relations too risky (costly). This means that social monitoring will eventually give way to more contractual Western-type relations both within and across firms. Similar effects would result from societal changes away from group orientation towards more individualistic values and value systems.

3. Cultural values, even when operationalised as behavioral traits or institutional peculiarities should, nevertheless, be treated with some caution if not reservation. For a large number of social and work norms readily identified as 'culturally determined' have rational explanations in terms of governance relations with low transaction costs. Similarly, the rigidity of and adherence to these norms over extended periods of time can be analysed and explained within the framework of X-efficiency theory (Leibenstein, 1984; Leibenstein and Weiermair, 1988). Norms can change over time and sometimes also vary across different groups in society. For example, groupism may be stronger among blue collar workers in comparison to white collar employees. Clearly more work along the lines of a generalised theory of norms and conventions would be needed to gain a better operationalisation for the use of cultural variables (see Schotter, 1981).

4. This represents an interesting illustration of inter-relationships between managerial strategy setting and cultural influence, between cultural values as means and as ends. As such it also throws light on the circumstances leading to changes in social norms. In the fifties, when Japanese managers decided on the democratisation of the workplace, they did so under considerable duress approaching dimensions of crisis (a destroyed economy, liberated and militant unions and pressures from the allies). It appears that management's change of philosophy had been based on long-term efficiency considerations, even though it may also have been conditioned culturally. Once, however, these new norms or conventions were set they became an end rather than a means of organisational life. We hypothesise that the efficiency-enhancing properties of an organisational culture are higher and more stable when they represent an end rather than being used instrumentally. At the same time we may infer that the inability to create new norms and organisational paradigms is likely to be related to a lack of environmental shocks and cultural conditioning (Leibenstein, 1987). While reference will be made later to an evolutionary theory of managerial response to environmental shocks (Nelson and Winter, 1982) clearly more work needs to be done to advance a dynamic theory of norm setting.

Part III
Market Structure and
Welfare Effects

4 Strategic Trade Policy and the Multinational Enterprise in Developing Countries

Edward M. Graham

4.1 INTRODUCTION

A recent paper by Wells and Encarnation (1986) examines a number of investments by multinational firms in one developing country from a social cost/benefit point of view, and concludes that a sizeable percentage of these impart net negative benefits to the local economy. The sectors in which these investment undertakings were made generally benefited from high levels of protection from imports of substitutes for the final output of the undertakings. The authors conclude that the major reason for the outcome is that the scale of the undertakings is sub-optimal, resulting in average costs of production of output substantially above the landed price of imported substitutes.

In this paper the (rather obvious) observation is offered that negative benefits will accrue to the economy even if the investment undertaking is able to operate at efficient scale (such that marginal costs of output are no greater than the landed costs of imported substitutes) if the structure of the local industry is highly oligopolistic or monopolistic. This can be easily demonstrated to be true even if the relevant firms 'compete' rather than 'collude' and the MNE is able to produce locally at costs equal to the landed price of imported substitutes. It is asked if there exist circumstances where it is optimal for a host country to encourage foreign direct investment via import protection when the local industry structure is oligopolistic. The situation is examined from the point of view of the emerging concepts embodied in 'strategic trade policy'. 'Strategic trade policy' has largely been developed in the context of oligopoly industries in the advanced industrial countries. The central issue is, do these concepts

79

ever make sense for developing countries when the key actors are multinational firms? The reader will recognise that this is essentially a re-examination of the 'infant industry' argument.

4.2   INDUSTRY STRUCTURE AND SOCIALLY SUB-OPTIMAL BEHAVIOUR BY THE MNE

The simplest case would be one where an MNE is allowed to invest directly in a nation so that it operated as a monopoly. This would generally require that the firm was granted protection from imports. Suppose that the resulting undertaking could produce at (constant with respect to volume of output and time) marginal cost $c = p_w$, where p_w is the landed price of imported substitutes. (The assumption of constant marginal cost is relaxed later in this article to account for economies of learning.) If demand for the product is linear and invertible, such that it can be written $P = A - bQ$, where A and b are constants, P is the price charged by the local subsidiary of the MNE, and Q is amount demanded at price P, it is straightforward that the firm would charge a price $P = (A + c)/2$.

If $A > c$, then $P > p_w$ and the undertaking will be sub-optimal from a social point of view, assuming only that the firm attempts to maximise profits, even though it produces 'efficiently'. If $A < c$, the firm cannot produce profitably, and the investment would not be made. If $A = c$, then $P = p_w$, and the investment would yield a pricing outcome identical to that of allowing free trade; this latter-most, however, would be a rather improbable occurrence. These results follow from elementary considerations of monopoly pricing and are completely standard. The outcome would be socially sub-optimal even if the host government taxed away all 'rents' garnered by the MNE; in this case, the level of output $Q = (A - c)/2b$ would be sub-optimal.

The result can be extended quite easily to the case where the local subsidiary of the MNE must compete with a local rival. Assume for simplicity that the end product of the MNE and that of the local rival are perfect substitutes and that each of the two firms produces at constant marginal cost, that of the MNE now denoted by c_1 (which again is equal to p_w) and that of the local rival c_2 (which we shall assume is greater than c_1.) We also assume that the two firms do not collude to achieve monopoly rents. Demand again can be represented by $P = A - bQ$, but now Q is total demand, which in equilibrium must be equal to the combined output of the two firms, where output of the MNE is denoted Q_1 and that of the local rival Q_2. The likely outcome is a Cournot equilibrium, wherein $P = (A + c_1 + c_2)/3$. Again, because by assumption $c_2 > p_w$, $P > p_w$ only if $A > c_1$, and this latter condition must hold if the MNE is to make any investment at all. In this analysis, we assume that the MNE does not choose to set price so as to put the (higher cost) local firm out of business. That this latter possibility could under appropriate circumstances be an optimal strategy for the MNE has been demonstrated by Casson (1987b). In this situation, the MNE becomes a monopoly, and the pricing behaviour of the MNE is as indicated above.

Analogous results extend readily to the case where the MNE must compete in an oligopoly consisting of n firms. It is a well established property of the Cournot equilibrium that if the number of firms in an oligopoly is n and each firm has constant marginal cost c, then in the limit as n becomes large, $P = c$. (In other words, the Cournot equilibrium is the perfect market equilibrium if the number of firms is 'large' and each firm has constant marginal cost c.) The results above can be easily extended to show that if the number of firms in the oligopoly is n such that n is finite and the marginal costs of any one firm are greater than p_w, then the equilibrium price will also be greater than p_w.

Because in this example the MNE is a lower cost producer than any local firm, it is entirely possible that the MNE could act as a Stackelberg price leader. In the case of duopoly under the assumptions above, the MNE will set price equal to $(3A + 3c_2 + 2c_1)/8$ which could be above or below the Cournot price depending upon the difference between c_1 and c_2 but again will always be above p_w.

The point here is that under favourable assumptions about costs and outcome (the MNE is able to produce at 'world costs' and all firms in the local industry actually compete, rather than collude to maximise profits jointly), the industry structure will lead to a socially unfavourable outcome with respect to pricing and output decisions of firms in the industry. Further rather obvious points are that any rent that accrues to the MNE in this context represents not simply a redistribution of income among domestic residents, but rather a transfer of income from these residents to the foreign shareholders of the MNE, a situation that clearly is undesirable from the point of view of host nation welfare. The analysis to this point suggests that a developing nation should never grant import protection to a MNE operating within its boundaries; open trade would reduce or eliminate rents that otherwise would accrue to the MNE, while if the MNE could produce at a cost $c \leq p_w$ its presence in the developing country could bring the usual social benefits to the nation (for example, externalities associated with technology transfer, greater inter-firm rivalry within the domestic market, exports, and so forth).

This outcome, however, depends upon the assumption that the cost structure of the MNE is static. Trade protection in developing nations is, however, often based upon the assumption that local economic activities will undergo learning, such that they will lower their costs as they accumulate production experience. This is, of course, the 'infant industry' argument for protection. It is by now well established that there can be a case for import protection when costs decline as a function of accumulated output; such an argument is at the heart of recent literature on 'strategic trade policy'. The question is, do these results ever make sense for the MNE in the developing country?

4.3   THE MNE IN THE DEVELOPING COUNTRY WHEN THERE EXIST DYNAMIC SCALE ECONOMIES

'Strategic trade policy' deals with a number of situations where the standard tenets of international trade theory break down. Among the situations are imperfect competition (Brander and Spencer, 1981), economies of scale (Krugman, 1984), and declining average cost in industries with constant marginal costs where threat of entry ('contestability') forces competitive pricing (Venables, 1984). The Brander and Spencer case and variants on it (for instance, Dick, 1988) do not really fit the circumstances of MNEs operating in developing countries, but rather are concerned with duopolists based in different countries operating in industries characterised by high rates of technological innovation. Similarly, the high fixed cost/constant marginal cost case of Venables is of questionable relevance to developing countries because of the assumption of 'contestability'. The most relevant circumstances are where some sort of scale economy is extant. One should note that the mere existence of a scale economy implies that the structure of the industry in question will be something other than 'competitive'.

From an analytical point of view, probably the most interesting situation to examine is that in which scale economies are dynamic – that is, where there is some sort of 'learning curve' affecting average and marginal costs such that each of these declines with accumulated output of the firm. (In this paper I consider the 'learning curve', the 'experience curve', and 'learning by doing' all to be the same thing, although there are authors who make subtle distinctions among these.) This situation apparently also is one that actually exists in a wide number of industries, or at least this is so if one believes the evidence as presented by several of the major international management consulting firms.

Krugman (1984) is the pioneering work on trade under learning-based scale economies. This work supposes that there are two firms based in different (advanced) nations, each of which operates under a similar learning curve. In this case, it might pay one nation to grant trade protection to the local firm in order that that firm accumulate volume of production as quickly as possible and 'win' the 'game' of international competitiveness. In this case the import protection acts *de facto* as an export subsidy.

It is clear that this holds only if one nation, but not the other, protects the local market. It would be mutually destructive for both nations to protect their home markets (each nation would suffer from both high costs and monopoly). For this reason, the Krugman reasoning works really only as a 'single-shot' game; the game has a prisoner's dilemma – like structure, and in a repeated game context, if one nation protected its market, in subsequent 'games' it is likely that the other nation would also protect its own home market, to the detriment of both nations.

The concern here, of course, is with multinational firms in developing countries. It is clear that we must ask ourselves whether the relevant learning curve is one that applies to the MNE as a whole or to the local subsidiary only. That is, is the relevant accumulated volume that governs the learning curve that of the global operations of the MNE or simply that of the local subsidiary?

If it is the former, it is unlikely that the welfare of the host nation would be enhanced by granting trade protection to the MNE so that it could increase local market share. For one thing, the additional local market share would probably not contribute greatly to world cumulative production of the firm, and hence local production for local consumption probably would not greatly affect costs of the firm. This story could change, of course, if the local subsidiary were to export output. Even if it did so, however, it is not clear how protection would help the host country. The protection would act to reduce competition within the host market, and even if the local subsidiary exported output, it would be able to charge monopoly (or oligopoly) prices domestically. Thus, protection of the home market could lead to the local subsidiary using domestic market sales to cross-subsidise export sales.

This is not to claim that there would be no benefits to the host nation from the dynamic scale economies in this situation. As Spence (1981) notes, the relevant marginal cost for a monopolist facing a learning curve is the unit cost of output after all learning has taken place. Because learning is a function of accumulated output, the greater the output, the lower will be this marginal cost. But, as will be demonstrated, if the marginal cost approaches an asymptotic limit c, then the MNE will engage in exactly the same pricing behaviour in the host country domestic market as described in the first section of this paper.

What about the case where the relevant accumulated volume is that of the subsidiary and not the whole enterprise? The issue facing the host government is likely to be whether or not the MNE is willing to make an investment in the local economy to serve as an export base. A further issue then would be whether or not the granting of local trade protection will help tilt the MNE towards making a favourable decision. To deal with these issues, it helps to look more closely at the dynamics of the firm's costs and resulting optimising conditions given the demand conditions facing the firm. The relevant question then is by how much will the granting of trade protection increase the total profits of the MNE over what it would achieve were there to be no trade protection? One can safely assume that because of the exports the undertaking can deliver net benefits to the economy even if trade protection is granted. If this is so, a further pertinent question is, could the increase in profits resulting from trade protection move the MNE to make the investment to establish the subsidiary under circumstances where with no trade protection no investment would be made?

To proceed further, it is necessary to model explicitly the learning process. A relatively simple way to view a 'learning curve' is to assume that unit costs consist of a term that is linear in volume (this component of costs might include raw materials plus some asymptotic value of those costs subject to learning) plus a term that depends upon accumulated total volume of production of the good by the firm. Following Spence (1981), this second term can be written as $c_0\theta(y)$, where y is accumulated volume of output x up to the present time t.

If x = x(t), then

$$y(t) = \int_0^t x(\tau)d\tau$$

The term $\theta(y)$ is bounded so that $1 \geq \theta(y) \geq 0$. If $\theta(y)$ were to decline 'forever' such that it actually did approach zero as y became large, the resulting industry structure might evolve towards a world-wide monopoly, and such issues as whether the host country should protect the local market would be somewhat moot. A monopoly is, however, not the only possible outcome (see Spence, 1981). Clearly, more than one firm can exist even if there is a dominant firm (this would be the firm with the greatest accumulated experience, assuming that all potential entrants faced the same learning curve) so long as marginal revenue for the non-dominant firm exceeds its marginal cost.

Spence (1981) assumes, for reasons of tractability but with little economic justification, that the firm maximises its profits over a fixed time horizon T. Under this assumption, the objective function of the firm is to maximise a profit function of the following sort:

$$V = \int_0^T S(x,t)dt - c_0\Gamma(y(T))$$

where $S(x,t)$ is a revenue function composed of total revenues at time t minus the constant marginal cost component of variable costs (the linear term referred to above, which could be written as $mx(t)$ where m is a constant), and $\Gamma(y(t))$ is given by

$$\Gamma(y(t)) = \int_0^{Y(t)} \theta(v)dv$$

and can be interpreted as the total 'learning sensitive' costs, equal to the area under the learning curve (with $c_0 = 1$) up to the accumulated output y (t).

This is not wholly satisfactory for our purposes, given that there is no particular reason why T should be fixed. It is more reasonable to assume that $c_0\theta(y)$ approaches some limit c, which one might think of as the equivalent cost component in the most efficient plant in the MNE's operations (this might be adjusted for, say, a labour cost differential). An interpretation is that a newly created local subsidiary over time 'learns' to operate at the same levels of technical efficiency as its long-established sister operations elsewhere in the MNE's network.

The problem with this is that in the general case there would be introduced into the mathematics a discontinuity (the 'learning-sensitive' component of variable cost at some level of y would drop to c.) One way to approximate the desired effect without introducing a discontinuity is to make the following explicit assumption about the behaviour of θ:

$$\theta(y(t)) = \exp(-\alpha y(t)) + c/c_0$$

which now implies that θ is bounded between $1 + c/c_0$ and c/c_0 rather than 1 and 0. However, this simply implies that the 'learning-sensitive' component of variable costs asymptotically approaches c, and thus c can be incorporated in m without loss of generality (as suggested earlier). θ then simply becomes $\exp(-\alpha y)$. We note that this is an approximating technique in that θ never quite gets to zero and hence the 'learning-sensitive' component of variable costs never quite gets to c.

We can then solve for V above by choosing an arbitrary but large value of T such that for any candidate trajectory x(t), $\theta(y)$ is arbitrarily close to 0. Under these assumptions standard calculus of variations techniques can be used to solve for V. The relevant Euler condition is for x(t) to be an extremal

$$S_x(x(t), t) = c_0\theta(y(T)) \approx 0$$

from which the optimal x(t) can be derived. We note that this result differs from the results given in Spence (1981) because Spence assumes a fixed time T. One might object to our treatment (which, incidentally, simplifies the solution) on grounds that for any given T, there is a value of θ other than zero that would maximise profits. This indeed might be true, but we argue here somewhat heuristically that if the firm faces a demand that is stationary or that grows with time, as T becomes large the only profit-maximising $c_0\theta(y)$ that can maximise total accumulated profits (not discounted) is the minimum possible such cost. This by assumption is 0[1].

To proceed further, we need some specific assumptions. Without loss of generality, set $C_0 = 1$, and scale other price and cost variables accordingly. To keep things as simple as possible, assume that the relevant subsidiary of the MNE in a host country is to be established primarily as an exporter but that it will service a domestic market as well. In the export market it will be a price taker, and it will receive a price p. In the domestic market it faces an instantaneous linear demand function $P(x) = a - bx$. (One must keep in mind that $x = x(t)$.) We must put a bound on the amount of product that can be exported (otherwise, if $P > M$, profits will be maximised when the subsidiary exports an infinite quantity!), and we can justify this by noting that it might be economical for this facility to supply some fraction of the MNE's world-wide production of the product to markets external to the host country at the price p, the price and the quantity determined exogenously from the perspective of the subsidiary. Call this quantity $Q = Q(t) =$ a constant, so that the cumulative volume of product shipped in time T is QT.

If $x(t)$ is the rate of product shipped to the domestic market at time t, it is clear that $X(t)$, the total rate of plant production at time t is just $X(t) = x(t) + Q$ and that the relevant profit-maximising condition is simply to choose $x(t)$ so as to maximise

$$V = pQT + \int_0^T [ax(t) - mx(t) - b[x(t)]]dt - \Gamma(y(T))$$

where now

$$y(T) = \int_0^T (Q + x(t))dt.$$

Because the export and the domestic market revenue functions are independent, V can be maximised in principle by considering the two revenue functions separately and setting the marginal revenue in each market equal to a common marginal cost. But because the export market is constrained by volume exogenously limited to a maximum of Q units per unit time, it is clear that profits in this market are maximised (at any cost below P) by selling all Q units. In the domestic market, the relevant Euler condition simply comes down to

$$S_x (x(t), t) = 0,$$

which implies that if a is constant one simply sets

$$x(t) = (a - m)/2b,$$

which is exactly the condition for profit maximisation if the firm is a monopolist with constant marginal cost m! This rather remarkable result (it comes from a more complex calculus than simply setting current marginal revenue equal to current marginal cost, where the latter is defined as current unit variable cost) is interpreted as follows: (current) marginal revenue is set equal to marginal cost after all learning has occurred (again, see Spence, 1981). By construction, this latter concept of marginal cost is just simply m, given that the 'learning sensitive' component of marginal cost is driven to zero after 'sufficient' time has passed.

If the firm does not receive trade protection, we assume that the product must be sold in the domestic market at price p or lower, in which case the firm will maximise profits by setting x(t) equal to either (a − p)/b or (a − m)/2b. The latter is unlikely (it implies that the monopoly price in the domestic market is lower than the world price p) and so we assume the former. The former implies that without trade protection, the MNE captures the whole domestic market of the host nation. This is consistent with the assumption that there is no locally made substitute. Then, with trade protection, the MNE will earn total profits to time T equal to

$$V = pQT + \int_0^T [(a-m)2/4b]dt - \int_0^{y(T)} \exp(-\alpha v)dv$$

where

$$y(T) = \int_0^T [Q + (a-m)/2b]dt$$

Likewise, if the firm does not receive trade protection, it will earn total profits to time T equal to

$$V = pQT + \int_0^T [(p-m)(a-p)/b]dt - \int_0^{y(T)} \exp(-\alpha v)dv$$

where now

$$y(T) = \int_0^T [Q + (a-p)/b]dt$$

These integrals are readily evaluated, and solving through we find that the difference in profits between the case where the firm receives trade protection and it does not is equal to:

$$(1/4b)(a2+m2+4p[p-a-m])T - (1/\alpha)(\exp[-\alpha(Q+[a-p]/b)T - \exp[-\alpha(Q+[a-m]/2b)T])$$

This last expression is one that only a masochist could love. It, nonetheless, is subject to a straightforward explanation. The first term represents the additional profits garnered by the MNE as a result of trade protection. These profits result from the ability of the MNE subsidiary to price monopolistically in the domestic market. The second term represents additional costs associated with monopolistic pricing. These costs result from the subsidiary moving down its learning curve more slowly under monopoly pricing than under competitive pricing; to achieve the monopoly price, the subsidiary supplies less to the domestic market than if it must supply at the world price p. Clearly, the second term is diminished the faster is the learning (that is, the larger is the term α).

Equally clearly, if the second term is greater that the first, the firm would never engage in monopoly pricing. Both intuition and a close examination of the algebraic terms reveal that this is an improbable outcome. If, however, the MNE discounts its earnings using a high discount factor, it is not wholly implausible that the net present (absolute) value of the second term could exceed that of the first.

4.4 SOME CONCLUSIONS

The major point indicated by the analysis of the subsidiary of the MNE affected by dynamic scale economies is that trade protection reduces the rate at which the subsidiary moves down its 'learning curve'. This is, of course, the opposite effect sought by advocates of the 'infant industry' argument. How does this perverse result come about? Here, one must note three key assumptions: (1) the subsidiary only 'learns' to the point where it becomes as efficient as other units of the MNE; (2) the subsidiary makes no substantial contribution to the overall 'learning' of the entire MNE; and (3) the output of the subsidiary shipped to 'world' markets (export markets from the perspective of the host nation) is invariant with respect to the rate at which the subsidiary comes down its learning curve. As always, the strength of the conclusion is dependent upon the strength of the assumptions.

Given these assumptions, what can be said for host country policy? The analysis points us in the direction of recommending against a protected domestic market for the local subsidiary of the MNE. The major reason is that suggested immediately above: the protection is likely to reduce the rate at which the subsidiary 'learns', and effectively, the MNE will use the domestic market to cross-subsidise export sales.

Two qualifications are in order. The first is that if the MNE requires some sort of subsidy as an inducement to get it to locate its subsidiary in the developing country in the first place, trade protection might be one way of effecting the subsidy. The second is that the assumption made in this analysis that the output exported by the subsidy is invariant of the rate at which the subsidiary moves down the learning curve may not be correct. If this assumption is indeed not correct, however, the implication for policy can swing in either of two directions. If the subsidy is initially so high cost that unit cost exceeds world price, it could be that a cross-subsidy would be necessary to induce the management to export from the subsidiary. (Close analysis here is likely to reveal that this conclusion rests on an implicit assumption of a certain amount of myopia on the part of the firm's management.)

But more likely, lack of a subsidy will induce the firm to increase its output (including that destined for export) more rapidly so as to come down the learning curve faster. And if this latter is indeed correct, the bottom line is again, trade protection is counterproductive. In a word, under a number of quite reasonable assumptions, the 'infant industry' argument just does not seem to apply to MNEs in developing countries.

Given this conclusion, what should developing countries do to attract MNE investment that is desired but where it is believed that some sort of incentive to the MNE is necessary? It follows from the analysis that the best approach would be direct front-end subsidies in the minimal amount necessary to induce the MNE to make the investment. But anyone who has had experience in developing nations knows that this approach can be unrealistic: developing country public revenue often is highly dependent upon collection of import duties and taxes from MNEs and front-end subsidies might simply not be acceptable politically. Thus, some sort of trade protection might be decided upon as the only feasible incentive. If so, this protection should be treated for what it is: an incentive that should be kept to minimal levels necessary to get the investment. Developing nation officials in particular should not delude themselves into thinking that the trade protection will actually provide the firm with an incentive to come down its learning curve faster than it would in the absence of the protection. The delusion is as likely as not to lead to a problem that has become endemic in many developing nations; the 'infant industry' that refuses to grow up.

Note

1. If a firm having constant returns to scale with marginal cost $= c$ faces invertible demand $P = a - bx$ and maximises profits π, then $\pi = (a-c)^2/4b$ and $d\pi/dc = -(a-c)/2b < 0$ if the firm makes positive profits. Thus, a decrease in costs always increases profits, a result that generalises to any firm facing a downward sloping demand curve.

5 Market Rivalry, Government Policies and Multinational Enterprise in Developing Countries

Homi Katrak

5.1 INTRODUCTION

The governments of less developed countries (LDCs) often complain that the subsidiaries of foreign multinational enterprises (MNEs) employ capital-intensive, rather than labour-intensive, techniques of production. The reasons for this concern are that the capital-intensive techniques generate relatively little employment, entail more expenditure in terms of scarce foreign exchange and the products made with those techniques yield relatively little benefit (in a sense discussed below) to consumers.

This concern about capital-intensive techniques could be interpreted in two ways. It may be taken to mean either that the MNEs' subsidiaries use techniques that are more capital-intensive than those of the indigenous enterprises (in the same industry), or that the MNE employs a capital-intensive technique even though another relatively labour-intensive technique is also available to the enterprise. The latter interpretation is rather more interesting because (i) it leads to a detailed analysis of the MNEs' choice of technique and (ii) as surveys by Lall (1978) and Jenkins (1988a) have shown, MNEs' techniques are not, in general, more capital-intensive than those of the indigenous enterprises.

The literature suggests a number of reasons why the foreign-owned subsidiaries may employ capital-intensive techniques; (some of those considerations apply also to large indigenous enterprises). Most of the explanations emphasise the role of LDCs' government policies, for instance, minimum-wage legislation, over-valued exchange rates, competition-restricting policies, and so on. However, the role of market rivalry, enterprises' conduct and their conjectures about rivals' responses appear to have been ignored.

Minimum-wage legislation (and/or tacit support for labour unions) causes the wage rate to exceed the market equilibrium rate and so is expected to reduce the advantage of labour-intensive techniques. Correspondingly, over-valued exchange rates offer an implicit subsidy for the use of imported, rather than indigenous, inputs and so create a preference for those techniques that require relatively greater use of imported inputs. Thus the over-valued exchange rate may encourage the use of imported machines, particularly those that require relatively smaller use of indigenous labour (and other) inputs.

Competition-restricting policies, for instance, import tariffs and controls, may have an indirect effect. An MNE could reduce its costs and enhance its profits by adapting its initially capital-intensive techniques to the LDC factor prices or by searching the international market for more labour-intensive techniques. However, such adaptive and search efforts are like innovative activity in that they may entail some costs and are stimulated if the pressures of market-competition have driven profits down to unsatisfactory levels. But the lack of competition in LDC markets allows enterprises to earn substantial profits and so reduces the incentives for reducing costs and using labour-intensive techniques.

Now although the above arguments seem intuitively appealing, they have not been adequately examined in the context of a theoretical model. What needs to be examined is (i) what factors influence an MNE's decisions about the choice of technique and then (ii) how those decisions may be affected by government policies.

This chapter employs a simple theoretical model to examine how an MNE's choice-of-technique decisions may be influenced by considerations of market rivalry and how the latter, in turn, may be affected by LDC government policies. The analysis focuses on the decisions of MNEs, but it also enables some comparisons with the competing indigenous enterprises. The role of market rivalry in the analyses of LDCs' technological choices has been briefly examined in Katrak (1989) and is emphasised further here.

The plan of the chapter is as follows. Section 5.2 draws upon Salter's (1960) well-known vintage capital model to examine the influence of minimum-wage legislation and over-valued exchange rates. Section 5.3 uses Dixit's (1979) analyses and standard hypotheses about conjectural variations to show how the choice of techniques may be influenced by an MNE's strategies of entry barriers and its conjectures about rivals' responses. Section 5.4 discusses the implications of the analyses for LDC policies and welfare, and considers comparisons between MNEs' subsidiaries and indigenous enterprises. Section 5.5 summarises the main findings. Appendix 5.1 gives a formal proof of the arguments in section 5.2.

5.2   MINIMUM WAGES, OVER-VALUED EXCHANGE RATES AND THE MNE'S CHOICE OF TECHNIQUES

To begin with it is helpful briefly to discuss Salter's (1960) vintage capital model. An enterprise may employ a number of machines, each of which was built at a different point of time. Each machine embodies the best practice technique of the time and the prevailing factor prices: machines built in earlier years, when wages were relatively lower, will have relatively higher unit labour requirements. For simplicity all machines are assumed to produce a single homogeneous product and employ a single uniform type of labour.

The range of machines employed at any time is determined as follows. When acquiring (or deciding to build) a new machine the enterprise takes account of the fixed and variable costs of using that machine. After some time, however, the fixed costs will have been fully amortised and thereafter only the variable costs will matter; the machine may now be called an 'old' machine. Thus average total costs are relevant for new machines but only unit variable costs matter for old machines. The enterprise will then be indifferent between continuing to use an old machine and acquiring a new one if the unit variable cost of the former (plus its scrap value) are just equal to the average total cost of the latter.[1]

Now let us apply this framework to analyse the technology transfer decision of an MNE. Suppose that a parent company can build a new machine such as could produce the same level of output as an older, more labour-intensive, machine (that has been fully amortised) and such that if both of the machines were used in the parent country, the average total costs of the newer one would just equal the unit variable costs plus scrap value of the labour-intensive one. The parent would thus be indifferent between using the two techniques in its own country.

The parent company now wishes to employ one of those two

machines (techniques) in its subsidiary in an LDC. Which technique will entail lower costs in the LDC, given that the parent is indifferent between their use in its own country? Could the LDC's minimum wage legislation and/or over-valued exchange rate induce the parent to transfer the capital-intensive technique to the LDC?

The outcome is illustrated in Figures 5.1a and 5.1b, and then formally proved in Appendix 5.1. OV_0 and NV_n in Figure 5.1a are respectively the per unit variable costs of employing the old and new machines in the parent country. These variable costs are assumed to consist of wage costs only. V_0S_0 is the scrap value of the old machine per unit output and V_nF_n is the fixed cost per unit output of the new machine. The two machines thus have the same level of total costs when employed in the parent country. Note that this presentation treats the scrap value and the fixed costs as annual opportunity costs that are constant over some finite time period.[2]

Now consider how these costs compare if the machines were to be used in the LDC subsidiary. Suppose initially that the per unit labour requirements in the LDC, for each machine, are the same as in the parent country. However, as the LDC will have a relatively lower wage rate, the unit variable costs of both machines will be lower in the LDC than in the parent country. The important point now is that this cost advantage will be comparatively greater for the machine with the higher per unit labour requirement, that is, for the old machine. These LDC costs are shown in Figure 5.1b where OV_0 and NV_n have the same interpretation as in Figure 5.1a. The other element of the costs, namely the opportunity costs associated with the scrap value of the old machine and the fixed costs of the new machine, are incurred in the parent country and so their magnitudes in figure 5.1b are the same as in 5.1a. So the total unit costs are OS_0 and NF_n for the old and new machines respectively.

It is rather obvious then that if the two machines have equal unit costs when employed in the parent country, the older machine would have a cost advantage if both were to be employed in the LDC subsidiary.

The LDC's minimum-wage legislation and/or over-valued exchange rate will reduce this cost advantage of the older machine. However, as long as the LDC wage rate (in terms of the parent's currency) remains lower than the wage rate in the parent country the older machine would continue to have relatively lower costs in the LDC. Thus in the absence of a labour-productivity gap, the LDC's minimum-wage legislation and/or over-valued exchange rates could

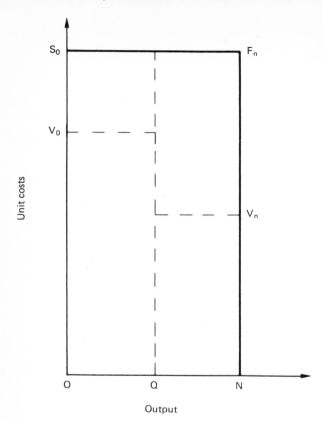

FIGURE 5.1a　*The fixed and variable costs of employing the old and new machines in the parent country*

not induce the parent to transfer the capital-intensive machine.

Next allow for a labour-productivity gap. For each technique the LDC subsidiary may have a relatively lower labour productivity. A productivity gap may be viewed either as a parameter for the parent company, or as an indicator of the costs that may need to be incurred to train the subsidiary's labour force.

If the productivity gap is greater for the new machine, the subsidiary's comparative costs would continue to be lower with the old machine. And this outcome would also hold if the gap were equal for the two techniques. It is only if the productivity gap were greater for

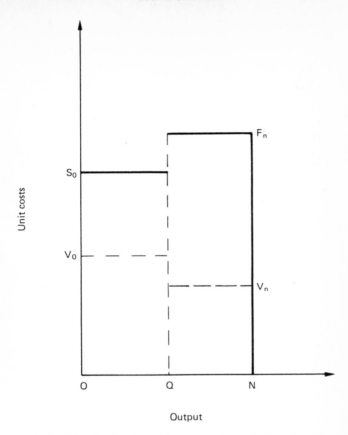

FIGURE 5.1b *The fixed and variable costs of employing the old and new machines in the LDC host*

the old machine that the subsidiary's costs *may* (but need not) be lower with the new machine.

But this last possibility is rather unlikely. The more likely case is that the productivity gap (and the cost of transferring technology) will be smaller for the older techniques. The reason for expecting this is that, as Teece (1977) has shown, the older the technique the greater is the likelihood that some aspects of its know-how will have been disseminated to other parties and the greater also will be the likelihood that the parent will have had some previous experience in transferring the know-how.

The costs of transferring technology also suggest another point. It may be that the installation of full capacity will require a learning process and may entail some delays. Such delays will reduce the present discounted values of the future profits obtained from a particular machine. Now, in view of Teece's empirical findings, it seems plausible that delays in installing full capacity may be relatively greater with the new machine. This possibility would thus reinforce the advantage of using the old machine in the LDC subsidiary.

It may also be worth adding that the above result is not restricted to the particular example chosen. To illustrate, suppose that the MNE's choice-set did not include a new machine. Suppose instead that the MNE was indifferent between two old machines, both of which had been fully amortized, such that one was of a relatively older vintage with a higher per unit labour requirement and a lower scrap value. In such case too, the MNE would find it more profitable to transfer the more labour-intensive of those machines. The MNE would not transfer the relatively capital-intensive one (of those two machines).

How then can we explain the LDCs' concern that MNEs transfer capital-intensive techniques? It will now be shown that our above result was a special case and was the consequence of an underlying assumption, namely that the alternative techniques would be used to produce the same level of output. That assumption was helpful in isolating the effects of minimum-wage legislation and over-valued exchange rates. Nevertheless, the assumption was rather forced, particularly as the capital-intensive technique has relatively lower per unit labour requirements and hence lower marginal costs.

The next section allows for the possibility that the technique with lower marginal costs will make it worth producing a higher level of output. The analysis also introduces the effects of market rivalry. The earlier assumption of a given level of output will be incorporated as a special case arising because of the MNE's conjectures about its rivals.

5.3   LDC MARKET RIVALRY AND MNEs' CHOICE OF TECHNIQUES

The MNE's output and choice-of-technique decisions may be affected by market rivalry in the LDC. The rivals may be established enterprises or potential entrants, and may be producers in the LDC

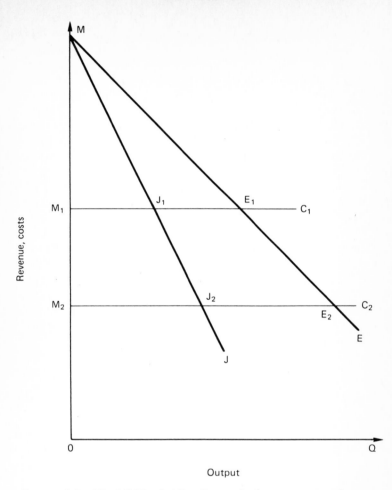

FIGURE 5.2   *The MNE subsidiary's marginal cost curves and revenue
marginal curves with and without rivalry*

or suppliers of competing imports. For expositional convenience the
influence of established rivals is considered first.

In Figure 5.2, the line M_1C_1 is the subsidiary's marginal costs when
using the older, more labour-intensive, technique and M_2C_2 is the
costs with the more capital-intensive technique. ME shows the marginal revenue when the subsidiary expects that the rivals will not

respond to its output changes, while MJ is the marginal revenue when the subsidiary expects that rivals will expand output in response to its own output increases. The greater is the output response expected from the rivals the lower will be the perceived marginal revenue curve MJ in relation to the curve[3] ME.

If the MNE expected that rivals would not respond to its own output increases, its equilibrium output would be M_1E_1 with the labour-intensive technique and M_2E_2 with the capital-intensive one. The corresponding operating profits (defined as the excess of revenue over the variable costs) would be M_1E_1M and M_2E_2M respectively. So the area $M_1E_1E_2M_2$ shows the extent by which the operating profits would be greater with the capital-intensive techniques.

In comparison, if the MNE expected that the rivals would follow its own increases in output, its equilibrium outputs would be M_1J_1 and M_2J_2 with the labour-intensive and capital-intensive techniques respectively. Once again the operating profit will be higher with the capital-intensive technique, though now this difference is only equal to $M_1J_1J_2M_2$.

Next we allow for the fixed costs of the new machine and the scrap value of the old machine and then deducting these from the operating profits we will arrive at the overall profits.[4] Let β denote the extent by which the fixed costs of the new machine exceeds the scrap value of the old one; $\beta > 0$. It is then possible to have the following interesting result.

It could be that in the absence of market rivalry the overall profits will be greater with the capital-intensive technique, that is,

$$M_1E_1E_2M_2 > \beta \qquad (1)$$

and yet with competitive output responses from rival enterprises the overall profit would be lower with that technique, that is,

$$M_1J_1J_2M_2 < \beta \qquad (2)$$

This suggests that market rivalry (or the expectation or rivals' output responses) may induce the MNE to transfer the labour-intensive technique, but the absence of sufficient rivalry may induce it to choose the capital-intensive one.

More generally, the more aggressive the output response expected of the rivals, the steeper (ignoring sign) would be the perceived marginal revenue curve MJ, the smaller would be the area $M_1J_1J_2M_2$, and so the greater would be the likelihood that inequality (2) would be satisfied and hence that the MNE would choose the labour-intensive technique.

The results of the previous section may now be interpreted as a special case of the above. The MNE may expect that a decrease in its own price will induce such a large decrease in the rivals' price as to induce no increase in its own sales.[5] In such case its level of output would not be affected by the choice of technique.

It may be worth emphasising that the argument has focused on enterprise conduct and .conjectures rather than on market-concentration. These two are not the same thing, though they may be related. A market with, say, high concentration may consist of different types of suppliers, namely indigenous enterprises, subsidiaries of MNEs and suppliers of competing imports. A particular MNE's conjectures may differ as between these different types of rivals and such different conjectures may affect its choice of techniques.

Too much should not be claimed for the details of the above results. The analyses had been built upon the simplifying assumption that older machines are relatively labour intensive (and have relatively lower set-up costs) and then proceeded with a simple model of conjectures about rivals' responses. Further research could examine the robustness of the results under alternative situations and attempt a calibration exercise. Bearing these points in mind let us next examine further the influence of market rivalry on the MNE's choice of technique.

5.4 BARRIERS TO ENTRY AND MNEs' CHOICE OF TECHNIQUE

Up to this point it had been assumed that the MNE faces a given number of rivals and cannot deter the entry of additional enterprises. However, the Industrial Economics literature has shown how established enterprises may be able to prevent the entry of potential rivals. What interests us is whether an MNE's choice of technique may be influenced by such entry-barrier strategies. The analysis that follows builds upon Dixit's (1979) entry-barrier model where an established enterprise faces a single potential rival. In the present context the established enterprise is an MNE subsidiary.

Each enterprise incurs certain fixed costs and constant marginal costs. (The former may be either the cost of acquiring a new machine or the opportunity cost of transferring an old machine). The important significance of the fixed costs is that enterprises have to produce some minimum level of output in order to earn positive profits. The higher the fixed costs the greater is this minimum level of output.

In Figure 5.3 OE_1 is the MNE's 'monopoly' output, that is, the amount that it would produce if there were no rival. $E_1B_1b_1$ is the reaction schedule showing the profit-maximising levels of output that the MNE would produce given alternative levels of output of the rival enterprise (the latter being measured on the vertical axis). The reaction schedule is discontinuous at the point B_1, indicating that the MNE must produce at least the amount b_1B_1 if production is to be profitable.

$E_2B_2b_2$ is the reaction schedule of the potential rival. It is discontinuous at the point B_2. The significance of this is that if the incumbent enterprise's output was equal to Ob_2 the entrant would just be able to produce its minimum output level B_2b_2, but if the MNE produced more than Ob_2 the potential rival's response would be a nil output, that is, not to attempt entry. So if, as drawn in Figure 5.3, the MNE's monopoly output exceeds Ob_2, it could safely produce that level of output and yet the other enterprise would not attempt entry. The rival's entry would be blocked.

The implication of all this for an MNE's choice-of-technique is rather obvious. An MNE wishing to block the entry of a potential rival will prefer a technique that enables it to produce a relatively high level of monopoly output. The larger the level of that output, the greater becomes the likelihood that the point E_1 will lie to the right of the point b_2, and so the greater becomes the likelihood that the MNE can block the entry of the potential rival. And since, as seen above, capital-intensive techniques lead to a higher level of output, the entry-barrier strategy creates a preference for such techniques.

5.5   SOME FURTHER QUESTIONS

The preceding analyses of MNE's conjectures and conduct may help discuss three further questions. Do capital-intensive techniques have a relatively adverse effect on LDC welfare, do LDC policies that restrict market-competition encourage the use of capital-intensive techniques and are MNEs likely to use more capital-intensive techniques than the indigenous enterprises (in the same industries)?

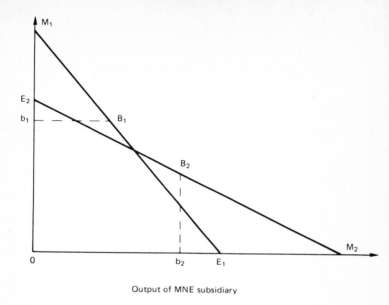

FIGURE 5.3 *Barriers to entry and MNEs' choice of technique*

Consider first how capital-intensive techniques may affect host country welfare. Are they likely to create relatively little employment, provide relatively little benefit to consumers and entail high foreign exchange costs? The preceding analysis suggests that these effects need to be examined at the level of the individual enterprise and also for the industry as a whole. The reason is that capital-intensive techniques may have lower marginal costs and so may enable a particular enterprise to produce a higher level of output but, at the same time, may also enable it to blockade the entry of potential rivals.

At the enterprise level the effects are as follows. First, although capital-intensive techniques will have lower labour requirements per unit of output, they also enable a higher level of output and so *may* be able to provide a higher level of employment.[6] Secondly, there are the effects on consumer welfare. One possibility is that capital-intensive techniques are associated with 'quality' products that have a 'high' price and so are not within the budget of the majority of LDC consumers. But there is also another possibility that, as assumed in the present Chapter, the alternative techniques produce a homogeneous product and that the capital-intensive technique, having lower marginal costs, will lead to a lower price. In such a case the capital-intensive technique may enable a larger number of consumers to purchase the product (though it could still be that the product may be beyond the budget of some consumers). Thirdly, there are foreign exchange considerations, which are of importance for at least some LDCs. It is likely that capital-intensive techniques entail higher import costs (because of their higher import content). But their relatively lower marginal costs may also make it easier to compete in export markets and so to earn foreign exchange. Thus considered together, these arguments suggest that at the level of a particular MNE the welfare effects of capital-intensive techniques need not be less beneficial than those of the more labour-intensive ones.

However, this picture becomes less favourable when the perspective shifts from the individual MNE to the industry as a whole. The use of capital-intensive techniques makes it more likely that an individual enterprise will be able to block the entry of potential rivals. Consequently the industry's employment could be lower than otherwise and its exports could also be lower. The only favourable effect of blockaded entry would be that with fewer enterprises the foreign exchange outlays for imported machines may be lower than otherwise.

The overall picture then is that, although we cannot rule out the possibility that capital-intensive techniques may generate relatively more favourable welfare effects, the likelihood of this becomes reduced if those techniques also enable an MNE to deter the entry of potential rivals.

Next consider the effects of government policies. Do import restrictions (and other measures that limit competition) induce the MNE to choose a capital-intensive technique? Let us envisage a scenario where an LDC market is served by an established subsidiary, a rival producer and competing imports. The MNE wishes to transfer another machine from the parent company to expand the subsidiary's output and/or to replace the existing machine. The MNE's choice of technique may be influenced by its conjectures of those rivals' responses. But how would those conjectures be influenced by the LDC's import restrictions (or even by the likelihood of such restrictions)?

Import restrictions may lead the MNE to expect a relatively less aggressive response from the supplier of the competing imports. In addition, the restrictions may also increase the likelihood of a market-sharing arrangement with the other local producer. Then *if* both these conjectures hold, the import restrictions may induce the MNE to choose a relatively capital-intensive technique. However, these possibilities would also need to be set against another one, namely that the restrictions may induce the supplier of the imports to set up local production and engage in a relatively more aggressive response.[7] This latter possibility may in fact induce the MNE to transfer its relatively labour-intensive technique.

Thus the overall outcome of the above is that import restrictions are more likely to favour the use of capital-intensive techniques if those restrictions also make it more difficult for potential rivals to set up production. But that qualification, in turn, leads to another question.

Can import restrictions help established producers' entry-barrier strategies? Import restriction will *ceteris paribus* enable local producers to sell larger quantities at their initial prices. Thus those restrictions will enhance the profit-maximising output of an established enterprise and also enhance the minimum level of output of a potential rival: in terms of Figure 5.3 above, import restrictions will enable an increase in the output levels OM_1 and Ob_2. But unfortunately, on *a priori* grounds, it is not possible to say which of those outputs will increase by a larger amount.[8] Thus there is no presumption that import restrictions will help the entry-prevention strategies of established enterprises.

The remaining question is whether MNEs are likely to employ more capital-intensive techniques than indigenous enterprises. The evidence from several empirical studies has been rather mixed. Our analyses in terms of market rivalry may offer some explanations of this.

Suppose first that an LDC market is served only by an MNE subsidiary and an indigenous enterprise. The former may have some firm-specific advantages (for instance, better managerial skills, easier access to finance, and so on) that enables it to expand production relatively quickly and also to maintain a lower price-cost margin. It may consequently be able to respond aggressively to any increase in output of its rival. Both enterprises may come to recognise this. The indigenous enterprise would thus have expectations of a relatively aggressive response while the MNE will expect a less aggressive rival. The former may then decide upon a more labour-intensive technique than the latter.

But now allow also for another MNE's subsidiary and suppose that the products of the two MNEs are closer substitutes for each other than is the product of the indigenous enterprise. Each MNE may expect that the other will respond aggressively to its own increases in output. In comparison, the indigenous enterprise may believe that the MNEs will be less concerned with its own output increases and so will come to expect relatively less aggressive responses.[9] In such case there would be no presumption that both of the MNEs will employ more capital-intensive techniques than the indigenous enterprise. The main point here is that if there are more than two enterprises, the industry may become divided into sub-groups and enterprises' choice of technique may then depend on the rivalry within and between the sub-groups.

A final point. It is likely that some indigenous enterprises may also have acquired certain firm-specific advantages. They may do this by initially using imported know-how and then building upon that with their in-house technological efforts. An interesting example is the Bajaj motor-scooter producer in India which started with foreign collaboration and has since become a major producer and exporter. Katrak's (1985) study also suggests such building-up of technological capabilities by indigenous enterprises.

5.6 SUMMARY

This chapter has drawn upon models of Industrial Economics to examine why MNEs sometimes transfer capital-intensive techniques to their LDC subsidiaries. The analyses considered the influence of market rivalry and enterprise conduct as well as those of LDC minimum-wage legislation and over-valued exchange rates.

Drawing upon a vintage capital model a distinction was made between 'old' and 'new' machines (or techniques), the former having relatively higher labour requirements per unit of output but lower fixed costs. It was then shown that if the two machines had been designed to produce the same level of output and the parent company was indifferent between their use in its own country it would always be more profitable to transfer the old machine to the LDC subsidiary. LDC policies such as minimum-wage legislation and/or over-valued exchange rates could not by themselves induce the MNE to transfer the machine with the more capital-intensive technique.

The influences of market rivalry and enterprise conduct were considered by allowing for the possibility that the new capital-intensive techniques, having lower labour requirements per unit of output, would have lower marginal costs and so would allow a relatively higher level of output. This, in turn, was of importance for two reasons. First, the higher output of capital-intensive techniques would mean a higher operating surplus which, in some situations, could more than offset their higher fixed costs: the outcome depended on the MNE's conjectures about its rivals' responses to its own increases in output, such that expectations of unaggressive responses may induce the MNE to transfer a capital-intensive technique. Secondly, because of the relatively higher level of output, the capital-intensive technique would also be more likely to deter the entry of a potential rival (who itself may have high fixed costs and so may not envisage entry below some minimum level of output).

The analysis also suggested that the relationship between the MNE's choice of technique on the one hand and LDC welfare and policies on the other could depend on the enterprises' entry-barrier strategies. It was argued that the use of capital-intensive techniques *per se* need not have an adverse effect on host country welfare, but that such an effect would become more likely if those techniques enabled established MNEs to blockade the entry of potential rivals. And the LDC's import restrictions *per se* may not encourage the use of capital-intensive techniques but that possibility was more likely if those policies enabled first entrants to block the entry of others.

Notwithstanding its limitations the main contribution of the chapter has been to show that introduction of the role of market rivalry greatly enriches (and complicates) the technology transfer decisions of the MNE. The influence of market rivalry may override those of host government policies and may induce similar technology choices by domestic enterprises. The significance of the latter conclusion is borne out by the empirical findings of Jenkins (1988) who, surveying a wide range of situations in LDCs, concludes that there is little evidence that MNEs generally use more capital-intensive techniques than the domestic enterprises.

Notes

Helpful comments on this chapter from two anonymous referees are gratefully acknowledged.
1. The new machine embodies more recent technological developments (in

the machine-tool industry). This makes it possible that the average total cost of using such machines may be equal to (or even less than) the marginal cost of old machines.

2. The expenditure (that is, fixed costs) on the new machines will entail interest payments (or interest income foregone). These interest charges are an opportunity cost which may be constant annual flows over some finite time period. Correspondingly as the decision to transfer an old machine to the subsidiary amounts to a decision not to scrap the machine, the interest income from that scrap value is foregone and so entails an opportunity cost.

3. The relation between the two marginal revenue curves may be formally shown as follows. An enterprise's revenue depends on its own output and that of its rivals. So we have

$$R_f = q(Q_f, Q_r)$$

where R and Q are respectively revenue and quantity sold and subscripts f and r denote the firm and its rivals. Differentiating totally and dividing throughout by dQ_f yields

$$dR_f = \partial R_f/\partial Q_f + [(\partial R_f/\partial Q_r)(dQ_r/dQ_f)]$$

where (dQ_r/dQ_f) is positive if the rival makes an aggressive response, in which case the expression in the squared bracket will be negatively signed. The term dR_f/dQ_f is the enterprise's marginal revenue if the rival has a non-zero response while $(\partial R_f/\partial Q_r)$ is the corresponding revenue in the case of no response, and so the more aggressive the rival's response the smaller is the former term relative to the latter.

4. The fixed costs and the scrap value are treated as annual opportunity costs (as explained above) and can thus be added to the variable costs to give total costs per unit period of time.

5. This may be formally seen as follows. The demand for the enterprise's product depends on the price of its product and that of its rival(s), namely, $D_f = p(P_f, P_r)$ where D and P are respectively quantity demanded and price and subscripts f and r denote the firm and its rival. On total differentiation and dividing throughout by dP we get

$$dD_f/dP_f = (\partial D_f/\partial P_f) + [(\partial D_f/\partial P_r)(dP_r/dP_f)]$$

The expression in the squared bracket on the r.h.s. will be positively signed if the rival makes an aggressive response and so if that expression is sufficiently high the entire r.h.s. could equal zero.

6. The capital-intensive techniques will be more likely to lead to higher employment the greater (ignoring sign) is the price elasticity of demand for the enterprise's product and the greater the share of labour costs in variable costs.

7. There are two reasons for expecting that local production will lead to more aggressive behaviour. First the enterprise will no longer face the threat of import restrictions, which it may have faced earlier. Secondly it

will now have lower marginal costs (because of lower transport costs, lower LDC wages and no tariffs) and so can expand output at a lower cost than before.

8. The outcome may depend, in part, on the degree of substitution between the product of each enterprise and the competing imports whose price is now increased by the import restrictions.

9. And even if the MNEs, with their firm-specific advantages, tried to expand their outputs at the expense of the indigenous enterprise, they could be restrained by the LDC government policies regulating the capacity and output expansion of larger enterprises.

APPENDIX 5.1

The appendix examines a question discussed in section 5.2. Can the LDC's minimum-wage legislation and/or over-valued exchange rate induce the parent to transfer the new machine to the LDC given that it is indifferent between using the two techniques in its own country. Stated formally the above question is

can
$$F_n + L_{nh}W_h/E < S_o + L_{oh}W_h/E) \qquad (1)$$
given that
$$F_n + L_{np}W_p = S_o + L_{op}W_p \qquad (2)$$

where F_n is the fixed cost of the new machine per unit of output, S_o is the corresponding scrap-value of the old machine, L_{nh} and L_{oh} are respectively the unit labour requirements for the new and old machines in the host country subsidiary, L_{np} and L_{op} are the corresponding requirements in the parent country, W_h and W_p are respectively the wage rates in the two countries and E is the LDC's exchange rate, that is, the number of units of its currency that exchange for one unit of the parent country's currency and so (W_h/E) is the LDC wage rate in terms of the parent's currency.

With slight re-arrangement (1) and (2) can be written as

can
$$(F_n - S_o) < (L_{oh} - L_{nh})(W_h/E) \qquad (1a)$$
given that
$$(F_n - S_o) = (L_{op} - L_{np})W_p \qquad (2a)$$

or more simply

can
$$(L_{op} - L_{np})/(L_{oh} - L_{nh}) < (W_h/E)/W_p \qquad (3)$$

Now if there is no labour-productivity gap between the two countries, that is, $L_{oh} = L_{op}$ and $L_{nh} = L_{np}$, equation (3) will reduce to

can
$$1 < (W_h/E)W_p \qquad (4)$$

Clearly as long as the LDC wage rate, in terms of the parent's currency, is less than that in the parent country, inequality (4) can never be satisfied. The parent company would not choose to transfer the new machine.

A labour-productivity gap would, for reasons given in the text, most probably cause the subsidiary's labour requirements to be relatively greater for the new machine, that is, make $(L_{nh} - L_{np})$ greater than $(L_{oh} - L_{op})$. The l.h.s. of (3) would thus continue to exceed the r.h.s. and so once again the parent would not choose to transfer the new machine.

6 The Impact of Foreign Investment on Less Developed Countries: Cross-Section Analysis versus Industry Studies

Rhys Jenkins

6.1 INTRODUCTION

The last two decades have seen a mass of studies of the impact of transnational corporations (TNCs) on host less developed countries (LDCs). A central issue in any discussion of the impact of TNCs is 'Does ownership matter?'. Do foreign subsidiaries behave differently from locally-owned firms and if so, what are the implications of such differences for development?

Critics of the TNCs argue that 'domestic firms offer a package of behavioural and structural traits that tend to capture for the nation a greater share of the benefits of growth and transmit them to lower income groups – domestic firms are unlikely to avoid taxes through transfer pricing and they tend to operate in more competitive markets, to rely less heavily on advertising, and to behave in their technology and trade activities in a way that has greater domestic linkages' (Gereffi and Newfarmer, 1985: pp. 424–5).

This view is hotly disputed by others, however, who claim that 'whenever we find, rightly or wrongly, that in any particular aspect the behaviour of the MNC differs from that of the traditional capitalist undertaking, the specific character of the MNC is generally to its [development's] advantage' (Emmanuel, 1980: p. 149).

The purpose of this paper is to review the empirical evidence concerning differences in the behaviour of foreign and locally-owned firms.[1] The implicit assumption is that differences in behaviour have implications for both firm performance and more general social goals.[2] However, in order to highlight some of the methodological

111

and interpretative problems involved the paper focuses on the link between ownership and behaviour rather than offering a more general survey of the impact of TNCs.[3]

Despite the growing number of empirical studies in this area, the picture remains confused. Lall's conclusion on reviewing the evidence on the choice of techniques illustrates this. 'The mass of conflicting evidence, the occasional use of imprecise methodology, the inherent problems of definition and measurement, all do not support any strong statement about the relative performance of TNCs and local firms' (Lall, 1978: p. 241).

It will be argued here that this confusion is in large part due to the inherent limitations of the kind of cross-section studies that have been used to analyse such questions, and that a more fruitful approach for future research is through longitudinal industry studies. In order to illustrate this, the paper focuses on four key areas of firm behaviour: technology, marketing, trade and employment.

These four areas are all crucial to the debate on economic development in the Third World. Decisions on technology affect employment creation and the development of local technological capabilities. Marketing decisions, particularly concerning the amount of advertising, have consequences for the development of local consumption patterns. The export and import strategies of firms have a major impact on the host country's balance of payments and the development of local linkages, while employment policy influences training, wages and class formation locally.

6.2 METHODOLOGICAL ISSUES

At first sight it might seem that the question of whether or not foreign and locally-owned firms behave differently in crucial respects could be easily resolved through appropriate empirical research. On closer examination, however, the issue involves problems both of methodology and of interpretation.

A simple comparison of mean values of the relevant variables for different types of firms is of little use as an indicator of the impact of ownership on behaviour. The distribution of foreign subsidiaries by industry and size is very different from that of locally-owned firms, so that observed differences may be the result of factors other than ownership.[4] Published census data is therefore not an appropriate source for such analysis.

Data on a firm-by-firm basis is required in order to take into account variables other than ownership. One approach is to use analysis of variance or multiple regression, which have the added advantage of permitting significance testing of any differences between types of firms. The problem with regression analysis, using ownership as one of the independent variables explaining behaviour is that it requires strong assumptions underlying a complicated theoretical model. If, for example, there are large differences in size between foreign and locally-owned firms, the use of a common regression model will involve extrapolation beyond the range of existing observations (Willmore, 1986: p. 491).

Another approach based on firm-level data involves selecting a sample of 'matched pairs' of foreign and local firms – matching usually in terms of size and product line. These are then compared in order to identify any systematic differences of behaviour between the two types of firm. While in some respects this is the most satisfactory approach in that it compares like with like, it does give rise to other problems.

First, it is often applied to a limited number of firms which may mean that differences are not statistically significant because of the small size of the sample. Secondly, it can only be used in those product lines where there are similar local and foreign firms which can be compared. If large sectors of the economy are the exclusive preserve of either foreign or local capital, focusing only on those industries where the two coexist may be misleading. In general then, this technique may lead to differences between local and foreign capital being played down.

In surveying studies from a variety of different countries it is necessary to be aware of the possibility that different conditions in specific countries (for example, in terms of the type of development strategy pursued or the level of economic development) might lead to differences in comparative behaviour. Thus, for example, in Latin America it has been found that the wage gap between TNCs and local firms is inversely related to the level of development of the host country (Taira and Standing, 1973).

6.3 CROSS-SECTION STUDIES

Choice of Technique

The aspect of behaviour on which there has probably been most empirical research comparing local and foreign-owned firms has been the choice of techniques. Critics of the TNCs often allege that foreign subsidiaries in the Third World use more capital-intensive (and hence by implication less 'appropriate') techniques than locally-owned firms. This it is claimed is due to the fact that one of the main 'advantages' which TNCs enjoy is the possession of advanced technology which they are reluctant to adapt for small LDC markets, and that due to their market power, they are able to pass on the higher costs of inappropriate techniques to consumers (Lall, 1980; Newfarmer, 1985). Against this, some writers have argued that TNC managers are more alert to ways of cutting costs by substituting labour for capital than those of locally-owned firms (Pack, 1976).

Although there is considerable evidence from a number of LDCs that for manufacturing as a whole, foreign firms tend to be more capital-intensive than local firms,[5] the studies in Tables 6.1 and 6.2 suggest a more mixed picture.[6] The most common result, particularly in Table 6.2, where firms which are similar in terms of factors other than ownership are compared, is for there to be no difference in terms of capital-intensity. The most detailed studies have been carried out for Brazil, and although these indicate that in aggregate foreign subsidiaries are more capital-intensive than local firms, when disaggregated by industry, significant differences are only found in a minority of cases (Morley and Smith, 1977; Newfarmer and Marsh, 1981; Willmore, 1986).

Research and Development

In recent years interest in technology issues has shifted somewhat away from static questions of choice of technique towards concern with the development of local technological capability. Critics of the TNCs point to the concentration of R&D in home countries and the limited amount of technological activity carried out by their subsidiaries in Third-World countries which is attributed to the 'appropriation problem'. Since technology is an important source of TNC power, parent companies seek to control R&D activity tightly in order to avoid leakages to their competitors. Since it is more difficult to control geographically dispersed facilities this can be best achieved through centralisation of R&D in the home country (Newfarmer, 1985).

From the point of view of the TNC subsidiary in an LDC, access to the parent company's technology, it is argued, reduces the need to undertake local R&D compared to a domestically-owned firm. There

TABLE 6.1 Choice of technique – results of studies using samples of firms (excluding matched pairs)

Country	Author	Variables	Method	Results*
Brazil	Morley & Smith (1977)	Kwh/L	ANOVA	FF > DF in 5 of 17 industries
	Newfarmer & Marsh (1981)	Fixed assets/L	Regression	FF > DF not disaggregated by industry
Brazil, Colombia, Central America and Mexico	Sosin & Fairchild (1984)	Net fixed assets/L	Regression	FF > DF in 2 of 7 industries
Hong Kong	Chen (1983a)	Fixed assets/L Kwh/L	ANOVA ANOVA	FF > DF in 1 of 4 industries DF > FF in 2 of 4 industries
Indonesia	Chen (1983a)	Kwh/L	t – test (no control for firm size)	FF > DF in 1 of 3 industries
Malaysia	Lim (1976)	Capital service/L	No significance test	
Singapore	Cohen (1975)	Kwh/L	No significance test	FF and DF no different
South Korea	Cohen (1975)	Kwh/L	No significance test	FF and DF no different
Taiwan	Koo (1985) Cohen (1975)	Total assets/L kwh/L	z – test No significance test	FF > DF in 3 of 27 industries FF > DF
	Riedel (1975)	Fixed assets/L Fixed assets/L	ANOVA Multivariate analysis	FF > DF in 1 of 6 industries FF and DF no different

continued on p. 116

TABLE 6.1 *continued*

Country	Author	Variables	Method	Results*
	Ranis & Schive (1985)	Fixed assets/L Machinery & equipment/L	No significance test	FF > DF in 6 of 6 industries FF > DF in 5 of 6 industries
	Chen (1983a)	Fixed assets/L	t – test (no control for firm size)	FF and DF no different in any of 6 industries
Thailand	Chen (1983a)	Fixed assets/L	No significance text	FF > DF in 3 of 3 industries
	Lecraw (1977)	Capital stock/L	No significance test	FF and DF no different
Ghana	Forsyth & Solomon (1977)	Plant & machinery/L	Discriminant analysis ANOVA regression	FF > DF in 1 of 10 industries DF > FF in 1 of 10 industries DF > FF in 1 of 11 industries
	Ahiakpor (1986)	Fixed Assets/L	Regression	DF > FF in 1 of 11 industries
Nigeria	Biersteker (1978)	Machinery & equipment/L		FF > DF in 1 of 3 industries
Uganda	Gershenberg & Ryan (1978)	Net capital assets/L	t – test (no control for firm size)	FF > DF

* Differences significant at the 5% level

TABLE 6.2 Choice of technique – results of studies using matched pairs

Country	Author	Observations	Variables	Results*
Brazil	Willmore (1986)	248	Kwh/L	FF > DF
	Morley and Smith (1977)	28	Kwh/L	No diff. Brazil/US subsidiaries
Costa Rica	Willmore (1976)	19		No diff. Brazil/W. Europe
		33	Equipment/L	FF and DF no different
			Fixed assets/L	FF and DF no different
			Total assets/L	FF and DF no different
Brazil, Colombia Mexico and Central America	Carvalho (1977)	98	Total assets/L	FF and DF no different
			Fixed assets/L	FF and DF no different
Malaysia	Chen (1983a)	15	Fixed assets/L	FF and DF no different
Philippines/Mexico	Mason (1973)	14	Equipment/L	FF and DF no different
			Equipment and buildings/L	
South Korea	Chung and Lee (1980)	9	Replacement value of capital stock/	FF and DF no different
				No diff. Korea/US subsidiaries
		8	Output	No diff. Korea/Japanese subsidiaries

* Differences significant at the 5% level

are relatively few cross-section studies which have addressed this hypothesis and as Table 6.3 indicates the results are very mixed. As with the choice of technique therefore, there is no strong empirical support for the view that the TNCs' behaviour differs systematically from that of local firms.

Advertising and Competitive Strategies

A frequently heard criticism of TNCs is that they promote consumption of inappropriate products through heavy advertising in low income countries (Jenkins, 1988b). However, despite considerable evidence that TNCs account for a substantial share of commercial advertising in many LDCs (see, for example, Jouet, 1984 on Kenya; Bernal, 1976 on Mexico), there are very few studies which compare their marketing behaviour with those of locally-owned firms.

The most sophisticated aggregate study by Willmore on Brazil finds that foreign-owned firms spent slightly more on advertising relative to sales than domestic firms (Willmore, 1986: Table 1). However, when disaggregated by industry, the difference was significant in only three out of 20 sectors (Willmore, 1986: Table 4). Other studies of single industries show a variety of patterns. In the Kenyan soap industry TNCs spent six times as much (in relation to sales) as local firms on advertising (Langdon, 1981: p. 68). In the pharmaceutical industry in both Argentina and Turkey there was little difference in behaviour between foreign and local firms and amongst the largest firms in Argentina, local firms advertised more heavily (Chudnovsky, 1979; Kirim, 1986). Again it seems that cross-section studies provide very little basis for asserting that ownership matters.

Trade Strategy

It is often claimed that foreign subsidiaries are well placed to promote exports from LDCs because they produce internationally known brand names and can take advantage of the distribution networks of their parents overseas (Vernon, 1971: p. 107; De La Torre, 1972). Critics of the TNCs, on the other hand, argue that their global rationality militates against their playing a major role in promoting exports of manufactures, except in the case of the relatively limited investments in export-processing zones. Restrictive clauses in technology contracts are seen as evidence of the reluctance of TNCs to export from LDCs.

TABLE 6.3 *Results of studies of research and development*

Country	Author	Method	Results*
Hong Kong	Chen (1983a)	No significance test	FF > DF in 3 of 4 industries
India	Lall (1985a)	Regression	Foreign ownership positively correlated with R & D in 1 of 2 industries
	Kumar (1987)	Wilcoxon signed-rank test	DF > FF in 26 out of 36 industries
Mexico	Fairchild (1977)	Matched pairs	FF and DF no different
Brazil, Colombia and Mexico	Carvalho (1977)	Matched pairs	FF and DF no different

* Difference significant at the 5% level.

Table 6.4 summarises a number of studies of export performance. Only two cases, one of Brazil and the other of Costa Rica, support the view that foreign subsidiaries are significantly more export-oriented than locally-owned firms. The remaining studies, including two other studies of Brazil, either found no statistically significant difference between foreign and local firms, or only managed to find them in a minority of industries. Some examples of superior export performance by local firms were also found. Once again therefore the evidence to support the view that behaviour varies systematically with ownership is lacking.

Turning to imports, there are strong *a priori* reasons for expecting foreign subsidiaries to have a higher import propensity than local firms, particularly where such imports are provided by the parent company (or another affiliate). It is the internalisation of international transactions that gives rise to TNCs, and the desire to capture suppliers' profits and to take advantage of the opportunities for transfer pricing offered by intra-firm trade that makes it likely that such transactions will be more extensive than in the case of local firms.

A number of the studies in Table 6.5 confirm the *a priori* expectation. Those that fail to do so are either based on matched pairs which, as already mentioned, tend to minimise differences, or were not tested for significance. This therefore appears to be an area in which ownership does make a difference. However a note of caution is in order here. As one survey concludes, 'the balance of evidence does suggest TNCs do have a greater import propensity, – though in some cases the differences may be minimal' (Newfarmer, 1985). It has also been concluded on the basis of a comparison of import propensities of firms in six less developed countries, that the level of industrial development of the country concerned and host country policies are likely to be more important factors determining the level of imports than ownership (Lall and Streeten, 1977: p. 145).

Wages

A final major difference between foreign and local firms is often alleged to be the level of wages. A number of explanations of the apparently higher level of wages paid by foreign subsidiaries have been put forward. These include the skill composition of the labour force, the productivity of individual workers (TNCs tend to pay higher wages in order to obtain the 'best' workers), the need to

TABLE 6.4 *Results of studies of export performance*

Country	Author	Method	Results*
Brazil	Newfarmer & Marsh (1981)	Regression	FF and DF no different
	ECLA (1983)	Matched Pairs	FF and DF no different
	Willmore (1986)	Matched Pairs	FF > DF
Costa Rica	Willmore (1976)	Matched Pairs	FF > DF
Mexico	Fairchild (1977)	Matched Pairs	FF and DF no different
	Jenkins (1979a)	z – test	DF > FF in 2 of 4 industry groups
Brazil, Colombia Mexico & C. America	Carvalho (1977)	Matched Pairs	FF and DF no different
Latin America	Morgenstern & Muller (1976)	Regression	FF and DF no different
Hong Kong	Chen (1983a)	ANOVA	FF > DF in 1 of 4 industries DF > FF in 2 of 4 industries
Malaysia	Chen (1983a)	Matched Pairs	FF and DF no different
Singapore	Cohen (1975)	No significance test	DF > FF
South Korea	Cohen (1975)	No significance test	FF > DF
Taiwan	Cohen (1975)	No significance test	FF and DF no different
Thailand	Riedel (1975)	ANOVA	FF > DF in 1 of 6 industries
	Lecraw (1977)	No significance test	FF > DF
Uganda	Gershenberg & Ryan (1978)	t-test	FF and DF no different

* Difference significant at the 5% level

TABLE 6.5 *Results of studies of import propensities*

Country	Author	Method	Results*
Brazil	Newfarmer & Marsh (1981)	Regression	FF > DF
	ECLA (1983)	Matched Pairs	FF > DF
Costa Rica	Willmore (1976)	Matched Pairs	FF and DF no different
Brazil, Colombia	Carvalho (1977)	Matched Pairs	FF and DF no different
Mexico and Central America			
Malaysia	Lim (1976)	No significance test	FF > DF in 18 of 30 industries
Philippines/Mexico	Mason (1973)	Matched Pairs	FF > DF
Singapore	Cohen (1975)	No significance test	FF and DF no different
South Korea	Cohen (1975)	No significance test	FF > DF
Taiwan	Cohen (1975)	No significance test	DF > FF
Thailand	Riedel (1975)	ANOVA	FF > DF in 4 of 6 industries
Nigeria	Lecraw (1977)	No significance test	FF > DF
	Biersteker (1978)	Regression	FF > DF
Ghana	Ahiakpor (1989)	ANOVA	FF > DF in aggregate but not for individual industries

* Difference significant at 5% level

reduce labour turnover, the bargaining power of organised labour, and state intervention (Dunning, 1981: pp. 282–3).

Table 6.6 confirms that higher wages paid to TNC workers are the rule, although this may reflect differences in the skill composition of the labour force between foreign and local firms. Unfortunately these studies have not thrown much light on the reasons why TNCs pay higher wages.

PRELIMINARY CONCLUSIONS

If the evidence from cross-section studies can be taken at face value, it seems as though the significance of foreign ownership has been overrated in discussions of development. Apparently on many of the key issues, there is no systematic relationship between ownership and behaviour. Even where systematic differences in behaviour have been found, the magnitudes involved are small and factors other than ownership appear to be more significant determinants of behaviour.

This, however, would be a false conclusion based on the inherent limitations of the cross-section approach itself. By definition, this provides a snapshot at a point in time and cannot capture the dynamics of the impact of TNC penetration on host economies. Furthermore, it assumes that the behaviour of foreign and local firms are independent of each other so that differences in behaviour are a good indicator of the way in which local firms would have behaved in the absence of foreign subsidiaries. When TNC competition leads to the elimination of local firms, no comparisons can be made, further complicating the picture, since local firms which survive are not necessarily typical.

These limitations can be overcome through detailed industry case studies examining the ways in which the behaviour of foreign and locally-owned firms interact and the ways in which they evolve over time. This is, of course, a time-consuming process and is unlikely to generate the same level of quantitative data as the other approaches discussed. However, it does open the possibility of examining the dynamic of the process of internationalisation of capital in a way that cross-section analysis does not.

TABLE 6.6 *Results of studies comparing wages*

Country	Author	Method	Results
Brazil	Willmore (1986)	Matched Pairs	FF > DF
Costa Rica	Willmore (1976)	Matched Pairs	FF > DF on average; no differences when disaggregated by type of labour
Peru	Vaitsos (1981)	No significance test	Differences mainly due to firm size
Brazil, Colombia Mexico and Central America	Carvalho (1977)	Matched Pairs	FF > DF
Latin America	Taira and Standing (1973)	No significance test	FF > DF
Philippines/Mexico	Mason (1973)	Matched Pairs	FF > DF for each type of labour
Malaysia	Lim (1977)	Step-wise Regression	FF > DF for gross wages
	Chen (1983a)	Matched Pairs	FF > DF for managers & skilled workers; no difference for unskilled workers.
Ghana	Forsyth & Solomon (1977)	Discriminant analysis	FF > DF for shop floor workers in 2 of 10 industries
Uganda	Gershenberg & Ryan (1978)	t – test	FF > DF
South Korea	Koo (1985)	z – test	FF > DF in 19 of 27 industries

6.4 INDUSTRY STUDIES

There is now a growing body of industry case studies which analyse the impact of TNCs in LDCs. In this section the issues discussed in the previous section are re-analysed using evidence from some of these case studies. The aim is to provide an interpretation of the confused pattern that emerges from cross-section studies.

The studies show that often TNC entry has a significant effect on the behaviour of local firms in an industry. In the Kenyan soap industry the entry of three TNCs producing well-packaged, heavily advertised products put pressure on locally-owned firms who found that they were unable to sell hand-made soap in urban markets. The response of the Kenyan firms 'placed them increasingly in the mnc mode. . . . To compete with sophisticated, brand-name mnc products, local firms required similar mechanized production and packaging techniques. They became much more import-intensive as a result. They felt they probably had to move to large-scale advertising to succeed' (Langdon, 1981: p. 76).

This is by no means a unique example. In the footwear industry in Kenya and the textile industry in Brazil, TNC competition has led to increasing capital-intensity of local firms (Langdon, 1981: p. 88; Evans, 1979: pp. 138–43). In Argentina large local pharmaceutical companies have successfully competed with TNC subsidiaries through imitating their strategies of heavy sales promotion and product differentiation (Chudnovsky, 1979).

Introducing differentiated Western products often leads to increased reliance on imported inputs. In the cigarette industry international brands often require imported packaging materials and filters (Shepherd, 1985: p. 101) while in Kenya machine-made soap used more imported tallow instead of local vegetable oils (Langdon, 1981: p. 70).

Not only is there evidence that local firms replicate TNC behaviour in order to compete with foreign subsidiaries, but conversely that not to do so often leads to commercial failure. In the Kenyan soap industry local firms which failed to mechanise found their market share reduced (Langdon, 1981: Table 4.3). Similarly in Mexico, Derivados de Leche (Delsa), which was the first firm to introduce yogurt on the local market in the late 1960s, faced problems following the entry of Chambourcy (a Nestlé subsidiary) and Danone in the early 1970s. While both TNCs launched major advertising campaigns,

Delsa did no advertising and rapidly lost its share of the market (Montavon, 1979: p. 55).

These case studies suggest that a number of situations can exist at a point in time when making comparisons between the behaviour of local and foreign firms. Soon after the initial entry by TNCs in an industry it is likely that they will be more capital-intensive than local firms, spend more on advertising and have a higher propensity to import. This situation is liable to change over time, however, as local firms alter their behaviour to imitate TNCs, or shift to segments of the market where they are not in direct competition with TNCs, or go out of business altogether. In these cases either differences between foreign and local firms are minimal, or differences exist but are the result of foreign and local firms producing different products (for example, synthetic versus cotton textiles in Nigeria, Biersteker, 1978), or it is impossible to find comparable firms.

This dynamic process explains why cross-section studies have produced such a mixed bag of results. Different countries and industries are at different stages in the process of TNC penetration. It also explains why studies based on matched pairs, which are careful to compare similar firms, so often fail to reveal any difference in behaviour between local and foreign firms.

In addition to showing the dynamic inter-relation between foreign and locally-owned firms, industry case studies can also illustrate the point made earlier that the behaviour of surviving local firms may be atypical. In the 1960s the Brazilian pharmaceutical industry included a number of locally-owned firms which were regarded by observers as technologically progressive. Moreover, amongst the larger firms in the industry, a higher proportion of locally-owned companies were involved in R&D than of foreign subsidiaries.

Between 1957 and 1974 the number of Brazilian firms among the leading 35 companies in terms of sales fell from 11 to 1. This was largely the result of acquisitions by TNCs and the first firms to be taken over were those with the most respected scientific record and which were strong both technologically and commercially. The Brazilian firms which survived are no longer noted for their technological capabilities but seem to be successful mainly because of their commercial and marketing skills. 'They make no pretense of trying to develop "original" products and are perfectly willing to admit that their product lines are "similars", that is, products originally developed by other companies' (Evans, 1979: p. 128).

That local firms are able to develop a technological capability of their own when cut off from foreign sources of technology is illustrated by a case study of the Argentinian tyre industry (West, 1985). During the Second World War a shortage of tyres led to a local firm, FATE, starting to manufacture treads for retreading tyres. After the war the company began to produce tyres without any foreign technical assistance, at a time, under Peron, when the climate for foreign capital in Argentina was generally viewed as unfavourable. Although the quality of its tyres was initially poor, FATE developed a considerable technological capability, which was maintained even after signing a technical assistance agreement with General Tire in 1957. Thus, unlike the foreign subsidiaries in Argentina, FATE has continued to do R&D locally and to introduce its own new products.

Both these examples come from Latin American countries with a fairly high level of development and as such cannot be generalised to all Third World countries. Even within Latin America it has been found that firms in Mexico and Brazil tend to spend more on R&D than in Colombia and Central America (Fairchild and Sosin, 1986). It is probable that in Africa, where local R&D is very limited, the differences *vis-à-vis* the Latin American countries would be even more marked. Biersteker (1978) found, for example, that only 13 per cent of the firms in his Nigerian sample did any R&D.

The role of government policy may be a crucial factor in determining the relative behaviour of foreign and local firms.[7] This is most obvious in the case of exports. As already indicated, the role of TNCs as far as exports is concerned is something of a two-edged sword. In terms of ability to export they are probably better placed than their local competitors. However, in terms of willingness to export, global strategic considerations may militate against a good export performance.

In these circumstances export performance may well reflect host country policies. In South Korea, for instance, where rapid export expansion began well before foreign investment became significant (Westphal, Rhee and Pursell, 1979; Cohen, 1973), the more export-oriented nature of foreign subsidiaries reflects the government's policy of reserving the domestic market for Korean firms. Similarly, in the Mexican motor industry the fact that in the mid-seventies foreign subsidiaries exported a higher proportion of their output than local firms (Jenkins, 1979b: p. 120), could be explained by the specific policies pursued by the Mexican government which led to increasing foreign domination of the industry (Bennett and Sharpe, 1985: pp. 176–8).

Finally, even where cross-section data show differences in behaviour between local and foreign firms there are difficulties of interpretation. This is illustrated by the case of wage payments. Much of the debate regarding wages has focused not on whether such differences exist, but on the implications of the differences. In particular, some critics have argued that TNC activities in less developed countries have tended to create a relatively well paid 'labour aristocracy', which as well as receiving higher wages, enjoys better working conditions, receives more fringe benefits and has greater security of employment. They form a privileged minority who are politically and ideologically divided from the mass of the working class and the peasantry, with an interest in preserving the status quo (Arrighi, 1970).

Cross-section studies are not well suited to evaluating such an argument. Once more case studies of particular industries, this time with a focus on labour, industrial relations and wages, can throw much more light on these issues. A study of the Brazilian motor industry, for instance, found that high wages, far from being an indicator of a privileged position, were associated with insecurity of employment and intense exploitation (Humphrey, 1982: ch. 3). This could only be understood in the light of the strategy of 'labour rotation' practised by the TNCs in the specific conditions of Brazil in the 1970s. As a result, far from being a conservative labour aristocracy, Brazilian car workers played a vanguard role in terms of working class struggle in the late seventies.

6.5 CONCLUSION

This paper has looked at differences in the behaviour of foreign subsidiaries and locally-owned firms with regard to technology, marketing, trade and wages. Generally the picture that emerges from cross-section studies is a confused one, and even where, as in the case of wages, there is general agreement as to differences in behaviour, there are still major differences over how these should be interpreted.

In addition to reviewing the available empirical evidence, a major thrust of this paper has been to argue that case studies of specific industries are likely to throw much more light on the impact of foreign investment on host less developed countries, than further static comparisons of local and foreign firms. Such industry studies have a number of specific advantages. First, it is at the level of the industry that competition and complementarity between TNCs and local firms often exist and therefore industry studies are the best means of analysing the interdependence between the two types of firms. Second, a longitudinal approach to a specific industry permits an analysis of changing relationships and strategies over time. Third, by focusing on a single industry, it is possible to establish links between different aspects of behaviour, for instance, the way in which producing differentiated products to compete with the TNCs leads local firms to change production techniques and import intensity. Finally, a growing number of industry studies would make it possible to identify different patterns in different industries.

In conclusion it seems appropriate to quote the words of Richard Caves:

> Easily spurned by sophisticated computer buffs, . . . it is not likely that we can uncover the long run effect of the multinational corporation. . . . except through the patient assembly of information on individual industries over time . . . One hopes that the necessary skills have not become entirely passé among economists: a flexible command of simple theoretical tools; foreign languages; and a willingness to grub for obscure and diffuse kinds of information (Caves, 1974: pp. 142–3).

Notes

1. It would have been interesting to consider differences between different types of foreign and locally-owned firms, for example, between wholly-owned subsidiaries and joint ventures, between local private and state-owned firms, or between the subsidiaries of US, Japanese, European and Third-World firms. Unfortunately few of the studies reviewed make such distinctions.
2. Analytically this can be thought of in terms of a modified structure-conduct-performance model in which foreign ownership is included as a market structure variable and performance is broadly defined (Newfarmer, 1985: Diagram 1).
3. For three recent comprehensive surveys of literature on the impact of TNCs on LDCs see Grieco (1986), Casson and Pearce (1987) and Helleiner (1989).
4. See Ingles and Fairchild (1977) for this argument and a simulation exercise which illustrates the point.
5. See Luiz Possas (1979) on Brazil, Fajnzylber and Martinez Tarrage

(1975) on Mexico, Vaitsos (1981) on Peru, Meller and Mizala (1982) on US subsidiaries in Latin America, Lin and Mok (1985) on Hong Kong, Agarwal (1976) on India, Balasubramanyam (1984) on Indonesia, Radhu (1973) on Pakistan, Jo (1976) on South Korea and ILO (1972) on Kenya.

6. Only studies which include direct indicators of capital-intensity such as fixed assets per employee or electricity consumption per employee have been included in these tables. Although value added per employee is sometimes used as a proxy for capital-intensity, it is also often used as a measure of productivity and has therefore not been included here.

7. Government policy may also be an important factor in determining the distribution of foreign and locally-owned firms across industries (Levy, 1988).

Part IV
Trade and Investment

7 Countertrade: Theory and Evidence

Mark Casson and Francis Chukujama

7.1 INTRODUCTION

Countertrade involves a contractual arrangement under which the export of a good is linked to the import of other goods. Lecraw (1988a) distinguishes seven main types: counterpurchase, barter, buy-back, production sharing, industrial offsets, switches, and the unblocking of funds. Only the first four types are discussed in this chapter.

Counterpurchase is the dominant form of countertrade between developed market economies (DMEs) and less developed countries (LDCs). It involves two linked contracts, in the second of which the exporter under the first contract (normally a DME) agrees to purchase a selection from a basket of commodities supplied by the importer (normally an LDC). The commodities are delivered later, subject to availability, at pre-arranged prices. Claims on the commodities can normally be transferred to another purchaser, and selection can be deferred until near the time of delivery.

Counterpurchase involves a two-way flow of money payments which, if the exports and imports are of equal value, cancel each other out. If payment for the export is deferred until payment for the import is made then the importer receives, in effect, an interest-free loan for the period during which only the delivery of exports has been completed. Deferred payment is by no means universal, but it is the case assumed in the analysis below.

Barter, by contrast, involves no money payments, except to balance a discrepancy between export and import values. A typical deal involves the export of minerals, agricultural products or standardised manufactured goods from a centrally planned socialist economy (CPSE) – including both East European countries and relevant LDCs

133

– in return for goods of a similar kind from another country. Barter may involve either a one-off bulk transaction or a long-term contract – the latter being the case analysed here.

Buy-back arrangements have the special feature that an input is exchanged for an output. The contract may specify that the output must be produced using the imported input and not a substitute for it. Buy-back arrangements are commonly connected with the supply of capital equipment, technology or training from a DME to a CPSE – often as part of a turn-key project or industrial collaboration agreement (Buckley, 1985).

Production sharing is similar to buy-back, except that the import supplier receives a proportion of the output rather than a pre-specified quantity of it.

This chapter seeks to explain countertrade by synthesising four main strands of theory:

monetary theory, which explains how the advantages of money-mediation vary across different types of transaction;

price theory, which explains how the negotiation of forward discounts and premia, which is implicit in countertrade transactions, enhances information flow and so improves the intertemporal allocation of resources;

the theory of market structure, which suggests that countertrade may be motivated by covert price discrimination and cheating on cartel arrangements; and

the theory of transaction costs, which interprets countertrade as a response to asymmetric information and, in particular, to the need for quality assurance in the provision of high-technology goods and services.

Monetary theory (sections 7.2 and 7.3) suggests that counterpurchase deals can be understood, to some extent, as an attempt to put 'commodity money' into circulation. These attempts are initiated by the governments of countries whose financial institutions lack reputation. This leaves unanswered, however, the question of why such currency should be put into circulation exclusively through countertrade contracts rather than by being offered as collateral for international loans.

Price theory (section 7.4) suggests that countertrade arrangements of all kinds have a valuable role in 'completing the market'. They can be understood as an alternative to organised futures markets, concentrating on the long-term rather than the short-term aspects of commodity trading.

The theory of market structure (sections 7.5 and 7.6) suggests that countertrade is a response to price distortions in the economic system. Such distortions can stem from imperfect competition, nominal price rigidity, government regulation, and so on. Distortions can explain why countertrade is so common in cartelised industries such as oil, and in the export trade of countries with endemic price distortions, such as CPSEs.

Transaction cost theory (section 7.7) can explain how buy-back and production-sharing arrangements emerge as non-equity alternatives to foreign direct investment for the transfer of technology to industrialising countries.

The analysis provides little support for the widely-held view that countertrade is an instrument of export promotion. Section 7.8 argues that under most conditions there are more effective means for promoting exports than the encouragement of countertrade.

Synthesising the different aspects of theory provides a multifaceted explanation of countertrade which is subjected to empirical testing in sections 7.9 and 7.10. Section 7.9 offers an econometric analysis of the determinants of counterpurchase, whilst section 7.10 provides a similar analysis of buy-back arrangements. These tests rely on original data, painstakingly collected from a wide diversity of sources. The econometric results provide significant support for the general theoretical approach. They clearly identify a relatively small number of factors as being of particular significance. The conclusions are summarised in section 7.11.

7.2 THE ROLE OF MONEY IN INTERNATIONAL TRADE

Economic liberals often criticise countertrade on the grounds that it substitutes a primitive form of exchange – namely barter – for a more sophisticated one – namely monetary exchange. Objections to barter stem from the difficulty of identifying a double coincidence of wants. Transaction costs are high under barter, in other words, because of the time required to search out a suitable partner. Coincidences, however, do happen, and when they do it is certainly efficient to make the most of them. The inference, therefore, is not that barter should never occur, but rather that it should occur only as a response to serendipity and not as a systematic policy.

The importance of money-mediated trade is that money facilitates multilateralism. Multilateralism is important because efficient trade cannot usually be sustained on the basis that each agent has a zero balance of trade with every other agent individually, rather than with all other agents as a whole.

Money is not, however, indispensable to multilateralism. Multilateralism can be achieved, for example, by the negotiation of a single comprehensive contract involving all agents in the system. This is the approach commonly adopted in international treaty-making, for instance. In an economic system dominated by bulk trade between a small number of agents in just a few commodities, it may be quite efficient to establish multilateral trade through an agreement of this kind.

When multilateral negotiation is difficult, the obvious alternative is to decompose the multilateral arrangements into a set of distinct but related bilateral arrangements. It is this approach that calls for the use of money, because money permits maximum flexibility in the negotiation and completion of the various bilateral arrangements.

If all bilateral trades were negotiated and completed simultaneously then the decomposition of the multilateral arrangement would simply require that in each bilateral arrangement goods are exchanged for units of account. Each transactor would face a budget constraint that his debits and credits across all transactions cancel out. The clearing of debts upon completion of the trades would then leave everyone in balance. Such decomposition is a rational response to search costs in a world where many traders exchange many products, and a changing environment necessitates continual adjustment in the pattern of trade.

Because of bounded rationality, each transactor may prefer to negotiate sequentially, completing one set of negotiations before he embarks upon another. This can be risky, however, because each negotiation is based upon expectations of future negotiations which may not be fulfilled. Nevertheless, in many cases these risks will be lower than the risks of misjudgement induced by simultaneous participation in several different negotiations.

The completion of different transactions can be effected sequentially too. This calls for a significant institutional change. To facilitate sequential completion, the unit of account must become a means of payment as well. This requires that the transfer of a unit of account in any transaction is final. It is sufficient to discharge all the buyer's obligations to the seller. Should the seller subsequently find that he cannot use these units of account in the way he planned, he has no recourse against the buyer: once completed, trades cannot be undone.

With sequential completion, some parties go into credit, and others into debt, as the sequence evolves. Because future plans can always fall through, there is a risk in allowing anyone to accumulate debt. The ability to issue debt on a large scale is therefore a privilege. When a reputable agent goes into debt his debts can be used by other agents as a means of payment. A seller will prefer to receive credits denominated in this reputable debt rather than in the debt of a less reputable buyer. Buyers will in turn find it advantageous to acquire this debt because they will be offered better terms by sellers. The agent issuing this debt will therefore be encouraged to put more and more of his debt into circulation, by running a payments deficit, until other agents have a sufficient stock of debt to provide the liquidity needed to sustain their trade with each other. At this point the less reputable debt will be driven out of circulation and all major transactions will occur in reputable debt. The reputable agents will then balance his payments, with a stable stock of his debt being in circulation, equivalent to the cumulated value of previous payments deficits.

Reputable debt functions most readily as a medium of exchange when ownership is easy to transfer, and for this reason it is typically issued as a 'bearer' claim. It also helps if it is available in the form of tokens that are homogeneous, divisible and difficult to counterfeit.

Hard currencies fill the role of medium of exchange in the international payments system. They are typically put into circulation by the central banks of DMEs, being sold for deposits which are in turn secured by the depositors' claims on certain assets. They are put into international circulation by the cumulative effect of short-term balance of payments deficits in the country of issue. The wide acceptability of hard currencies means that it is natural, in any international transaction, to buy or sell goods in terms of hard currencies. Prices are quoted in hard currency and, in particular, payment is made in hard currency. Although soft currencies may play a useful role in mediating domestic transactions in their country of issue, the attempted use of such currencies in international transactions will simply result in much higher transaction costs.

7.3 COUNTERPURCHASE AS THE ISSUE OF COMMODITY MONEY

One of the advantages of issuing hard currency is that the issuer can borrow at negligible cost simply by putting more debt into circulation. Provided that the currency continues to circulate at the same velocity, the issuer obtains an indefinite interest-free loan. Furthermore, in so far as the additional currency induces inflation, the penalties are borne by holders of existing debt and not by the issuer concerned. The obverse of this is that confidence in the value of a hard currency depends not only upon the quality of the assets it is secured on but also upon voluntary restraint on issue.

The security for most modern currencies is only partly provided by stocks of precious metals and of other hard currencies. Most of it is underpinned by the power of the government to tax its citizens. Poor countries with weak governments and little reputation for restricting issue command little confidence and are therefore normally obliged to conduct their external trade in hard currencies issued by wealthier countries.

For a poor country with a weak government the cost of borrowing can be very high. Imports can be purchased only with hard currency, and when domestic gold and foreign exchange reserves are low, repayment of the hard currency may be difficult to assure (Mirus and Yeung, 1987). Potential lenders may be sceptical of its ability to repay hard currency out of subsequent export earnings, and so they demand a high risk premium as part of their interest payment. One way of partially reassuring lenders is to offer repayment in commodities whose availability is already assured, rather than a currency that has still to be acquired. Availability may be assured by natural endowments (for instance, minerals) or previous irreversible decisions (for example, planting of agricultural crops).

Counterpurchase may be regarded as a mechanism for reducing borrowing costs by securing loans on future commodity supplies. By basing the claims upon homogeneous commodities of assured quality, they may be rendered widely acceptable. Furthermore, by making the claims transferable, and allowing the redemption of the claims to be extended indefinitely, lenders may be encouraged to circulate the claims as a medium of exchange. This 'secondary market' empowers the poor country, in effect, to put a commodity-based currency into international circulation. The country considerably increases its borrowing power because many of the claims will never be presented for redemption but remain in circulation instead. Instead of borrowing hard currency at potentially high interest rates, it can borrow interest free by issuing its own commodity currency instead. Few, if any, counterpurchase agreements approach this limiting case of currency issue, but many of them do involve transferable claims against a country which command greater confidence than does its official currency of issue.

7.4 FORWARD MARKETS

Forward selling is an element of all the major countertrade arrangements considered here. The claims on future commodity supplies offered in counterpurchase deals can be interpreted as complex forward contracts (Parsons, 1985). Barter deals also involve forward sales as well as spot sales because they are typically completed in a number of instalments.

Forward contracts have a dual role in coordinating intertemporally the activities of the buyer and the seller, and in allocating the risks between them. Coordination is effected through the price signals generated through the negotiation process. The allocation of risks is governed by the number of contingencies allowed for in the contract. In a simple contract the seller bears the risks associated with future shortages of the commodity, and the buyer the risks associated with future gluts. A more complex contract allows risks to be shifted between buyer and seller according to their different subjective expectations and their relative risk aversion.

A forward contract that can be easily resold is akin to a futures contract. Resale is facilitated by the fact that the typical futures contract conforms to one of a small number of standard types. A resaleable contract reduces the buyer's risks by allowing him readily to dispose of his obligation to purchase. Futures contracts are, in fact, usually bought back by sellers just before maturity. Because the repurchase price is highly correlated with the spot price that could be obtained in the open market, a futures contract still supplies the same information, and the same degree of insurance, as does an ordinary forward contract, even if it does not come to maturity.

Another type of forward contract is the option, which allows the buyer to defer his decision as to whether or not he will complete the purchase. Counterpurchase schemes typically involve a bundle of options on different commodities, subject to a constraint on the total value of the options that are exercised. Like futures contracts, these bundles of options are normally resaleable.

Forward contracts are most likely to benefit the parties when the price of the commodity concerned is relatively volatile. This often occurs where short-run supplies are inelastic, as in agricultural production. A combination of inelastic supply and demand raises particularly acute problems. This case is exemplified by multi-stage processing with economies of continuous flow production. Demands and supplies for intermediate products are both liable to be inelastic, particularly when the operations are running close to full capacity. The forward contracting element of countertrade is therefore likely to be particularly useful for both agricultural products and semi-processed products generated within multi-stage production.

A major objective of LDC governments is the stabilisation of export earnings (Newbery and Stiglitz, 1981). The narrower is the range of export commodities, the more limited are the opportunities for diversifying the risks of price volatility. This suggests that the higher is the commodity concentration of a country's exports, the greater is the impetus towards exploiting the forward contract element in countertrade. Furthermore, because fluctuations in economic activity in different countries are less than perfectly correlated, price risks are likely to be greater for countries which – because of tariff preferences, transport costs or political considerations – have access to only a limited number of foreign markets. A high geographical concentration of a country's exports may therefore provide a stimulus to countertrade as well.

It should be emphasised, however, that none of the arguments so far presented explains why forward claims should have to be marketed through countertrade. A simple assertion that conventional forward markets are missing is quite inadequate, as it does not explain why they are missing. If they are missing because of high transaction costs, why is it that transaction costs of forward trading are lower with countertrade? In practice, they may be even higher.

The obvious way to sell forward claims, for example, is through hard currency payments made at the date of delivery. Use of hard currency provides convenience and flexibility for the buyer, whilst deferring payment until delivery reduces the moral hazard that the seller will deliberately default. Yet counterpurchase schemes require that forward claims be bartered for current imports. Because payment is required in advance of delivery the forward purchaser is effectively required to advance a loan. Although the loan element in counterpurchase can be rationalised as an attempt to put commodity-backed money into circulation (see section 7.3), this still leaves unresolved the issue of why it cannot be put into circulation by using it to purchase hard currency. The bartering of forward claims for goods still needs to be explained.

One line of reasoning would argue that barter is a method of indexing the price of exports to the price of imports. Barter can indeed effect such indexation, but only when deliveries of imports are timed to match deliveries of exports. Indexation may therefore be a motive in the case of long-term barter deals, but not in counterpurchase deals where typically the imports are supplied in advance.

It must also be recognised that long-term barter is not the only way of achieving indexation. The price of future exports could be linked to an index of import prices, yet payment for exports still made in hard currency. The reason for preferring barter must ultimately rest on transaction economics. Barter is most likely to be chosen when there are difficulties in finding a suitable price index, and the costs of arbitrating disputes over the correct value of the index at future delivery dates are high.

It seems therefore, that although forward selling is an element in both counterpurchase and barter, it is really only in the special case of long-term barter deals between two distrustful parties seeking a simple mechanism of indexation that the superiority of countertrade over conventional forward trading is clear.

7.5 DISCOUNTING

There are two main situations in which a buyer may wish to offer a discount on an official quoted price.

(1) Quoted prices are sticky, and the discount represents a realistic response to the current market situation; this is an argument for a general discount offered to all buyers.
(2) The seller wishes to discriminate between different buyers. The quoted price applies to those who must pay the higher price, so that a discount can be offered to those who pay the lower price.

In the first case, countertrade may help to 'keep up appearances' by maintaining official prices for money-mediated transactions whilst allowing most trade to occur through barter at flexible prices dictated by short-term market conditions. This motive applies mainly – but not exclusively – to CPSEs. It raises complex issues which are discussed in the following section.

In the second case, countertrade is a method of concealing the selective discounts from those who are paying the higher price. This second motive applies in two main situations.

In the first, the seller has monopoly power against a relatively small number of buyers. The presence of just a small number of buyers reduces the administrative costs of discrimination, since there are few individual demand schedules to discover and reselling between buyers is easy to detect. This case too applies to CPSEs exporting specialised raw materials required by just a few major industrial buyers.

The second situation is cartel cheating. Here the sellers' market is segmented between the cartel-controlled market and a 'black market' where sales are made at below the cartel price. Secrecy is most important in this case. Most cartel members recognise that the maintenance of a price in excess of marginal cost provides other members with an incentive to undercut the official price. As a deterrent, punishments for culprits who are detected can be quite severe. A similar sort of situation arises when a non-member of a cartel has been threatened with reprisals if he continues to 'dump' in the cartelised market. He may wish to make some conspicuous sales at the official price whilst continuing to dump covertly at the lower price. Countertrade can provide a suitable mechanism for this. The nominal values of both exports and imports are inflated so that the nominal export price corresponds to the normal cartel price; but this inflated price is paid only in return for a commitment from the seller to purchase an equal value of the buyer's own output at a similarly inflated price.

There are certain conditions under which *both* parties may wish to discount. When there is a global deflation, for example, nominal price rigidities may cause prices to remain too high in many countries. Following Barro and Grossman (1976), there is global excess demand for money balances associated with global excess supply of labour and goods. Everyone wants to sell for money, but no one wishes to circulate the money by using it to buy other goods. This *impasse* can be resolved by bartering one set of goods, which are overpriced in nominal terms, for another set of goods which are equally overpriced in nominal terms. Because of its barter element, countertrade is thus a means of sustaining world trade under conditions of excess demand for money. In this sense, countertrade can be regarded as a rational response to a world-wide Keynesian deflation caused by a deficiency of aggregate demand at fixed nominal prices.

7.6 TRADE POLICY IN CENTRALLY PLANNED ECONOMIES

A key feature of government policy in many CPSEs is to thrust the burden of financing industrialisation on to foreign capitalist economies through the attempted exercise of market power in foreign trade. A combination of downward rigidity in the nominal exchange rate and downward rigidity in nominal prices in the export sector maintains export prices at a premium relative to the world level. (This analysis follows closely the treatment of 'repressed inflation' in Cuddington, Johansson and Lofgren (1985)). At the same time the downward rigidity of the exchange rate, coupled with upward rigidity in nominal prices in the import-competing sector, maintains import prices at below their world level. Internal relative prices are thus distorted away from world relative prices, with exportables being too dear and importables too cheap.

Exports appear so profitable to domestic producers that they are in excess supply, so production quotas need to be allocated amongst producers to discourage discounting. Imports appear so cheap to domestic consumers that they are in excess demand. This problem is particularly acute when a high proportion of domestic production of importables is taken up by investment goods – as under forced industrialisation – and when excess production of exportables cannot be diverted to consumer use – as in many natural resource-based economies. To prevent importers from bidding up prices, a system of licenses can be used; the licensing system can also be used to 'fine-tune' discrimination in favour of capital equipment.

Excess demand for consumer goods leads to non-price rationing, typically through a combination of queues and an official coupon system. Domestic currency is of limited value to consumers, and so they are keen to exchange it for foreign currency at a rate well below the official one. Foreign currencies – particularly hard currencies – can be used to obtain imported goods which it is difficult for the government to license – for example, personal services purchased whilst travelling abroad. Thus foreign exchange controls are normally required to supplement the licensing system.

Exporters have an incentive to trade illicitly in terms of foreign currency at a price which reflects an implicit discount on the official exchange rate. Foreign currency acquired by an exporter can be sold through a domestic black market (possibly mediated by illicit bank accounts overseas) to domestic importers who obtain supplies at a foreign currency price which also reflects a discount on the official exchange rate. The importer covers his expenses by selling the product at a premium in a domestic black market for consumer goods. The implicit discount which matches the foreign currency flows of the exporters and the importers determines an equilibrium exchange rate in the domestic black market.

It is difficult for the government of a CPSE to resolve these problems through piecemeal liberalisation. Raising official prices of importables brings the domestic relative price of exportables and importables more into line with world prices. By reducing excess demand for consumer goods it shortens queues and may even eliminate the need for coupons. But unless the domestic currency is simultaneously devalued, it does not make exports any more competitive. Conversely, whilst devaluing the currency without altering the official price of importables makes exports more competitive, it exacerbates consumer problems.

Complete liberalisation, despite its advantages, may be ideologically unacceptable to the governing élite. They may prefer to 'fine-tune' discrimination by organising additional foreign trade deals at world prices to obtain incremental efficiency gains. The natural way to organise these deals is through hard-currency transactions, along the lines described earlier in the context of illicit trade. Selective authorisation of otherwise illicit deals would allow the official policy to exploit the logic of the market system in controlled fashion. A more discreet alternative is to devise a three-way countertrade deal involving a foreign exporter, a foreign importer and the CPSE government. The values of the flows involving the foreign exporter and the foreign importer are matched, with the aid of a private broker or the foreign government concerned. Such an arrangement restricts the flow of foreign currency to within the foreign country, leaving the CPSE government a party to what appears to be a simple barter arrangement with a foreign consortium. Although the relative price of the imports and exports can be ascertained from a comparison of the export and import volumes that constitute equivalent value, the nominal price of exports and imports in terms of hard currency cannot, because the hard currency payment is internal to the consortium.

Many variants of this sort of arrangement are possible. The key feature is that exports and imports are revalued relative to each other in a covert fashion, and that mediation by foreign currency flows is restricted to beyond the borders of the CPSE.

7.7 BUY-BACK AND PRODUCTION SHARING

Some of the issues discussed above take on a rather different complexion when the countertraded products are an input and an output of the same production process. In particular, the problem of rationalising the barter element in countertrade is much less acute. When there are economies of vertical integration within a multi-stage production process, it may be efficient for one firm to assume overall control of production, from the early stages of processing through to the wholesaling and distribution of the finished product. An important source of such economies is the internalisation of forward markets in intermediate products (Arrow, 1975), though this is by no means the only motive. There may, however, be a special reason for subcontracting one stage of this sequence to an independent firm. If economies of scale are much greater at this stage than at adjacent stages, for example, then it may be efficient to utilise equipment which can handle other types of product too. The vertically integrated sequence is interrupted at the stage at which economies of scale are greatest. The owner of this stage purchases intermediate inputs from the integrated firm and resells the output to it. Thus the firm which supplies the input to the independent firm is also the natural customer for the output. The introduction of money-mediation is superfluous: recourse to a barter-type arrangement is the obvious solution.

The analogy between buy-back and subcontracting should not be pushed too far, however. Under conventional subcontracting the supplier of the input retains ownership of the input while it is being worked on by the subcontractor. Under buy-back arrangements, by contrast, the input becomes the property of the subcontractor – or the processor, as he should now be called – and the supplier of the input simply has the status of a customer so far as the repossession of the input is concerned.

Buy-back is inferior to subcontracting under these conditions, so far as the supplier is concerned, because the moral hazards are so much greater. The supplier has less justification for visiting the processor's premises, and so the processor has greater opportunity to switch the supplier's input to other uses and substitute inferior inputs of his own. The processor also has greater power to hold up the entire process by accumulating input stocks and then refusing to release them until better terms are agreed.

Buy-back arrangements are therefore unlikely to occur except as a response to forced devolution of processing as a result of government policy. Given the hazards of this contractual arrangement, the firm is unlikely to acquiesce unless it has already made irrecoverable investments in the country, or is offered compensating benefits of another kind.

Buy-back arrangements most commonly occur in the context of technology transfer. A combination of licensing rights and training are bartered for a proportion of output from the project. The exploitation of proprietary technology raises two distinct issues (Casson, 1987a). The first is the importance of coordinating the marketing of the output in order to maximise monopoly rents. This implies that a firm which devolves production should either buy back all the output, or at very least ensure that producers who retain output collude by, for example, agreeing to segment the global market into non-overlapping areas.

The second issue is quality uncertainty, and this is the one that has received most attention in the literature (see especially Kogut, 1986; Mirus and Yeung, 1986; Yavas and Vardiabasis, 1988). Given that the owner of the technology is prepared to relinquish ownership of output, the recipient may be concerned about the quality of the technology. False claims may be made about the performance of the technology, and where the supplier has access to several technologies he may deliberately supply an inferior one in order to retain his own competitive edge (cf Akerlof, 1970).

The case for buy-back rests upon the fact that the quality of the technology input is reflected in the quality of the output. Given that conventional forms of quality guarantee may be difficult to enforce, a requirement that the supplier takes back the output as payment may prove the best insurance for the buyer. An honest licensor who is concerned to get the best price for his technology may, indeed, voluntarily offer such an undertaking simply to reassure prospective buyers.

The technological input is unlikely to be the only input that affects the quality of the output, however. It is possible for the supplier of technology to over-insure the producer, so that the producer uses inferior inputs or generally supplies too little effort. One solution is for the supplier of the technology to impose a tied input restriction on the producer, but such restrictions may prove difficult to enforce if there is no right of access to the producer's premises. The fact that the producer is taking some of the output himself then provides a measure of reassurance to the technology supplier over the producer's input quality. This principle is institutionalised most conveniently by replacing the buy-back of a fixed quantity of output with a production-sharing arrangement. Production-sharing also benefits the producer because it makes the supplier of technology bear the consequences of low quantity as well as low quality.

Production-sharing is still asymmetrical, however, in that the producer holds equity in the plant and the technology supplier does not. This gives the producer the power to implement the production-sharing arrangement, and makes it difficult for the technology supplier to monitor him. On the other hand, the producer bears all the consequences associated with higher than expected costs of production. Since the technology supplier has no equity involvement, his attitude to technology transfer is likely to be 'quantity and quality at any cost'.

These incentive problems are resolved through joint ventures. Although shared ownership can generate ambiguities over control, a division of responsibilities can often be specified in the joint venture agreement. Joint ventures also have the advantage that they are particularly good at helping to engineer trust between the two parties (Buckley and Casson, 1988). On these grounds it can be argued that buy-back and production sharing arrangements are normally inferior to joint ventures where technology transfer is concerned. Resort to buy-back and production-sharing must therefore be rationalised chiefly as a response to constraints on foreign equity participation in local production plants. Buy-back and production-sharing arrangements can be expected to emerge chiefly where government policies not only preclude wholly-owned foreign subsidiaries, but are unsympathetic to joint venture operations too. This does not necessarily mean that joint ventures are formally prohibited – the government attitude may be sufficiently hostile that the technology supplier opts for buy-back because he fears expropriation of his equity share at a future date.

7.8 COUNTERTRADE AND EXPORT PROMOTION

The preceding analysis provides only limited support for the view that countertrade arrangements promote export marketing. Although the forward selling element in counterpurchase can reduce the risks of price volatility in export markets, the bartering of these claims for import supplies reduces rather than enhances the effectiveness of the strategy.

The idea that countertrade can promote exports seems to have become influential in the period leading up to the formation of the OPEC cartel. Countertrade was perceived as a suitable mechanism for selling Middle Eastern oil to non-traditional markets such as Eastern Europe. It should be recognised, however, that these markets were almost certainly less profitable than the traditional Western markets, and that the choice of countertrade was largely a response to the trading policies of the centrally planned economies of Eastern Europe. Countertrade was therefore more of an improvisation to meet specific circumstances than the first step in a coherent exporting strategy.

The idea that countertrade systematically promotes exports seems most cogent in connection with buy-back arrangements. Foreign technology is often necessary to produce goods of export quality in non-traditional export industries (for example, engineering products) or to increase productivity in traditional export industries (for example, mining). The analysis shows, and the empirical results below confirm, however, that buy-back is efficient only in response to a previous commitment to exclude foreign equity participation. In technology-intensive industries producing differentiated products, restrictions on foreign equity participation can deny the exporting country access not only to the foreign technology but also to the distribution channels controlled by multinational enterprises in the importing countries. While buy-back arrangements may help to mitigate the worst effects of equity restrictions, they cannot in any sense be interpreted as offering an improvement upon equity-based arrangements.

One of the key aspects of successful export marketing is the continuous updating of information about trends in the export market. Information feedback from the export market is normally best secured from a network of foreign sales offices. These may be operated either by independent agencies – as joint ventures with indigenous partners – or as wholly-owned sales subsidiaries. Evidence suggests that with a successful product being exported to a growing market, the exporter's degree of equity participation in foreign sales operations will increase over time (Nicholas, 1983). This almost certainly reflects the increasing importance of feeding back large amounts of information from the market in order to 'fine-tune' the export strategies.

Overseas sales offices may form the basis on which the exporter develops a distribution channel that bypasses existing channels and so reduces the channel leader's market power. An alternative strategy is to use the information collected by these offices to bargain more effectively within existing channels for a higher share of the rents. Both of these strategies are likely to be superior to relying upon countertrade arrangements. Countertrade does not guarantee access to the kind of information needed either for bargaining or for the establishment of independent distribution channels, and therefore offers limited potential for the development of export markets.

7.9 AN EMPIRICAL STUDY OF COUNTERPURCHASE

Empirical analysis of countertrade is scant. There has been some discussion of the policies of individual countries (Business International, 1984) – in particular the Soviet Union (Hannigan and McMillan, 1984; Rontanen, 1983) – and of the role of buy-back arrangements in East-West industrial cooperation (OECD, 1981; Paliwoda, 1981). Lecraw (1988) has analysed countertrade arrangements in general, using firm-level data, but unfortunately he does not use regression techniques, and so fails to measure the relative size of the separate influences that simultaneously impinge on the firm.

Empirical study of counterpurchase has been particularly lacking. As a first step towards remedying this defect, this section reports a cross-section regression study of counterpurchase arrangements based upon a sample of 35 countries over the period 1982–85. The sample comprises 20 LDCs that are significantly involved in counterpurchase and 15 developed countries (DCs) that trade with them through counterpurchase arrangements. The sample is confined to countries on which definite evidence of involvement in counterpurchase was available. The sample is therefore truncated, and there is a potential problem of selection bias. This problem could not be avoided, given the limitations of the data. Data sources are described in the appendix.

The dependent variable, CP, is the propensity of a country to engage in counterpurchase arrangements. It measures the proportion of a country's exports that are matched by imports of goods under a counterpurchase arrangement. This measure nets out from recorded counterpurchase the value of any exports or imports within the arrangement that are sold for cash.

The forward selling element in counterpurchase suggests that the incentive to engage in counterpurchase is greater, the lower is the country's ability to diversify the risks of export price variability. Inability to diversify is likely to stem from a high commodity concentration of exports, CN, and, to a lesser extent, from a high geographical concentration, GN, too. Thus CP is likely to depend positively upon CN and GN, which can be proxied by the respective Gini-Hirshmann indices

$$CN = \{\Sigma_j (X_j/X)^2\}^{\frac{1}{2}}$$

$$GN = \{\Sigma_k (X^k/X)^2\}^{\frac{1}{2}}$$

where X is the total export earnings of the country concerned, X_j its export earnings from the jth commodity, and X^k its export earnings from the kth country. An alternative approach is to use a measure of export earnings instability directly as an explanatory variable. The disadvantage of this is that if the theory is correct, the propensity to engage in countertrade should influence the observed level of export instability, whereas it is less likely to feed back on CN or GN – at least in the short run.

The currency aspect of counterpurchase suggests that claims upon primary products are more readily traded than claims on manufactured products or services. Manufactured products are more highly differentiated, and their quality is not only more variable, but is particularly difficult to assess by inspection. Thus CP is likely to be positively related to an index of primary commodity specialisation, PS, where PS is the proportion of export earnings derived from primary products.

The loan element in counterpurchase suggests that involvement in counterpurchase will be positively related to the country's cost of borrowing. This can be proxied by DB, the external debt liability of the country normalised with respect to its Gross Domestic Product. Theory predicts a positive relation between CP and DB.

The barter element in counterpurchase suggests that attempts to exploit market power through price discrimination, or to cheat on cartel-type arrangements, are both potential influences on CP. To capture these effects, two indices were constructed. The index CT measures the extent to which a country's exports are marketed through cartels. It is a dummy variable which takes the value unity when the country's major export market is dominated by a price-fixing institution of some kind, and is zero otherwise. MP is a dummy variable designed to indicate the market power of the buyers faced by the country in its export markets. MP takes on a value of unity when the buyer concentration in the major export market exceeds a threshold level, and is zero otherwise. Theory implies that because buyer concentration facilitates price discrimination when the seller has market power, MP is positively related to CP.

It was noted earlier that the preceding considerations do not provide a comprehensive rationalisation for counterpurchase. The policy stance of the exporting country must also be taken into account. It is therefore postulated that CP is related to a dummy variable PL, which assumes the value unity when the government energetically promotes countertrade policies – either by mandating countertrade or providing fiscal incentives – and is zero otherwise. If government strategy is entirely a rational response to the economic environment, then within a multiple regression in which all relevant economic variables have been included, PL will carry a coefficient of zero. On the other hand, when political and ideological consider-ations are important in their own right, theory predicts that PL will carry a positive sign.

Finally, an attempt is made to assess the overall validity of the preceding theory by comparing it with an alternative naive hypoth-esis. The naive alternative is that CP is entirely explained by the country's level of development, as measured by its per capita national income, Y. The naive hypothesis asserts that CP is negatively related to Y.

The regression was estimated using Ordinary Least Squares, and standard diagnostic procedures were followed, with particular atten-tion to outlying residuals. Apart from multicollinearity (discussed below), no major problems emerged. Because the dependent vari-able CP is constrained to the unit interval, the effects of a logit transformation were investigated, but the results proved quite robust to this change.

Equation 1 in Table 7.1 shows that commodity concentration of exports, CN, indebtedness, DB, and policy stance, PL, are all significant at the 5 per cent level and take the expected sign. About 94 per cent of variation is explained by this equation which, for a cross-section regression, is a relatively high figure. The naive hypothesis is refuted: the coefficient on per capita income, Y, is insignificant, though it carries the right sign. There is a very high correlation between commodity concentration, CN, geographical concentration, GN, and commodity specialisation, PS, and this partially explains why the coefficients on GN and PS are insignificant when CN is included in the regression.

Suppressing the three least significant variables – GN, CT and Y – gives equation 2. As expected, the coefficient on CN becomes more strongly significant with the suppression of the collinear variable GN, and the other variables become marginally more significant too. The index of primary commodity specialisation PS, however, takes the wrong sign. Suppressing the remaining variables that are insignificant at the 5 per cent level – MP and PS – gives equation 3. It is worth noting that reducing the number of explanatory variables from eight to three reduces the proportion of sample variation explained by only 1 per cent, while the F-ratio increases nearly three-fold as a result, from 50.4 to 136.9.

Equation 3 provides convincing support for the view that it is a combination of forward selling, cheap borrowing and political and ideological appeal that makes counterpurchase attractive. The insignificance of cartel involvement CT and market power MP suggests that price discrimination and cartel cheating are not significant motivations. Despite the fact that the majority of sample countries are strongly specialised in primary product exports, PS is not a major influence on countertrade. One reason for this may be that when counterpurchase is mandated it is often used to promote non-traditional exports such as clothing, footwear and other low-technology manufactured products. The schedule of countertraded goods offered by the LDC may be manipulated to offer the largest implicit discounts on these goods, so biasing countertrade towards manufactures and away from primary products.

Intuition suggests that the determinants of counterpurchase may differ between the LDCs and the DCs that trade with them. On the other hand, the theory developed above is sufficiently general that it

TABLE 7.1 *Regression analysis of the propensity to engage in counterpurchase in a cross-section sample of 35 countries*

Equation Number	Constant	CN	GN	PS	DB	CT	MP	PL	Y	R^2	F
1	−2.19	0.17 (3.94)*	0.01 (0.18)	−0.05 (−1.45)	0.20 (2.29)*	1.26 (0.82)	1.64 (1.05)	5.58 (3.27)*	−1.05 (−0.77)	0.94	50.4
2	−3.27	0.18 (6.12)*		−0.06 (−1.59)	0.22 (2.81)*		1.85 (1.23)	6.28 (4.09)*		0.94	84.9
3	−3.85	0.17 (7.68)*			0.19 (2.46)*			5.77 (3.85)*		0.93	136.9

Note: * indicates significance at 5 per cent in a two-tailed test.

TABLE 7.2   *Regression analysis disaggregated by type of country*

Sample	Constant	CN	DB	PL	R^2	F
LDCs	4.56	0.16	0.08	–	0.66	16.77
		(5.71)*	(0.79)	–		
DCs	–2.06	0.08	0.26	3.37	0.86	23.2
		(3.62)*	(1.68)	(4.31)*		

Note: LDCs (20 observations):
Algeria, Bangladesh, Brazil, Colombia, Ghana, Honduras, Iran, Iraq, Indonesia, Jamaica, Libya, Malaysia, Nigeria, Philippines, Pakistan, Peru, Turkey, Tanzania, Uruguay and Venezuela.
DCs (15 observations):
Australia, Belgium, Canada, Denmark, France, Germany, Italy, Japan, Norway, New Zealand, Spain, Sweden, Switzerland, United Kingdom and United States.

should be able to cope with this. Although the initiative for counter-purchase may well come from an LDC, the response of a prospective DC trading partner should be governed by the same factors that influence the LDCs. To test this, the sample was split into two sub-samples, comprising 20 LDCs and 15 DCs respectively, and the equations re-estimated.

Table 7.2 shows that the equation for the DCs remains basically satisfactory, the main change being that indebtedness DB becomes insignificant, though it continues to take the expected sign. Figure 7.1 shows, however, that this regression is 'anchored' at one end by a single observation, whose removal would substantially reduce the significance of commodity concentration, CN. It is bad statistical methodology to simply eliminate such observations, however, because they contain potentially precious information. In the present case, while such sensitivity is clearly a cause for concern, the observation concerned is economically meaningful. It shows that New Zealand, a DC with very high commodity concentration and a significant primary commodity specialisation in the export of butter, lamb and so on, has opted for a higher level of counterpurchase than any other DC in the sample.

Rather surprisingly, it is the equation for the LDCs that changes most. One reason is that all the LDCs in the sample have a pro-countertrade policy, which means that the PL variable is unity throughout the sub-sample, so that the coefficient on PL cannot be identified.

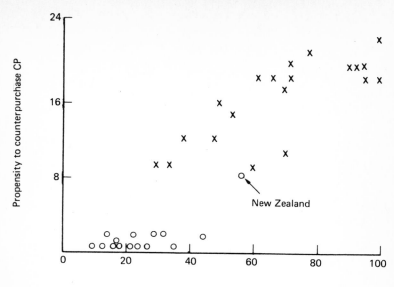

Note: O denotes DC observation

x denotes LDC observation

FIGURE 7.1 *Scatter diagram of commodity concentration and propensity to engage in counterpurchase*

Suppressing the unidentified variable PL leads to an estimated constant term for LDCs which exceeds the constant term for DCs by 6.62. Whilst it seems reasonable to impute some of this difference to the impact of the policy variable PL, it is not reasonable to impute all of it in this way. The low proportion of variation explained in the two sub-samples ($R^2 = 0.66$ and 0.86 for LDCs and DCs respectively) relative to that in the full sample ($R^2 = 0.93$) suggests that, independently of policy, LDCs have a higher autonomous propensity to engage in counterpurchase than do DCs. This difference seems to be captured in the full regression by indebtedness, DB, which is on average higher for LDCs than for DCs (it is not captured by *per capita* income, Y, which is insignificant in the full sample regression). The fact that DB is insignificant within both sub-samples, however, suggests that it is not indebtedness *per se* that influences counterpurchase, but rather certain fundamental aspects of underdevelopment of which indebtedness – in excess of some threshold level – is a symptom. One probable candidate is the degree of domestic price distortion. Excessive distortion will inhibit adjustment to world recession and so lead to high indebtedness. It is some such fundamental aspect of underdevelopment which accounts for that part of the difference in the size of the constant term that cannot be attributed to the policy variable PL.

Despite these qualifications, the impact of commodity concentration remains strongly significant, suggesting that the basic interpretation of counterpurchase as a risk reduction instrument is sound.

7.10   AN EMPIRICAL STUDY OF BUY-BACK ARRANGEMENTS

This section reports a cross-section regression study of buy-back arrangements involving 30 countries over the period 1980–86. The sample comprises 17 DMEs, eight CPSEs from the CMEA bloc, and five LDCs. The dependent variable BB is the propensity to engage in buy-back, as measured by the ratio of the total value of counterpurchase deals involving the country concerned over the seven-year period, normalised by the total exports of the country in the final year.

There are seven independent variables, one of which, DB, was used in previous regressions, and is expected to take the same sign. The theory of section 7.7 suggests that BB will vary positively with the incidence of host-country restrictions on foreign ownership, as measured by the dummy variable RF. A high risk of expropriation will also encourage the use of buy-back as an alternative to foreign investment; this is captured by the variable RK, which measures the relative riskiness of the foreign environment. RK is the 'Investment Environment Score' published by Business International, which ranges from zero (high risk) to 100 (no risk). Theory predicts that RK is negatively related to BB.

Since buy-back is closely associated with technology transfer, it is likely to be stimulated when the host country's indigenous technological capability is low relative to the sophistication of local demand and the requirements of the export market. It is therefore postulated that BB is negatively related to indigenous technological capability, TC, as proxied by the share of manufacturing in GDP, and positively related to the sophistication of the local market, MS, as measured by *per capita* GNP. The issue of export quality is addressed by constructing a dummy variable QS, set equal to unity when the country's reputation for export quality is high, and zero otherwise. QS is estimated judgementally by combining other people's published assessments, with the result that all DMEs in the sample have QS = 1. Since it is widely believed that buy-back can be used by non-reputable producers to establish overseas market links, it is postulated that QS is negatively related to BB.

The results shown in Table 7.3 provide qualified support for the theory. Once again, a high proportion of sample variance is explained ($R^2 = 0.90$). Restrictions on foreign equity ownership, RF, quality reputation, QS, and indigenous technological capacity, TC, are all significant and take the expected sign. The signs are confirmed by the LDC and CMEA sub-sample, but unfortunately all the variables lose significance. This is not unexpected, however, given the very low degrees of freedom. Focusing on DMEs alone, equity restrictions become less critical and the riskiness of the environment dominates instead. Indigenous technological capacity continues to be a significant negative influence, but indebtedness also becomes significant and takes the wrong sign. In this sense, the buy-back regression is less successful than its counterpurchase equivalent.

Overall, the buy-back regression analysis is useful in explaining why LDCs and CMEA countries as a whole have a higher propensity to engage in countertrade than do DMEs, but it cannot provide a finely-tuned account of why some countries within one of these groups engage in countertrade more heavily than do the others.

7.11 POLICY IMPLICATIONS

The empirical evidence suggests that counterpurchase provides a useful service in managing risks and in mitigating liquidity problems, whilst buy-back can assist technology transfer and industrialisation. There is one important sense, however, in which the empirical evidence is incomplete, for this chapter has been confined to cross-section analysis. Time series data on countertrade is extremely difficult to obtain, because it is only since the recent growth in countertrade that press information on the subject has been collated on a global level. It is fairly clear, however, from the scant evidence available, that countertrade has a strong cyclical element, rising at the onset of depression and – on the evidence of the 1930s – falling as

TABLE 7.3   *Regression analysis of the propensity to engage in buy-back*

Equation Number	Sample	Constant	RF	MS	RK	QS	TC	DB	R^2	F
1	Full	24.6	3.78 (2.15)*	−0.25 (−0.86)	0.05 (0.87)	−10.2 (−3.64)*	−5.03 (−2.10)*	−4.23 (−0.80)	0.90	36.2
2	Full	25.5	3.49 (2.22)*			−10.09 (−4.00)*	−5.14 (−3.31)*		0.89	74.6
3	LDCs and CMEAs	14.62	3.55 (0.80)	−1.17 (−0.45)	0.05 (0.62)	−5.7 (−0.88)	−0.79 (−0.07)	18.48 (−0.23)	0.50	1.4
4	DMEs	−9.25	−3.35 (−1.55)	0.06 (0.28)	0.34 (2.29)*		−7.32 (−3.57)*	−6.35 (−2.27)*	0.69	4.86
5	DMEs	−9.79			0.14 (1.88)*		−4.48 (−3.54)*		0.51	7.3

Note: LDCs (5 observations); Brazil, China, India, Indonesia, Nigeria.
CMEAs (8 observations); Bulgaria, Czechoslovakia, East Germany, Hungary, Poland, Romania, USSR, Yugoslavia.
DMEs (17 observations); Australia, Austria, Belgium, Canada, Denmark, Finland, France, Italy, Japan, Netherlands, Norway, Spain, Sweden, Switzerland, UK, US, West Germany

recovery begins. A simple explanation of this cyclical behaviour, in terms of nominal price rigidities and loss of confidence in soft currencies, was advanced in sections 7.3–5, but it has not been possible to test this rigorously here.

The theory and evidence in this chapter are sufficient, however, to show policy issues in a somewhat novel light. Some DME governments with a strong commitment to multilateralism have denounced countertrade as detrimental to world welfare. A more appropriate approach, it would seem, is to tolerate countertrade and at the same time to promote institutional innovations in the free market system which provide benefits similar to those of countertrade, but without the costs of bilateralism. If intervention is deemed necessary, it is better to intervene to promote new alternatives rather than to restrict one of the alternatives already in use.

Nor does the evidence suggest that intervention is desirable to *promote* countertrade. In the context of counterpurchase, restricting hard currency transactions in order to promote countertrade increases transaction costs and reduces economic efficiency. Such a policy can be condoned only as a 'second best' response when, because of rigidities in foreign trade management, hard-currency transactions would take place at the wrong prices.

Restrictions on foreign equity participation which stimulate the development of buy-back arrangements are also liable to reduce efficiency. Liberalisation of ownership would go a long way, in many industries, to reducing the incidence of buy-back, as it would allow technology transfer to be effected using first-best contractual arrangements, such as joint ventures and wholly-owned subsidiaries.

It was noted in section 7.8 that countertrade is of limited value so far as export promotion is concerned. The discussion above suggests that in a 'second best' environment of missing futures markets, disequilibrium pricing of hard-currency exports and restrictions on foreign ownership, countertrade is, however, of potential value in import procurement. In some cases, of course, import procurement may be the first step in a development process which leads to export generation. This is particularly true in the context of technology imports. In this sense – and in this sense only – countertrade may have a role in (indirectly) promoting exports from industrialising countries.

APPENDIX 7.1

Statistical Sources and Methods

The appendix provides additional information on the specification and measurement of the variables used in the econometric analysis.

CP: Consider a single counterpurchase agreement between a party in country A and a partner in the rest of the world (country B). Let x be the value of the goods (according to the agreement) exported from A to B, and y the corresponding value of goods imported from B by A. Let $m = x - y$ be the net flow of cash from B to A. Define the counterpurchase component of the agreement $cv = min(x,y)$ and the transaction value $tv = max(x,y)$. Note that $cv \neq tv$ if and only if $m \neq 0$. Let CV be the total counterpurchase value of country A's exports. It is equal to the sum of all cv components taken across A's transactions with B. Let X be the total exports of country A. This is the sum of all x components of counterpurchase agreements *plus* all exports under non-counterpurchase agreements. A's propensity to engage in counterpurchase is $CP = CV/X$. Note that this differs, in general, from the measure derived from the alternative concept $CP' = TV/X$ where TV is the total value of all tv elements.

Sources: A, B, C, D, E, F, G, I, J, L

CN, GN: The calculation of concentration indices uses Michaely's method (M1) applied to 1985 data.

Sources: I_1, J_1, J_2.

PS: Sources: H_2, J_1, J_2.

DB: Sources: H_1, H_2.

CT: A country's major export product was identified. If the major domestic producers belong to an international cartel, or any restrictive commodity agreement designed to raise prices, then $CT = 1$. If the major export product was not subject to any such agreement, or if domestic producers were not members of such an agreement, then $CT = 0$.

Sources: J.

MP: The major export product was identified as above. If fewer than eight firms purchase more than 60 per cent of world production of this product then $MP = 1$, otherwise $MP = 0$. The critical number of eight firms was chosen because, of the 15 product markets surveyed, nine had between three and six leading firms and the remainder had between ten and 15 leading firms, making a 'natural break' over the interval between six and ten. The figure of 60 per cent was chosen because it is typical of four-firm buyer concentration in the most highly concentrated markets.

Sources: K_1, K_2

PL: Source: M_2

Y: Source: H_2

BB: Sources: A, B, H, I, J, N, P, Q_1, Q_2, Q_3, Q_4

RF: Sources: B, P

MS: Sources: H, N

RK: Sources: B_4

QS: Sources: A, P, Q_2, Q_3, Q_4

TC: Sources: J, N

Key to Sources

A	Organisation of Economic Cooperation and Development (OECD).
A_1	*Developing Countries' Attitudes Towards Countertrade* (1985).
A_2	*External Debt of Developing Countries* (1984).
A_3	*East-West Trade in Chemicals* (1980).
A_4	*East-West Trade: Recent Developments in Countertrade* (1981).
A_5	*Developing Countries' Attitudes Towards Countertrade* (1985).
A_6	*Statistics on External Indebtedness: The Debt and Other External Liabilities of Developing, CMEA and Certain Other Countries.*
B.	Business International
B_1	*Countertrade with Developing Countries* (1983).
B_2	*Countertrade and Buy-back Transactions* (1984).
B_3	*Exploring Countertrade Opportunities in Africa* (1984).
B_4	*Managing and Evaluating Country Risk* (1987).
B_5	*Licensing and Trade Publications* (1986).
B_6	*Market Size Indicators* (1986).
C	Financial Times.
C_1	Financial Times Survey (6 Feb. 1985).
C_2	Financial Times Survey (23 March 1987).
D	Countertrade and Barter Quarterly.
D_1	No. 1, Summer 1983.
D_2	No. 3, Spring 1983.
D_3	No. 5, Spring 1985.
D_4	No. 6, Autumn 1983.
D_5	No. 9, Spring 1986.
E	Business Week International.
E_1	Business Week International Report, 30 Sept. 1985.
F	News Watch.
F_1	Keeping Step with the Past (15 July 1985).
F_2	Countertrade Boom in Third World Trade (6 Oct. 1986).
F_3	Japan's Countertrade Boom with Latin America (17 May 1986).
G	US International Trade Commission.
G_1	*Analysis of Recent Trends in US Countertrade: Report on Investigation*, No. 382–125, USITC Pub. 1237, Washington, March 1982.
H	World Bank.
H_1	World Debt Tables (1987).
H_2	World Development Report (1987).
I	International Monetary Fund (IMF).
I_1	*International Financial Statistics* (various issues).
J	United Nations (UN).
J_1	*Yearbook of International Trade Statistics* (1985).
J_2	*Commodity Trade Statistics* (1985).
J_3	*Handbook of International Trade and Development Statistics*, 1985 (pp. 406–13).
J_4	UNESCO Statistical Yearbook (1987).
K	UNCTAD.
K_1	Document TD/229/Supp. 3 (1979).
K_2	Document TD/184/Supp. 3 and Corr. 1 (No date).

L   Economist Intelligence Unit (EIU).
L$_1$ *North/South Countertrade* (1982).
M   International Monetary Fund.
M$_1$ *Report on Exchange Arrangements and Exchange Restrictions* (various issues).
N   National Statistical Yearbooks.
N$_1$ *Statistical Pocket Book of Hungary* (1986).
N$_2$ *Concise Statistical Yearbook of Poland* (1986).
N$_3$ *Statistical Pocket Book of Yugoslavia* (1986).
N$_4$ *Statistica Moscow* (English edn) (1985).
N$_5$ *Comecon Foreign Trade Data* (1986).
N$_6$ *Statistical Yearbook of China* (1985).
P   Country Reports (weekly)
P$_1$ *Business Asia.*
P$_2$ *Business Europe.*
P$_3$ *Business Latin America.*
P$_4$ *Overseas Business Report.*
Q   *Miscellaneous.*
Q$_1$ Michaely, M. (1984) *Trade, Income Levels and Dependence*, Amsterdam: North Holland.
Q$_2$ *Kostecki, M.* (1987) Should One Countertrade?, *Les Cahiers du CETAI*, No. 87–02.
Q$_3$ Verzariu, P. (1980) *Countertrade Practices in East Europe, the Soviet Union and China: An Introductory Guide to Business*, Washington: US Dept. of Commerce, International Trade Administration.
Q$_4$ Matheson, J. *et al.* (1977) Countertrade Practices in Eastern Europe, in *Eastern European Economies Post-Helsinki*, Washington, DC; US Congress Joint Economic Committee.

Note

The research is based upon a thesis 'The Case for Countertrade Agreements' by Francis Chukujama, submitted for PhD at the University of Reading. The preparation of this paper was supported by the WIDER Institute, Helsinki. The authors are grateful to Gerry Helleiner, Nick Rowe, Winston Frisch, Lorraine Eden, Don Lecraw, Rolf Mirus, Danny van den Bulcke, Bernard Yeung, and many others, for their constructive comments and suggestions.

8 Factors Influencing FDI by TNCs in Host Developing Countries: A Preliminary Report

Donald J. Lecraw

8.1 INTRODUCTION

The relationship between foreign direct investment (FDI) by transnational corporations (TNCs) and developing countries continues to be a controversial one among both researchers on TNCs and government policy-makers in developing countries.[1] The governments of some developing countries have viewed FDI by TNCs as one means of accelerating economic growth, increasing investment, expanding and diversifying their exports, and accessing product and process technology; they have promoted rather than restricted investment by TNCs.[2] Others have allowed some FDI, but have placed restrictions of varying severity on TNC operations.[3] Others have actively discouraged, if not prohibited, FDI in most sectors of their economies.[4]

Through the early 1980s, inward FDI flows to developing countries rose from $2 billion in 1970 to $6.3 billion in 1975, and to $15 billion in 1981. By 1983, however, inflows had fallen to $10.3 billion, from which point they recovered marginally to $11.5 billion in 1985 (the last year for which there currently is comprehensive data).[5] At the country level, there were much wider variations. In Mexico, for example, inward FDI fell from $2.5 billion (in 1981) to $0.390 billion (1984), but, for Colombia, inflows increased from $0.265 billion (1981) to $1.02 billion in 1985, while for Indonesia inflows were more or less constant in the $250 million range.[6] These wide variations in the inflows of FDI both over time and among developing countries raise the question of what factors influence FDI inflows to developing countries.

Since the mid-1970s the governments of many developing countries have made substantial changes in their policies and regulatory

163

systems toward TNCs (UNCTC, 1983, 1988; Lecraw, Grosse and Cantwell, 1990). China's 'Open Door' policy towards trade and FDI is the most dramatic example of such a change, but the trend towards more openness to FDI was quite general. In the mid-1980s the debt crisis, a change in many developing countries' economic policies from import substitution towards export promotion and diversification, and a trend towards deregulation and liberalisation, led many developing countries to undertake further measures to attract investment by TNCs. They instituted a wide variety of promotional measures towards TNCs on the one hand and relaxed many regulatory restrictions on TNC operations on the other.

These policy and regulatory changes raise the question: what have the effects of these policies been on inward flows of FDI?

There is little systematic evidence on the effects of government regulatory or promotional policies on the flows of FDI into host countries. Based on surveys of businessmen, Reuber *et al.* (1973) and Guisinger and Associates (1985) found that tax incentives influenced footloose, export-oriented FDI, while tariff rates influenced FDI oriented towards the domestic market.[7] Only the direction, not the magnitude, of the effects of changes in these variables was measured in these two studies. At present there is little systematic knowledge concerning the factors that influence the *flows* of FDI to developing countries. Policy-makers in developing countries then have little information on which to base their decisions when they design policies to attract and to regulate the flows of FDI. Guisinger (1986), a co-author of the World Bank study, concluded (p. 94):

> The World Bank study did not tackle the 'normative' side of foreign investment policies . . . The study focused on what countries do, not what they should do . . . The main implication is that our level of ignorance of investment incentives and performance requirements is unacceptably high.

The purpose of the research reported here is to reduce this level of ignorance somewhat by trying to identify in a systematic manner the factors that influence FDI flows, particularly such factors as the tax and tariff rates and the basic openness of the country's policy towards FDI, factors that are under the host country's control.

The research reported in this paper follows Dunning (1981) in attempting to estimate the factors that have influenced the gross inflow of FDI to developing countries. Its contributions are:

(1) it uses more recent and more comprehensive data than was available to Dunning;

(2) building on his seminal work, the number of variables tested was expanded and the proxies for some of the variables were changed;

(3) it uses a flow model of FDI in which TNCs are hypothesised to respond to *changes* in conditions in host developing countries, rather than to their absolute level.

8.2   THE THEORY OF FDI IN DEVELOPING COUNTRIES

There is an extensive literature on the factors that influence the level of FDI investment by TNCs and the effects of this investment in high-income countries.[8] There is also a growing literature on the relationships between market structure in developing countries and the levels of TNC ownership in their industries and the effects of this investment on the economies of these countries. As yet, however, there has been little empirical testing of the determinants of the *flows* of FDI into developing countries. Theory would indicate that, barring restrictions on investment inflows, TNCs would allocate their investment capital among countries so as to maximise their risk-adjusted profits over their world-wide operations. Flows of capital to any one developing country would then depend on the (risk-adjusted) marginal return on the additional TNC capital relative to the returns available on that capital in other countries. This paper tests this basic hypothesis.

The marginal rate of return on capital for the TNC investment in a country may depend on three groups of factors: factors in the host country (such as changes in the value of natural resources, changes in wage rates, the size and growth of its domestic market, changes in the exchange rate, the availability of domestic capital, the growth rate of the labour force, infrastructure development), factors within the TNC (such as proprietary technology, access to markets, capital cost, and management expertise), and factors that influence the return to direct investment abroad relative to retaining investment in the home country and servicing other countries via exports and licensing (such as transaction costs and barriers to trade). Dunning (1981), in his 'Eclectic Theory of the TNC', has classified these three groups of factors as: locational advantages, ownership advantages and internationalisation advantages.

Focusing on the locational advantages of host countries, assume that foreign capital is a perfect substitute for domestic capital.[9] Then the stock of FDI would increase with the stock of other complementary resources (such as labour), decrease with the amount of domestically supplied capital, and increase with a variety of productivity-raising factors, such as infrastructure development, the education and discipline of the workforce, and government policies that shift the marginal productivity of capital. The desired stock of capital would also increase with such factors as a growth in demand (leading to short-term upward pressures on prices and long-term demand for greater output), or increases in the prices of the output of natural resource projects. The *flow* of FDI that is observed would then be an adjustment of the stock of FDI in response to changes in the optimum stock of FDI in the country.

If we assume that the stock of FDI in each country was at its equilibrium level at the beginning of the period, then flows (changes in stock) of FDI would be related to *changes* in the resource stock variables of the country (capital and labour) and in the country's locational advantages (ΔLA) that change the marginal product of capital. Under this assumption, flows of FDI would *not* be related to *levels* of the country's locational advantages or the size of its labour force and domestic investment. In equation form:

(1) $FDI = F(\Delta L, \Delta Kh, \Delta LA)$

where L is the labour force, Kh is host country capital, and LA are the set of locational advantages that raise the marginal product of capital.

On the other hand, if we assume that there is a gap between desired long-run, steady-stocks and actual stocks of FDI at the beginning of the period, then the flows would represent an equilibration process to fill this gap. Under this assumption, FDI inflows would be negatively related to start-of-period *stock* of FDI (FDKo) and positively related to the end-of-period *levels* of the locational advantages (LA_t).

(2a) $FDI = G(FDK^*, - FDKo)$

where $FDK^*, = g(LA)$ and FDK^* is positively related to the *level* of all LA at the end of the period and g( ) is a positive function in the LA. For empirical testing, FDK^*, an unobserved variable, could be replaced with the end-of-period values of the locational advantages (LA). Hence Equation 2a can be re-written:

(2b) FDI = H(LA$_t$, − FDKo).

Equations 1 and 2b present different assumptions concerning the factors that determine inward flows of FDI. Of course, there is no reason why both these models could not be correct or represent part of the picture; they are not mutually exclusive. If the model is specified using *levels* of the locational advantages, as in equation 2b, then a case must be made why there is a gap between desired investment (FDK*) and actual investment (FDKo). One rationale for the gap would be changes in the country's locational advantages but, as we have seen, these changes are not explicitly incorporated in this particular model. It happens to be the case that data on the stock of FDI in developing countries are generally not reliable and are not comparable among countries, a fact which precludes any satisfactory test of the hypothesis that the inward foreign direct capital stock is explained by the variation in the level of LAs between hosts.

In view of the above discussion, this paper employs changes in locational advantages as a way of explaining inward flows of FDI. This can be presented as a capital stock adjustment process, using the following basic definitions:

FDK = inward foreign direct capital stock
FDI = inward foreign direct investment flows (net investment inflows) being given by FDK$_t$ − FDK$_{t-1}$
FDK* = optimal inward foreign direct capital stock

According to this process, observable net FDI inflows are some fraction of the difference between the optimal capital stock (FDK*$_t$) and the actual capital stock in the previous period (FDK$_{t-1}$). As we assumed above that the stock (FDK*$_t$) was at its equilibrium level at the beginning of the period, it follows that FDK*$_{t-1}$ = FDK$_{t-1}$. The adjustment process is unlikely to be completed within a single year, and here we denote the proportionate shortfall by λ. The essential propositions are that:

(3) FDI$_t$ = (1 − λ) (FDK*$_t$ − FDK$_{t-1}$) and

(4) FDK*$_t$ = f(L$_t$, Kh$_t$, LA$_t$).

It was argued above that FDK* is unobservable, while FDK is not measurable with sufficient accuracy. As the process is now assumed to be preceded by an equilibrium capital stock, FDI inflows can therefore be written as:

(5) $FDI_t = (1 - \lambda)\ f\ (\Delta L_t,\ \Delta Kh_t,\ \Delta LA_t).$

This forms the basis of the model tested, although host-country capital stock (Kh) is eventually dropped, while the lags are later allowed to vary between the independent variables.

We now turn to the locational advantages themselves and how they might influence inflows of FDI. Here it is useful to distinguish three types of FDI: natural resource-seeking (FDIR), market-seeking (FDIM), and export-oriented, efficiency-seeking (FDIE). These three types of FDI might be motivated by both common and different locational advantages. Common locational factors would include any factor that changes the return on capital for FDI regardless of which type it was. These would include: a change in the tax rate, the growth rate of the labour force, a change in the openness of a country's policy towards FDI, a change in perceived country risk, a change in the real exchange rate, and the growth rate of infrastructure.

Market-seeking FDI might be influenced by factors in the domestic market such as a change in tariff and non-tariff protection, changes in domestic demand, or some combination of these factors. Efficiency-seeking FDI (most particularly export-oriented FDI) and natural resource-seeking FDI might be influenced by such factors as a change in the wage rate relative to wages in other countries and/or a change in the human capital per worker relative to other countries. These two factors might be combined into a quality-adjusted wage rate. Natural resource-seeking FDI inflows might be influenced by changes in the value of the country's natural resource products, as reflected in changing prices for its natural resource exports.

The most comprehensive theoretical and empirical work on the determinants of FDI in developing countries was conducted by Dunning as part of his broader work on the patterns of inward and outward FDI among countries and over time (Dunning, 1981a).[10] In this research Dunning reported that, for countries with per capita incomes of between $1000 and $2499, for the 1967–75 period, per capita inward FDI averaged $38.60. For countries with per capita income of $500–$999, FDI averaged $21.60, while for countries with per capita incomes of less than $125 the figure was $1.30. Within each income group, countries which Dunning classified as 'resource rich' had two to three times as much inward FDI as countries he classified as 'industrialising'.

Dunning (1981a, p. 123) advanced the hypotheses that:

> From the viewpoint of GII (Gross Inward Investment), one might hypothesise that countries with the same level of GNP per capita, which are (1) rich in natural resources and/or human resources, (2) have a large home market, (3) offer a congenial environment for foreign investment, (4) have a well-developed infrastructure, and an acceptable legal and/or commercial framework, and yet (5) whose indigenous firms are not able (or do not choose) to generate the kind of ownership advantages to enable them to compete with foreign enterprises, will be those that record an above average level of inward investment.

Dunning used correspondence analysis for the countries in his sample and identified three clusters of countries based largely on 1971 GNP per capita and net outward investment (NOI). For the period 1967 to 1975, for the first group of countries (high income countries, high NOI), there was substantial inward and outward FDI, with positive net outward FDI; for the second group of countries (middle income countries, negative NOI), there was considerable inward FDI but little outward FDI; for the third group of countries (those with the lowest income levels and little NOI), there was only a small amount of inward FDI. The focus of this paper is on cluster 2 and cluster 3 countries, the developing countries.

Using stepwise OLS regression, Dunning found that for cluster 2 countries, the factors that influenced GII for the 1967–75 period were: per capita exports of primary products plus tourism receipts (1973), growth in manufacturing output (1960–77), and an infrastructure index of the percentage of urban to total population plus the percentage of secondary school children in the relevant age group (average of 1960 and 1975). These three variables accounted for 78 per cent of the variance in GII among the 15 countries in cluster 2. For cluster 3 countries the results were not as good: only one variable, natural resource endowment, was statistically significant and only 16 per cent of the variance was explained. For the developing countries in Dunning's sample (clusters 1 and 2), only locational variables were found to have a significant influence on inward FDI.

There are problems with Dunning's model specification, however, which make interpretation of the results difficult. One problem with Dunning's analysis is that it is not clear whether some of the variables used as proxies for locational advantages represented levels or changes in the variables. The natural resource variable may have compounded both effects. Over the 1967–75 period of Dunning's data, natural resource prices increased dramatically, and hence there might have been a *change* in this locational advantage. Were FDI inflows responding to the level of natural resource endowments or to the change in the return to investing in natural resource industries due to higher prices? Similarly, there is a question of whether the country risk used should be its level (as used by Dunning) or changes in its level.

8.3 METHODOLOGY

The analysis in this paper follows the general thrust of Dunning (1981a) in that it relates FDI inflows to country locational advantages. It departs from Dunning's model in that it focuses on *changes* in the locational advantages rather than on their level as the determinant of FDI inflows. Inflows of FDI were related to *changes* in the country's locational advantages, the labour force and domestic capital, and to *changes* in barriers that might impede TNCs from investing in the host country, such as government restrictions on FDI. Under this hypothesis, the *level* of the locational variables was not viewed as the driving force behind FDI inflows. This assumption may be open to challenge. As examples, it implies that FDI is not attracted to a country by the size of its market *per se*, but rather by changes in the size of its market; inflows of FDI are not attracted by the size of a country's natural resource base, but by changes in its economic size.

It can also be argued that multinationals investing in a host for the first time are reacting to levels of locational advantages and not to changes in these. In view of this it must be assumed that the bulk of FDI inflows are accounted for by existing investors. Clearly this assumption is open to question, especially for LDCs with little inward FDI.

Operationalising the Dependent Variable

There is a problem with selecting an appropriate dependent variable to capture the determinants of inward FDI for developing countries. The problem lies in the dimensionality of the variable measuring FDI flows. Inflows of FDI are measured in dollars and would therefore depend on the size of the economy. Most of the independent variables, such as changes in perceived risk, wage rate, and so on, are not dependent on the size of the economy. Consider a country with an inflow of FDI of X. If the country were divided in two, then each new country would receive FDI inflows of X/2, but wages rates, risk levels and so on would not change. For estimation purposes, the FDI inflow variable must be standardised among the countries – as must the independent variables that vary with country size. Dunning (1981a) used Gross Inward Investment *per capita* as the dependent variable. This choice, however, may lead to problems with the choice of the independent variables and their statistical significance and the dimensionality of the reported coefficients. Among other things, as wage rates increase as a country develops, the capital output ratio would increase, demand for investment, FDI included, would increase, and a significant relationship between GNP per capita and FDI per capita would be expected. There seems to be no obvious way around this problem, especially since capital stock data (whether the FDI or domestic investment) are not generally available. In these circumstances, the variable chosen was FDI/GNP.

Another problem arises in the selection of the dependent variable. Three types of inward direct investment were identified: natural resource-seeking, market-seeking, and export-oriented. These three types may be motivated by both common and by different locational advantages. For example, investment to supply the host country market may increase if trade protection is increased, while for export-oriented investment, trade barriers may be of no value or have a negative impact if these barriers raise the cost of imported capital equipment and intermediate raw materials inputs. Standard data sources, such as the *International Financial Statistics*, do not disaggregate FDI into these three categories. Country reports from several sources were used to estimate the proportions of the total investment flows that fell into each category.

The Independent Variables

The independent variables used in the regression analysis to proxy location-specific advantages were:

(1) *Risk*. The greater the decrease in country risk, the greater FDI inflows. Changes in the BERI index were used as a measure of country risk.

(2) *Infrastructure development*. The changes in level of infrastructure development may also influence inward flows of investment. It is difficult to capture changes in the state of a country's infrastructure development in any one variable. Dunning used a combination of the percentage of the population in urban centres (presumably as some measure of the ease of accessing the market and/or the ease of attracting workers to an urban plant site) and the percentage of secondary school children in the relevant age group. The relevant infrastructure variables will depend on the type of FDI. If it is oriented to the domestic market, then urbanisation and the internal road network may be relevant. If it is export-oriented, then the level of development of the ports may be more important. If it is resource-seeking, then the developmental state of the internal transportation and port facilities may be important. Data to capture these effects, however, were not generally available. The change in government expenditures on 'transportation services' (TRANS) was used as a proxy for changes in infrastructure development.

(3) *Government policy towards foreign investment*. Whatever the locational advantages of a country, government policy towards TNCs (ISFI) may have a strong influence on inward investment. There are several examples of dramatic changes in openness of a country's policy towards foreign investment, such as in China, Korea and Sri Lanka where a change in government policy towards FDI led to significant changes in the flows of inward investment. As part of another research project, an index of the openness of the foreign investment incentives system for the LDCs was constructed based on a one-to-ten scale. Changes in this index were included as an independent variable.

(4) *Labour force and domestic capital*. Inflows of FDI should be positively related to increases in the labour force (LAB), and negatively related to increases in the stock of domestically owned capital (DCAP). Data on changes in the labour force in the mining sector (LABR) and manufacturing sector (LABM) were used separately. DCAP was set equal to the growth rate of domestic investment minus FDI inflows, a procedure which relies heavily on the accuracy of investment series.

(5) *Taxes*. All else equal, decreases in the tax rate (TAX) should raise the return on capital and increase inflows of FDI. There was a problem in determining the appropriate measure for this variable

since tax rates in many developing countries vary over the life of the project: tax holidays at the beginning of the investment, higher taxes later on. As one example, in 1984 Indonesia changed its tax system such that the basic corporate tax was lowered to 30 per cent, but at the same time tax holidays for new investment were abolished. Two alternative measures were used: the tax rate in the first three years of the investment (TAX3) and the tax rate over the first ten years (TAX10) of the investment. Tax rates may also differ depending on the sector and the orientation (export-oriented/domestic-market oriented) of the investment. These effects were incorporated into the analysis.

(6) *Growth rate of the domestic market, tariffs, and the real exchange rate*. Flows of FDI oriented to the domestic market, should increase with the growth rate of domestic demand minus imports, although we might note that inflows of such FDI would themselves tend to raise this variable in subsequent periods. Imports should be affected by the tariff rate and the real exchange rate. The growth rate of domestic demand (DEMD), changes in the tariff rate (TAR), and changes in the real exchange rate (RFX) were used. This second specification was used to isolate the effects of tariffs and the real exchange rate on inward FDI.

(7) *Natural resource base*. Dunning found that the natural resource base of the host country was a locational advantage that attracted FDI. In Dunning's overall regression equations, this variable and ECSTR (the percentage natural resources in the country's exports) sometimes were, but sometimes were not significant. This latter measure of natural resources is a rough proxy for the country's comparative advantage in natural resources. Flows of natural resource-seeking FDI should be positively related to increases in the prices of a country's natural resource products (PNAT).

(8) *Wage rates*. For TNCs engaged in export-oriented industries, the wage rate in a country may be a locational advantage. The educational level of the population may also influence the attractiveness of the work force for export-oriented TNCs. Wage rates and education levels might also influence natural resource-seeking FDI, since ultimately, for many developing countries, most production of natural resources are exported. Wage rates and human capital may also affect inward flows of FDI oriented to the domestic market to the extent that domestic production competes with imports. A composite

variable was used to test for the joint effects of wages rates and human capital: HC/W. HC was the percentage of the relevant age group enrolled in secondary schools four years previously; W was the wage rate in the manufacturing sector. Changes in this ratio relative to changes in the same ratio in the United States were used.

Foreign direct investment may not respond instantly to changes in the locational advantages in host developing countries. Rather it may respond with a lag structure. If flows of FDI among different investors respond with different lags, then, in any one year, FDI flows would be the sum of the responses to changes in previous years. One way to approach this problem would be to introduce lagged independent variables. But, as usual in these situations, following this procedure uses up degrees of freedom and there is a high degree of correlation among the lagged variables. Several procedures were tried to handle this problem. They all essentially involved specifying some lag structure, running the regressions, and examining the results to see which lag structure gave the best fit.[11]

Table 8.1 presents a list of the variables that may influence inward foreign investment, their definitions, how they were measured, their expected signs, and whether they were expected to influence flows of FDI in general or only one type of FDI.

A Generalised Least Squares analysis was performed on the pooled cross-sectional, time series data, with the three types of FDI inflow that were identified used as the dependent variables. As described above, some of the independent variables were hypothesised to influence only one type of FDI, for example, natural resource prices would only affect natural resource-seeking FDI, whereas others, such as the openness to FDI and country risk, were hypothesised to affect the flows of all three types of FDI. The statistical technique placed dummy variables in front of these variables to turn them 'on' and 'off' depending on whether they were expected to influence the particular form of FDI. This technique enabled using the full data set in one regression run: no. of countries x no. of years x no. of types of FDI. For reasons discussed in the following section the dependent variable was converted to three-year moving averages.

Sample Size and Data

The countries in the sample were chosen to be all the countries with per capita income of below $2200 (most of the countries classified by

TABLE 8.1 *Variable definition and sign*

		Sign	Type
BERI	Denoting changes in the BERI index, measuring changes in risk levels	−	All
TRANS	Changes in percent of GNP spent on transportation	+	All
ISFI	Changes in the openness of the country to FDI	+	All
LABR	Growth of the labour force in mining	+	FDIR
LABM	Growth rate of manufacturing labour force		FDIE
		+	FDIM
DCAP	Growth rate in domestic investment	−	All
TAX	Changes in the tax rate (E = export oriented, M = market seeking R = natural resources)	−	All
DEMD	Growth of domestic demand − imports	+	FDIM
TAR	Changes in the tariff rate	+	FDIM
RFX	Changes in the real exchange rate	−	All
PNAT	Changes in the relative price of natural resource exports	+	FDIR
HC/W	Changes in the quality-adjusted wage rate relative to the US	+	All

Note: the *higher* the BERI index, the *lower* the risk

the World Bank as being low and middle income countries). FDI data were not available for 15 of the countries listed in the World Bank *World Development Report 1988*, with per capita incomes below $2200. These were largely countries with centrally planned economies which did not report data on a regular basis and some of the small low-income countries. The sample size was further reduced for lack of foreign direct investment data for several of the developing countries. This reduced the sample size to 55 developing countries. Since different factors in the host country influenced different types of FDI flows, data were required on FDI by type – market-seeking, resource-seeking, and efficiency-seeking – and, in the case of the tax rates, to differentiate between the tax rates applied to these three types of investment. Data of this degree of disaggregation could only be obtained for 27 countries and 13 years – 1974–86.

8.4　RESULTS

There were several problems in interpreting the results of the statistical analysis. To take them in order:

(1) *Domestic capital.* One of the assumptions in the model was that FDI was a substitute for domestic capital. Under that assumption, FDI would be inversely related to domestic capital formation. When the regression equation was estimated with DCAP among the independent variables and inflows of FDI as the dependent variable, however, the sign on DCAP was positive and significant, and most of the other independent variables were either not significant or were only significant at the 0.10 level. When DCAP was dropped from the regression equation, many of the other independent variables became significant. When DCAP was used instead of FDI as the dependent variable, the signs on the independent variables did not change. It would seem that domestic capital was responding to many of the same factors that influenced FDI. This result does not necessarily imply that FDI and domestic investment were complements rather than substitutes, but rather it may indicate that both responded similarly to the same factors that raised the return on capital.

(2) *Lag structure.* There were no *a priori* expectations about the lag structure nor of the influence of the lag structure on FDI in response to changes in the independent variables. For several of the variables, such as infrastructure development and the quality-adjusted wage rate, the lag structure did not influence the significance of the coefficient. For other variables it did. In fact, the lag structure was longer than had originally been expected, for instance, a lag of up to three years was found to have the greatest explanatory power for some variables and influences were found up to five years. There is a danger here of changing the lag structures until the 'best' one is found, that is, the one for which the variable has the highest significance. To impede this tendency, checks were made with Chow tests to determine if the coefficients were stable on data sets from different time periods and groups of countries.

(3) *Common factors influencing FDI.* A similar problem was encountered with the variables for the quality-adjusted wage rate and the real exchange rate. HC/W was expected to have its strongest influence on export-oriented FDI, but a case could be made that it would

also influence natural resource-seeking FDI. The real exchange rate could affect not only export-oriented FDI, but also natural resource-seeking FDI (since natural resource production is also largely destined for international markets) and market-seeking investment. Chow tests were used to test for differences and stability of the coefficients model under different specifications and data sets.

(4) *Instability of FDI flows.* For many countries, FDI flows experienced wide year-on-year variations. These variations were particularly severe for natural resource-seeking FDI, perhaps reflecting the lumpiness of natural resource investments. This raised the problem of stability of the model under different data sets and compounded the problem of the lag structure of some of the independent variables. This problem was addressed by examining the stability of the coefficients when three-year moving averages in the variables were used instead of yearly data and by splitting the period into two and comparing the results. Therefore the results reported in Table 8.2 are for the three-year moving averages.

Table 8.2 presents the results of the regression equation analysis. Although all the variables took the expected sign, not all of them were significant, even at the 90 per cent level. Some patterns did emerge, however. Changes in the value of a country's natural resource endowments (as reflected in changes in prices) had a significantly positive influence on natural resource-seeking FDI. Changes in the real exchange rate were found to have a negative effect on export-oriented and resource-seeking FDI, but did not affect market-seeking FDI. Alterations in the tariff rate had a positive influence on market-seeking FDI, but not on the other two types. Adjustments in tax rates did not have a significant influence on market-seeking FDI, but did have a significant influence on export-oriented FDI and natural resource-seeking FDI.

Changes in domestic demand were found to influence market-seeking FDI, while changes in country risk had a significant influence on FDI of all three types. Changes in the openness of a country's foreign investment incentive system also had a positive and generally significant influence on all types of FDI, and therefore it would seem that governments can influence inward flows of investment via changes in the openness or the restrictiveness of their incentives systems. Variation in the quality-adjusted wage rate for workers relative to the United States only had a significant influence on efficiency-seeking FDI. The change in the labour force also had the

TABLE 8.2 *Statistical results*

	Coefficient	t-stat	lag (years)
BERI	−2.34 (A)	2.10*	1
TRANS	+1.70 (A)	.53	3
ISFI	+15.16 (A)	2.97*	2
LABR	+2.18 (R)	1.20	2
LABM	+2.72 (E,M)	1.01	2
TAXE	−2.53 (E)	1.31*	3
TAXM	−.42 (M)	1.12	3
TAXR	−3.04 (R)	1.67*	2
DEMD	+8.73 (M)	1.81*	0
TAR	+.72 (M)	1.67*	3
RFX	−1.92 (E,R)	2.14*	1
PNAT	+5.43 (R)	2.35*	3
HC/W	+14.15 (E)	1.52*	3
R2	.65		

A = applies to all types of FDI
E = efficiency-seeking FDI
R = resources-seeking FDI
M = market-seeking FDI

* denotes significance at the 90 per cent level or above.

expected sign, but was not a statistically significant influence on inward FDI of all three types. Lastly, the variable measuring changes in the level of infrastructure development was also not significant.

8.5 CONCLUSIONS

What does all this mean for the research question at hand: the relationship between foreign investment flows and country characteristics of the developing countries? Despite the uneven statistical results, some generalisations seem to be supported by the data:

(1) Locational factors, such as the value of the natural resource base and the rate of growth of the labour force, that are outside the control of government, seem to have influenced inward investment.
(2) Locational factors, such as the rate of growth of the consumption, the perceived risk of the country, and the real exchange rate,

over which the government may exercise some degree of control, also influenced the inward flow of investment.

(3) Locational factors, such as the tariff rate, the tax rate and the 'openness' of the country's foreign investment incentives system, which are under the direct and immediate control of the government, also influenced inward flows of investment.

This analysis gives some indication of the effects of the basic locational advantages of developing countries on inward flows of FDI and of the scope for government policies in these countries to increase the flows of inward foreign investment by changing some of the variables under their short- and long-term control.

Notes

This study was partially funded by the Centre for International Business Studies, the School of Business Administration, the University of Western Ontario, the Special Programme for Least Developed, Land-locked and Island Developing Countries, UNCTAD, and the United Nations Centre on Transnational Corporations.

1. Rugman (1980, 1981, 1982) and Hennart (1982) typify those who emphasise the efficiency-enhancing aspects of TNCs. Dunning (1981, 1985, 1988a), Casson (1987), and Teece (1981, 1985) typify those who find both efficiency-enhancing and efficiency-reducing aspects of TNC operations (although they most often see the TNC as efficiency-enhancing), and Jenkins (1987), Hymer (1976), Lall and Streeten (1978) and Dutt (1988) emphasise the negative aspects of TNCs both on efficiency and on income distribution.
2. For example, Singapore, the province of Taiwan, and Hong Kong.
3. Indonesia, Malaysia, Thailand, Brazil and Mexico are typical of this group.
4. Until recently, most countries with centrally-planned economies, such as the Soviet Union and the People's Republic of China, fell into this group. Currently, North Korea, Albania and Ethiopia typify this group.
5. Based on UNCTC (1988), Table A.2, pp. 504–7. The same source shows inward FDI to developed market economies of about $9 billion in 1970, $15 billion in 1975, $42 billion in 1980, falling to $31 billion in 1982, and rising to $37 billion in 1985.
6. For Brazil the fall was from $2.9 billion (1982) to $1.36 billion (1985); Venezuela: $257 million to $48 million; Argentina: $823 million to $184 million; Peru: $128.5 million to –$88.2 million; Malaysia: $1.4 billion to $0.695 billion; Hong Kong: $1.1 billion to –$0.216 billion.
7. See also Guisinger (1986), Guisinger and Farrel (1985) and especially Wells (1986).

8. For reviews of this literature see Caves (1982), Dunning (1981, 1988a) and the United Nations, Department of Economic and Social Affairs (1973), United Nations, Economic and Social Council (1978) and United Nations, Centre on Transnational Corporations (UNCTC) (1983 and 1988).

9. This assumption is incorrect at the microeconomic level, but is relatively harmless at the macroeconomic level.

10. See also articles by Lall (1985b for India), Koo (Korea), Simoēs (Portugal), and Lecraw (Singapore) in Dunning (1985a).

11. The results of this trial and error procedure will be discussed further on in the paper.

Part V
Empirical Studies of Foreign Direct Investment in Less Developed Countries

9 Foreign Multinationals and Industrial Development in Africa

John Cantwell

9.1 THE SIGNIFICANCE OF FOREIGN DIRECT INVESTMENT IN AFRICA AND ITS SECTORAL DISTRIBUTION

In an earlier paper (Cantwell, 1986), it was argued that despite a shift in investment towards the newly industrialising countries of South East Asia and Latin America, investment in Africa has remained important for European multinationals. The firms of the UK and France, and to a lesser extent West Germany and Italy, have had traditional historical links with Africa.[1] Although these links have been relatively weakened in the last 20 years or so, they have not been completely broken. This paper further develops the statistical evidence on the investment of foreign multinationals in Africa, drawing upon a variety of sources. It is particularly concerned to establish the sectoral distribution of foreign direct investment in Africa, by comparison with other developing regions. The existing structure of investments by foreign multinationals in Africa is then related to the prevailing pattern of economic activity in African countries, and their current and future impact on local development is discussed in the light of this.

The data on the sectoral composition of foreign direct investment in Africa reveal the kind of multinationals which have been involved in the past. An assessment is made of which other types of foreign multinationals are most likely to be attracted in the future, and of the prospects for further investments by established firms. In this context some suggestions are made for sector-specific policies on the part of African countries aimed at promoting those investments which have the greatest potential for assisting local industrial development. This is not to deny that there may be a case for countries setting out an overall policy framework (going beyond sectoral strategies) for the

183

encouragement and regulation of foreign multinationals in general. However, this raises a variety of issues such as the linking of incentives to appropriate macroeconomic and exchange rate policies, the desired balance between public and private sectors in the economy as a whole, and so forth which go beyond the scope of this paper.

Of the total stock of foreign direct investment (FDI) of firms of the eight major industrialised countries in 1981 just over a quarter was located in developing countries. Of this stock of FDI in all developing countries, 12.7 per cent was directed to Africa. However, British, French, German and Italian companies had above average shares of their investment in less developed countries (LDCs) in Africa. Of the total stock of FDI in the LDCs, Africa accounted for 58.7 per cent in the case of France, 30.7 per cent for the UK, 28.4 per cent for Italy, and 19 per cent for Germany. This illustrates that despite recent trends Africa is still significant in the calculations of many European multinationals. In fact, in the case of British firms there is evidence to suggest that Africa has not slipped back all that much as a host region to FDI *vis-à-vis* other developing regions. Whereas 30.7 per cent of the UK stock of FDI in LDCs was located in Africa in 1981, this had only been a little higher at 33.3 per cent in 1962. British multinationals have not redirected their activities towards South East Asia and Latin America as much as others.

It should also be noted that although their African operations do not carry the same relative weight in their global productive activity, the investments of US and Japanese multinationals are also important to many African countries. The total stock of US FDI in Africa is about the same as that of the UK, and in absolute terms they are the two leading source countries for investment in Africa. Japanese investment has been rising to the point where 8 per cent of Japan's FDI in the LDCs in 1981 was in Africa, above the 7.5 per cent equivalent figure for the US. At the moment, though, Japanese FDI is much more geographically concentrated, a very high proportion being in Liberia, and much of the rest in Zaire and Nigeria.

Information on FDI flows also suggests that in the aftermath of the Latin American debt crisis Africa's share of new FDI in developing countries has risen back to a level almost sufficient to maintain its existing share of FDI stocks. This is not so much because of any dynamism of FDI in Africa in the early 1980s, as because of the slipping back of Latin America and more recently the Middle East (Saudi Arabia in 1985). Table 9.1 sets out the full position of African countries in FDI flows from 1974 to 1985. Between 1974 and 1978 Africa accounted for 17 per cent of all new FDI in developing

TABLE 9.1 *Average annual flow of inward foreign direct investment, 1974–85 (US $m)*

	Average 1974–78	Average 1979–83	1984	1985
Developed Areas	15 875.9	31 682.2	39 845.2	33 852.5
Developing Areas	5 043.2	15 816.2	15 500.2	13 322.2
Africa (except S. Africa)	859.8	1 410.1	1 520.1	1 582.9
Asia & Pacific (except Japan)	1 764.5	3 887.2	4 492.6	4 720.3
Latin America & Caribbean	2 733.3	5 738.6	3 476.8	4 055.3
Middle East	–374.5	4 664.8	5 871.3	2 828.7
Australasia	60.1	115.5	139.4	135.0
Botswana	25.9	77.3	62.5	58.9
Burkina Faso	100.9	239.5	N.S.A.	N.S.A.
Cameroon	22.8	129.5	17.4	
Central African Republic	4.8	9.1	5.1	
Congo	30.2	34.0	34.9	Not
Egypt	136.3	807.6	728.8	separately
Gabon	75.4	76.9	8.2	available
Ghana	23.5	2.9	2.1	6.1
Kenya	45.8	69.0	62.5	87.3
Liberia	54.8	42.0	39.0	N.S.A.
Libya	–256.6	–628.0	N.S.A.	N.S.A.
Malawi	13.0	6.9	N.S.A.	N.S.A.
Mauritius	3.3	1.4	5.1	8.1
Morocco	70.8	110.4	47.2	N.S.A.
Nigeria	342.7	180.0	272.7	341.2
Senegal	20.5	3.9	N.S.A.	
Seychelles	5.5	7.6	5.1	Not
Sierra Leone	11.7	2.3	6.2	
Tanzania	N.A.	11.5	N.S.A.	separately
Togo	15.0	34.6	N.S.A.	
Zaire	83.3	137.3	7.2	available
Zambia	25.0	42.1	N.S.A.	
Zimbabwe	5.2	12.3	9.8	

Source: J.H. Dunning and J.A. Cantwell, *The IRM Directory of Statistics of International Investment and Production*, London: Macmillan, and New York: New York University Press, 1987; IMF, *Balance of Payments Statistics Yearbook, 1986*, Volume 37, Part 2.

countries, ahead of its estimated share of 12.7 per cent of FDI stock at the end of 1981. FDI flows into Nigeria alone were 6.8 per cent of the total, probably due to new investments in the oil sector. However, as investment in the newly industrialised countries took off in the late 1970s, Africa's share of FDI inflows into developing areas fell back to 8.9 per cent over the period 1979 to 1983. Yet by 1984 FDI inflows into Africa had risen back to 9.8 per cent of the developing country total, and in 1985 to as much as 11.9 per cent. The share of Nigeria rose from 1.1 per cent from 1979–83 to 2.6 per cent in 1985, while the share of Kenya was 0.4 per cent and then 0.7 per cent at the equivalent times, indicative of the slowdown of FDI in Latin America and the Middle East in the mid-1980s.

The significance of Africa in the international division of labour is also appreciated more clearly once it is realised that the sectoral composition of its stock of FDI is distinctive. In certain sectors it is difficult to ignore the role of African countries. FDI in Africa is much more oriented to resource-based activities than is the case in Asia or Latin America. This becomes clear from an inspection of Tables 9.2 to 9.5. It is estimated in Table 9.5 that in 1982 over half the total stock of FDI in Africa was in extractive sectors (agriculture, mining and oil). In non-African LDCs extractive activity accounts for about 20 per cent of FDI or just under (see Table 9.5 and Table 9.6, where an adjustment is made for the exclusion of oil from the FDI data of some Asian countries). This suggests that if Africa is the location for 12.7 per cent of FDI in developing regions, then it is responsible for not much short of 40 per cent of foreign-owned ventures in primary commodities in the LDCs.

FDI in extractive sectors appears to be especially important in the case of Botswana, Egypt, Gabon, Liberia, Libya, Malawi and Nigeria. It is in mining and oil, even more than agriculture, forestry and fishing, in which Africa is at present particularly prominent as a host to FDI. In the case of US investment the emphasis is on oil; this sector was responsible for 67.5 per cent of the total stock of US FDI in Africa at the end of 1983, compared with 32.5 per cent in all LDCs taken together (Cantwell, 1986). It seems that the effect of forced divestments in the African oil industry between 1970 and 1977 had been reversed by 1983. For European multinationals Africa is also crucial for other types of mining as well. A very large proportion (over 95 per cent in the official statistics) of the total stock of UK FDI in mining in the developing countries is located in Africa. A high proportion of this is in Zimbabwe. The leading British companies involved are Lonhro, Rio Tinto Zinc, Falcon Mines, and Turner and Newall (Clarke, 1980).

Four basic minerals are mined by foreign firms in Africa: copper, iron, bauxite and uranium. The production of bauxite (chiefly in Guinea) and uranium (in Namibia, Gabon and Niger) has essentially

TABLE 9.2   *Sectoral distribution of foreign direct capital stock, 1975 (US $ million)*

	Primary	Secondary	Tertiary
Developed Areas	34 824.0	79 943.9	48 672.1
Developing Areas	10 014.7	19 907.4	7 469.7
Africa (except S. Africa)	4 191.2	2 598.7	1 246.4
Morocco	26.8	78.8	96.6
Nigeria	4 164.4	2 519.9	1 149.8
Asia and Pacific (except Japan or			
M. East)	1 096.1	4 455.2	2 324.0
India	341.1	1 195.2	627.6
Indonesia	585.9	1 425.4	273.9
S. Korea	9.0	459.7	100.4
Philippines	83.9	236.3	165.0
Singapore	neg.	987.3	879.1
Thailand	76.2	151.3	278.0
Latin America and Caribbean	4 185.0	12 816.9	3 831.9
Argentina	134.1	1 561.7	588.2
Brazil	176.4	5 400.5	1 313.1
Chile	71.2	234.3	115.9
Colombia	347.4	426.5	191.1
Mexico	196.8	3 723.6	879.6
Peru	1 348.0	240.0	112.0
Venezuela	1 911.1	1 230.3	632.0
Australasia	542.4	36.6	67.4
Papua New Guinea	542.4	36.6	67.4
TOTAL	44 838.7	99 851.3	56 141.8

Source: J.H. Dunning and J.A. Cantwell, *The World Directory of International Investment and Production Statistics*, London: Macmillan, and New York: New York University Press, 1987.

developed since the 1970s, while due to the state of world demand the production of copper (in Zambia and Zaire) and iron ore (especially significant in Liberia and Mauritania) has contracted somewhat in recent years (Yachir, 1988). While mining in larger countries (Zimbabwe and Nigeria) has been reasonably broadly based, the shift away from the traditional mining of gold and diamonds towards the extraction of metallic ores has created some mono-export economies. For example, in selected recent years, copper represented 91 per cent of Zambia's exports, iron ore accounted for 86 per cent of Mauritania's exports, and bauxite for 87 per cent of Guinea's exports (Yachir, 1988).

TABLE 9.3   *Percentage distribution of foreign direct capital stock, 1975*

	Primary	Secondary	Tertiary
Developed Areas	21.3	48.9	29.8
Developing Areas	26.8	53.2	20.0
Africa (except S. Africa)	52.2	32.3	15.5
Morocco	13.3	39.0	47.7
Nigeria	53.1	32.2	14.7
Africa and Pacific (except Japan or M. East)	13.9	56.6	29.5
India	15.8	55.2	29.0
Indonesia	25.6	62.4	12.0
S. Korea	1.6	80.8	17.6
Philippines	17.3	48.7	34.0
Singapore	neg.	52.9	47.1
Thailand	15.1	29.9	55.0
Latin America and Caribbean	20.1	61.5	18.4
Argentina	5.9	68.3	25.8
Brazil	2.6	78.3	19.1
Chile	16.9	55.6	27.5
Colombia	36.0	44.2	19.8
Mexico	4.1	77.6	18.3
Peru	79.3	14.1	6.6
Venezuela	50.7	32.6	16.7
Australasia	83.9	5.7	10.4
Papua New Guinea	83.9	5.7	10.4
TOTAL	22.3	49.7	28.0

Source: J.H. Dunning and J.A. Cantwell, *The World Directory of International Investment and Production Statistics*, London: Macmillan, and New York: New York University Press, 1987.

TABLE 9.4   *Sectoral distribution of foreign direct capital stock, 1982*
(US $ million)

	Primary	Secondary	Tertiary
Developed Areas	70 165.3	164 374.0	141 127.5
Developing Areas	26 664.9	63 936.7	27 544.5
Africa (except S. Africa)	6 697.0	3 619.7	2 549.2
Botswana*	310.2	12.5	12.5
Burkina Faso	192.6	481.6	349.1
Cameroon	85.4	718.6	1.6
Central African Republic	47.0	56.6	35.2
Congo	70.6	94.8	165.3
Egypt	2 983.9	105.3	355.4
Gabon	736.6	299.2	17.1

TABLE 9.4 (*continued*)

	Primary	Secondary	Tertiary
Kenya	71.4	252.2	175.8
Liberia	633.5	120.4	120.4
Libya	573.6	17.3	15.1
Malawi	206.0	123.0	46.0
Morocco	80.4	244.7	310.6
Tanzania*	17.9	156.9	41.0
Zambia*	69.4	257.5	165.2
Zimbabwe	618.5	679.1	658.9
Asia and Pacific (except Japan or M. East)	2 889.9	11 751.3	9 230.1
China	29.3	886.8	853.9
Hong Kong	113.9	1 435.3	2 778.6
Indonesia	1 176.0	2 996.7	472.5
S. Korea	13.8	880.3	249.1
Malaysia*	797.5	4 133.3	1 885.3
Pakistan	12.7	334.5	490.6
Philippines	516.6	911.2	506.9
Singapore	neg.	1 083.3	1 132.0
Sri Lanka	3.4	89.8	131.7
Taiwan	neg.	881.4	63.7
Thailand	226.7	440.8	665.8
Latin America and Caribbean	13 950.6	39 106.4	14 697.4
Argentina	1 825.0	3 219.7	1 735.3
Barbados*	39.8	53.3	106.5
Brazil	865.3	18 249.3	2 525.4
Chile	770.1	469.5	623.4
Colombia*	530.3	1 051.0	530.3
Dominican Republic	61.8	355.9	358.0
Ecuador	49.2	410.2	220.2
Jamaica	176.6	236.2	472.5
Mexico	317.8	11 308.9	2 817.2
Panama	1 108.7	506.4	3 798.7
Paraguay	38.1	116.5	105.7
Peru	1 878.1	494.4	323.5
Trinidad and Tobago	3 114.7	184.4	68.9
Venezuela	3 175.1	2 450.7	1 011.8
Middle East	3 115.6	9 392.7	778.9
Saudi Arabia	3 115.6	9 392.7	778.9
Australasia	11.8	66.6	288.9
Fiji	11.8	66.6	288.9
TOTAL	96 830.2	228 310.7	168 672.0

Note: * Represents authors' estimate.

Source: J.H. Dunning and J.A. Cantwell, *The World Directory of International Investment and Production Statistics*, London: Macmillan, and New York: New York University Press, 1987.

TABLE 9.5   *Percentage distribution of foreign direct capital stock, 1982.*

	Primary	Secondary	Tertiary
Developed Areas	18.7	43.7	37.6
Developing Areas	22.6	54.1	23.3
Africa (except S. Africa)	52.1	28.1	19.8
Botswana*	92.6	3.7	3.7
Burkina Faso	18.8	47.1	34.1
Cameroon	10.6	89.2	0.2
Central African Republic	33.9	40.7	25.4
Congo	21.3	28.7	50.0
Egypt	86.6	3.1	10.3
Gabon	70.0	28.4	1.6
Kenya	14.3	50.5	35.2
Liberia	72.4	13.8	13.8
Libya	94.6	2.9	2.5
Malawi	54.9	32.8	12.3
Morocco	12.6	38.5	48.9
Tanzania*	8.3	72.7	19.0
Zambia*	14.1	52.3	33.6
Zimbabwe	31.6	34.7	33.7
Asia and Pacific (except Japan or M. East)	12.1	49.2	38.7
China	1.7	50.1	48.2
Hong Kong	2.6	33.2	64.2
Indonesia	25.3	64.5	10.2
S. Korea	1.2	77.0	21.8
Malaysia*	11.7	60.6	27.7
Pakistan	1.5	39.9	58.6
Philippines	26.7	47.1	26.2
Singapore	neg.	48.9	51.1
Sri Lanka	1.5	39.9	58.6
Taiwan	neg.	93.3	6.7
Thailand	17.0	33.1	49.9
Latin America and Caribbean	20.6	57.7	21.7
Argentina	26.9	47.5	25.6
Barbados*	19.9	26.7	53.4
Brazil	4.0	84.3	11.7
Chile	41.3	25.2	33.5
Colombia*	25.1	49.8	25.1
Dominican Republic	8.0	45.9	46.1
Ecuador	7.2	60.4	32.4
Jamaica	19.9	26.7	53.4
Mexico	2.2	78.3	19.5
Panama	20.5	9.4	70.1
Paraguay	14.6	44.8	40.6
Peru	69.7	18.3	12.0
Trinidad and Tobago	92.5	5.5	2.0

TABLE 9.5 (*continued*)

	Primary	*Secondary*	*Tertiary*
Venezuela	47.9	36.9	15.2
Middle East	23.4	70.7	5.9
Saudi Arabia	23.4	70.7	5.9
Australasia	3.2	18.1	78.7
Fiji	3.2	18.1	78.7
TOTAL	19.6	46.2	34.2

Note: * represents author's estimate
Source: J.H. Dunning and J.A. Cantwell, *The World Directory of International Investment and Production Statistics*, London: Macmillan, and New York: New York University Press, 1987.

The high share of FDI in Africa in extractive sectors is also indicative of the slower pace of post-war industrialisation in Africa, by comparison with Latin America or Asia. Historically, the bulk of FDI was located in the LDCs and was associated with primary commodity production (Dunning, 1983). It was often linked with colonial ties, and for this reason Africa featured prominently, especially for French, British and other European investors. In the post-war period there has been a gradual shift towards FDI in manufacturing production in the LDCs, which has accompanied a typically import-substituting industrialisation in Latin America, and a typically export-oriented industrialisation in Asia. Africa has been left behind by this process, but at the same time has if anything become more attractive as a centre of mining activity; for example, the mining of bauxite has been switched away from the Caribbean (Jamaica, Guyana) and relocated in Africa (Guinea) despite a fall in the world demand for aluminium (Yachir, 1988). To the more limited extent that direct investments in manufacturing have taken place in Africa, they have tended to follow the Latin American model of import substitution (Swainson, 1980). Import-substituting FDI in manufacturing has tended to make greater inroads in the larger more developed African economies, and in doing so has contributed to that development.

On average, just over a quarter of the FDI stock in Africa is now based in manufacturing activities, as opposed to a half in Asia and well over a half in Latin America (Tables 9.3 and 9.5). By African standards, manufacturing seems to be of above average importance in FDI in Burkina Faso (formerly the Ivory Coast), the Cameroon,

TABLE 9.6   *The sectoral distribution of foreign direct capital stock in 16 non-African developing countries in 1982 (%), for comparative purposes.*

	9 LDCs in Asia[1]	7 LDCs in Latin America[2]	Total 16 non-African LDCs
Primary	19.8	18.2	18.7
Agriculture	3.4	0.9	1.7
Mining and quarrying	5.1	2.7	3.5
Oil	11.4	14.6	13.5
Secondary	50.1	65.7	60.5
Food and drink	6.0	6.9	6.6
Chemicals and allied	7.7	14.7	12.4
Metals	3.6	6.2	5.4
Mechanical engineering	2.6	6.4	5.1
Electrical equipment	8.4	5.6	6.5
Motor vehicles	2.2	10.0	7.4
Other transportation equipment	0.4	2.2	1.6
Textiles and clothing	7.9	2.3	4.2
Paper and allied	0.6	2.3	1.8
Rubber and plastic products	1.8	2.3	2.1
Stone, clay and glass	3.9	2.2	2.7
Coal and petroleum products	2.7	2.9	2.9
Other manufacturing	2.1	1.7	1.8
Tertiary	30.1	16.2	20.8
Construction	4.6	1.2	2.3
Transport and communications	3.3	0.3	1.3
Distribution trade	7.7	6.3	6.8
Property	0.5	0.4	0.5
Banking and finance	12.0	6.4	8.2
Other services	1.9	1.6	1.7
TOTAL	100.0	100.0	100.0

Notes:
1. Hong Kong, India, Indonesia, S. Korea, Malaysia, Philippines, Singapore, Taiwan and Thailand. The data for India are for 1974. The total stock of FDI in these 9 countries was US $27,862.4 m.
2. Argentina, Brazil, Colombia, Ecuador, Mexico, Peru and Venezuela. The total stock of FDI in these 7 countries was US $56,632.4 m.
Source: J.H. Dunning and J.A. Cantwell, *The Directory of International Investment and Production Statistics*, London: Macmillan, and New York: New York University Press, 1987; and author's estimates where appropriate.

the Central African Republic, Kenya, Malawi, Morocco, Nigeria, Tanzania, Zambia, and Zimbabwe. There is also some evidence that this FDI in manufacturing involves not only a process of import substitution, but also the downstream diversification of companies previously established in extractive sectors (Swainson, 1980; Clarke, 1980). Certainly, manufacturing FDI in Africa appears to be much more resource-related than in Asia or Latin America. In the case of US FDI in Africa, metal products is a relatively favoured sector (related to mining), while Africa is relatively attractive as a host to UK FDI in the textiles, paper products, rubber products, wood products and building materials sectors, and holds its own in food products (Cantwell, 1986).

There are also signs that, despite its difficulties in recent years, Africa has been able to move a little further down the development path in terms of the evolution of the industrial structure of its FDI. Although it has a long way to go to catch up with the developing regions of Asia and Latin America in investment directed towards engineering, chemicals and transportation equipment, it has made a start. Since the early 1970s, UK FDI in Africa has expanded relatively fast in the chemicals and mechanical engineering sectors, while US multinationals have witnessed comparatively rapid growth in the electrical equipment industry, although in all three cases starting from a very low base. Meanwhile, German and Italian firms have invested substantially in the textiles and clothing sector in North Africa, a form of export platform FDI more normally associated with South East Asia (Fröbel, Heinrichs and Kreye, 1980; Acocella *et al.*, 1985). French multinationals, however, do not seem to have moved so readily from their traditional style of operations in Africa. They remain most heavily involved in agriculture, mining, oil and food processing linked to agribusiness. There has been a limited diversification into the resource-based building materials and metals sectors (cement crushing and canning), and as yet still weak development in the areas of textiles, plastics and car assembly (Savary, 1984).

About a fifth of the stock of FDI in Africa is in services, which is roughly equivalent to the position in Latin America, but well behind the proportion in Asia (Tables 9.3 and 9.5). The main difference between Asia and the other two regions is the greater expansion of FDI in banking and financial services that has characterised this area (Cantwell, 1988). Investment in trade has been traditionally important in LDCs in general, and it remains so in Africa. A greater share of French and British FDI in Africa is involved in trade than is the case for other developing regions, which again goes back to former colonial ties. Today, the service sector that has witnessed the fastest expansion of UK and French FDI in Africa is construction, which has also been growing steadily in other developing countries. Despite the lesser role played by FDI in finance and insurance in Africa by comparison with elsewhere in the developing world, it is still significant, especially in the case of US FDI.

9.2   THE SECTORAL COMPOSITION OF FDI IN AFRICA: SELECTED HOST COUNTRY EVIDENCE

Because of the less developed state of FDI data collection in Africa, it is much harder to form a precise overall impression of the industrial specialisation of multinationals operating there, by comparison with Asia or Latin America. However, recent research (Dunning and Cantwell, 1987) has improved the situation. Drawing on this, this section presents some individual country evidence on the sectoral distribution of FDI in Africa, in contrast with what is already known at a more aggregative level in the case of FDI in Asia and Latin America. Although there are still too many observations missing to be able to aggregate over African countries with any degree of confidence, the more important sectoral characteristics of FDI in Africa can be seen by examining evidence from the leading recipient countries. This helps to elaborate on the general picture described above.

Resource-based manufacturing FDI predominates in the Cameroon. Agriculture and food processing accounted for 35.3 per cent of FDI stock in 1981 (compared to 8.3 per cent in 16 leading non-African LDCs in 1982), wood products were responsible for 14.2 per cent (as opposed to less than 1 per cent in the non-African countries), and building materials for a further 5.2 per cent (UN Economic Commission for Africa, 1981). Foreign involvement is also relatively important in the metals and textiles sectors, and significant in chemicals even though in this instance it is (at 9 per cent) below the Latin American proportion. Within the Cameroon itself, foreign firms are responsible for a very high proportion of total equity capital in the sectors that have been mentioned. Foreign penetration stands at 81 per cent in food products, 80 per cent in wood products, 48 per cent in building materials, 76 per cent in metals, 73 per cent in textiles, and 57 per cent in chemicals.

In the case of the Congo it is a little difficult to be sure of the value of FDI in services. However, considering just the investment in primary and secondary activities, resource-based and import-substituting investments are again to the fore. Mining and quarrying accounted for 42.7 per cent of the stock of FDI in primary and secondary sectors in 1983 (which compares with 4.4 per cent in the selected group of non-African countries), drink and tobacco for 24.1 per cent (compared to 8.3 per cent for all food products in other developing regions), and wood products for 12.6 per cent (as opposed to about 1 per cent in LDCs outside Africa). Data on the Congo are again due to UN Economic Commission for Africa (1981). The share of chemicals was 9.2 per cent (15.7 per cent elsewhere), mechanical engineering 2.7 per cent (6.4 per cent in other LDCs), and textiles 8.7 per cent (5.3 per cent outside Africa, although 11.3 per cent if considering the Asian LDCs alone). In these fields the degree of foreign penetration appears to be even greater than in the Cameroon. The foreign share of equity capital is believed to be 100 per cent in tobacco and mechanical engineering, and is estimated at 83 per cent in mining, 70 per cent in wood products, 89 per cent in chemicals, and 70 per cent in textiles.

Investment in the oil industry dominates FDI in Egypt, with US firms playing the leading role. Oil companies were responsible for over 70 per cent of all FDI in Egypt in 1982, and for 85.5 per cent of US FDI in 1983 (Dunning and Cantwell, 1987; US Department of Commerce, 1984). This is way above the 13.5 per cent equivalent figure for the 16 non-African LDCs, and indeed well above the average for other African countries. Foreign participation in manufacturing industry has been encouraged through the Free Zone project scheme, but this has not succeeded in attracting very large investments by comparison with the extractive sectors. The most significant areas for such export-oriented FDI have been chemicals, textiles and metals.

Extractive activities are also heavily featured in FDI in Gabon. Oil accounted for a 39.2 per cent share of total FDI (compared with 13.5 per cent in LDCs outside Africa), and mining and quarrying for 28 per cent (as against a much smaller 3.5 per cent in non-African LDCs) (UN Economic Commission for Africa, 1981). The most important manufacturing sectors have been building materials (8.8 per cent as opposed to 2.7 per cent outside Africa), and wood products (7.7 per cent compared to around 0.8 per cent elsewhere). The foreign share of total equity capital in Gabon in 1979 was 75 per cent in oil, 85 per cent in mining, 49 per cent in building materials, and 83 per cent in wood products. Foreign multinationals were also present in the manufacture of food products (26 per cent of equity capital), chemicals (71 per cent), textiles (71 per cent), and metals (89 per cent).

Kenya has followed the development path from FDI in extractive activities (mainly agricultural plantations) and trade before 1945 through to import-substituting industrialisation after 1945, and especially after 1963 (Swainson, 1980). Since the 1970s there has been some evidence of export-oriented FDI in the food processing sector. British companies have moved downstream from agriculture to food processing, and in 1981 the food sector accounted for 26.7 per cent of UK FDI in Kenya (UK Department of Industry, 1981), which is very high in comparison with the average 6.6 per cent share of FDI that the industry attracts in non-African LDCs. In 1976 foreign firms held 28.9 per cent of total equity capital in the food products sector, 71.2 per cent in chemicals and rubber products, 56.6 per cent in textiles, 50.9 per cent in fabricated metal products, 44.4 per cent in building materials, 40.5 per cent in paper products, and 15 per cent in wood products (Kaplinsky, 1979).

According to host country sources, primary commodity production accounts for getting on for three quarters of all FDI in Liberia, with mining and agriculture being proportionately much more important than in LDCs outside Africa. Mining, principally of iron ore, had a 42.7 per cent share of the stock of FDI in 1979, while forestry was responsible for 15.9 per cent, and the production of crude rubber for 13.9 per cent (Republic of Liberia, 1980). As yet, downstream processing activities have not been well developed by the multinationals involved. Investments in trade are also thought to be important, perhaps also linked to the exploitation of natural resources. Indeed, Japanese sources suggest that Japanese FDI in Liberia, at US $1257 million in 1981, now outweighs the total FDI of all other countries (US $859.6 million in 1979); and most of this Japanese FDI is in trade and shipping (Dunning and Cantwell, 1987). However, it is unclear to what extent this investment is simply a matter of legal convenience, and without further evidence on the involvement of Japanese firms in Liberia, it is wise to keep an open mind on just how important the role that they play is.

Libya is rather like Egypt, in as much as its FDI position has been dominated by US investment in the oil sector, which has recovered somewhat since the mid-1970s. In the 1970s a limited movement of FDI into light industry and mechanical engineering began, and European multinationals have also been involved in this area, in construction and energy supply as well as manufacturing (Dunning and Cantwell, 1987; US Department of Commerce, 1983).

Malawi follows the by now familiar pattern for FDI in the less developed African LDCs. Agriculture (mainly sugar and tea plantations) accounts for 54.8 per cent of FDI, and food products for 16.4 per cent (of which half is in tobacco) (US Department of Commerce, 1983.) Construction, trade and banking and finance together constitute 12.3 per cent of the remaining FDI, while the development of the manufacturing sector outside agribusiness is as yet little developed.

Mauritius, on the other hand, represents a country in which a measure of foreign led export-oriented industrialisation has been successful. The export receipts from the Export Processing Zone comprised 32 per cent of total such income in 1982 (Currie, 1986). The textiles and clothing sector was essentially responsible, generating around 83 per cent of all EPZ employment in 1982, and 71 per cent of EPZ exports. These exports have been directed primarily to the European Community countries, assisted by preferential trade arrangements. The leading source of FDI has been the Third-World multinationals of Hong Kong, and their establishment of textile production in Mauritius is as much a function of trade discrimination against Hong Kong as it is the favourable agreements enjoyed by Mauritius.

In Morocco the share of FDI in primary commodity production (at 11.2 per cent) is below the equivalent proportion in non-African LDCs (18.7 per cent), and well below the average for Africa as a whole (52.1 per cent) (Dunning and Cantwell, 1987). The traditional investments of French companies were in this case relatively small, and they have been surpassed by the role of foreign firms in import-substituting industrialisation. FDI has steadily grown in a range of light industries, and as early as 1973–74 the share of capital held by foreign-owned firms was reported to be about 60 per cent in the metals sector, 70 per cent in paper products, 50 per cent in food processing, 60 per cent in pharmaceuticals, 40 per cent in other chemicals, and 20 per cent in textiles (Socialist Party of Morocco, 1974).

Nigeria is the most important host country for FDI in Africa, though its position has been obscured by the depreciation of the local currency. Oil and mining once again stand out as the leading sectors, accounting for 30.5 per cent and 16.2 per cent of FDI stock in 1978 respectively (Central Bank of Nigeria, 1981). Import-substituting industrialisation has proceeded as elsewhere, to the point where manufacturing activities were responsible for 31.6 per cent of FDI stock in 1978, above the African average. UK firms, whose investments account for a high proportion of total FDI in Nigeria, have moved into manufacturing even more strongly. In recent years they have shifted away from the food sector (which accounted for 20.2 per cent of UK FDI in 1974, but 11.7 per cent in 1981), and towards chemicals (which rose from 8 per cent to 16.8 per cent over the same period) and rubber products (UK Department of Industry, 1974 and 1981).

Sierra Leone is another African country whose FDI is heavily resource-oriented, in that the most significant investment shares lie in mining (of diamonds, bauxite, iron ore and other precious metals), and food products. There is also some foreign involvement in oil refining, chemicals and light industries (textiles, metals, printing and plastic products) (US Department of Commerce, 1983.) By contrast, in the case of Tanzania such manufacturing activities are proportionately more attractive to FDI, and mining proportionately less attractive, which can presumably be explained in part by a different endowment of natural resources (see the evidence on British investment, UK Department of Industry, 1981).

British investment is over half of the total FDI in Zambia (Dunning and Cantwell, 1987), and it has moved as much into manufacturing (52.3 per cent of UK FDI in 1981) as has FDI in the Asian LDCs (50.1 per cent of the investment in which was in manufacturing), if not those of Latin America (65.7 per cent). The traditional investment in trade has undergone particular decline, from 34.6 per cent of FDI in 1974 to 19.5 per cent in 1981 (UK Department of Industry, 1974 and 1981). Food products and textiles and clothing are again significant sectors, but about as large a share of FDI has been directed to the chemicals and electrical equipment sectors as it has outside Africa.

Zimbabwe is one of the major traditional host countries to FDI in Africa, and established companies have for the most part retained their interests in the period after UDI in 1964 and the change of government in 1980. As elsewhere in Africa, the traditional extractive investments are still of the utmost importance, and mining especially accounted for 22.3 per cent of the total FDI stock in 1981 (compared to 3.5 per cent in non-African LDCs) (Dunning and Cantwell, 1987; Riddell, 1986). Foreign-owned mining in Zimbabwe covers gold, copper, nickel, chrome, tin, iron ore, lithium, asbestos, emeralds, and coal (Clarke, 1980). The movement of FDI into import-substituting manufacturing ventures has in this case been encouraged not only by the growth of local markets, but also by the restrictions on capital withdrawal (which compelled local reinvestment) and the tariff barriers of the sanctions economy. Within this, there seems to have been a move away from light industry (in food products, textiles and clothing, and paper products) towards heavier industry (in chemicals, steel and mechanical engineering). Wood products, building materials and electrical equipment have also been important areas for FDI. In services, FDI has been prominent in banking and finance and trade. The UK is the leading source country for FDI in Zimbabwe with a share of 46.6 per cent in 1978, but the future role of South African investments which accounted for a further third of FDI in 1978 has been called into question amidst the political changes of the 1980s.

9.3   THE SECTORAL COMPOSITION OF FDI IN AFRICA: THE FIRM LEVEL EVIDENCE

Information on the numbers of foreign affiliates in Africa, arranged by host country and sector of activity, is set out in Table 9.7. In fact it might be more correctly described as information on numbers of parent companies involved in each case, as the procedure followed where the multinational had more than one affiliate in the same country was to count only one. Because of the limited number of sources scanned it is not comprehensive, but it gives a better coverage in the case of the world's largest multinationals, and for the firms of Britain and France. The problem with this kind of data is, of course, that it makes no allowance for the size of firm; it simply adds together very large and very small affiliates, and related groups of affiliates counted as a single unit. However, in this instance it may be a useful supplementary source, in view of the lack of a detailed sectoral disaggregation of FDI in Africa. It can itself be complemented by information on particular companies where case study evidence of their significance is available.

Considering the sectoral distribution of the total 1513 companies recorded as having operations in African countries, it is noticeable that extractive activities do not come out as strongly as might have been expected. Affiliates in extractive sectors are just under 20 per cent of the total number, which is well below the share of over 50 per cent of FDI stock for which they are responsible. This is probably due

TABLE 9.7   *The sectoral distribution of numbers of foreign affiliates in Africa based on counts for 1982–83*

Sector	Algeria	Angola	Benin	Botswana	Burundi	Cameroon	Congo	Djibouti
Extractive	4	8	2	2	1	14	5	0
Agriculture and forestry	0	0	0	0	0	3	0	0
Fishing	0	0	0	0	0	0	0	0
Mining	0	1	0	2	0	2	0	0
Oil and Gas	4	7	2	0	1	9	5	0
Manufacturing	2	4	1	4	4	20	8	0
Food, drink & tobacco	0	0	0	1	2	4	2	0
Chemicals and allied	1	2	0	1	0	5	2	0
Metals	0	1	0	0	0	0	0	0
Mechanical engineering	0	0	0	1	0	1	2	0
Electrical engineering	0	1	0	1	0	3	0	0
Motor vehicles	1	0	0	0	0	2	0	0
Other transport equipment	0	0	0	0	2	0	0	0
Textiles and clothing	0	0	1	0	0	1	1	0
Paper and allied	0	0	0	0	0	3	1	0
Wood products	0	0	0	0	0	1	0	0
Rubber and plastic	0	0	0	0	0	0	0	0
Building materials	0	0	0	0	0	0	0	0
Professional instruments	0	0	0	0	0	0	0	0
Services	18	4	0	11	1	30	17	1
Energy supply	0	0	0	0	1	2	0	0
Construction	16	3	0	3	0	8	4	1
Distributive trade	0	1	0	3	0	4	2	0
Transport and communications	0	0	0	1	0	4	1	0
Financial services	2	0	0	4	0	10	9	0
Other services	0	0	0	0	0	2	1	0
TOTAL	24	16	3	17	6	64	30	1

TABLE 9.7 continued

Sector	Burkina Faso	Egypt	Ethiopia	Gabon	Gambia	Ghana	Guinea	Kenya	Liberia
Extractive	15	7	5	18	1	11	6	7	10
Agriculture and forestry	2	0	0	0	0	0	0	1	1
Fishing	0	0	0	0	0	1	0	1	1
Mining	0	1	1	1	0	3	5	0	2
Oil and Gas	13	6	4	17	1	7	1	5	6
Manufacturing	33	19	6	16	0	21	1	56	3
Food, drink & tobacco	6	1	2	2	0	5	0	9	1
Chemicals and allied	9	3	0	2	0	5	0	16	1
Metals	2	2	2	4	0	3	0	3	0
Mechanical engineering	2	2	0	1	0	1	0	5	0
Electrical engineering	6	3	1	3	0	3	0	9	1
Motor vehicles	2	2	1	1	0	2	0	2	0
Other transport equipment	0	0	0	0	0	0	0	0	0
Textiles and clothing	2	2	0	1	0	0	0	1	0
Paper and allied	2	0	0	2	0	0	1	3	0
Wood products	1	0	0	0	0	0	0	1	0
Rubber and plastic	1	2	0	0	0	2	0	4	0
Building materials	0	1	0	0	0	0	0	2	0
Professional instruments	0	1	0	0	0	0	0	1	0
Services	39	24	24	30	10	11	2	37	15
Energy supply	3	3	0	2	0	0	2	0	0
Construction	5	9	0	7	2	1	0	5	0
Distributive trade	7	3	17	1	5	3	0	6	1
Transport and communications	4	0	4	3	1	0	0	5	4
Financial services	19	7	1	15	2	7	0	20	10
Other services	1	2	2	2	0	0	0	1	0
TOTAL	87	50	35	64	11	43	9	100	28

continued on p. 202

TABLE 9.7   *continued*

Sector	Libya	Lesotho	Madagascar	Malawi	Mali	Mauritania	Mauritius	Morocco	Mozambique
Extractive	8	0	1	1	5	8	2	11	3
Agriculture and forestry	0	0	0	0	0	0	0	0	1
Fishing	0	0	0	0	0	0	0	0	1
Mining	0	0	0	0	0	5	0	3	0
Oil and Gas	8	0	1	1	5	3	2	8	1
Manufacturing	3	1	0	14	2	0	7	47	7
Food, drink & tobacco	0	0	0	5	0	0	3	3	1
Chemicals and allied	1	1	0	1	1	0	1	17	2
Metals	0	0	0	1	0	0	0	5	1
Mechanical engineering	2	0	0	3	0	0	0	6	0
Electrical engineering	0	0	0	3	1	0	0	8	2
Motor vehicles	0	0	0	1	0	0	3	0	0
Other transport equipment	0	0	0	0	0	0	0	1	0
Textiles and clothing	0	0	0	0	0	0	0	0	1
Paper and allied	0	0	0	0	0	0	0	3	0
Wood products	0	0	0	0	0	0	0	0	0
Rubber and plastic	0	0	0	0	0	0	0	1	0
Building materials	0	0	0	0	0	0	0	3	0
Professional instruments	0	0	0	0	0	0	0	0	0
Services	10	4	2	19	3	2	6	40	7
Energy supply	2	0	0	0	1	0	0	4	0
Construction	7	0	1	1	0	0	0	10	1
Distributive trade	0	1	0	13	0	0	5	4	2
Transport and communications	0	0	0	1	0	1	0	2	0
Financial services	1	3	0	4	2	1	1	19	2
Other services	0	0	1	0	0	0	0	1	2
TOTAL	21	5	3	34	10	10	15	98	17

TABLE 9.7 . *continued*

Sector	Namibia	Niger	Nigeria	Rwanda	Senegal	Seychelles	Sierra Leone	Somalia	Sudan	Swaziland
Extractive	50	6	19	0	6	2	7	4	9	0
Agriculture and forestry	7	0	0	0	0	0	0	0	0	0
Fishing	8	0	1	0	3	0	0	0	0	0
Mining	28	2	4	0	0	0	4	0	2	0
Oil and Gas	7	4	14	0	3	2	3	4	7	0
Manufacturing	6	4	94	3	13	0	9	1	3	1
Food, drink & tobacco	0	1	11	1	2	0	4	1	0	1
Chemicals and allied	1	0	23	0	5	0	0	0	2	0
Metals	1	1	17	0	0	0	2	0	1	0
Mechanical engineering	4	0	0	0	1	0	0	0	0	0
Electrical engineering	0	2	17	0	1	0	0	0	0	0
Motor vehicles	0	0	10	0	1	0	0	0	0	0
Other transport equipment	0	0	1	2	0	0	0	0	0	0
Textiles and clothing	0	0	3	0	2	0	3	0	0	0
Paper and allied	0	0	4	0	1	0	0	0	0	0
Wood products	0	0	0	0	0	0	0	0	0	0
Rubber and plastic	0	0	3	0	0	0	0	0	0	0
Building materials	0	0	5	0	0	0	0	0	0	0
Professional instruments	0	0	0	0	0	0	0	0	0	0
Services	6	4	96	0	21	0	9	5	16	0
Energy supply	0	0	2	0	0	0	0	0	0	0
Construction	0	0	31	0	3	0	0	1	5	0
Distributive trade	0	1	20	0	6	0	2	2	2	0
Transport and communications	0	1	7	0	6	0	2	0	1	0
Financial services	6	2	34	0	5	0	5	1	6	0
Other services	0	0	2	0	1	0	0	1	2	0
TOTAL	62	14	209	3	40	2	25	10	28	1

continued on p. 204

TABLE 9.7   *continued*

Sector	Tanzania	Togo	Tunisia	Uganda	Zaire	Zambia	Zimbabwe	TOTAL
Extractive	3	3	9	2	9	7	8	299
Agriculture and forestry	1	0	0	1	0	0	0	17
Fishing	0	0	0	0	0	0	0	16
Mining	0	1	1	0	2	4	4	78
Oil and Gas	2	2	8	1	7	3	4	188
Manufacturing	16	2	17	17	23	42	50	580
Food, drink & tobacco	3	0	1	2	4	9	10	97
Chemicals and allied	3	1	3	3	4	12	8	136
Metals	0	0	1	0	1	2	2	52
Mechanical engineering	0	0	1	1	1	5	4	43
Electrical engineering	5	1	4	3	3	6	10	97
Motor vehicles	2	0	2	3	5	3	3	46
Other transport equipment	2	0	0	0	2	1	1	12
Textiles and clothing	0	0	2	0	1	0	1	22
Paper and allied	0	0	1	1	0	0	4	26
Wood products	0	0	0	1	1	0	0	5
Rubber and plastic	1	0	0	2	1	2	3	22
Building materials	0	0	2	0	0	1	3	17
Professional instruments	0	0	0	1	0	1	1	5
Services	13	12	22	4	8	17	34	634
Energy supply	0	1	0	0	0	0	0	23
Construction	2	2	7	1	2	3	3	144
Distributive trade	2	1	4	1	0	3	3	125
Transport and communications	1	2	2	0	1	2	2	58
Financial services	8	6	6	1	4	9	26	258
Other services	0	0	3	1	1	0	0	26
TOTAL	32	17	48	23	40	66	92	1,513

Source: UN Economic Commission for Africa/UNCTC Joint Unit, *List of Major TNCs in Selected African Countries*, UN unpublished document, 1984; J.M. Stopford, *The World Directory of MNEs, 1982–83* (Volumes 1 and 2), London: Macmillan, 1982; *Who Owns Whom*, 1984, London: Dun and Bradstreet, various editions; for individual company names see Appendix 2.

to a greater concentration of investment in mining and oil, such that a smaller number of large multinationals have bigger groups of related affiliates in the countries in which they operate, and these affiliates are of a larger average size.

Within manufacturing, food products and metals rank highly as would be anticipated, as would the reasonably important role of chemicals (which accounts for about 9 per cent of affiliates, compared with 12.4 per cent of the FDI stock of non-African LDCs). The strength of the electrical equipment sector (at 6.4 per cent of affiliates) is perhaps a little surprising, as is the comparative weakness of the presence in textiles and clothing, wood products and building materials. The reason for this is probably the exclusion of smaller multinationals based in countries other than Britain or France, and the smaller scale of electrical equipment production in Africa by comparison with other developing regions.

The host country sources mentioned in section 9.2 also sometimes provide details of the role played by leading foreign companies in the local economy, and their contribution to FDI. Sometimes just one company is crucial in determining the focus of the FDI position of the country; Botswana, Gabon and Ghana all provide examples of this. In Botswana the US firm Amax had an investment of $117 million in 1981, in a total stock of FDI of only a little over $300 million. Amax is involved in the mining of copper and nickel. Gabon's FDI position is dominated by the French oil company Elf, which had an equity capital stake in Elf Gabon of $322 million in 1985. The US oil company Amoco also has an investment in Gabon of about $120 million, and US Steel has a 37 per cent interest in the foreign-owned manganese mining affiliate Comilog which is worth around $110 million.

In Ghana the Valco Aluminium Smelting Company (which is 90 per cent owned by Kaiser Aluminium and Chemicals, and 10 per cent by Reynolds Metal) accounted for about 70 per cent of the total stock of US FDI in 1978. Valco is the largest primary aluminium producer in Africa, and a major supplier of the world market. Valco utilises the large bauxite reserves of Ghana (which are used in making the raw material alumina), and it has recently been expanding its local operations to cover aluminium processing activities. The company has planned to extend the manufacture of aluminium utensils and roofing equipment for the local market, and also hoped to diversify its activities to other sectors. It is already the largest single producer of manufactured exports from its existing operations.

Some foreign companies are also well known in Africa because of their historical role in the continent. This is especially true of some British companies in extractive and trading activities, as well as in the construction of railway systems. A list of some of the most significant such companies has been compiled from various sources in Table 9.8. UK firms with investments in Africa before 1914 included Imperial

TABLE 9.8 *A list of some of the most historically significant investors in Africa*

Company name	Home country	Host country	Date of first establishment	Sector
Anglo-French Sisal Co.	UK/France	Kenya	1931	Sisal growing
Associated Portland Cement	UK	Kenya	1933	Building materials
BAT (Imperial Tobacco)	UK	Kenya	1907	Tobacco
BAT (Imperial Tobacco)	UK	Zimbabwe	1917	Tobacco
BOC	UK	Zimbabwe	1930s	Industrial gases
BP (APOC)	UK	Kenya	Inter-war	Oil distribution
BSA (British South African Co)	UK	Zimbabwe	Pre-1914	Railways, plantations
Balfour Beatty	UK	Kenya	1922	Power generation
Bird and Co.	UK	Kenya	1920	Merchant trade
Brooke Bond	UK	Kenya	1924	Tea & coffee processing
Brooke Bond	UK	Tanzania	Inter-war	Tea & coffee plantations
Brooke-Bond-Liebig (Liebigs)	UK	Zimbabwe	Pre-1914	Cattle ranching
Brooke-Bond-Liebig (Liebigs)	UK	Kenya	1935	Metal processing
James Finlay	UK	Kenya	1924	Tea manufacture
Firestone	USA	Liberia	1920s	Rubber plantations
Foote Minerals	USA	Zimbabwe	Pre-1914	Chrome mining
Forestal Land and Timber	UK	Kenya	1932	Wattle bark
Gibson and Co.	UK	Kenya	1920	Merchant trade
Guggenheim Enterprises	USA	Congo	Pre-1914	Diamond mining, rubber plantations
ICI	UK	Kenya	1911	Soda extraction & processing
Ind Coope Ltd.	UK	Kenya	1922	Beer manufacture
Mitchell Cotts	UK	Kenya	1906	Export of primary products

Company		Country	Date	Activity
RTZ	UK	Zimbabwe	1929	Mining
Schneider-Creusot	France	N. Africa	Pre-1914	Iron ore mining
Shell	UK	Nigeria	1951	Oil
Shell	UK	Tunisia	1951	Oil
Sinclair	USA	Angola	1920s	Oil exploration
Sinclair	USA	Ghana	1920s	Oil exploration
Société Générale	Belgium	Congo	Pre-1914	Copper & non-ferrous metal mining
Tate and Lyle	UK	Zimbabwe	1940s	Sugar estate
Turner and Newall (Turner Bros.)	UK	Zimbabwe	1917	Asbestos mining
Unilever (Lever Bros.)	UK	Congo	1910	Vegetable oil trading
Unilever (Lever Bros.)	UK	Nigeria	1910	Coconut and palm oil plantations
Unilever (United Africa Co.)	UK	Kenya	1924	Import & servicing machinery; Unilever food investment in 1952.

Source: H. Archer, *An Eclectic Approach to the Historical Study of UK MNEs*, Ph.D. dissertation, University of Reading, October, 1986; M Wilkins, *The Emergence of Multinational Enterprise*, Harvard University Press, 1970; M. Milkins, *The Maturing of Multinational Enterprise*, Harvard University Press, 1974; L. Franko, *The European Multinationals*, London; Harper and Row, 1976; D.G. Clarke (1980); N. Swainson (1980).

Tobacco (BAT today), The British South African Company in Rhodesia, Liebigs (which became part of the Brook Bond group), Mitchell Cotts, and Lever Brothers (now Unilever).

The most accessible source of information on foreign-owned companies across African countries is a survey of the largest firms operating in Africa reported in the December 1986 issue of the French journal *Jeune Afrique Économie*. The largest 20 African companies in terms of sales which are 40 per cent or more foreign-owned are listed as being: Elf Gabon (in oil in Gabon), Société Ivoirienne de Raffinage (in oil refinery and petrochemicals in Burkina Faso), Scoa Nigeria (a Nigerian trading company), Sté Chérifienne des Pétroles (in oil in Morocco), Sar (in oil refinery and petrochemicals in Senegal), Total Nigeria Limited (in oil distribution in Nigeria), Cfao (a Nigerian trading company), Sté Shell du Maroc (in oil distribution in Morocco), SA des Brasseries du Cameroun (a drinks company in the Cameroon), Sitep (in oil in Tunisia), Sogora (in oil refinery and petrochemicals in Gabon), Cfci (a trading company in Burkina Faso), Scoa Gabon (in trade in Gabon), Zaïre Fina (in oil distribution in Zaïre), Comilog (in mining in Gabon), Shell Côte d'Ivoire (in oil distribution in Burkina Faso), Anambra Motor Manufacturing Company (in motor vehicles in Nigeria), Alucam (in aluminium and non-ferrous metals in the Cameroon), FSN (in food products in Nigeria), and Ceca-Gadis (in distributive trade in Gabon). While the larger companies that operate in some African countries (such as Zimbabwe, Kenya and Egypt) appear to have been missed, the continuing significance of the traditional types of FDI in oil, mining and trade once again comes over clearly.

As might be expected this source provides better coverage of those countries in which French investment is most important. It is interesting to examine a little more closely Burkina Faso and Zaïre, to which a great deal of French FDI is directed, to see the extent to which multinationals have moved beyond their traditional spheres of activity and into manufacturing. In Burkina Faso the foreign-owned manufacturing companies listed are Ets R. Gonfreville (36 per cent foreign-owned) in textiles, Capral in drinks, Solibra in drinks, Sonaco in paper products, Africycle in motor cycle manufacture, Sofaco in chemicals, Ivoiral in non-ferrous metals, Mac in motor cycle manufacture, Sicable in electrical equipment, Sicobel in chemicals, Sivoclim in electrical equipment, and Simap in building materials.

In Zaïre the leading foreign-owned manufacturing firms are said to be Tabazaïre in tobacco, Sté des Ciments du Zaïre in building materials, Cib in drinks, Peugeot Automobiles Zaïre in motor manufacture, Utema Travhydro in metals, Tubetra Zaïre in metals, Brikin in building materials, Asco in paper products, Safem in paper products, and Mazadis in plastic products (records).

There is also some evidence that some foreign companies have increased their use of joint ventures and non-equity contractual agreements in Africa, and that in some cases this has led them to become more involved than they would otherwise have been (Cantwell and Dunning, 1985). One example is the British food company Booker McConnell, mainly in sugar and poultry, which has successfully expanded its operations in Kenya through the use of contract farming rather than the ownership of plantations. Another feature of joint ventures where they involve the local state is that they may give the company access to government contacts and support. Lonhro is a firm that has become known for its ability to develop useful political contacts in Africa, which has doubtless encouraged it to increase its African involvement.

In mining, collaborative agreements have taken the form of consortia in which some firms participate through management contracts, and in which investment is often financed through the involvement of banks, financial institutions and local state agencies rather than FDI by the mining multinationals. This is partly explained by the strategy of diversification on the part of foreign multinationals. Large firms which historically produced one specific mineral, sometimes from a position of colonial monopoly, are now investing in the production of others. Such investments may be in complementary activities (from iron to chromium or manganese), substitutes (from bauxite to copper), or in the related energy-producing sector including uranium (Yachir, 1988). Iron ore and bauxite consortia generally comprise firms from the same industry but different countries, while copper and uranium consortia normally include manufacturing firms and oil groups or state energy agencies. New projects entailing a relocation of mining and related activity have tended to work in Africa's favour where US (or occasionally Japanese) firms have been involved, which traditionally had less connection with African countries.

9.4 THE FUTURE POTENTIAL FOR FDI IN AFRICA, AND THE CASE FOR SECTOR-SPECIFIC POLICIES

It is fairly clear that in terms of the changing international division of labour, and of regional shifts in the location of productive activity,

Africa will not attract the levels of FDI flows that are directed to Asia and Latin America, at least not in the foreseeable future. This fact of life of the present world economy holds more or less irrespective of the various investment policies and incentives that governments in different LDCs decide to adopt. Although companies may be tempted to switch certain types of production away from the industrialised countries and towards developing regions partly due to wage differentials, this is not a major consideration when comparing the attractiveness of different LDCs in deciding upon the location for a footloose investment. The more important issues are the suitability of local forms of work organisation, the local capacity for organisational and related innovation, and the existence of an appropriate infrastructure of supporting activities. In this context there are African countries that have demonstrated that they have some scope to attract FDI, but for the most part they remain well behind the leading Asian and Latin American countries.

However, while it is important to understand that the potential for FDI in the immediate future is limited in terms of changes in the world division of labour, it is equally important to appreciate that FDI still plays a significant role within the African economies, and that from the perspective of these countries themselves even smaller-scale FDI may act as one of the crucial catalysts of development. When considering the kind of investments that countries would need to attract to fulfil this function, it must be remembered that Africa differs from other developing regions not only because it is at an earlier stage of development, but also because of the different type of development path that it has followed up until now. It differs from the NICs of South East Asia in that most FDI that has moved into manufacturing activities has been import-substituting rather than export-oriented, and it differs from Latin America in as much as foreign led import-substituting industrialisation has been far more allied to the previous structure of the existing FDI in extractive sectors. A number of African countries have begun to move towards more export-oriented FDI since the 1970s, and further foreign-assisted development may well rely upon the growth of new export-oriented but still distinctively resource-related FDI.

Whatever strategy the African countries adopt, it seems essential that they devise policies tailored to the needs of individual sectors in a way that fits in with their overall development objectives. This is for a variety of reasons. Firstly, there will be some sectors in which foreign firms are likely to play a positive role, interacting favourably with local énterprises and helping to stimulate local development, and others in which they will not. In the former it is appropriate to encourage FDI, in the latter it may be necessary to impose checks to prevent the abuse of monopoly power, and governments may wish to bargain with multinationals over the sharing of monopoly rents. Secondly, policies aimed at attracting new foreign firms and those aimed at retaining the interest or encouraging the expansion of those already operating in the country may be quite different. Thirdly, the form of FDI varies between sectors, and different types of FDI require different policies. The main division here is between import-substituting and export-oriented FDI. To attract the former may require the granting of local privileges to offset against the costs of building a plant of less than minimum efficient scale to serve local markets; while in the case of the latter, policies which encourage greater linkages and more cooperative arrangements with local firms may be called for (Casson and Pearce, 1987).

The existing patterns of trade in Africa may shed some light on the scope for attracting either import-substituting or export-oriented types of FDI, and they are examined at a broad level of disaggregation in Tables 9.9 and 9.10. Data on exports have been used to calculate an index of revealed comparative advantage (a concept first introduced by Balassa, 1965), and data on imports have been used to generate an equivalent index of revealed comparative disadvantage. Denoting the value of exports by X, and the value of imports by M, and using the subscripts A for Africa, W for the less developed regions of the world, I for a given industry, and T for the total of all industries, the relevant formulae are:

$$RCA_{AI} = (X_{AI}/X_{WI}) / (X_{AT}/X_{WT})$$
$$RCD_{AI} = (M_{AI}/M_{WI}) / (M_{AT}/M_{WT})$$

The changes in RCA and RCD between 1970 and 1983 are set out in the tables. Where the comparative advantage of Africa rises the implication is that its exports in the sector in question have grown faster relative to all LDC exports than have its total exports over all industries. Such a comparative improvement in export performance may suggest the potential for export-oriented investment, but only if it is in a buoyant faster growing industry. An increased RCA value may indicate only a slower relative decline in a contracting sector. Likewise, a rise in the RCD index may suggest opportunities for import-substituting FDI in the case of a sector in which imports have been growing quite rapidly. Of course, this kind of analysis cannot be taken too far. There may be sectors in which the change in RCA would have been much more favourable had export-promoting FDI taken place.

Tables 9.9 and 9.10 cover only trade in extractive and manufacturing sectors, and not services. Table 9.9 shows that from 1970–83 Africa had a rising comparative advantage in extractive exports relative to other developing countries, and that this was especially true in mining, particularly in the export of metallic ores. It has already been noted that FDI in mining remained strong throughout this period. At the same time, Africa's comparative advantage in the manufacture of non-ferrous metals declined, and its position in other metal products was further worsened. This suggests that there may be some scope for export-oriented FDI in metal processing downstream from the existing investments in the mining of metallic ores, which would help to shift the sectoral structure of African exports and to increase local industrial development. Much the same could be said about the potential for export-oriented FDI in food processing, though in this case a movement of companies downstream is already evident in trade performance, with comparative advantage having increased in both agriculture and food products.

Other sectors in which an improvement in the RCA of Africa has accompanied a rapid rate of growth of exports are chemicals, mechanical engineering, building materials, and clothing and footwear. The latter is particularly encouraging in view of the notable achievements (and consequently strong competition) of Asian countries in this sector in the period in question, and export-oriented FDI in the clothing industry would again seem to fit in with development aims extremely well. The existing comparative advantage, which grew further in the 1970–83 period, is in the resource-related textile fibre sector; but growth here appears to have slowed down, and it would be beneficial if investments were to be extended downstream into the production of made-up clothing in this industry also.

Turning to Table 9.10, it appears that the potential for FDI in metal products and food processing is not just limited to the possibilities for export expansion, but may also have something to gain from the growth of local markets in these areas, which until now have been served by an above average increase in imports and a rise in the RCD index. The same can be said of mechanical engineering, building materials and perhaps chemicals. However, it is of course inadequate to treat the potential for FDI solely in terms of market

TABLE 9.9 *The revealed comparative advantage of developing Africa in total developing country exports*

Sectors	RCA 1970	RCA 1983	Annual growth of exports from developing Africa over 1970–83 (%)
Extractive	1.00	1.51	15.5
1. Agriculture and forestry	1.12	1.37	5.8
Animal & vegetable oil & fats	1.15	0.52	1.9
Crude materials	1.08	1.36	5.5
Crude fertilizers and minerals	1.98	3.34	11.1
2. Mining	0.95	1.54	18.7
Mineral fuels and related materials	0.98	1.54	19.3
Metalliferous ores	0.71	1.50	9.0
Manufacturing	0.99	0.51	4.9
1. Food, drink and tobacco	1.02	1.05	6.4
Cereals	0.49	0.20	0.8
Oil seeds, nuts and kernels	2.22	1.34	−2.5
2. Chemicals	0.57	0.88	16.9
3. Metals	1.79	0.79	−0.2
Iron and steel	0.47	0.38	14.7
Non-ferrous metals	2.04	1.44	−1.7
Fabricated metal products	0.32	0.15	12.1
4. Mechanical engineering	0.34	0.51	18.4
5. Electrical engineering	0.09	0.09	24.5
6. Motor vehicles	0.49	0.10	4.1
7. Other transportation equipment	0.19	0.07	13.8
8. Textile and clothing	0.86	0.58	6.4
Textile fibres	1.67	2.35	2.7
Textile yarn and fabrics	0.44	0.33	7.6
Clothing and footwear	0.14	0.34	24.4
9. Paper and allied	0.74	0.27	4.9
10. Wood products	0.54	0.32	8.2
11. Rubber and plastic	0.28	0.12	8.1
12. Building materials	0.42	0.52	16.0
13. Professional equipment	0.21	0.12	19.2
14. Other manufactured goods	0.96	0.35	2.7
TOTAL	1.0	1.0	11.2

Source: United Nations, *Yearbook of International Trade Statistics, 1974* and *1984*.

TABLE 9.10   *The revealed comparative disadvantage of developing Africa in total developing country imports*

Sectors	RCD 1970	RCD 1983	Annual growth of imports from developing Africa over 1970–83 (%)
Extractive	0.64	0.63	18.9
1. Agriculture and forestry	0.73	0.97	15.7
Animal & vegetable oil & fats	1.21	1.53	17.1
Crude materials	0.66	0.84	15.0
Crude fertilizers and minerals	0.73	1.13	18.7
2. Mining	0.56	0.52	21.8
Mineral fuels and related materials	0.58	0.52	21.9
Metalliferrous ores	0.22	0.25	14.9
Manufacturing	1.04	1.07	15.1
1. Food, drink and tobacco	1.03	1.36	16.1
Cereals	0.86	1.28	17.4
Oil seeds, nuts and kernels	0.65	0.20	6.4
2. Chemicals	0.90	0.87	13.7
3. Metals	0.84	1.03	16.0
Iron and steel	0.71	0.94	15.4
Non-ferrous metals	0.64	0.53	10.5
Fabricated metal products	1.24	1.31	17.9
4. Mechanical engineering	0.93	1.41	19.3
5. Electrical engineering	0.86	1.00	20.7
6. Motor vehicles	1.27	1.30	15.6
7. Other transportation equipment	1.14	1.04	14.0
8. Textile and clothing	1.11	0.80	9.9
Textile fibres	0.50	0.67	12.8
Textile yarn and fabrics	1.23	0.82	8.2
Clothing and footwear	1.46	0.84	14.0
9. Paper and allied	0.99	1.09	13.5
10. Wood products	1.40	0.91	18.9
11. Rubber and plastic	1.59	1.18	13.7
12. Building materials	1.12	1.48	21.2
13. Professional equipment	0.62	0.72	20.5
14. Other manufactured goods	1.11	0.88	11.9
TOTAL	1.0	1.0	15.4

Source: United Nations, *Yearbook of International Trade Statistics, 1974* and *1984.*

growth. Above all, when considering the international location of production, foreign firms require the presence of a satisfactory local technological and organisational capacity to make their operations effective. This may exist in the case of building materials, linked to new construction projects, but it seems less likely that conditions are suited to attracting substantial FDI in mechanical engineering and chemicals, at least in the smaller African countries. Conversely, though, the fact that the comparative disadvantage of Africa in imports of wood products has disappeared at a time when imports in this sector have been rising fast, suggests that local productive capacity in this area has been improving, and that there may be opportunities for resource-related FDI here as well.

Clearly, such contentions are rather tentative, and cannot be supported simply on the basis of the very broad and general evidence of Tables 9.9 and 9.10. However, they do seem to fit in with the literature on developing country experience of the role of FDI in development (which until now has relied mainly on non-African evidence), and with the peculiarities of recent African development. There has been a shift in emphasis in all LDCs, including Latin America and beginning to affect Africa as well, that has led to export-oriented FDI becoming more favoured relative to the import-substituting types. This form of FDI also seems to have been more successful in promoting local development. Following the export-oriented FDI in Asia in the textiles and clothing and electrical equipment sectors, the most spectacular example in the case of Latin America has been export-oriented FDI in the motor vehicle sector, which now accounts for 10 per cent of the total stock of FDI in that region (see Table 9.6). Brazil, Argentina and Mexico now account for around four-fifths of total developing country production and exports of motor vehicles (Dicken, 1986).

There are consequently good precedents for African countries favouring export-oriented types of FDI as a means of helping to promote local industrialisation. Import-substituting FDI is more likely to encounter the problems of the emergence of a high degree of monopoly power, and dissatisfaction over higher consumer prices. However, the prescription for export-oriented FDI must take into account the African context. The investments of foreign firms in Africa are likely to remain much more resource-related than in other developing regions for some time to come. The sectoral evolution of FDI in Africa has been much more tied to existing investments in extractive activities, and has typically taken the form of a limited downstream diversification into simple resource-related manufacturing.

The further progression of this kind of development can easily be envisaged. The widespread agricultural, forestry and mineral resources in Africa all provide scope for downstream manufacturing investments in which there is some hope that local as well as foreign firms can become involved, thereby ensuring against an enclave development. There is also reason to believe that this type of development strategy would not only be locally beneficial, but would also prove attractive to the firms of certain foreign countries. These are the firms of countries which have a lack of natural resources, especially where they are themselves undergoing a relatively rapid industrial expansion, and are encountering resource constraints as a result (Ozawa, 1982). Multinationals from Japan, Germany and the NICs have an interest in FDI in resource-related development as a means of supplying their own domestic markets. Moreover, as their production in their home economies is steadily upgraded they have an interest in relocating their less sophisticated types of production in countries at an earlier stage of development. Although they still possess the technological and organisational know-how to sustain this simpler production, it may be more profitable to do so abroad, and to concentrate on higher value added activities in the now more developed home environment.

The driving force behind this process is the rise in wage and other costs with industrial development which render less economic the older activities characterised by lower labour productivity. This is often accompanied by greater environmental pressure as the full consequences of earlier industrial expansion are better appreciated. Apart from higher labour costs, the costs of energy provision have risen in the more developed countries. This may have created an opportunity in African countries such as Guinea or Zaïre which are well equipped with hydro-electrical resources, which may become a significant locational advantage. Relative transport costs also tend to favour a shift towards local downstream processing activities. Transport costs are responsible for 27 per cent of the price of imported iron ore, but only 12 per cent in the case of steel products; while two tons of bauxite are needed to produce one ton of alumina (Yachir, 1988). A similar comparison holds for ore concentrates as against blister or refined copper; or for agricultural produce as against processed food.

However, to sound a note of caution here technological change in established industries may reduce the cost advantages of relocation, and reduce the extent of pollution associated with them. Indeed, even the underlying extractive activity may be displaced from Africa by, for example, the development of the resources of the sea bed closer to the industrialised countries. It may also be that foreign tariff barriers are higher in the case of finished or semi-finished products than for raw materials, and that coordination with user firms favours a developed country location. The future for the local development of downstream processing depends to a large extent on the overall state of demand; a number of steel projects proposed for Africa in the 1970s were put on ice when world demand dropped. Perhaps the most important qualification is that new manufacturing facilities will only be established where the country has a suitable supporting infrastructure. Only certain African countries have the potential to attract new FDI, as is discussed in section 9.5 below.

To give an illustration of how the relocation of processing activity may occur, an engineering company in Asia may import metallic ores from Africa as a raw material, and as it expands African exports of ores increase. Eventually, as operations in Asia become more sophisticated, and perhaps widen to encompass electrical as well as mechanical engineering, a rise in domestic costs and environmental pressure begin to squeeze out its lower value added activities. At this stage, the company may wish to consider moving its basic metal processing activities close to the African site of the mining venture. From here it may be able to serve not only the parent company in Asia, but also other engineering companies in third countries. The possibilities for multinational expansion are in such a case very much in tune with an appropriate strategy for FDI and development in Africa. The objective of resource-based development is 'to convert foreign-owned enclave type ventures, which produce raw materials for export with relatively little dependence on domestically produced goods and services, into national industries exporting and selling domestically processed or manufactured products' (Mikdashi, 1976, as cited in Ozawa, 1982).

The notion that FDI should be given the role of gradually but systematically upgrading the productive capacity of a developing country, in accordance with the existing capabilities of local firms and the stage of development so far achieved is familiar from the literature on FDI in Asia (see, for example, Kojima, 1978, and Koo, 1985). In cultivating resource-related FDI Africa can learn from the development strategies of South East Asian countries, though from the perspective of an earlier stage of development. What African countries may particularly wish to emulate from the Asian experience is the way in which the gradual shift in the underlying industrial structure was in general supported by a sector-specific strategy towards FDI, which was encouraged in certain key target sectors that changed over time. Although such a selective policy stance was frequently implicit rather than explicit, it is quite clear that industrial policies have been assigned a prominent role in development in Asia (see Koo, 1985, on the case of sector-specific FDI policies in South Korea, and on how the choice of target sectors shifted).

9.5   THE SELECTION OF TARGET SECTORS TO ATTRACT FDI AND PROMOTE RESOURCE-BASED DEVELOPMENT IN AFRICA

The selection of target sectors for the encouragement of FDI and local development in Africa must depend upon individual host country appraisals, but three or four sectors stand out as particular candidates that are likely to have potential over a certain range of African countries, and not just in isolated cases. These are wood and paper products (linked to forestry), textiles and clothing (linked to textile fibres), and metal products (where mining is the leading extractive sector) or food processing (where agriculture is more important). The objective would be to attract both the downstream diversification of multinationals already in the relevant extractive sector, and the new investments of multinationals whose operations in the more developed countries are tending to move downstream and may wish to relocate what for them are now upstream activities.

In order to appreciate more precisely the potential for attracting new investment it is necessary to divide African countries into groups, as they are different from one another and the sector-specific strategies which are appropriate for each group will differ accordingly. The foreign multinationals likely to be involved in each group of countries have distinct characteristics. Leaving aside those countries which due to their backwardness or remoteness have little chance of attracting any significant industrial investments, the remaining African nations can be divided into three groups as set out in Table 9.11. The first consists of countries rich in natural resources in which resource-based multinationals have already invested heavily in extractive activity. The second comprises mainly larger countries, often as in the first case former colonial territories, in which foreign

TABLE 9.11 *A typology of foreign multinationals with interests in Africa, and the industrial and geographical characteristics of their investments*

Original type of investment	Type of firm	Type of country	Prospects for newer resource-related industrial investment	Examples of countries
Resource-oriented	Former colonial firms Firms from resource-rich industrialised countries Firms from resource-scarce newly industrialising countries.	Resource-rich countries	Related diversification (for example, from mining) Downstream processing (for example, metal processing, wood products, oil-related chemicals, agribusiness).	Gabon Guinea Liberia Namibia Nigeria Zaïre Zambia Zimbabwe
Local market-oriented and inter-firm trade related.	Expatriate firms. Trading companies. Construction and local service firms.	Larger countries with foreign entrepreneurs	Management contracts and 'new forms' of involvement (for instance, food processing).	Kenya Zimbabwe
Export-oriented and intra-firm trade related.	Offshore producers from industrialised countries. Newly industrialising country firms relocating activity. International service groups (shipping, finance, and so on).	Better developed countries with local skills, or smaller countries with taxation or legal advantages.	Trade barrier or preference-related (for instance, textiles).	Arab State of North Africa, Mauritius

entrepreneurs have a major presence. In this group expatriate firms with links with local élites and trading companies have established local market-oriented and trade-related investments in the past. The third group includes countries which are sometimes excluded from discussions of Africa altogether due to their different cultural backgrounds. These are more advanced countries with local skills and expertise (such as certain North African states) or smaller countries with various taxation or legal attractions, in which foreign multinationals have invested in export-oriented and trade-related activity.

The first possibility, then, is that in each of these cases established multinationals may extend their activity into related industries. Thus metallic mining companies may set up local processing facilities, plantation-linked firms may move out into a wider range of agribusiness and food processing, and offshore producers such as the German textile firms may broaden their operations. By comparison, the new multinationals not so far established in Africa may well come from less well known source countries, both the smaller industrialised countries and Third-World countries at a more advanced stage of development. The firms of Canada and Sweden come most immediately to mind in the case of wood and paper products, which have advantages that can be exploited in timber-rich countries. Meanwhile, Third-World multinationals are likely to be important in the textiles sector, in which better developed countries with local skills may be able to attract investment. The relocation of textiles production from the NICs of South East Asia to Africa has an additional motivation besides the general advantages of shifting simpler activity to a country at a lower stage of the development ladder which is attempting to follow in the footsteps of the home country. That is, trade policy within the industrialised countries has imposed quota arrangements on South East Asian textile exports, thereby compelling firms based there to diversify home production, moving in the direction of more sophisticated articles. The manufacture of more basic lines can be relocated to countries with more favourable conditions of access to industrialised country markets. This is what has already begun to happen in the case of Hong Kong investment in Africa, and in Mauritius in particular (Currie, 1986; Chen, 1983b).

Third-World multinationals have built up particular advantages in the production of textiles in Third-World conditions. They tend to be organisationally innovative and technologically adaptive in traditional small-scale industries, in which they have well developed managerial and marketing skills (Lall, 1983a). They have advantages that are well suited to extracting the greatest benefits from the resource-related potential of some African countries. Moreover, there is other evidence that the more advanced African countries have the local capacity to become involved in the new international division of labour in the textiles sector, in which they have already been host to German and Italian investment (Fröbel, Heinrichs, and Kreye, 1980; Acocella *et al*, 1985). Although this development has focused on North Africa so far it has extended to sub-Saharan Africa, and there appears to be an emerging opportunity that has not yet been fully exploited.

Textiles is a sector in which production has become highly internationally mobile, with the world division of labour in a process of continual change. One locational advantage of African countries in such a sector lies in their large reservoir of cheap unskilled labour. Simple manufacturing tasks which require little skill were initially the basis for the expansion of foreign-owned production in the NICs outside Africa. The rise in wages that has accompanied development in the NICs has improved the attractiveness of an African location, although this has been at least partly offset by organisational and productivity improvement in the NICs, which has altered the form of the contribution that they make. For some of this production now to shift to Africa would require a similar capacity for organisational innovation effectively to implement those simpler types of manufacturing activity that make the best use of its own local resource availabilities. While African enterprise is unlikely to be able to seriously challenge the NICs in this respect, it may still be capable of a small increase in its participation in the new international division of labour. Although this would not result in any substantial switch of activity at a global level, it may well be significant for African countries themselves, given the smaller scale of their existing manufacturing operations, and the correspondingly smaller scale at which development is likely to take place, at least initially.

In the wood products and textiles sectors the major sources of FDI are likely to be newer and smaller multinationals. The firms of higher growth countries have begun a particularly rapid international expansion in recent years. Much of this has been in innovative activity in the industrialised world, but resource-based firms have also been seeking investment opportunities in developing countries. Ozawa (1979) explains this phenomenon through the use of a Ricardian growth model in which expansion depends on the alleviation of resource constraints through the import of raw materials supported

by export-oriented FDI. This resource-based type of outward investment is likely to be more important relative to that FDI which relies
upon innovative advantages in the case of countries that are industrialising fast (Japan in the 1960s, and the NICs today) as opposed to
those countries that are rapidly upgrading the nature of their manufacturing and service activities (Japan and Germany now). Today the
multinationals of the NICs are growing faster than the multinationals
of any other group of source countries, in proportional terms even
exceeding the rapid international growth of Japanese firms (Dunning
and Cantwell, 1987). There is also evidence that they are attracted
beyond their home regions, and interested in Africa. The value of
Indian investments in Nigeria, for example, is the greatest in any
individual country outside Asia (Dunning and Cantwell, 1987; Lall,
1983b).

FDI in the metal products and food processing sectors would in
part be import-substituting (local market-oriented) as well as export-
oriented, depending upon the degree of international vertical integration which characterises the product concerned (iron and steel, for
example, are different from copper or aluminium). However, the
export-oriented feature of the investment potential is especially
important, as the objective would be to increase the local value
added in a vertically integrated chain that typically ends in marketing
in the industrialised countries. These activities may involve the
multinationals with traditional interests in Africa, perhaps under
contractual arrangements more favourable to local firms than have
prevailed in the past. Here there is evidence that the multinationals
with existing operations in Africa have an incentive to attempt to
diversify into downstream activities in the local economy, particularly
in the larger African countries (Clarke, 1980; Swainson, 1980). New
forms of cooperative ventures with local partners also seem to have
worked better and to have led to greater commitment on the part of
foreign firms in the case of resource-based production (Cantwell and
Dunning, 1985). The scope for encouraging vertical linkages between
foreign and local firms in developing countries has been further
discussed by Lall (1980) and Landi(1986).

Perhaps the most important criterion in selecting sectors in which
to seek out foreign participation is the need to encourage development in sectors in which indigenous firms already have some potential, or have potential in related and complementary sectors. In this
way the entry or expansion of foreign firms is liable to set in motion a
process of positive interaction, and a more rapid development of the

industry in question. If this happens then forced partnerships and regulations to prevent the monopolisation of local industry are unnecessary.

In each of the sectors proposed as potential targets for attracting greater foreign involvement increased FDI is likely to be associated with more collaborative agreements with local firms, to the benefit of local development. However, this is unlikely to go so far that foreign firms restrict themselves entirely to non-equity arrangements without any direct investment. FDI is necessary to take advantage of the experience that the multinationals in question have acquired in the simple manufacturing activities that they may now consider shifting to Africa. This is the case for both the traditional vertically integrated multinationals with long-standing investments in the extractive sector in Africa, but which until now have organised the bulk of processing activity in more developed regions; and for the newer multinationals who have accumulated organisational skills in running basic manufacturing operations in developing country or resource-rich country conditions. The transfer of knowledge and managerial capacity is likely to be costly even if the local environment (in terms of the growth of allied local firms and infrastructure) is ripe for such an initiative, but the costs will be very much less if such a transfer takes place within the firm with the established experience. Multinationals also have a major contribution to make to the success of local operations through their abilities to coordinate primary commodity production, manufacturing, finance and other supporting services, in a way that smaller African firms would not be able to manage themselves immediately.

The adoption of sector-specific FDI policy with chosen target sectors requires the development of differentiated policies designed to meet the needs of any particular local industry. It also requires a flexible approach towards FDI as the priorities for economic development change. The attraction of export-oriented FDI may well depend upon public investment in supporting infrastructure. However, the limits to what FDI policy can achieve must also be clearly understood so that governments do not become easily disillusioned. Policies can only successfully promote investments in those areas in which there is already an incipient potential in the local economy. At a general level in Africa the greatest current potential seems to be in the development of resource-based simple manufacturing activity. Given the historical presence of multinationals in extractive sectors in Africa, and given the desires for international expansion of many newer resource-based multinationals, this seems the likeliest way in which to involve foreign firms in the further development of African countries.

Notes

The author gratefully acknowledges the assistance of Paz Tolentino and Christina Varvias in preparing the tables in this chapter. He also wishes to thank the Foreign Investment Advisory Service, a joint venture between the International Finance Corporation (IFC) and the Multilateral Investment Guarantee Agency of the World Bank, for financial support and comments on an earlier draft discussed at an IFC meeting. He is grateful to Hafiz Mirza, Sanjaya Lall and other participants at the UK AIB annual conference and a seminar at Queen Elizabeth House, Oxford, for useful comments which have improved the paper.

The views expressed remain those of the author, and are not necessarily those of the organisations which provided financial support.

1. In what follows 'Africa' refers to developing Africa excluding South Africa.

10 Yugoslav Foreign Direct Investment in Less Developed Countries

Patrick Artisien, Matija Rojec and Marjan Svetlicic

10.1 INTRODUCTION

This study focuses on the relatively new phenomenon of Yugoslav direct investment in LDCs. The main purpose of this chapter is to discuss the origin, evolution, specific characteristics and motivation of Yugoslav firms in LDCs. The focus is on four issues: (1) What are the major historical, economic and political variables that help to explain the growth of Yugoslav FDI in LDCs? (2) What are the motives behind Yugoslav direct investments in LDCs? (3) What factors prompted minority-owned Joint Ventures as the preferred form of investment in LDCs? (4) What are some of the problems and reasons for divestment?

The data for this paper were collected from structured interviews with the Yugoslav partners of 20 minority-owned joint ventures in LDCs. Interviews were conducted in Slovene and Serbo-Croat with senior executives in charge of overseas operations, and in most cases with the chief executives of the firms as well. Company reports and statistical sources from the Federal Secretariat for Foreign Trade and the Social Accounting Service in Yugoslavia complement the interview-based data.

10.2 THE BACKGROUND

Few studies of East European and Yugoslav firms investing abroad have been conducted to date. The pioneering work of Carl McMillan (1979; 1987) links the growth of East European multinationals in the 1960s and 1970s to a new external strategy by the Comecon countries to improve the structure of their foreign trade with the more developed Western economies. McMillan argues that the growth of Comecon-based multinationals has been in response to many of the forces which motivated their Western counterparts in the immediate post-war years: the search for markets, raw materials and lower production costs. McMillan's evidence suggests that Comecon companies abroad do not behave significantly differently from the subsidiaries of Western multinationals: the predominant legal form of investments in both West and South is the joint stock company; there is a clear preference for majority ownership, and expansion and diversification are financed mainly through re-invested profits and local borrowing rather than through capital exports from the home country.

Studies of Yugoslav multinationals investing in LDCs (Svetlicic and Rojec, 1985; 1986) link the emergence of Yugoslav FDI to the post-1965 Economic Reform period in Yugoslavia which stimulated the expansion of Yugoslav firms in the international division of labour. This period of economic decentralisation provided Yugoslav enterprises with the necessary incentives and independence to intensify direct economic links with foreign enterprises. According to official Yugoslav figures, at the end of 1986 there were 335 wholly- or partly-owned Yugoslav subsidiaries abroad, mostly established since the mid 1960s. As Table 10.1 illustrates, the vast majority of Yugoslav subsidiaries abroad (80.9 per cent) are located in the developed market economies of Western Europe, North America and Japan; 18.8 per cent are established in LDCs, and only one subsidiary is situated in Eastern Europe.

The origin of Yugoslav outward direct investment dates back to the late 1950s: in 1959 Intertrade set up a trading and marketing subsidiary in India (Intraco), and in 1961 Generalexport set up Yugoarab in the Lebanon. Prior to 1954 Yugoslavia's external economic relations were strictly centralised and managed by federal ministries. Moreover, the latent xenophobia which persisted in the years following Yugoslavia's expulsion from the Cominform in 1949 acted as an impediment to innovative forms of industrial cooperation, which remained limited to traditional exports and imports. In the mid-1950s Yugoslavia initiated a network of licensing and long-term industrial cooperation agreements with its major Western trading partners with the objective of establishing qualitatively new relationships with a view to acquiring foreign technology (Svetlicic and Rojec, 1988). It was also during this period that Yugoslav firms entered into construction work agreements with firms in LDCs. The first such contract was

TABLE 10.1   *Number of Yugoslav economic entities abroad, end of 1986*

	Developed market economy countries	East-European socialist countries	Less developed countries	Total
Number of Countries	24	11	62	97
Number of Entities-Total	555	443	994	1,992
1. Subsidiaries	271	1	63	335
a. Wholly (Yugoslav) Owned	193	1	25	219
b. Majority (Yugoslav) Owned	27	–	4	31
c. Minority (Yugoslav) Owned	51	–	34	85
2. Entities for Construction Works	71	167	697	935
3. Representative Offices	202	253	198	653
4. Business Entities	11	22	36	69

Source: Social Accounting Service of Yugoslavia.

1/ Includes China and Mongolia.

2/ Entities for construction works and business entities are both set up to undertake construction projects abroad. Business entities, however, are not legally bound to draw up their balance sheet reports for the Yugoslav authorities.

signed with Turkey in 1952, but the share of direct investment in LDCs remained modest until the turn of the decade. In the 1960s the Yugoslav government signed a series of international credit agreements with the governments of LDCs in Asia and Africa through which Yugoslav firms secured contracts for the building of turn-key power generating and industrial plants. As a result, the LDCs became a major recipient of Yugoslav FDI: in the period 1960–65 the LDCs' share of Yugoslav construction projects abroad exceeded 25 per cent. By the mid-1980s LDCs accounted for 80 per cent (see Table 10.1). By 1988 Yugoslav enterprises were estimated to be represented by some 2000 entities abroad in just under 100 countries, 62 of which were located in the Third World.

Although the growth of Yugoslav investments in both developing and developed countries formed part of a new foreign economic policy approach which emerged in the 1960s and took shape in the 1970s, differing rationales for investments in the West and South have produced different patterns of investment in the two areas. Companies with Yugoslav equity participation in the West are primarily engaged in trading and marketing, whilst those in the South are concentrated in the manufacturing, construction and engineering industries, which function in support of Yugoslav capital development projects in the host economies.

Although by the early 1960s the Yugoslav economy had reached a level of industrialisation which prompted firms to intensify their international economic cooperation, the take-off stage for Yugoslav FDI was primarily the result of the 1965 Economic Reforms. The economic reforms marked the final phase of the transition to market socialism and proclaimed Yugoslavia's intention to integrate with the world economy: the Yugoslav market was opened to foreign competition in order to increase the industrial efficiency and competitiveness of Yugoslav enterprises. The Reforms carried out the process of decentralisation in the field of international economic cooperation which provided enterprises with the necessary independence to embark on a foreign investment strategy (Svetlicic and Rojec, 1988).

Thus, the reforms strengthened the economic profile of the enterprise as the main vehicle through which to intensify direct economic cooperation with foreign partners. Initially, the foreign subsidiaries of Yugoslav enterprises were trade-oriented, particularly in the developed market economies, where they were set up by large Yugoslav parents such as Generalexport and Interexport. The second half of the 1960s witnessed the fastest growth in Yugoslav FDI, with a new emphasis on the markets of the LDCs: the first production subsidiary in LDCs was established in 1969 by Energoinvest in Mexico. The growth of Yugoslav production ventures which ensued in LDCs was never matched in the developed West, suggesting that Yugoslav investors did not possess the necessary firm-specific advantages to internalise their production on Western markets. This observation rests on the premise that Yugoslav firms were unable to innovate processes or adapt products to operate successfully in the US and West European markets, or that if such advantages did exist, they were unable to penetrate the relevant segments of those markets. Studies of multinationals from LDCs have suggested that the competitive advantages of these firms are different from those based in industrialised countries (Lecraw, 1977; Wells, 1977; Kumar and Kim, 1984). The Yugoslav experience confirms the aforementioned: Yugoslav firms in LDCs do not manufacture new or exclusive products or operate under brand names, but as a general rule use standard technologies. Table 10.1 also reveals the preponderance of Yugoslav firms in LDCs in providing construction and engineering services for development projects (697 contracts out of a total of 994 at the end of 1986). Given Yugoslavia's relatively undeveloped industrial base in the 1960s, it came as no surprise that Yugoslav firms chose not to concentrate on the more capital- and technology-intensive manufacturing industries, and that the establishment of subsidiaries abroad was preceded by the setting up of representative offices and small business units as ways of minimising risks.

The significance of Yugoslav enterprises abroad is illustrated further by the share of exports and imports realised by these firms in Yugoslavia's overall foreign trade. In 1987 Yugoslav enterprises abroad accounted for 58 per cent of total exports and 30.9 per cent of total imports.[1]

10.3 PROFILE OF EXTERNAL INVESTMENTS BY YUGOSLAV FIRMS

Table 10.1 shows that at the end of 1986 Yugoslav firms had established 335 subsidiaries and joint ventures abroad, of which 63 were located in the LDCs. The majority of these enterprises are located in Africa, particularly south of the Sahara, which reflects to a certain extent the concentration of investments in Liberian shipping companies. This location strategy is broadly in line with Well's observation that LDC firms have a preference for investing in neighbouring countries (Wells, 1983): Africa is Yugoslavia's nearest LDC region. However, the concentration of Yugoslav FDI in low income, underdeveloped and thinly populated African countries does not accord with the prevailing world trend, whereby LDC firms tend to invest in the newly industrialised countries of Latin America and South East Asia (Svetlicic and Rojec, 1986). The tally of Yugoslav investments in Latin America is a mere ten enterprises, whilst only six firms have been set up in Asia. Distance and weak trading links with those two regions account for this low profile. The predominance of Africa as host to Yugoslav FDI is not a short-term transitory phenomenon, but falls within the broader framework of Yugoslavia's long-term industrial cooperation with the African continent: in mid-1987 as many as 90 (46.2 per cent) of the 195 representative offices of Yugoslav firms in LDCs were based in African countries. In terms of size, Yugoslav investments in LDCs are in general small when measured against international standards. This arises largely because many investments are located in countries with an undeveloped industrial base and poor infrastructure. There are, however, individual exceptions: Slovenia Bois, the tropical wood exploitation and processing joint venture in the Central African Republic, is one of the largest projects in that country and its major source of foreign investment. DAWA, the Krka Joint Venture in Keyna, is the largest pharmaceuticals factory in Africa south of the Sahara, contributing

TABLE 10.2 *Sectoral distribution of Yugoslav enterprises in LDCs, mid-1987*

Sector	Number	%
Trade	18	24.3
Production	23	31.1
Services (including engineering, construction and transport)	32	43.3
Banks	1	1.3
Total	74	100.0

Source: Federal Secretariat for Foreign Trade, Belgrade.

5 per cent to Kenya's GDP and employing approximately 3 per cent of its workforce. At the end of 1986 Yugoslav enterprises abroad employed 10 684 people, of which 5845 (54.7 per cent) were employed in LDCs, reflecting the predominance of labour-intensive manufacturing industries. It is also significant that as many as 84.6 per cent of the workforce in LDC enterprises were employed in joint ventures where the Yugoslav partner held a minority of the equity – the most common pattern of ownership.

Table 10.2 shows the sectoral distribution of Yugoslav FDI in LDCs as of mid-1987: of the total of 74 enterprises, 32 are engaged in the service industries (mostly construction and transport), 23 in production, 18 in trading and marketing and one in banking. In terms of invested Yugoslav capital, the picture which emerges is somewhat different, with 60.9 per cent of all Yugoslav invested capital concentrated in industrial production.

An examination of Yugoslav investment in LDCs by industrial sector shows a wide distribution across a variety of products, including pharmaceuticals, paints, electrical goods, hand machine tools, metal working machinery, clothing, meat processing and the assembly of motorcycles. The general impression gained is that Yugoslav industrial enterprises in LDCs are concentrated in skill- and technology-intensive sectors rather than in the more traditional labour-intensive industries. The same investments are rarely resource-oriented, in spite of Yugoslavia's limited natural resource endowment and its trade dependence for raw materials on LDCs – raw materials make up over 60 per cent of Yugoslav imports from LDCs (Centre for International Co-operation and Development, 1984a). The lack of sufficient financial resources and of expertise in

TABLE 10.3   *Ownership structure of Yugoslav FDI in LDCs, 1986*

Ownership pattern	Number	%
Wholly owned subsidiaries	25	39.7
Majority owned Joint Ventures	4	6.3
Minority owned Joint Ventures	34	54.0

Source: Social Accounting Service of Yugoslavia.

resource-based projects seems to account for this trend.

As alluded to above, minority- (Yugoslav) owned joint ventures have been the most common type of ownership in LDCs since the mid-1970s; before 1975, the bulk of Yugoslav FDI was in the form of wholly-owned subsidiaries. The growth of local ownership participation was the result of three sets of factors: the first two were policy-determined, namely a reappraisal by the Yugoslav authorities in 1974 of foreign investment policy which, in the context of South-South cooperation, was designed to meet the needs of LDCs, by lessening their economic dependence on majority-owned foreign interests and promoting a greater degree of 'collective self-reliance' (Svetlicic and Rojec, 1985). Second, Yugoslav investors had in some cases no option but to submit to the host countries' legal ceilings on foreign participation. The third factor is micro-economic in nature: our empirical evidence suggests that Yugoslav firms have a higher propensity to form minority-owned joint ventures in LDCs with low-technology, undifferentiated products, for which local partners are required to provide knowledge of the local marketing techniques and economic environment. This evidence concurs with Lecraw's findings (1977).

As Table 10.3 illustrates, 60.3 per cent of investments by Yugoslav enterprises in LDCs are owned jointly with host country partners, and in 54 per cent of cases the Yugoslav partner holds a minority of the equity; the other 39.7 per cent are wholly owned by the Yugoslav enterprise.

10.4   MOTIVATION FOR INVESTMENT

This section examines the main motives which have prompted Yugoslav enterprises to establish foreign subsidiaries and joint ventures in LDCs. The factors which motivate a LDC firm to make a direct investment in another LDC have received extensive coverage in the literature (Wells, 1983; Lecraw, 1977; Lall, 1983). The most quoted motives include threats to the parents' markets, risk diversification, limited home market growth, high local returns and the exploitation of labour-intensive technology.

The experience and motivations of Yugoslav enterprises in LDCs are less well documented. A survey was conducted by the Centre for International Co-operation and Development (1984b) among a sample of 86 Yugoslav enterprises in LDCs (including subsidiaries, joint ventures and representative offices). Although the reasons enumerated were extremely varied, over 85 per cent of motives fell within the aggressive category: these included opening up new markets for the firms' own products, securing imports of raw materials and intermediate products and avoiding transportation and tariff costs. The primary motive of many Yugoslav firms for making a direct investment in LDCs was clearly to exploit a present or anticipated opportunity abroad more effectively than was possible via exports. The survey also addressed the question of the deteriorating economic situation of many LDCs: the improvement of their balance of payments was reported to be a major factor, ranked as decisive by 45 per cent and very important by 39 per cent of the sample.

Institutional factors varied in importance: whilst the establishment of preferential treatment for Yugoslav imports from LDCs was deemed important (decisive: 19 per cent, very important: 39 per cent), intergovernmental agreements were less important. One third of respondents thought that the institutional framework had failed to stimulate long-term cooperation with LDCs, highlighting the unsatisfactory level of government incentives. In our survey of Yugoslav investors in LDCs we concentrated our interviews on minority joint ventures, which were the predominant type of ownership at the end of 1986 (as outlined in Table 10.3). The 20 sample joint ventures are fairly evenly distributed among manufacturing firms (8), trading organisations (5), the construction and engineering industries (4) and resource-based industries (3).

The motives for the investment are classified in three major groupings: market-related factors, cost and legal/institutional factors. Companies were asked to rate the importance of these factors in their decision to invest on a four-point scale ranging from very important (1), to important (2), to less important (3), to irrelevant (4).

Our findings in Table 10.4 demonstrate that firms were predominantly motivated by market considerations (average score 1.70), followed by cost considerations (average score 2.25), and institutional/legal factors. This evidence accords with the existing literature. A survey by Dunning (1973) of nine studies of the motivation of US multinationals overseas found that market-related factors (including market size, growth and the potential for an export base) prevailed, followed by cost considerations (among which the availability of cheap labour was predominant). The findings of a survey of West German investors in LDCs (Riedel, 1984) bear out this trend: the most important motive was the potential accessibility to new markets.

In our sample, by far the most important motive behind Yugoslav investments in LDCs is to increase exports to the host country market (listed by 65 per cent of interviewees as either important or very important). This is particularly the case for firms investing in manufacturing, trade and construction industries, whilst for resource-based investments this motive is practically irrelevant. The desire to protect existing markets is relatively unimportant in our sample and suggests that few Yugoslav firms succeeded in establishing a strong foothold in LDC markets.

Other motives, namely to secure a basis for exports to the host country and exploit the market more effectively than could be achieved via exports, illustrate the importance of the 'presence principle' (Newbould, Buckley and Thurwell, 1978).

As expected, firms with resource-oriented investments ranked the need to secure sources of raw materials and intermediate goods high in their motivation (average score: 2.0), whilst for other firms this motive was unimportant (average score: 3.0).

Although 75 per cent of interviewees regarded cost considerations as a very important segment of their motivation pattern, an analysis of individual cost-related motives across the full range of industrial sectors fails to confirm this trend, bar in the case of lower labour costs (which scored 2.75). The relative under-representation of cost considerations stems from a growing concern among Yugoslav investors to boost exports to the host country, and by implication to keep production costs down in Yugoslavia rather than in the host country.

Finally, Yugoslav investors in LDCs have in general only paid lip service to host government and legal regulations, except in cases where the local partner's knowledge of the host environment could be maximised to reduce risk and generate higher profits. This suggests that the incentives offered have not been sufficient to offset some of the constraints on dividend repatriation as well as import

TABLE 10.4 *Motives of Yugoslav investors in LDCs*

MOTIVES	Average score (*)	% share of interviewed firms which assessed individual motive as important or very important
Marketing Motivation	1.70	75.0
1. Protection of existing market	2.85	35.0
2. Increasing exports to host country market	1.95	65.0
3. Access to markets of neighbouring countries	3.30	20.0
4. Securing of long-term basis for exports to the host country	2.45	55.0
5. Realisation of business which otherwise would not have been secured via exports	2.60	60.0
6. Securing of raw materials and intermediate goods	3.35	25.0
7. Advantages of direct presence in the market (presence principles)	2.45	60.0
Cost motivation	2.25	75.0
1. Lower costs of local labour	2.75	45.0
2. Lower prices of raw materials	3.50	15.0
3. Lower transport costs	3.30	20.0
4. Economies of scale	3.25	25.0
5. Better exploitation of production capacity in Yugoslavia	3.00	40.0
6. Higher profits than in Yugoslavia	3.35	20.0
7. Developing of other activities in host country market	2.90	40.0
Institutional/legal motivation	2.60	45.0
1. Liberalisation of host country foreign investment legislation	3.00	30.0
2. Local partner provides better conditions for doing business in the host country market	2.30	55.0
3. Financial and other measures of host government	2.55	60.0
4. Existence of regional integration schemes which offer possibilities for exports to other countries	3.40	20.0
5. Better possibilities for local credits	3.40	15.0
6. Avoiding of import tariffs	3.30	25.0
7. Avoiding of other import		

TABLE 10.4   (*continued*)

MOTIVES	Average score (*)	% share of interviewed firms which assessed individual motive as important or very important
restrictions	3.70	10.0
8. Better contacts with local consumers	3.20	20.0

Source: Authors' interviews of Yugoslav investors.

(*) Average scores were derived as follows: (1) very important; (2) important; (3) less important; (4) irrelevant.

restrictions. It is also worth noting that the relatively high profile of the host partner's contribution reflects to a large extent the sample's bias towards Yugoslav minority-owned joint ventures, and it can be surmised that Yugoslav firms investing in wholly-owned subsidiaries would not subscribe to the same opinion. Finally, Yugoslav investors were asked whether the decision to invest in LDCs was 'an integral part of their firm's long-term strategy in a foreign market', or whether it was 'the result of the local partner's interest or of ad hoc business opportunities'. For most respondents, the former was the case, confirming the impression that firms are becoming increasingly aware that future overall development calls for a greater degree of internationalisation of their activities.

To sum up, our sample has illuminated some distinctive characteristics in the motivation of Yugoslav enterprises in LDCs: first, market-related motives fall within the general pattern of international investment (in terms of export promotion), although the modalities do differ: firm-specific advantages are not based on innovations, but rather on adapted technology, particularly with regard to the scale of production, inputs and managerial know-how. Second, cost considerations matter less to the Yugoslav investor; location-specific advantages including lower labour costs and access to raw materials and other sources of energy are pertinent to the local partner's contribution, but are not perceived as a source of technological rent. Finally, some Yugoslav firms have been induced to invest in LDCs by the draw of import-substituting markets. This has prompted firms which were previously exporting to those countries as well as those which hoped to establish themselves there to set up local production and assembly facilities.

10.5 OWNERSHIP PATTERNS

This section analyses the ownership patterns of Yugoslav direct investments in LDCs, in particular the reasons behind the decision to take up a minority share in the equity of joint ventures. Lecraw (1977) has argued that ownership and management control are the most controversial issues concerning foreign direct investment in LDCs as 'there is a constant struggle by the host country to wrest away as much equity and control as possible from foreign firms whilst still maintaining as many as possible of the benefits to the country which accrue from such investment'.

It seemed pertinent, therefore, to test whether the minority Yugoslav share of equity in LDC ventures was a result of host regulations or/and a function of firm-specific assets: Wells (1983) found that firms with low technology and undifferentiated products had a higher propensity to set up joint ventures in LDCs. As Table 10.1 showed, 34 out of 63 Yugoslav investments (54 per cent) in LDCs at the end of 1986 were minority-owned. This contrasted markedly with the ownership pattern of Yugoslav firms in advanced market economies where wholly (Yugoslav) owned enterprises are the norm (193 out of a total of 271, or 71 per cent), with minority ventures accounting for only 19 per cent. A number of reasons suggest themselves: first, developed market economies tend to impose fewer ownership restrictions on foreign investors: in our sample of 20 minority joint ventures in LDCs (see Table 10.5) 55 per cent of respondents reported that legal restrictions played an important part in their investment choice. Another factor is the sectoral distribution of Yugoslav investments in both country groups: minority joint ventures appear to be more suited to industrial entities (which prevail in LDCs) than to trade-related investments, which are predominant in the developed West. Financial constraints go some way towards explaining the greater frequency of minority joint ventures in industrial sectors, which by their very nature require larger capital outlays. The chronic scarcity of foreign exchange in Yugoslavia has constrained the availability of funds for foreign investments, and has contributed to an important feature of the investment strategy of Yugoslav firms in LDCs: on the one hand, a tendency to invest in small-scale manufacturing; on the other, to enlist local capital participation in Yugoslav ventures abroad, and by implication the greater involvement and interest of the local partner. Our sample confirms the above hypothesis: 65 per cent of respondents invested to 'reduce risk and increase the local partner's involvement', whilst retaining 'adequate control and mana-

TABLE 10.5   *Reasons for preferring a minority-owned joint venture*

FACTORS	Average score (*)	% share of respondents listing individual factors as important or very important
Joint Venture evolved out of previous cooperation	2.20	70.0
Host country legislation excludes foreign majority equity	2.55	55.0
Other host country institutional/ legal restrictions	3.40	20.0
Yugoslav investor's lack of capital	3.35	20.0
Host government incentives to minority (foreign) owned Joint Ventures	3.70	10.0
Result of Yugoslav government policy	2.40	65.0
To reduce risk and increase local partner's involvement	2.35	65.0
Lower financial commitment combined with adequate control and managerial influence	2.50	65.0
Other incentives to minority (foreign) owned Joint Ventures	2.90	35.0

Source: Authors' interviews of Yugoslav investors.

(*) Average scores were derived as follows: (1) very important; (2) important; (3) less important; (4) irrelevant.

gerial influence'. This would suggest further that Yugoslav investors are not unduly concerned about losing influence or control by drawing upon the local partner's experience and knowledge.

As the success and efficiency of the ventures are clearly not based on monopolistic advantages (such as brand names or trade secrets) but rather on undifferentiated products for which technology must be adapted to local needs, and the pooling of resources with local partners, Yugoslav investors do not have strategic reasons for insisting on majority equity shares. This accords with the findings of Lall (1983) for Indian multinationals, Wells (1981), and Lecraw (1977). But by far the most quoted motive for setting up a minority joint venture (listed by 70 per cent of respondents) was the existence of previous trading links, either in the form of exports or licensing. The 'full route', including the above-mentioned intermediary steps, to setting up a joint venture illustrates the importance of previous association, an observation of equal significance in the case of inward foreign investments into Yugoslavia (Artisien, 1985; Artisien and Buckley, 1985).

We argued in an earlier section that many of the motives listed by Yugoslav firms for investing in LDCs fell within the aggressive category. There are indications, however, that Yugoslav minority-owned joint ventures are also used as a defensive instrument. The Yugoslav firms' relatively weak technological base, their marginal share in the export of technology and limited experience in the internationalisation of production have been instrumental in the decision to seek the participation of local partners. In this sense, minority-owned joint ventures can be regarded as the only possible form of investment at the time, highlighting the fact that Yugoslav enterprises are relative newcomers to the internationalisation of production. This should not imply, however, that Yugoslav firms with a minority share of the equity cannot optimise their operations abroad. In many of our sample cases the choice of a minority-owned joint venture was the combined result of objective conditions in the international market, as well as of the choice of host country and of firm-specific decisions by the investing firm.

We conclude this section by examining the extent to which Yugoslav investments in minority joint ventures are the result of legal constraints in the host countries. To test this hypothesis, we compare the percentage share of Yugoslav equity in minority joint ventures with the legal limits operative in the 15 host LDCs under consideration. Table 10.6 shows that in at least 12 cases Yugoslav investors chose not to increase their investment to the legal maximum: in nine cases, the establishment of 100 per cent-owned sudsidiaries and of majority-owned joint ventures was permitted but not taken up; in another three cases the Yugoslav investment was below the legally permitted minority ownership ceiling. When asked to assess the success of the joint ventures both from their and their local partner's viewpoints, the group of investors who did not increase their share of the equity to the legal maximum were on average more successful. This evidence concurs with the findings of Beamish (1984), who in a study of joint ventures in LDCs, found that there was a greater likelihood of satisfactory performance when the multinational owned less than 50 per cent of the equity.

Predictably, the impact of host legislation on Yugoslav investors who chose not to increase their share of the equity to the legal limit was negligible; the opposite perception applied to the other group of firms. Finally, both groups of firms were asked about the extent to

TABLE 10.6 *Impact of legal constraints in 15 host countries (LDCS) on % share of equity in Yugoslav minority-owned joint ventures*

	Number of MIJVs*	Share of MIJVs in all entities (%)	Legal limits on foreign equity (at the time of establishment)	Yugoslav share in equity (in %)	Yugoslav share: below or up to legal limits on foreign share	Importance of legal restrictions**
1. ECUADOR electrical hand tools	1	100.0	49%. This is the major restriction on foreign ownership; in some cases above 50% foreign equity is allowed.			
2. EGYPT	1	50.0	Not specified; the law refers to a 'reasonable percentage of foreign ownership'.	50%	Up to limit	Not important
3. GHANA – two wheeled motor vehicles	2	66.7	Enterprises must be jointly owned by Ghanaians and foreign investors on terms to be approved by a competent body.	30% 50%	Below Below	n.a. Not important
4. GUINEA – bauxite ore – iron ore	2	100.0	Not available	49% 4%	– –	Not important Very important
5. INDIA – tanned fur skins	1	50.0	Yugoslav MIJV is totally export-oriented. 100% foreign equity is permitted if a firm exports all its production. India is not	49%	Below	Very important

continued on p. 240

TABLE 10.6 continued

	Number of MIJVs*	Share of MIJVs in all entities (%)	Legal limits on foreign equity (at the time of establishment)	Yugoslav share in equity (in %)	Yugoslav share: below or up to legal limits on foreign share	Importance of legal restrictions**
6. IRAN	1	100.0	enthusiastic about foreign investment in this field. Exact data not available, but there are indications that only 50% or less of foreign ownership is permitted.			
7. JORDAN – trade	1	100.0	49%	49%	Up to limit	n.a.
8. KENYA – pharmaceuticals	2	66.7	No specific regulations; wholly-owned foreign ventures are permitted, but the state insists on 'reasonable domestic participation'. Keynesian firms' participation in Joint Ventures tends to range from 35% to 50%.	33%	Below	Not important
– clothing				33%	Below	Not important
9. LIBYA – civil engineering	2	100.0	49%	40%	Below	Very important
– civil engineering				49%	Up to limit	Important
10. MEXICO – metal working	2	100.0	49%, except for certain industries. Activities of			

Country / sector	No.*	Equity limit (Yugoslav MIJVs are not in these exempted areas.)	%		Importance**
machinery					
– electric power equipment and switchgear			19%	Below	Important
11. MOROCCO	1	100.0	49%	Up to limit	Important
– trade		50%	37.5%	Below	Important
12. NIGERIA	6	100.0			
– pharmaceuticals		60%	50%	Below	Less important
– paints		40%	40%	Up to limit	n.a.
– civil engineering		40%	40%	Up to limit	Important
– civil engineering		40%	40%	Up to limit	Very important
– trade		40%	40%	Up to limit	n.a.
– transport		40%	40%	Up to limit	Not important
13. UGANDA	1	100.0			
– trade		No limits (100%)	40%	Below	Not important
14. TUNISIA	2	100.0			
– meat preparations		100%. Companies producing for the domestic market usually have majority Tunisian equity.	35%	Up to limit	Very important
– trade		No limits (100%)	50%	Up to limit	n.a.
15. ZAMBIA	1	20.0			
– civil engineering			49%	Below	Not important
TOTAL for 15 developing countries	26	76.5			
TOTAL for all developing countries	26	47.3			

* Minority-owned joint ventures.
** On the establishment of a MIJV from the Yugoslav investor's viewpoint.

which the setting up of the joint venture represented a 'logical step' in the evolution of their economic cooperation with their LDC partner. For those investors who did not invest up to the legal limit, previous cooperation was crucial in the decision to take up a minority equity; conversely, Yugoslav firms which invested up to the legal limit perceived their minority share of the equity as 'a compulsory form of investment', suggesting that for these firms minority ownership was a second best strategy. This would also go some way towards explaining the lesser performance of this group of respondents.

To sum up, the decision by Yugoslav investors to take up a minority equity position in LDC joint ventures was strongly influenced by several factors external to the firm: risk diversification, the desire to increase the local partner's commitment, and financial constraints on hard currency resources to finance the foreign investment. The availability of host government incentives was unimportant in the decision to set up the venture. A cross-evaluation of the performance of Yugoslav minority-owned joint ventures in LDCs and of the factors which impacted on ownership patterns revealed the following trends: first, minority joint ventures, particularly in industrial production, stand better chances of success if they are the logical step in the evolution of ongoing business cooperation between the partners; second, the decision to set up a minority joint venture in order to take advantage of host government incentives is generally ill-conceived, suggesting that such inducements have at best only a marginal effect on ventures' operations and performance. Thirdly, the choice of a minority joint venture as a 'last resort', namely because other forms of direct investment are not permitted, is unlikely to result in satisfactory performance. Finally, minority joint ventures can be an effective instrument in diversifying risk, increasing the local partner's involvement and reducing financial commitment, provided other objectives, such as appropriate control and managerial influence, are met.

10.6 PROBLEMS AND REASONS FOR DIVESTMENT

It came as no surprise that Yugoslav firms as relative newcomers to foreign investment in LDCs have been and are still confronted with a number of problems. Although some of our sample firms have recorded encouraging results, in other cases results have been below expectations. Table 10.7 summarises our findings. The most pressing

TABLE 10.7   *Major Problems of Yugoslav enterprises in developing countries*

	Average score (*)	Share of interviewed firms indicating individual problem as very important or important (in %)
1. *Insufficient elaboration of the project at the pre-investment stage*	2.60	50.0
a. Inadequate pre-investment analysis	3.05	30.0
b. Insufficient analysis of host country legislation and other regulations	3.20	25.0
c. Insufficient or inadequate analysis of future economic and political developments in host country	2.60	40.0
d. Inadequate analysis of natural resources and other local conditions	2.95	30.0
e. Inadequate analysis of existing local capacities and competitive situation	2.85	45.0
f. Inadequate analysis of political risk	2.90	35.0
g. Wrong estimation of local market's absorption capacity	3.20	30.0
h. Inadequate and insufficient information	3.45	10.0
2. *Infrastructural constraints*	3.45	20.0
3. *Inadequate production orientation of investment*	3.30	25.0
4. *Problems arising from institutional and legal framework in Yugoslavia*	1.95	85.0
a. Long and expensive administration procedures	1.85	75.0
b. Inadequate treatment of Yugoslav imports from Yugoslav enterprises in developing countries	2.70	50.0
c. Rigid and inadequate treatment of Yugoslav enterprises in developing countries in general	2.20	65.0
5. *Problems arising from institutional and legal framework in host country*	1.75	90.0
a. Import restrictions set by host country	2.00	70.0
b. Restrictions on profit repatriation	1.90	70.0
c. Long administrative procedures	2.55	50.0
d. Frequent changes in the legislation	2.80	40.0
e. Difficulties in interpreting legislation	3.50	5.0
6. *Financial problems*	2.25	65.0

continued on p. 244

TABLE 10.7	(*continued*)

	Average score (*)	Share of interviewed firms indicating individual problem as very important or important (in %)
a. Financing of equity capital	2.50	60.0
b. Financing of working assets	2.05	75.0
c. Restrictions on financing of Yugoslav exports to enterprises abroad	2.75	35.0
d. Financing of pre-investment activities	3.15	25.0
7. *Cadre problems*	2.35	60.0
a. Lack of Yugoslav cadres and/or insufficient interest of Yugoslav cadres prepared to work in developing countries	3.00	25.0
b. Lack of adequate local labour force and experts	2.15	70.0
c. Problem of securing adequate income for Yugoslav workers abroad	2.60	40.0
d. Linguistic barriers	2.30	40.0
e. Excessive fluctuations in Yugoslav cadres	3.40	15.0
f. Lack of legal, financial and accounting cadres is more pressing than the lack of technical and commercial cadres	3.15	25.0
8. *Organisational problems*	2.70	30.0
a. Inadequate organisation of Yugoslav firm	2.90	40.0
b. Internal administration in Yugoslav firm is unable to handle requirements arising from operating an enterprise abroad	2.65	45.0
c. Organisational problems of enterprise abroad	2.80	35.0
9. *Marketing and supply problems*	2.45	55.0
a. Non-competitive prices	2.75	40.0
b. Inadequate conditions for realising business operations	3.05	30.0
c. Problems associated with input supplies	2.65	45.0
d. Inadequacy of local inputs	3.15	25.0
10. *Problems of costs*	2.55	50.0
a. Excessive overhead costs	2.85	35.0
b. Necessary investment in infra-structure and related facilities	2.60	45.0
11. *Problems related to the relationship between Yugoslav and local partners*		

TABLE 10.7   (*continued*)

	Average score (*)	Share of interviewed firms indicating individual problem as very important or important (in %)
(for example, with regard to profit or loss distribution)	3.40	15.0
12. *Problems arising from applied technology*	3.80	5.0
13. *Management problems*	3.10	35.0

Source: Interviews of Yugoslav investors

* Average scores were derived as follows: (1) very important; (2) important; (3) less important; (4) irrelevant.

problems are linked to the institutional and legal frameworks, both in the host countries (listed by 90 per cent of respondents as 'important' or 'very important') and in Yugoslavia itself (85 per cent). Other factors listed include financial difficulties (65 per cent), problems with cadres (60 per cent), followed by marketing and supply problems (55 per cent), costs (50 per cent), and insufficient research at the pre-investment stage (50 per cent). At the other end of the spectrum, it seems that problems arising from disagreements with local partners and related to technology transfer were negligible. The preponderance of institutional and legal factors suggests that respondents have tended to minimise their own responsibility for failure whilst exaggerating the influence of external factors. On the other hand, the ranking of problems in Table 10.7 has a bias for 'reasonably successful' firms. Investors who withdrew from LDCs declined to take part in our survey, and it can be assumed that such factors as lack of information, inadequate pre-investment assessment and wrong product orientation would have figured highly on their lists of problems. The pre-investment stage is one of the weakest aspects of Yugoslav investment strategy in LDCs. Bearing in mind, as some estimates suggest, that the cost of information may account for up to 70 per cent of overall production costs, the quality and timing of information cannot be underestimated. Our sample responses suggest that Yugoslav investors are not fully aware of this prerequisite. The case of a Yugoslav minority-owned joint venture producing pharmaceuticals in Kenya illustrates the negative impact of insufficient information on product choice and overall performance. The Yugoslav partner produced a high quality pharmaceutical unaware that Kenya had no registration procedure for drugs, which resulted in the influx of cheaper substitutes with resulting heavy losses. Other comments showed that the information was too general and inadequately processed, or that the data collecting system was inadequate. Badly worded contracts frequently drawn up by inexperienced lawyers or engineers were another cause of poor performance.

It is also pertinent to point out that the majority of divestments have occurred in trade and construction-related investments. By definition, these two sectors are oriented to short-term operations; in the construction industry, Yugoslav firms have found that a local representation – in the form of a local enterprise – often helped secure a large construction project. As the objective of such ventures often consists of a one-off project, it is not infrequent for a firm to shut down operations on completion. Divestment in this sector is thus frequently inbuilt in the initial conception of the investment.

In industrial sectors where success normally depends on stability and long-term cooperation, fluctuations in investment flows have also been observed. Existing joint ventures are discontinued but new ones are set up. Thus, the relatively high rate of divestments is compensated for by new investments, resulting in a considerable proportion of enterprises being of recent origin.

Finally, Yugoslav direct investment in LDCs being a relatively new phenomenon, laws and regulations are in general ill-suited to this type of activity, and frequently set constraints on operations. Several respondents reported the harmful effects of institutional delays on business operations, which depend for their success on a high degree of flexibility and adaptation.

10.7 CONCLUDING REMARKS

Although recent studies on Joint Ventures in LDCs have focused on the multinational enterprise/host country interface (Wells 1977, 1981, 1983; Lecraw 1977; Lall 1983; Kumar and Kim 1984), it is our belief that the ongoing changes in host country regulations and resulting responses by multinationals call for additional research. Nowhere is this more evident than in the emergence from comparative isolation over the past two decades of East European and Yugoslav multinationals, which until now have received little serious academic attention.

An attempt has been made in this paper to raise and answer a number of questions about direct investment by Yugoslav firms in LDCs. In response to the first question – what are the major variables which help to explain the growth of Yugoslav direct investments in LDCs – we noted that the economic decentralisation process initiated by the 1965 Reforms had spurred enterprises to integrate more fully with the world economy. However, unlike their counterparts in the West, Yugoslav multinationals do not manufacture new or exclusive products, but rely on adaptations of standard technologies. This explained the under-representation of Yugoslav investors in manufacturing ventures in Western markets, where they lacked the necessary firm-specific advantages to internalise operations. Yugoslav government policies have also played a role in defining the objectives of overseas investments, although this could not be specifically quantified at the level of the firm.

Our second question addressed itself to the motives behind Yugoslav investments in LDCs; it was found that firms were predominantly motivated by market considerations with the objective of boosting exports to the host countries.

The third set of questions – related to ownership characteristics – established the Yugoslav investor's preference for a minority share in joint ventures: Yugoslavia's chronic scarcity of foreign exchange explains the tendency to invest – barring a few exceptions – in small-scale projects and to enlist local capital participation.

Finally, although the reasons for divestment were diverse, the most persistent problems arose from administrative and legal delays in both home and host countries.

Notes

The authors would like to thank Professor Carl McMillan and the anonymous referees for comments on an earlier draft.

1. *Source*: Federal Secretariat for Foreign Trade, Belgrade.

11 The Evolution of Multinationals from a Small Economy: A Study of Swedish Firms in Asia

Raj Aggarwal and Pervez N. Ghauri

11.1 INTRODUCTION

Swedish firms have been active in international business for almost a hundred years. Firms like AGA, Alfa Laval, and Ericsson have had manufacturing subsidiaries abroad since the 1890s. Firms like Swedish Match had established manufacturing operations in far away markets such as India, Pakistan, and Thailand as early as the 1920s. Most of the literature on multinational firms tends to focus on the nature and characteristics of traditional multinationals from large countries such as the United States. However, studies of small-country multinationals have burgeoned in recent years and prior studies have examined foreign operations of firms from small developed economies as well as the foreign operations of firms based in the developing countries.[1] Few of these studies have focused on the development of a conceptual framework that may be useful in understanding the evolution of multinational firms from a small developed economy such as Sweden. This chapter contributes to this gap in the literature by developing a product life-cycle-based conceptual framework for understanding the evolution of multinational firms from small countries and by applying that framework to examine the evolution of the Asian operations of Swedish firms.[2]

Prior research on Swedish firms' international strategies and activities has covered many areas. An early study (Swedenborg, 1979) examined the determinants of inter-firm differences in foreign production among Swedish firms. Another major study (Clegg, 1987) compared Swedish FDI and its determinants with FDI from the

USA, Japan, the UK and West Germany. In the early 1980s an official committee was appointed in Sweden to study the impact of inward and outward FDI on its society and it submitted its report in 1983. Another study (Hornell and Vahlne, 1986) analysed the impact of FDI on Swedish society. Other studies have dealt with the internationalisation process, the export behaviour of Swedish firms, and on their activities in Western Europe, linkage effects, and international business negotiations.[3] However, none of the prior studies of Swedish FDI have examined the evolutionary phenomena of the growth of the foreign subsidiaries to become independent of the parent firm.

In this chapter the operating characteristics and the recent evolution of Swedish MNCs are examined using a framework based on the product life-cycle theory of foreign direct investment. The implications of this theory for the evolution and growth of multinationals from small developed countries are used to explain the growth and nature of the Asian operations of Swedish multinationals. Statistical data on the level of foreign investment in each region or country at the firm or the industry level is unfortunately unavailable for Swedish firms.[4] Thus, this study is based on selected primary data gathered from Swedish firms having wholly- or partly-owned subsidiaries in Thailand, Pakistan, the Philippines and Indonesia. The data collection was done through personal interviews with the area managers at the head office of each firm in Sweden and with the managing director of each subsidiary in the respective foreign country. In some cases, the marketing managers of the subsidiaries were also interviewed. Because of the limited nature of data availability, this study perforce cannot be considered as definitive but rather as exploratory. However, there is good reason to believe that its conclusions regarding the independence of foreign affiliates of Swedish MNCs are likely to be overly conservative as they are based on data regarding Asian affiliates. Affiliates in large economies like the US are likely to be, if anything, even more independent. Thus, the findings of this study have much significance for future research.

This chapter is organised as follows. The next section reviews briefly the factors that influence foreign direct investment (FDI), the life-cycle model of the evolution of a multinational firm, and their implications for a small-country multinational. Section 11.3 is an examination of the nature of foreign operations of Swedish firms in the context of this framework. The chapter ends with some observations.

11.2 UNDERSTANDING THE FOREIGN DIRECT INVESTMENT PROCESS

This section first examines the factors that influence FDI. Second, it describes the life-cycle theory of firm evolution, and lastly it develops a framework based on these factors and the life-cycle theory to understand the evolution of a small-country multinational.

Factors influencing foreign investment

A multinational corporation (MNC) is a firm that controls resources in two or more countries. FDI is the use of long-term capital flows or its local formation to acquire control of productive capabilities by a foreign enterprise.[5] The resources and factor inputs transferred to accomplish this may be tangible as well as an intangible combination of technology, management skills, production processes, financial resources, and other factors scarce in the local economy.[6] There can be several reasons and motivations for a firm to undertake FDI including the need to overcome restrictions (imposed by local governments) such as tariffs, quotas and other discriminatory taxes and policies. However, in our view, consistent with the eclectic theory of FDI, MNCs undertake FDI as an integrated part of their international strategy.

In order to understand better the role of FDI in the overall strategy of the firm, we have organised the following brief discussion of these reasons for FDI into three categories, namely, factors related to market imperfections with financial market imperfections as a special case, behavioural and cultural influences.

Market imperfections and FDI

Imperfections in product markets and the need to respond to the advantages of foreign operations of competitors are two factors that may influence FDI by a firm.

Monopolistic Advantage and Internalisation Theories: These theories maintain that the existence of imperfections in the markets for factors of production result in the internalisation of such transactions by a firm (Buckley and Casson, 1976). These internalised markets may give such a firm a monopolistic advantage, usually unique technological or managerial skills generally developed initially for home use, to more than overcome the dual disadvantage of being a foreigner and the costs associated with operating at an economic (geographical, political and cultural) distance. Such MNCs often start with exporting before they decide to invest directly in a foreign market, especially since barriers to trade can cause technology to be traded through FDI.[7]

Market Structure and Protection of Markets: MNCs that engage in FDI are often characterised by their large size, by high expenditures for new product development and on product differentiation and other forms of non-price competition, and such firms generally belong to industries characterised by a few mutually interdependent firms in an oligopolistic relationship.[8] In such cases, when local markets have been fully exploited, firms in the oligopoly recognise that a firm going abroad will develop size, financing and other advantages that will help it dominate its home and foreign markets. A great deal of FDI may therefore be defensive in nature and may be taking place as a result of the 'bandwagon' effect.

The Eclectic Theory: As propounded by Dunning (1980 and 1981), this theory attempts to combine the various influences discussed above into an integrated theory of FDI combining the role of technology, imperfect competition and internalisation. It contends that firms undertake FDI as part of their overall business strategy whenever and wherever they derive the most from internalising activities in response to market forces and structures. Therefore it provides a framework in which to incorporate all the motives for FDI.

Financial market imperfections as reasons for FDI

Financial reasons for undertaking FDI can arise because of imperfections in financial markets and can be subdivided into three major categories, interest rate differences, diversification of assets, and investor preferences for strong currencies.[9]

Interest Rate Differences: This theory contends that interest rate and rate of return differences between countries are the causes of international capital movements. An MNC can use its access to efficient and free global capital markets to exploit opportunities in markets and economies that have limited availability of capital. This theory, however, does not explain the role of MNCs adequately as it limits itself to the explanation of how and from where firms decide to obtain the capital needed to finance their global plans, and it does not say much about the need for managerial control of production capabilities that is involved in FDI.

Portfolio Theory: In general terms, a firm that can operate in many different economies that are out of phase with each other is more likely to encounter opportunities for diversification than a comparable domestic firm. In many cases, individual investors are less likely than an MNC to have the knowledge, skills and opportunities for international diversification. MNCs can, thus, add value by engaging in FDI. One of the implications of this theory is that the relevant measure of the riskiness of a foreign investment is not its riskiness as an independent investment, but is the extent to which the addition of such a foreign investment changes the overall riskiness of the MNC.[10]

Currency Preference Theory: An MNC based in a country with such a strong and stable currency, will have a lower cost of capital because of investor preferences, seigniorage advantages, and lower currency risk as its assets are denominated in the preferred strong currency of the parent company. Another reason for investors to prefer assets in a strong currency may be a result of the greater efficiency of the capital markets in that currency and the existence of an efficient and large financial centre.[11]

Behavioural and cultural influences on FDI

Imperfections in human/managerial markets and international differences in behavioural and social characteristics can also influence FDI. The influence of these factors on FDI may be felt through organisational, social or environmental forces.[12]

Organisational Behaviour: Local market growth is often regulated and the size of the home market limited by anti-trust laws and other restrictions. Thus, firms seeking continued growth have to expand abroad. Other aspects of organisational behaviour, for example, the personal goals, attitudes and ambitions of the chief executive or of the head of an international division, may also encourage firm internationalisation.

FDI as Modern Imperialism: Many economists believe that FDI has been used by the advanced, industrialised nations to continue their imperialistic control over other, weaker nations. International control of local economies is sought to ensure sources of raw materials and to ensure captive markets for produced goods. Moreover, FDI may be used to develop and perpetuate an international division of labour and other forms of political and economic dependence. Although widely criticised, a milder view of this theory suggests that because of the natural identity of interests between the MNC and its home government, and because it is in the interest of the MNC to have freedom of movement internationally, home governments of MNCs are likely to help create and preserve an open and integrated international system.

11.3 AN EVOLUTIONARY VIEW OF FIRM INTERNATIONALISATION

As the above discussion indicates, different factors contribute to FDI and there can be many reasons for the decision by a given firm to engage in FDI. While the product life-cycle theory has been criticised by some as an inadequate and limited theory for explaining the determinants of FDI,[13] we feel that it is useful for understanding the evolution of the *process* of engaging in FDI.

The Product Life-Cycle Theory

The product life-cycle (PLC) theory of firm internationalisation has generally been associated with a transfer of technology from one country to another. However, here we focus on its role in explaining the successive introduction, sale, production and export of a product in a country. The PLC theory has been presented in different versions by different authors. Vernon (1966) presented a four-phase cycle to explain international trade, while Wells (1972) used a five-phase cycle. More recently, Aggarwal (1984) extended the PLC theory into a seven-phase cycle in an attempt to understand it more clearly. In this paper we apply Aggarwal's seven-phase international PLC to the internationalisation of Swedish firms (see Table 11.1).

Restrictions on the flow of information across national boundaries and relative factor endowments indicate where innovations of new products can normally be expected to take place. It should be noted here that the factor endowments optimal for the innovation of different products may be different and product innovations may take place in many different countries. According to the PLC theory, these new products are then successively demanded and used in other countries that may be less developed or have different initial endowments. The internationalisation of a firm's activities can be considered to be a set of sequential stages in the life-cycle of the product

TABLE 11.1   *The seven phases of the product life cycle theory*

Phase I	– Product Invented (or Innovated). No Domestic Sales. No Export Sales.
Phase II	– Domestic Sales Begin. No Export Sales. Production for Domestic Sales Increases from Pilot Plant to Full Production. Volume Dependent only on Domestic Demand (and/or Capacity).
Phase III	– Domestic Sales Continue to Grow at a Decreasing Rate. Export Sales to Similar Countries and LDCs Begin. No Overseas Production.
Phase IV	– Domestic Sales Level Off. Production Begins Overseas in Similar Countries. Innovating Country Continues some Exports while LDC Sales Begin to be Supplied from Other Countries.
Phase V	– Domestic Sales Continue. Sales in Similar Countries now from Local Production. Innovating Country Exports to LDCs Displaced by Exports and FDI from these Other Countries.
Phase VI	– Domestic Sales by the Innovating Firm Decline. Other Countries Begin Exporting to and Eventually Producing in the Innovating Country. Other Country Exports to LDCs Being Displaced by Local Manufacturers.
Phase VII	– Domestic Sales by the Innovating Company Reach a Minimum. LDCs Export to and Produce in the Innovating and Other Countries.

Source: Aggarwal, Raj, (1984), 'The Strategic Challenge of Third World Multinationals: A New Stage of the Product Life Cycle of Multinationals', in Richard N. Farmer, (ed.), *Advances in International Comparative Management*, Volume 1 (Greenwich, CT: JAI Press), pp. 103–22.

or process it develops initially for sale in its home country. Thus, the first phase of the PLC is that in response to domestic factor endowments and market conditions, product innovations take place in a country such as the US or Sweden.

The second phase, domestic sales growth, is critically important in the life of the product. During this stage the product undergoes test marketing, redesigning and re-engineering, and production scale-up. In case the product is not accepted in the domestic market, the question of an international PLC usually does not arise. If, however, the product is accepted in the home market and the domestic sales volume grows, the third phase of PLC starts. In this phase domestic sales continue to grow but most likely at a decreasing rate. Exports to other similar countries and perhaps even to some less developed countries (LDCs) begin. All of the production is, however, still in the home country where the innovation originated. Exports to other countries are based mainly on similarities in markets, the product becoming cheaper due to economies of scale with the increasing demand, and because the income levels of some of these countries may be increasing.

In the fourth stage, all of the competing firms in an industry in the innovating country or other similar countries by this time have gained enough knowledge of the product to start their own manufacturing facilities. Moreover, firms in these countries may have developed similar or substitutable products which compete with the original product. In addition, by this time foreign governments would have introduced tariffs or quotas against imports in order to encourage manufacture of the product in their countries. Thus, the innovating firm starts manufacturing facilities in other countries with similar factor endowments and markets. In this fourth phase, thus, the firm starts producing in some foreign markets where exports have stopped growing or even started declining. However, exports may continue to grow in other markets and foreign production in such markets need not be considered yet.

In the fifth stage, exports to non-producing countries are now being undertaken from plants in countries other than the innovating country. Markets in a number of countries become sufficiently large and local production initially through FDI and later by local firms seems justified as it would not entail small-scale manufacturing. In the sixth stage, markets in more importing countries grow and it now becomes feasible to start manufacturing the product in countries with factor endowments and levels of development much different from the country of innovation. In the later parts of this stage considerable FDI and product innovation and adaptation to local conditions may take place in these new countries. Production technology is well known by now and costs are so low in these countries that the transport and tariff protection of the innovating country can be overcome and production in the latter displaced by imports of the product from these other countries. In the final stage, most countries become net importers of the product and only countries that have the lowest comparative costs produce, export, and engage in FDI to supply not only the innovating country but also most other countries.

PLC theory and smaller-country multinationals

As our discussion of the PLC theory indicates, the process of FDI as undertaken by firms in the larger developed countries is likely to be repeated by firms from other smaller developed countries and eventually by firms from the LDCs. As these firms grow in their ability to develop, acquire and use sophisticated technologies, they become more likely to engage in FDI. It can therefore be expected that MNCs from the larger countries would face increasing competition from their counterparts based in smaller economies.

In the post-Second World War era, global economic and technological leadership has so far been provided by the United States of America. The US has used its dominance to encourage an environment of free trade and, despite several crises such as the oil crisis, world trade has increased dramatically. In 1960, world trade amounted to $136 billion. By 1980 this volume of trade had increased to over $2 trillion and the 1988 volume of international trade was estimated to be $5 trillion; a large proportion of this trade is carried out by firms engaged in FDI.[14] As Europe and Japan rebuilt their economies, American MNCs began to face competition from European and Japanese MNCs.[15]

The percentage of United States firms in the world's hundred largest industrial corporations is, therefore, declining (69 per cent in 1960, 59 per cent in 1970 and 45 per cent in 1980) while the proportion of firms from West European countries, Japan and other countries is increasing.[16] Moreover, as indicated by the PLC theory, European and Japanese firms are now being challenged by firms from Third-World countries. According to Wells (1983), in 1981 there were more than one thousand developing country firms which were operating in more than one country.

Another implication of the PLC theory of multinationals is that in the final stages, when production has moved completely away from the innovating country, the parent company in multinational firms based in the smaller economies, may have to share its influence with its foreign subsidiaries at an earlier stage of evolution than parent companies of multinational firms from large developed economies. A factor contributing to this phenomenon is that smaller MNCs are less likely to find it economic to develop and implement highly centralised control systems. Section 11.4 is an attempt to examine the pattern and recent trends in Swedish FDI in light of the above discussion of the PLC theory.

11.4 INTERNATIONAL GROWTH OF SWEDISH FIRMS

In the first part of this section the nature and growth of Swedish FDI is detailed while the second part discusses some recent developments and the continuing evolution of the foreign operations of Swedish firms.

The Nature and Growth of Swedish FDI

Some of the larger Swedish firms and banks were already known for their innovations and international growth before the two world wars.[17] However, Swedish involvement in international trade and investment increased greatly after the Second World War. Sweden was not involved in the world wars, was rich in raw materials, and had a strong tradition of innovation. Swedish firms found an easy market in Europe where countries reduced trade restrictions and needed Swedish raw materials and other products to rebuild their infrastructure after the war.

Recent Trends: Sweden emerged as an industrially advanced country and in the mid-1960s it had the highest per capita income. The 1950s and the 1960s saw increasing internationalisation of Swedish firms. In 1965 82 Swedish firms had over 800 overseas manufacturing and sales subsidiaries with more than 170 000 employees. The 1970s and 1980s were, however, turning points for Swedish multinational growth. The most important Swedish industries, such as forest products, steel and ship-building, began to face increasing competition from emerging nations such as Japan, Brazil and South Korea.

In retrospect it can be seen that the industrial rebuilding of Europe and Japan, the great increase in wages in Sweden (highest per capita income), an overvaluation of the Swedish currency, and the emergence of MNCs from the developing countries were important factors contributing to this decline in the international competitiveness of Swedish firms. As the ability of Swedish firms to serve foreign markets through exports declined, they had increasingly to engage in FDI to protect markets developed with exports from Sweden. Thus, as shown in Table 11.2, consistent with the PLC theory, FDI by Swedish firms increased greatly during the 1970s and the 1980s.

Geographic Distribution: In terms of the extent of geographic spread, there are two groups of firms. First, there are those firms which started their international activities a long time ago. This group includes firms such as Agfa, Alfa Laval, SKI, ASEA, and Swedish Match who now have operations all over the globe. The second group

TABLE 11.2   *Swedish foreign direct investment (in billions of Swedish Krona)*

Year	Inward	Outward
1975	2.0	0.53
1976	2.8	0.47
1977	3.8	0.65
1978	2.6	0.74
1979	3.3	0.70
1980	3.0	1.29
1981	5.0	1.10
1982	6.9	1.78
1983	9.2	1.48
1984	10.6	2.76
1985	14.3	5.37
1986	25.1	6.06
1987*	10.5	1.87

* Up to June
Source: *Kredit och Valutaoversikt*, various issues, Central Bank of Sweden.

consists of those firms which started internationalising after the Second World War and includes firms such as Volvo, Electrolux and Saab, which are still expanding geographically.

A major part of Swedish FDI is directed towards Europe, North America and Latin America. This overall geographic distribution is consistent with the PLC theory as firms try to establish their subsidiaries in nearby markets (EEC), in large markets (USA), and in markets with trade barriers (Latin America). Table 11.3 summarises the geographic distribution of Swedish FDI in recent years.

As indicated by the PLC theory, FDI by Swedish firms in manufacturing has generally followed the development of sales in a region or country. For example, in Indonesia Electrolux started with a sales agency which was converted into a sales subsidiary and has recently started manufacturing locally. The same firm has also chosen other ways to expand internationally. In the case of the Philippines, the firm started with a manufacturing subsidiary. In North America, after buying the American vacuum cleaner maker, National Union Electric (with the 'Eureka' brand) in 1974, Electrolux acquired Tappan in 1979, Zanussi in 1985, White Consolidated in 1986, and Roper in 1988. All US operations of Electrolux are centralised under the White Consolidated name.[18]

A number of other Swedish firms such as ASEA, Atlas Copco,

TABLE 11.3   *Swedish foreign direct investment by areas of the world*

Region	1981%	1982%	1983%	1984%	1985%	1986%	1987%	1988%*
Africa	0.9	1.1	0.6	0.9	10.0	1.2	0.1	--
Australia	1.3	1.5	1.5	0.5	0.3	0.7	0.6	0.1
Asia	6.1	3.7	3.2	3.5	3.7	2.2	1.6	0.4
Europe	52.1	51.6	58.8	67.3	46.4	45.9	74.0	88.6
Latin America	8.2	12.7	11.8	3.8	6.0	2.4	3.3	2.4
North America	31.4	29.5	24.2	24.1	33.6	47.7	20.4	8.5
Total	100.0%	100.0%	100.0%	100.0%	100.0%	100.0%	100.0%	100.0%

-- = less than 0.1%
* = January-September
Source: *Kredit och Valutaoversikt*, Central Bank of Sweden, Stockholm, Various
Issues.

Sandvik, Nitro Nobel, and Volvo have also gone international in this traditional way. They started their activities first in the nearby markets of Europe and later went to South East Asia. Moreover, they followed the traditional modes of internationalisation as they started first with a sales agency which was then converted into a sales subsidiary and only later started manufacturing locally.

Role of Firm Size: Swedish MNCs are generally specialised firms and world leaders in their product areas. In the market for specialised products, quality, knowledge of the market, customers' needs, and service are more important competitive strategies than price or low cost factors of production. The foreign operations of large firms such as Alfa Laval, Electrolux, Ericsson, Sandvik, SKF, Swedish Match and Volvo are good examples.

The high cost of Swedish labour seems to have influenced the decision to engage in FDI only for Swedish firms with products having the lowest technological content. As implied by our discussion of the PLC above, for most Swedish firms undertaking FDI, factors such as import restrictions, high import taxes and duties, high transport costs, and the size of the market seem to have been more important than labour costs. However, in the textile industry it is easier to find support for the argument that FDI was influenced by cheaper production costs overseas. Swedenborg (1979) contends that for the more technically advanced products, Swedish FDI has been lower as such products could be exported directly from Sweden.

Table 11.4 provides a list of the 30 largest Swedish firms ranked in terms of their total sales. While these firms are quite large even when compared to other international firms, they face increasing levels of

TABLE 11.4 *Largest Swedish firms in terms of 1986 sales (millions of SEK)*

Rank	Name	Sales	Foreign Sales	%FS
1	Volvo	84,090	70,604	84
2	Electrolux	53,090	43,434	82
3	Asea	46,031	33,447	73
4	Saab-Scania	35,222	23,247	66
5	Ericsson	32,278	25,177	78
6	KF	29,476	4,185	14
7	ICA	28,469	na	--
8	Televerket	26,340	na	--
9	Carnegie	20,411	na	--
10	SKF	20,232	19,220	95
11	SJ	16,431	na	--
12	Skanska	16,103	2,632	16
13	SCA	15,303	10,406	68
14	Procordia	15,299	4,950	32
15	Nordstjernan	15,251	7,000	46
16	Vattenfall	15,207	na	--
17	Stora	13,238	6,863	52
18	SSAB	13,010	5,204	40
19	Sandvik	12,721	11,652	92
20	Boliden	12,384	6,232	50
21	Postverket	11,956	na	--
22	Systembolaget	11,922	na	--
23	A Johanson & Co.	11,543	na	--
24	Nobel Industries	11,535	6,865	60
25	Esselte	11,251	7,421	66
26	Swedish Match	10,912	7,976	73
27	Flakt (Asea)	10,352	8,075	78
28	Atlas Copco	10,351	na	--
29	Alfa-Laval	10,300	na	--
30	ABV	9,661	1,700	18

na: not available.
%FS: Foreign Sales as a Percent of Total Sales.
SEK: Swedish Krona.
Source: *Veckans Affarer* nr. 38/17 (September 1987) and Company Annual Reports.

financial risks as each new product takes longer in the development stage but has a shorter life-cycle in the market. Thus, most of these firms work on special products for relatively small international market niches where quality and product characteristics are more important. According to Jagren (1981) a number of Swedish firms

TABLE 11.5 *Employment abroad in foreign subsidiaries of Swedish firms*

Year	1965	1970	1978	1981	1985
Number of employees (thousands)	171	222	301	326	329
Percent of employment in manufacturing industry in Sweden	18	24	33	39	43

Source: Government Proposition 1986/87, Central Bank of Sweden, 74/3, p. 299.

specialise in industrial products and complex systems with quality and technical sophistication and not price as the dominant marketing characteristics.

The large part of Swedish FDI is undertaken by the larger Swedish firms (about 30 firms) such as Volvo and Electrolux. Among the firms with more than 500 employees abroad, the largest 30 firms have between 2000 and 60 000 employed out of Sweden. Some of these large firms now have 85 per cent of their employees abroad. According to Swedenborg (1979), approximately one third of the 118 Swedish firms having production abroad, accounted for 90 per cent of the employees of Swedish firms outside Sweden. Table 11.5 shows the trend in employment by Swedish establishments abroad.

Importance of Reinvestments and Acquisitions: As the data in Table 11.6 indicate, reinvestment in already existing markets and acquisitions of suppliers, competitors and distributors has become important in recent years. For example, Swedish Match had two factories in different parts of the Philippines. In 1977 it sold off some of the factories and instead acquired one of its suppliers as it considered it more important to have a secure source of inputs and raw materials than to have a bigger market share. The importance of acquisitions has also greatly increased in the last two decades, as illustrated by the data in Table 11.7. Forsgren (1988) concluded that most acquisitions by Swedish firms have taken place in the countries where these companies were already well established.

Impact of International Expansion on Domestic Growth: As indicated by the prior discussion of the theories of FDI, there has been considerable growth in Swedish firms engaged in FDI as compared to the firms which are not involved in FDI. Not only have Swedish MNCs expanded their international activities but they have also

TABLE 11.6   *Reinvested profits in Swedish foreign direct investments*

Region	Millions of SEK		Industry	Percent
USA	780	(17.0%)	Mechanical	48
Northern Europe	570	(12.4%)	Chemical	11
EEC	2020	(43.9%)	Paper & Pulp	15
OECD	3270	(71.1%)	Financial Institutions	7
Others	1330	(28.9%)	Social Services	4
Total	4600	(100.0%)	Others	15

SEK: Swedish Krona
Source: *Kredit och Valutaoversikt*, Central Bank of Sweden, Stockholm
   Various Issues.

TABLE 11.7   *Acquisitions of foreign production companies by Swedish companies (with more than 500 employees abroad in 1982)*

Period	Number
1971–1973	39
1974–1976	55
1977–1979	64
1980–1982	101
1983–1985	113

Source: Forsgren, M., (1988), *Managing the Internationalization Process: The Swedish Case*, London: Routledge.

grown in their home markets. According to Jagren and Horwitz (1984) one of the factors contributing to this domestic growth is the supply of components to their foreign subsidiaries. Swedish firms that have developed expertise in managing FDI are also well positioned for further economic growth. In recent years such Swedish firms have increased their FDI in new areas that are opening up, such as China, and in traditional areas such as North America and European countries partly in anticipation of the scheduled 1992 integration of the EEC.[19]

As the above discussion indicates, most Swedish FDI is consistent with traditional theories of the MNC. However, as hypothesised by Aggarwal (1984) in his discussion of the life-cycle of multinational firms, and as implied by our discussion of the PLC above, Swedish MNCs are also beginning to exhibit some of the characteristics of MNCs that are in the late stages of their life-cycles. The next section reviews additional evidence in this regard.

Recent developments in the life-cycle of Swedish FDI

As hypothesised earlier, Swedish FDI has begun to exhibit some aspects of the later stages of the life-cycle of MNCs. In particular, FDI is now being undertaken by smaller Swedish companies, some Swedish MNCs' foreign operations are becoming quite important, and in some cases Swedish MNCs are becoming polycentric groups with only a weak influence by the headquarters. These trends in the evolution of Swedish MNCs are supported by primary data about their Asian operations.

FDI by Small Swedish Firms: The number of small Swedish firms engaged in FDI has increased in recent years. Contributing to this development is the increasing specialisation of international trade and the increasing sophistication of Swedish industry. In a research project undertaken on behalf of STU (Styrelsen for Teknik Utveckling) by Elisson (1982), it was found that a typical newly established Swedish firm after ten years has a turnover of around SEK 20 million, sells 80 per cent of its production out of the country, and has 5 per cent of its employees working out of Sweden. After 14 years such a firm has a turnover of SEK 80 million and has 30 per cent of its employees working out of the country.

The Rise of Foreign Regional Centres in Less Developed Countries: For a number of Swedish multinationals, as forecast by the PLC theory, foreign subsidiaries have become larger than their head office in terms of sales and number of employees. In some cases, a number of subsidiaries have grouped together into a regional network. This is especially popular in South East Asia where a number of Swedish firms have established their regional offices in Singapore. These regional subsidiaries often have their own research and product development programmes and work as independent firms with commercial power rivalling that of their head offices.

Swedish Match, a Swedish international concern with 150 wholly- or partly-owned subsidiaries in about 40 countries, has 75 per cent of its total sales and 55 per cent of its production outside of Sweden. Swedish Match started international production with manufacturing subsidiaries in markets as far away as India, Pakistan and Thailand as early as the 1920s and 1930s. In the early years, the foreign subsidiaries of Swedish Match faced numerous problems in obtaining material of the right quality with reliable delivery schedules from local suppliers. However, they have now succeeded and have developed reliable local suppliers. Although these foreign subsidiaries are fully owned by Swedish Match (except in India, due to government restrictions), they work rather autonomously. They purchase most of their inputs from local markets while the imported material is from international markets such as Germany, Finland, China and Japan. This decentralised approach to the management of foreign operations at Swedish Match is also reflected in the decentralised nature of the finance function which is normally highly centralised in large-country MNCs.[20]

The growth of foreign operations to become large enough to demand independence from the home-country parent may not be smooth and can be accompanied by many conflicts as illustrated by the case of a producer of farm equipment. This company established ten sales subsidiaries in major overseas markets during the 1970s as outlets for its home production. Soon, however, these sales subsidiaries began to modify the parent company's products to adapt them to local demands. This evolved into local production. In some cases, the production facility has led to research facilities for the development of new products adapted to local and regional conditions. Most of these subsidiaries also buy parts and components from local suppliers, especially because of competition in their region from other international companies such as Massey Ferguson, John Deere, International Harvester and Caterpillar. At one time, clearly against the policy of the parent firm, a subsidiary in England was buying 65 per cent of its components and parts from local suppliers. These developments eventually led to conflicts between the parent company and its overseas subsidiaries with regard to sourcing and optimal product mix. The parent company believed that affiliates should preferably purchase from each other. In terms of the product line, the parent company felt that some of the products offered by competitors were at prices and qualities which were hard to beat and, therefore, the parent company wanted to focus its resources and know-how on product lines with higher technological content. However, purchasing policies and product mix strategies of the subsidiaries continued to be dictated by local market considerations.

Similar parent-regional developments are also illustrated by the case of Electrolux's subsidiary in the Philippines. In the beginning (1979), the subsidiary was importing all of its components from the parent company or from affiliated sister companies around the world. As it gained more experience, not only did it start buying from local suppliers but, in fact, it helped local suppliers develop their technical competence so that they could supply to Electrolux. As a result, in

1987 the local subsidiary was buying more than 85 per cent of the components locally. Because of continuing product development at the local subsidiary, the vacuum cleaner manufactured in the Philippines was quite different from the one Electrolux was manufacturing in its subsidiaries in Europe. As an example of how the product was being adapted to the local market, the Philippine vacuum cleaner has reusable dust containers. As an example of differences in product mix, the product category with the second largest sales in the Philippines are water purifiers which are not even sold in the home market.

The case is not much different with the Nobel industries subsidiary in the Philippines. This local subsidiary is now buying almost all of its components and raw materials from local, Japanese and American suppliers. Only a very small part of the input is bought from Sweden. In 1984 the subsidiary started its own Research and Development department and, as the local market was declining in the Philippines, the subsidiary started exporting to nearby countries. This led to some conflicts with sister affiliates of Nobel in the countries where the Philippine subsidiary wanted to export. Eventually, because of this conflict the head office established a sales subsidiary to sell in Indonesia and Thailand, countries where there was no existing Nobel subsidiary.

These are some examples of the growth of independent decision-making among subsidiaries of Swedish MNCs and illustrate factors that influence the evolving nature of these relationships among headquarters and subsidiaries. In addition to the factors discussed above, foreign subsidiaries of Swedish firms often seek trade with other local companies in order to spread the risk on the supplier side. From the parent company's point of view, loyalty means buying from the parent company, or from other units within the group, or at least giving priority to such sources. On the other hand, the subsidiaries have often perceived such loyalty as costly dependence while independence from the parent company appears to offer many benefits to the foreign subsidiaries.

The MNC as a Polycentric Group in Less Developed Countries: As these examples show, it can be contended that the concept of a centre with strong influence on its peripheries is fading away in many Swedish MNCs as they enter the later stages of the PLC. In many MNCs several centres in the same company are emerging.

The South East Asian group of subsidiaries for Tetra Pak, a well known packaging company, is very active and independent of the parent corporation. Tetra Pak has binding contracts that specify that local firms using their machines should buy and use raw material only from Tetra Pak. The packaging material used in these machines throughout South East Asia including Thailand, the Philippines, Malaysia and Indonesia is produced and supplied by Tetra Pak's subsidiary in Singapore. The sales and maintenance subsidiaries in all of these South East Asian countries deal only with the subsidiary in Singapore and not with the parent firm. The 'centre' or parent company for these subsidiaries is, thus, Tetra Pak-Singapore and not the parent company in Sweden.

The case of Electrolux, where the subsidiary in the Philippines is working independently is very much the same. The Philippine subsidiary has excellent manufacturing facilities and it is exporting extensively to other Electrolux subsidiaries in the region, for example, Thailand and Indonesia. The parent company, in view of the independent status of the Philippines subsidiary and because it is one of the most successful subsidiaries for the whole concern, has chosen not to interfere in that subsidiary's business with other regional companies. For Electrolux subsidiaries in that area, the Philippines subsidiary is acting as a 'centre', especially because the products manufactured in that subsidiary have been adapted to the local market and are more suitable for the regional market than the products manufactured in Sweden or in another European subsidiary.

Sandvik, another big Swedish firm, started its sales operation in the Philippines in 1966 and began manufacturing locally in 1968. Most of the raw material used in the Philippines is made in Sweden. The Philippine subsidiary has, however, no contact with the parent company in Sweden as all of the raw materials, including any material which is not available in Sandvik's own group of companies, are bought from Sandvik South East Asia located in Singapore. All Sandvik subsidiaries in South East Asia report to Singapore, which compiles the regional results and sends a consolidated report to the parent company.

As the above indicates, while there are many instances of parent-subsidiary conflict in MNCs, Asian affiliates of Swedish MNCs have much greater autonomy than is typical for MNCs from the larger economies such as the US, UK or Japan.[21] This pattern of relatively weak control of foreign affiliates has also been documented for the foreign affiliates of MNCs based in another group of small economies, the developing countries.[22] Interestingly, the use of data on Asian affiliates of Swedish MNCs is conservative in this situation as affiliates of Swedish companies in large economies such as the US are likely to exhibit even stronger signs of independence from their Swedish parent firms.[23] Nevertheless, it should be noted that this is an exploratory study and further research on parent-subsidiary relations is needed before definitive conclusions can be drawn. For example, such research could document more extensively these trends and differences in small- versus large-country MNC procedures for managing foreign affiliates and determine if the data support an explanation of this phenomenon not based on the PLC theory. In such research, it would be useful to examine parent-affiliate relations in MNCs based in other small economies like Switzerland and Holland that are similar to Sweden and where the foreign sales of their larger companies are greater than domestic sales.

11.5 SUMMARY AND CONCLUSIONS

This chapter has reviewed the nature and extent of FDI by Swedish firms. It found that most trends and characteristics of Swedish FDI are consistent with traditional theories of the MNC as they apply to traditional large country MNCs. This chapter has contended that the foreign operations of MNCs based in small economies have become independent centres and have evolved to challenge the parent firm's influence sooner than in MNCs from large economies. Recent developments regarding the foreign operations of Swedish firms in Asia were shown to be consistent with these implications of the product life-cycle theory of the evolution of multinational firms. The evidence presented in this exploratory study indicates that further research on parent-subsidiary relationships in MNCs from small economies is likely to be very useful.

Notes

The authors are grateful for comments from Peter Buckley, Jeremy Clegg, Mo Yamin, and two anonymous reviewers. However, the authors remain responsible for the contents.

1. For reviews of the extensive literature in this area see, for example, Agmon and Kindleberger (1977); Wells (1983); Aggarwal and Weekly (1982); and Aggarwal (1985, 1988).
2. While there are numerous instances of small-country firms from many

nations that operate in many areas of the world, in order to keep the length manageable, this paper focuses only on the Asian operations of Swedish firms. In addition, this paper does not deal with the more commonly examined phenomenon of large multinational firms in small countries. For a recent discussion and review of the latter issue see, for example, Goodman (1987).

3. See, for example, Swedenborg (1979), Hakansson (1982); Jansson (1982); Ghauri (1983); Hornell and Vahlne (1986); Clegg (1987); and Kaynak, Ghauri and Olofsson, (1987).

4. Studies of foreign direct investment from smaller countries, indeed countries other than the US and UK, are often limited by availability of data. For detailed discussions of this issue, see, for example, Agmon and Kindleberger (1977); Wells (1983); and Aggarwal (1988).

5. For additional discussion of these definitions see Dunning (1981) for this definition of the MNC, and Kindleberger (1969) for this definition of FDI.

6. See, for example, Hymer (1960); Caves (1971); Shapiro (1983); Aggarwal (1984), and Buckley and Casson (1985).

7. See, for example, Kindleberger (1970) and Krugman (1983).

8. See, for example, Horst (1972), Knickerbocker (1973), Buckley *et al.* (1978), Graham (1978), Dunning (1981) and Casson (1987a).

9. See, for example, Ivanson (1953), Aliber (1971), Agmon and Lessard (1977), Aggarwal (1980), and Reed (1983).

10. This theory also implies that national policies towards FDI should be clearly spelled out and should not change very often since a stable policy, irrespective of its harshness, would reduce the risks faced by MNCs.

11. See, for example, Aliber (1971), Richardson (1971), Agmon and Lessard (1977), and Reed (1983).

12. See, for example, Magdoff (1969), Weekly and Aggarwal (1987), and Dunning (1988).

13. For the limitations of the PLC as a general theory of FDI see, for example, Lall (1979), Swedenborg (1982), Buckley and Casson (1976 and 1985), Clegg (1987) and Dunning (1988a). For opposing views and a reappraisal of the PLC see, for example, Vernon (1979) and Aggarwal (1984).

14. See Weekly and Aggarwal (1987).

15. See, for example, Franko (1978).

16. See, for example, Aggarwal (1987).

17. See, for example, Lundstrom (1986).

18. See, for example, Ariana Sans, 'Scharp's cutting edge: The man behind the Electrolux success speaks out on future strategy', *Sweden Now*, January 1989, pp. 16–17.

19. See, for example, Christina Fagerstrom, 'A convenient division of labor' *Asian Finance*, 15 July 1989, pp. 34–5; Erroll G. Rampersad, 'The multinationals gear up', *Sweden Now*, January 1989, pp. 13–15; Christina Fagerstrom, 'Swedish Companies Engineer a Push Into China', *Asian Finance*, 15 August 1988, pp. 58–60; 'Swedish Companies Aid U.S. Economic Growth', *The Wall Street Journal*, 18 April 1988, pp.

17–18; 'Swedish Takeovers: A European Smorgasbord', *Economist*, 9 April 1988, pp. 58–61; and Lipsey *et al.* (1987).

20. See, for example, 'How Swedish Match Adopts an Innovative Approach to the Finance Function', *Management Europe*, 29 August 1988, pp. 12–16.

21. See, for example, Negandhi (1987).

22. See, for example, the references cited in note 1.

23. Foreign affiliates in larger economies are likely to be larger in sales, profits and, thus, influence.

12 Multinational Activity in the Mediterranean Rim Textile and Clothing Industry

Jim Hamill

12.1 INTRODUCTION

Over the last decade or so, a number of Mediterranean Rim countries have emerged as major textile producers and exporters. Turkey, for example, has recently replaced Hong Kong as the leading foreign supplier of textiles to the European Community (EC) (in volume terms). Textile exports from Tunisia have increased by more than 1000 per cent since the early 1970s; while for countries such as Morocco, Greece and Malta textile exports have increased at a significantly faster rate than the world average. Even in Algeria and Egypt, where textile exports have grown less rapidly, recent investments in new plant and equipment have added considerably to domestic textile capacity and improved long-term export prospects.

Although the emerging textile industries in the Mediterranean Rim present a clear competitive challenge to Western producers, their growth also provides opportunities for the latter. The growth in textile production in the region has resulted in an increase in demand for imported raw materials, including high quality yarns and fabrics. Many Rim countries are large importers, as well as exporters, of textiles. This is particularly true in those countries with a developing clothing sector, such as Tunisia and Morocco, which rely heavily on yarn and fabric imports. Most Rim countries actively encourage the direct involvement of foreign textile multinationals in their domestic industry and attractive incentives are available to foreign investors in many countries. Foreign licensing arrangements and other forms of technology transfer are encouraged, while opportunities to reduce production costs through offshore assembly (processing) are available in several countries, especially with the establishment of export processing zones.

This chapter examines the growth and future prospects of the emerging textile and clothing industries in seven Mediterranean Rim countries, with particular attention being paid to the role and impact of foreign textile multinationals in the region. The countries examined include Algeria, Egypt, Greece, Malta, Morocco, Tunisia and Turkey. The chapter is divided into four main sections. Section 12.2 provides an overview of the growth and characteristics of the textile and clothing industry in the region focusing mainly on export performance and export markets. Section 12.3 examines industry structure in the countries studied, especially the pattern of multinational textile involvement in the region. Section 12.4 examines the threats and opportunities currently facing the industry; with the final section discussing future prospects.

The issues examined in this chapter are important in three respects. First, the rapid growth in textile and clothing exports from the Mediterranean Rim has led to concerns within industrial countries regarding the high level of imports from this source and pressures have grown for the introduction of protectionist measures. The Turkish industry, in particular, has been severely affected by quota restrictions imposed by both the EC and the US. Second, the textile and clothing industry is central to the process of economic development in the region, accounting for a very high proportion of total manufacturing output, employment and exports. While the industry has grown rapidly in recent decades, there is growing concern regarding the ability of Mediterranean Rim textile producers to maintain their international competitiveness in the rapidly changing environment of the late 1980s. Third, the involvement of foreign textile MNEs in the region is becoming the subject of closer scrutiny, from both a home and host country perspective. As regards the former, there is growing concern (especially in Europe) of the home country employment effects arising from the offshore assembly activities of MNEs in the region. From a host country perspective, the dependency of many Mediterranean Rim countries on foreign textile investment and technology is a source of concern, with future growth prospects being dependent on multinational investment and sourcing policies.

The evidence presented in this chapter is derived from a more detailed Special Report on Mediterranean Rim Textiles and Clothing prepared for the Economist Intelligence Unit (Hamill, 1989). A wide variety of data sources were used in the preparation of this report including information guides prepared by banks, the Economist Intelligence Unit and management consultants; British Overseas Trade Board publications; UN and OECD statistical sources; World Bank reports; newspaper and journal articles; academic studies, together with information obtained directly from leading experts in the industry, foreign embassies, export promotion and foreign investment agencies and various textile manufacturers in the countries concerned. This report (Hamill, 1989) provides a full list of the data sources used below.

12.2   MEDITERRANEAN TEXTILES AND CLOTHING: AN OVERVIEW

The importance of the textile and clothing industry to economic growth and development in the Mediterranean Rim region cannot be overstated. For each of the countries examined in this chapter the industry is one of the leading industrial sectors, accounting for a very high proportion (20–45 per cent) of total manufacturing output and employment (Table 12.1). More importantly, given the foreign debt and balance of payments problems of most of these countries, the textile industry accounts for a very high proportion of total export earnings. Textiles have been identified by most national governments as a priority growth area, with the low-technology and labour-intensive nature of the industry being particularly suited to the factor endowments of each nation. To this end, most national governments are actively encouraging additional capital investment in the industry, not only through state-owned textile enterprises, but also through grants and loans to the private sector. In some countries, such as Algeria, Egypt, Morocco and Tunisia, such investment is in the form of new capacity. In others, such as Greece and Turkey, the investment is more orientated towards a restructuring and modernisation of the industry, involving the installation of up-to-date plant and equipment, with the aim of maintaining the international competitiveness of indigenous producers.

Growth

The growth in textile exports from the region is shown in Table 12.2. In all countries (except Algeria and Egypt), textile exports have increased at a significantly faster rate than the world average. The most rapid increase in exports occurred in Tunisia and Morocco, although Turkey and Greece remain the largest exporters in value terms. With the exception of Turkey, export growth has been less rapid during the 1980s compared with the period 1974 to 1980. This has been due to a combination of external difficulties (for example, the world recession; protectionism and so on) and internal efficiency problems (see later). The seven countries examined now account for just over 5 per cent of world-wide textile exports to OECD countries and for just under 10 per cent of total textile exports from developing countries.

The only two countries in which overall textile exports have not increased significantly are Algeria and Egypt. The Algerian industry has experienced major problems which have severely curtailed its exports, although recent large-scale investments have improved considerably the country's export prospects. The increase in Egyptian textile exports shown in Table 12.2 is somewhat misleading. While overall textile exports increased by only 10 per cent between 1974 and 1986, this disguises rapid export growth in the yarn and fabric, and clothing sectors. The low 10 per cent increase in overall textile exports is due to a significant reduction in fibre exports.

Product Categories

In terms of products, clothing represents the dominant export of the countries examined, accounting for two-thirds of total exports in 1986. It is also the fastest growing sector, with most countries experiencing a rapid increase in clothing exports over the period covered. Several of the countries are significant yarn and fabric exporters including Egypt, Morocco, Greece and Turkey; while Egypt and Turkey are also major fibre exporters.

Export markets

The EC is the dominant export market for Mediterranean Rim textiles, accounting for 85 per cent of total exports in 1986 (Table 12.3). Both Egypt and Turkey, however, have expanded their ex-

TABLE 12.1 *Growth and characteristics of Mediterranean Rim textiles: summary table by country*

Country	Importance of textile industry	Textile export growth	Export markets	Principal exports	Industry structure
Algeria	20% of manufacturing employment but very small proportion of total exports (1%)	Slowest rate of growth of any Rim country; fall in textile exports since 1981	EC (96%)	Not a significant textile exporter	State-owned and controlled; growing importance of private sector (mainly small, family-owned firms)
Egypt	40% of manufacturing employment; 40% of total exports	Rapid growth in yarn fabric and clothing exports. Fall in fibre exports	US; EC; Yugoslavia, Japan	Cotton yarns & fabrics; rapid growth in clothing exports	State owned and controlled plus large number of small privately-owned enterprises; limited foreign investment in joint ventures
Greece	40% of manufacturing employment; 25% of total exports	Rapid growth during 1970s; slower rate of growth since 1979; recent increase in exports	EC (West Germany, Italy and France); increase in exports to USA	Natural & manmade fibres; cotton & synthetic fabrics and yarn; threads; clothing	Fragmented structure (large number of small enterprises) but largest 20 firms account for half of output; limited foreign investment
Malta	32% of manufacturing employment; 40% of total exports	Rapid growth during 1970s; fall in exports during 1980s; recent increase in exports	EC (West Germany, UK)	Clothing (93%)	Exports dominated by foreign-owned firms

Morocco	33% of manufacturing employment; 17% of total exports	Rapid growth during 1970s; slower rate of growth after 1979; recent increase in exports	EC (France, West Germany)	Clothing; woollen fabrics; knitwear; cotton thread	Predominance of small manufacturers; extensive use of sub-contracting and licensing with European textile enterprises
Tunisia	27% of manufacturing employment; 20% of total exports	Rapid growth during 1970s; slower rate of growth during 1980s; recent increase in exports	EC (West Germany, France, Italy)	Ready-to-wear clothing	Mixed structure – state-owned and controlled; small and medium-sized private enterprises; wholly-owned subsidiaries and joint ventures with foreign firms
Turkey	33% of manufacturing employment; 25% of total exports	Rapid growth during 1970s and 1980s despite protectionism	EC (West Germany, Italy); USA	Cotton yarns and fabrics; rapid growth in clothing exports	Mixed structure – state-owned Sumerbank; private conglomerates; private textile companies both large and small; limited foreign investment

Source: Hamill (1989)

TABLE 12.2   *Textile[1] exports of selected Mediterranean Rim countries to the OECD: 1974–86*

	1974	1976	1978	1980	1982	1984	1986
				Exports ($ mn)			
Algeria	6.5	4.5	2.2	1.0	3.7	0.7	0.5
Egypt	355.8	206.8	224.4	403.4	364.2	488.0	391.6
Greece	378.3	644.4	927.4	1458.8	1161.3	1165.3	1775.2
Malta	46.6	95.6	160.0	211.6	172.6	127.6	155.7
Morocco	77.9	119.8	159.3	245.7	254.8	290.2	538.0
Tunisia	47.5	131.6	240.4	442.7	401.8	371.4	598.8
Turkey	381.3	662.5	585.1	596.4	866.8	1284.3	2001.1
World Textile exports to the OECD	38,870.2	45,706.2	60,854.1	80,833.7	72,195.8	82,474.8	108,819.2

	1974–80	1980–86	1974–86
		% change in exports	
Algeria	–84.6	–50.0	–92.3
Egypt	13.4	–2.9	10.0
Greece	285.6	21.7	369.3
Malta	354.1	–26.4	234.1
Morocco	215.4	119.0	590.6
Tunisia	832.0	35.3	1160.6
Turkey	56.4	235.5	424.8
World Textile exports to the OECD	108.0	34.6	180.0

Note 1:   Includes textile fibres; yarns and fabrics; and clothing
Source: Derived from 'Foreign Trade by Commodities', OECD, 1988.

TABLE 12.3   *Textile exports from selected Mediterranean Rim countries: by destination (1986)*

	Total textile exports ($ mn)	Share of total exports destined for:		
		EC (%)	USA (%)	Others (%)
Algeria	0.5	95.6	0.0	4.4
Egypt	391.6	60.4	9.8	29.8
Greece	1775.2	85.0	4.4	10.6
Malta	155.7	89.1	3.9	7.0
Morocco	538.0	95.9	2.3	1.8
Tunisia	598.8	97.7	0.4	1.9
Turkey	2001.1	82.6	10.9	6.5
Total	5460.5	84.9	6.5	8.6

Source: As Table 12.2.

TABLE 12.4   *Distribution of Mediterranean textile exports within the EC*
(1986)

	Total textile exports to the EC ($ mn)	Share of total exports to EC destined for:				
		West Germany (%)	France (%)	UK (%)	Italy (%)	Others (%)
Algeria	0.5	0.8	39.2	0.4	11.9	47.7
Egypt	236.7	21.8	10.7	7.0	36.5	24.0
Greece	1509.7	58.6	13.6	7.0	11.9	8.9
Malta	138.7	64.4	2.4	17.0	9.0	7.2
Morocco	516.2	27.2	60.2	0.6	1.9	10.1
Tunisia	585.1	34.9	36.5	0.2	6.2	22.2
Turkey	1651.3	55.2	9.2	8.1	14.7	12.8
TOTAL	4638.2	49.2	19.6	6.1	12.2	12.9

Source: As Table 12.2

ports to the US which now accounts for 10 and 11 per cent respectively of total exports. Within the EC, West Germany, France and
Italy are the principal markets, accounting for 81 per cent of all
exports to EC countries (Table 12.4). The relative importance of
these markets, however, varies by country. West Germany is the
dominant export market for the Maltese, Greek and Turkish textile
industries. For Morocco and Tunisia the French market remains
dominant, with Italy being the dominant market for Egyptian textile
exports. This country concentration is also true on the import side.

12.3   INDUSTRY STRUCTURE AND MULTINATIONAL ACTIVITY IN THE REGION

The structure of the textile industry in the countries being examined
varies enormously with respect to such characteristics as firm size, the
relative importance of state versus privately-owned textile enterprises, and the role and importance of foreign multinational enterprises (see Table 12.1). As regards the latter, foreign textile
enterprises have played an important role in the growth of textile
production in the region. This involvement has taken a number of
different forms including FDI, joint ventures, licensing, offshore
processing and other forms of technology transfer and assistance.
The nature and extent of multinational activity, however, varies
considerably by country, as summarised in Table 12.1.

Algeria

Like most other sectors of the Algerian economy, state-owned and controlled enterprises (known as Sociétés Nationales or Entreprises Nationales) occupy an important position in the textile industry – especially in fibres, yarns and fabrics. Unlike most other sectors, however, there is a large and growing number of privately-owned textile companies – most of which are small-scale, family concerns operating in the clothing sector. State-owned enterprises account for approximately 60 per cent of fibre, yarn and fabric output, with the remainder being accounted for by privately-owned companies (20 per cent) and imports (20 per cent). The relative importance of the state- and privately owned sectors is reversed in clothing given the large number of privately-owned clothing concerns.

Two of the leading textile enterprises in Algeria are the state-owned Entreprise Nationale des Industries de Confection et Bonneterie (Ecotex) and the Société Nationale des Industries du Textile (Sonitex). The former employs approximately 9000 people in 32 different locations throughout the country. The company's two principal product categories are clothing and knitwear, together with a limited involvement in spinning, with an annual production capacity of approximately 26 billion articles. Sonitex was established by the Algerian government in 1966 to promote the development of an indigenous textile industry (which had been almost non-existent prior to independence) and to save foreign exchange through import substitution. At its inception, the company's activities were restricted to the manufacture of a limited range of textile products, mainly textile fabrics, with all production being sold to the Société Nationale de Commercialisation du Textile et du Cuir – a state-owned distribution company. Since the early 1970s, however, Sonitex has broadened its product range, including a range of ready-to-wear clothing and has taken over responsibility for its own distribution and marketing. Currently, the company employs approximately 20 000 people at various locations including 42 production plants, 13 commercial departments, 18 distribution depots, and approximately 100 retail outlets scattered throughout the country. Both Ecotex and Sonitex are concerned mainly with supplying the domestic market, with exports accounting for an extremely small proportion of total output.

In comparison with the other Mediterranean Rim countries examined below, there is almost no foreign investment in the Algerian textile industry. The country has traditionally adopted a highly restrictive approach to inward investment with Law (1979) 78–01 prohibiting foreign companies from establishing subsidiaries or branches in the country. A more liberal policy towards inward direct investment was introduced in 1982 aimed at encouraging foreign joint ventures. The take-up rate, however, has been very low.

Egypt

The textile industry in Egypt consists of three main sectors in terms of company ownership: a publicly-owned and controlled sector, a privately-owned and controlled sector and joint venture companies involving foreign equity participation.

All of the largest textile enterprises in Egypt are state-owned and controlled, with spinning and weaving operations being established as a state monopoly during the nationalisation programme of the 1960s. Such state-owned companies account for well over three quarters of total textile output.

The private sector of the Egyptian textile industry consists of over 2000 small-scale establishments, most of which are cottage industries, artisan workshops or small mechanised factories employing fewer than ten workers. Such private enterprises are geographically concentrated in three main areas – El-Mahala Al Kobra, Kafr-El Dawar and Greater Cairo. The private sector of the industry has grown rapidly in the last decade or so as a result of the government's more liberal approach towards private ownership and investment. Since 1974 a total of 2089 licences, involving investment of £E329 million, have been granted to private-sector textile companies under the 'Open Door' policy.

Joint ventures between Egyptian and foreign-owned textile enterprises have also grown in importance with the more liberal attitude towards inward direct investment adopted by the Egyptian authorities. However, the degree of foreign direct investment in the industry by US and European textile enterprises is still limited, (8 per cent of total investment) with most inward investment in textiles originating from other Arab nations (25 per cent of total investment).

There has also been some divestment by foreign-owned textile companies in Egypt. The UK-based Tootal Group, for example, established a joint venture (The Nile Ready-Made Clothing Co) in Egypt in the late 1970s, with the aim of utilising low-cost Egyptian labour to supply the UK market. The company, however, has recently withdrawn from the country following major disagreements with its Egyptian partners and frustrations in its dealings with the authorities.

Significant technological linkages exist between the three sectors of the Egyptian textile industry. For example, although the level of FDI has been limited, foreign-owned firms have played an active role in recent attempts to restructure and modernise the industry through turn-key projects and machinery sales. Rhône Poulenc of France, for example, was involved in a £E44 million turn-key project with Misr Rayon Co. for the building of a continuous polyester filament plant at Kafr El Dawar, while a consortium headed by Kloechner Ind. of Austria was involved in a $6.8 million expansion of a textile factory belonging to the El-Ameriya Spinning & Weaving Co. Japanese and European textile machinery manufacturers have been actively involved in sales of spindles and looms used in the modernisation of the industry and in the supply of new equipment to the Egyptian clothing industry.

Greece

The textile industry in Greece is highly fragmented, consisting of over 400 companies, 95 per cent of which employ fewer than 50 workers. Almost half of the industry's output, however, and a higher percentage of its exports are accounted for by the largest 20 enterprises, employing more than 500 workers each. By far the largest producer is Piraiki-Patraiki whose principal products include cotton and synthetic yarns and fabrics. Other major producers include Aegean Mills, Athenian Knitting Mills, Athena Spinning and Weaving, Barco Textile Industries, Hellenic Fabrics, Kazantis, Les Filteries de Greece, Michailidis, Naglo-Hellenic, Roca, Tsirozides and Volos. Most of these companies are actively involved in exports.

The involvement of foreign multinationals in the Greek textile industry is limited. There are approximately 300 foreign-owned manufacturing companies operating in Greece. Few of these, however, are engaged in textile or clothing production with the main sectors attracting inward investment including petroleum, mining, metals, chemicals and transport.

Foreign textile multinationals, mainly from Europe, were actively engaged in outward processing activities in Greece during the 1960s and 1970s. In recent years, however, the country has lost its locational advantage as a low-cost production base as a consequence of

TABLE 12.5 *Foreign participation in the Maltese textile industry (1985)*

	Number of companies	Total employment	Sales (LM000s)	
			Export	Local
Wholly-owned foreign subsidiaries	31	4485	39 053	1043
Foreign/Maltese joint ventures	14	1706	16 658	974
Wholly Maltese-owned	43	2108	4 527	1365
Total	88	8299	60 238	3 382

Source: Malta Development Corporation.

spiralling inflation, increased labour costs, an overvalued drachma and competition from other low-cost Rim countries such as Tunisia, Morocco and Malta. Indeed, the increase in production costs has been so severe that several Greek manufacturers themselves – including Piraiki-Patraiki – are becoming involved in outward processing with fabrics being exported to Northern Italy for manufacturing into clothing.

Malta

The Maltese textile industry is characterised by a high degree of foreign ownership. According to data provided by the Malta Development Corporation, there were 88 companies actively involved in the production of textiles and clothing in 1985. As Table 12.5 shows, more than one third of these were the wholly-owned subsidiaries of foreign multinationals, with a further 14 per cent being joint ventures between Maltese and foreign partners. In nine of these joint ventures the foreign firm held a majority equity stake, with a further four joint ventures being 50 per cent foreign-owned. In only one joint venture was there a majority Maltese equity stake. While foreign-owned companies account for just over half of all companies in the industry, their contribution in terms of employment and exports is significantly greater. No less than three-quarters of all employment in the industry is in wholly-owned foreign subsidiaries or joint ventures. More importantly, foreign firms (including joint ventures) account for 91 per cent of total textile and clothing exports. Almost all of the output

TABLE 12.6   *Stock of foreign direct investment in the Maltese textile industry by country of origin (1985)*

	Value (LM,000s)	% of total
UK	662	3
West Germany	1 277	6
Italy	64	–
Netherlands	195	1
Other EC	51	–
US	17 558	86
Libya	449	2
Others	197	1

Source: Malta Development Corporation.

of foreign-owned textile companies in Malta is exported with domestic sales accounting for only 3 per cent of the total. Indigenous companies, on the other hand, are more orientated towards the domestic market with over one fifth of sales within Malta.

Table 12.6 shows the value of foreign direct investment in the Maltese textile industry by country of origin, with the US being the dominant source country, accounting for 86 per cent of the total stock of FDI in textiles. By far the most important foreign investor in the industry is the jean manufacturer Blue Bell of the US which uses Malta as a sourcing point for European markets.

Morocco

In its formative years following the end of the Second World War, the Moroccan textile industry was dominated by family groups based mainly in the Fez area; although two thirds of current manufacturing is now based in the Casablanca area. Such family groups have since grown into large holding-type companies such as the Kettanis, Sebtis, Alami Tazis, Bouftas and Sekkat groups. Few of these are involved in exporting, however, being concerned mainly with supplying the domestic market. In addition to the above companies, there is an estimated 860 small-scale textile enterprises, most of which are not included in the official statistics.

Although the actual volume of foreign direct investment in Moroccan textiles is limited (see Table 12.7), a distinguishing feature of the industry is its extensive links with European manufacturers, retailers

TABLE 12.7   *Foreign investment in Morocco: 1985 and 1986*

	1985		1986	
	DH 000	*% of all investment*	*DH 000*	*% of all investment*
Food processing	88 061	13	279 899	29
Textiles & leather	88 603	11	120 655	12
Chemical industry	149 837	21	231 625	29
Mechanical industries	108 505	27	210 500	40
Others	16 173	–	281 452	13.5
Total	451 179	16	880 320	25

Source: Ministry of Finance, Rabat; reported in *Financial Times*, July 13, 1987.

and fashion houses through subcontracting and licensing agreements. Indeed, much of the recent growth in Moroccan textile exports, especially clothing, can be explained in terms of such linkages. Many Moroccan textile and clothing enterprises act as subcontractors or manufacture under licence for firms located in France, Belgium, the Netherlands and Italy. European firms known to be actively involved in subcontracting or licensing agreements in Morocco include such well-known names as Christian Dior, Pierre Cardin, Louis Vuitton, Benetton, Cacharel, Daniel Hechter, Emilio, Fendi, and Eminence. In addition to the advantage of low-cost labour (approximately \$4–\$5 per day), the growth of subcontracting and licensing agreements has been encouraged by the close proximity of Morocco to major European markets, generous quota limitations on Moroccan textile exports to the EC, and the liberalisation of Moroccan policy towards inward investors. Although the nature of such arrangements varies between companies, the normal pattern is for the Moroccan enterprise to import raw materials (yarns, fabrics, and the like) and re-export the final product manufactured to well-defined specifications laid down by the European partner. Equity participation by the foreign licensor or subcontractor is the exception rather than the rule – a situation which is markedly different from that in Tunisia where there are more extensive ownership linkages. One result of such arrangements is that Morocco is a large importer of raw materials – especially yarns and fabrics to be made-up into ready-to-wear clothing. In the clothing sector, over 90 per cent of all materials used are imported – most of which are tied imports under subcontracting or licensing arrangements.

Tunisia

The Tunisian textile sector is characterised by a mixed industry structure comprising state-owned enterprises, small- and medium-size, privately-owned enterprises, and the subsidiaries and associated companies of foreign-owned multinationals.

The largest textile enterprise in Tunisia is the state-owned Société Genérale des Industries Textiles (Sogitex) whose principal products include bed linen and tablecloths. Sogitex also acts as a holding company for a group of smaller enterprises engaged in spinning, weaving and finishing operations including Sitex, Somotex, Tissmok, and Siter although only the former is actively engaged in export activity. The large number of small to medium-sized clothing and knitwear enterprises, many of whom are highly export-orientated include MPP, Makni, MTPP, Chavic, Moncef Barcous, Mac, Nov-Nov Coutour, Pantaloisir, Sovel, VTL, Sopic, Sportswear Manufacture, Sotvintex, Sibac, Sogemon Socoto-Bucotex and Sotib.

Foreign investment and offshore processing have played a crucial role in the growth and development of Tunisian textiles, especially in the clothing sector. Since the liberalisation of foreign investment policy in 1972, approximately 300 foreign-owned companies have located in Tunisia. Over 85 per cent of these are in the clothing sector with the principal source countries being France, West Germany, the Netherlands and Belgium. Most of this investment has taken the form of outward processing, with fabrics being imported from the parent company which are then cut and sewn for re-export back to Europe. Although most foreign investment in Tunisian textiles has come from Continental Europe, one of the largest foreign-owned firms in the industry is the UK-owned Lee Cooper who employ over 600 people at their Tunisian subsidiary with a production capacity of 3.2 million jeans per annum. Lee Cooper's exports from Tunisia are in excess of TD 11 million most of which is exported to the EC.

The extent of offshore processing in Tunisia is reflected in the country's import statistics. The rapid increase in clothing exports since 1974 has been accompanied by an equally rapid growth in yarn and fabric imports – which now account for almost 80 per cent of total textile imports. The major suppliers of yarns and fabrics are those countries most actively involved in offshore processing in Tunisia. West Germany and France together account for two thirds of total textile imports with the Benelux countries accounting for a further 18 per cent.

As part of the government's privatisation programme, several parastatal textile enterprises have recently been partially denationalised. This has included the partial privatisation of the Société Industrielle des Textiles (Sitex) – the largest producer of denim jeans in Africa; the selling-off of a 25 per cent interest in the Société des Industries Textiles Réunies (Siter) to the World Bank's International Financial Corporation bringing external control of Siter to 51 per cent; and the encouragement of private equity investment in the Société Monastiriènne de Textiles (Somotex).

Turkey

Four broad categories of domestic producer can be identified in the Turkish textile industry. First, the state-owned Sumerbank which is the largest textile enterprise in Turkey, with an annual turnover in excess of $400 million. Second, conglomerate companies such as KOC, Sabanci, Cukyrova, Anadolu Endustri, and Yashar Holdings with extensive textile interests, although being highly diversified into other business areas. Third, a group of large and medium-sized companies whose principal activities are in textiles including Altinyildiz, Soktas, Mensucat Santral, Guney Sanayii, Pektas and Akin. Finally, a large group of very small (mainly family-owned) textile enterprises employing ten or fewer workers often in cottage-type enterprises. There is also some foreign involvement in the industry. Between 1983 and 1986, the number of foreign-owned textile enterprises doubled from 14 to 29, representing an increase in foreign direct investment in the industry from TL4.3 billion to TL8.5 billion (Table 12.8). This is reflective of the more liberal attitude towards

TABLE 12.8   *Foreign investment in Turkey's textile industry*

Year	Number of firms	Foreign investment stock (TL mn)
1983	14	4 303
1984	15	6 326
1985	21	7 846
1986	29	8 611

Source: State Planning Organisation, Ankara.

inward foreign investment being adopted by the Turkish authorities, including the establishment of free trade zones.

12.4   INTERNATIONAL COMPETITIVENESS AND FUTURE PROSPECTS

A number of factors have contributed to the emergence of the above countries as major textile producers and exporters and these are summarised in Table 12.9. Most Mediterranean Rim countries possess specific locational advantages in the production and export of textiles relating to the availability of indigenous raw material supplies (for example, cotton in Greece, Turkey and so on); an abundant supply of low-cost labour; and close proximity to the important markets of the EC. Such locational advantages have been reinforced by government policies which have encouraged the growth of textile exports through export subsidies and the funding of capital investment projects. EC restrictions on textile imports from MFA countries, and the 'preferential' trade agreements negotiated with most Mediterranean Rim countries provided a further stimulus to the growth in textile exports from the region. Finally, the export propensity of the region has been enhanced by the involvement of foreign multinationals through inward direct investment, offshore assembly, licensing and the like, which has complemented the growth and development of large indigenous textile enterprises with international marketing experience, as in Turkey, Greece and Egypt.

Despite such advantages and the rapid growth in textile exports over the last decade and a half, future prospects for many of the above countries are uncertain and there are major doubts regarding the ability of some countries to maintain their competitiveness in the rapidly changing international trade environment of the late 1980s. The textile industries of most Rim countries are currently facing a number of severe difficulties which are threatening their future competitiveness. The nature and seriousness of such difficulties will obviously vary by country. However, there are a number of problems common to most countries as shown in Table 12.9. The geographical concentration of Mediterranean Rim textile exports on EC markets is a high-risk strategy and may require efforts at geographical diversification. Similarly, the dependency of many countries on foreign textile enterprises – although providing short-run benefits regarding output and exports – may give rise to long-run problems arising from

TABLE 12.9 *Factors influencing the future competitiveness of Mediterranean Rim textile producers*

Positive	Negative
Raw material supplies	Geographical concentration on few major markets
Labour availability and costs	Dependency on foreign investment, technology, raw material supplies and the like
Proximity to EC markets	Inefficiency and low productivity (fragmented industry structure; outmoded machinery; shortage of skilled labour)
Government investment policies	
Export incentives	
Export processing zones	Poor product quality
Preferential trade agreements with EC	Limited international marketing networks and experience
Foreign investment; subcontracting; licensing and so on	Entry of Spain/Portugal into EC
	Threat of protectionism
	Technological developments reducing labour cost advantage
	Domestic economic problems (high inflation; balance of payments and international debt problems; IMF-imposed deflationary policies and the like)

Source: Hamill (1989)

changes in multinational investment and sourcing policies. Despite the rapid growth in exports, the textile industries of many Rim countries continue to suffer from major problems relating to inefficiency and low levels of labour productivity, which reduce their labour cost advantage. Several factors contribute to such difficulties including the fragmented industry structure in many countries, limited investment in modern plant and equipment, and a shortage of skilled manpower. In countries such as Turkey and Egypt, such problems are compounded by long-standing inefficiencies within the state-owned and controlled sector. Difficulties also exist in the marketing of Mediterranean Rim textiles which continue to suffer from a poor quality image abroad. In addition, most companies lack the international marketing networks and experience necessary to penetrate new markets such as the US.

The above difficulties are all internal to the industry. Future prospects for Mediterranean Rim textiles will also be influenced by external pressures. The recent entry of Spain and Portugal into the EC provides a major competitive challenge to Mediterranean producers through allowing duty-free access to European markets for Iberian producers. Most Mediterranean countries have negotiated preferential trade agreements with the EC covering textile exports. There is, however, an ever present threat of protectionist measures being introduced, especially in the US where the Textile Trade Bill – which would severely restrict the growth of textile imports into the US – was recently passed by the House of Representatives – although subject to presidential veto. Finally, technological developments, especially the introduction of automated production processes, will erode the historic labour-cost advantages of Mediterranean producers by reducing the importance of labour costs as a proportion of total costs.

In addition to the above factors, most Mediterranean Rim countries suffer from major domestic economic problems including high and persistent rates of inflation, recurrent balance of payments problems, shortages of foreign currency and so forth, which will have adverse effects on textile output and exports.

Future prospects for Mediterranean textiles and clothing will depend on the introduction of appropriate government and industry/company-specific policies to deal effectively with these threats. This issue is considered in the final section.

FUTURE PROSPECTS

The countries examined in this report have introduced a series of measures aimed at maintaining or improving textile competitiveness in response to the threats identified in the previous section. These have included attempts at industry restructuring and modernisation, involving substantial capital investment; improving efficiency, especially in the state-owned sector; improved quality and design; and the further encouragement of inward direct investment, in some cases through the establishment of Export Processing Zones. In a number of countries such measures have enhanced long-term growth and export prospects in textiles and clothing. In other countries, serious constraints on future growth remain (see Table 12.10).

The *Egyptian* and *Greek* textile and clothing industries are currently in the throes of a major restructuring and future growth prospects remain uncertain. In *Malta*, the industry has peaked and the country is becoming less attractive as an offshore processing location. The opposite is the case for *Morocco* and *Tunisia* where short-run growth prospects remain high given the locational advantages of both countries as a sourcing point for European markets. Long-term growth prospects in both countries, however, will be dependent on the development of a stronger indigenous industry which will reduce their reliance on MNE sourcing and investment policies. In *Turkey*, both the government and the industry itself have adopted an aggressive approach to the problems facing textile and clothing producers and this is a major source of concern for textile manufacturers in the industrialised countries of Europe and the US. Clothing and knitwear exports from Turkey were forecast to rise by no less than 80 per cent in the three-year period 1987–89 and the industry was aiming for a total of \$10 billion in textile and clothing exports. The great unknown in all of this remains *Algeria*. The Algerian textile industry remains lacking in international competitiveness and is orientated mainly towards the domestic market. There is evidence, however, of a shift in government policy away from import substitution towards export promotion. In the long run this may create the necessary infrastructure for the Algerian textile industry to develop along the lines followed by its Maghreb neighbours, Morocco and Tunisia.

CONCLUSIONS

The Mediterranean Rim countries will continue to be major textile producers and exporters and, as the above paragraphs have shown, future prospects for export growth are promising in most countries. The countries examined, therefore (together with other Rim countries such as Portugal, Spain and Israel) will continue to present a major competitive challenge to USA and EC textile producers already suffering from a rapid increase in low-cost imports from the Far East. The Mediterranean Rim region, however, also presents attractive opportunities to Western producers wishing to exploit local markets through imports or to reduce production costs through local manu-

TABLE 12.10   *Mediterranean Rim textiles and clothing: industry restructuring and future prospects*

Algeria   : *Industry restructuring*: additional capital investment (especially in fibres) but little change overall; government policy remains import-substituting, but recent evidence of minor shift towards export promotion.

: *Future prospects*: prospects limited due to fragmented industry structure; inefficient public-sector management; lack of international marketing experience; domestic market orientation; and limited foreign involvement.

Egypt   : *Industry restructuring*: major restructuring of the industry in recent years involving a large number of capital investment projects aimed at increasing capacity, upgrading and modernising plant and equipment and improving quality; improved efficiency in state-owned sector through decentralising decision-making, reduced manning levels and price controls; geographical diversification of export markets; encouragement of private-sector and foreign investment through the establishment of EPZs.

: *Future prospects*: good prospects for further increase in textile exports as a result of the above reforms but major problems remain including public-sector inefficiency; fragmented industry structure; increasing labour costs; macroeconomic problems; continued bureaucratic delays in joint-venture approval; quality, design and international marketing issues.

Greece   : *Industry restructuring*: largest textile enterprises respond to EC membership and EC enlargement (Spain and Portugal) by investing in new plant and equipment, cost reduction, improvement in productivity and quality; pace of change slow elsewhere in the industry and small-firm sector remains uncompetitive.

: *Future prospects*: improved prospects as result of the above plus drachma devaluation; major concerns remain regarding the ability of small-firm sector to compete in an enlarged EC.

Malta   : *Industry restructuring*: limited change; focus of inward investment policy shifted towards higher-technology industries; declining locational attractiveness compared to other Rim countries, such as Morocco, Tunisia.

: *Future prospects*: industry may have peaked; future growth dependent on continued attraction of FDI and MNE sourcing and investment policies.

Morocco : *Industry restructuring*: continual promotion of country as offshore processing zone; evidence of marginal improvement in international marketing skills of indigenous companies.

TABLE 12.10 *(continued)*

	: *Future prospects*: short-term prospects very good due to locational attractiveness; longer-term prospects dependent on the development of an indigenous textile industry, geographical diversification and reduced reliance on foreign technology and MNE sourcing policies.
Tunisia	: Similar to Morocco.
Turkey	: *Industry restructuring*: wide range of restructuring measures introduced by both the government and the industry itself, including an aggressive approach towards trade negotiations; large-scale capital investments; Lira devaluation; countertrade deals; economic liberalisation, including the planned privatisation of Sumerbank and the partial removal of textile import controls (allowing access to lower cost/higher quality inputs); the establishment of EPZs (and other incentives to exporters) and Regional Textile Resource Centres; shift towards higher value added products.
	: *Future prospects*: high level of optimism within the industry (target of $10 billion in textile exports).

Source: Hamill (1989).

facturing. Most host country governments in the Mediterranean Rim are actively encouraging the involvement of foreign multinationals in their domestic textile industries. The extent to which Western producers respond to the opportunities available will have a significant impact on their future international competitiveness, and on the future for Mediterranean Rim textiles.

13 Service Sector Multinationals and Developing Countries

Peter Enderwick

13.1 INTRODUCTION

This chapter examines some of the principal issues in the relationships between multinational enterprises (MNEs), the service sector and developing countries. The linkages are both complex and important. There is sizeable investment by developed country MNEs in the service industries of developing countries. Increasingly, developing country-based MNEs are operating in the service sectors of the developing and more advanced economies. The importance of this investment results from the growing significance of the service sector in the world economy, its considerable fluidity and the role that services play in the development process (UNCTAD 1985). MNEs enter the picture as major suppliers of services in the developed nations and, because of the particular economic characteristics of services (Enderwick, 1988a), as a principal mode for transfer of service technologies and output to the developing nations.

The chapter is organised around six substantive sections. The next section examines the role of services in the economic development process. Sections 13.3 and 13.4 deal, respectively, with inward and outward service sector investment and the developing nations. Important policy issues in the regulation of service trade and investment are the subject of section 13.5. Finally, some conclusions are offered in section 13.6.

13.2 SERVICES AND THE DEVELOPMENT PROCESS

Conventional views of development seriously understate the importance of the service sector in economic growth. The most widely held view interprets a growing service sector as a result rather than a source of development. The stages concept of development which envisages a transition from pre-industrial to industrial and eventually post-industrial status, clearly elevates the role of the manufacturing sector. The eventual expansion of the tertiary sector follows from the rise in per capita incomes created by the manufacturing sector (UNCTAD, 1985).

This view of the limited development potential of services is reinforced by the low trade level of services and constraints on export-led growth. In 1980 only 8 per cent of world production of services was traded internationally compared with figures of 45 per cent for agricultural products and 55 per cent for mining and manufacturing output. Such comparisons are not terribly helpful: they overlook the fact that international transactions in services occur through direct investment to a much greater degree than is the case for agricultural or manufactured goods. Estimates for US overseas sales of services suggest that in excess of 80 per cent are attributable to affiliate operations (Enderwick, 1988a). In addition, technological changes and the growing importance of economies of scale in the supply of services are increasing their tradeability (Grosher, 1987; Rada, 1987).

The implications of such views on the role of services are unfortunate. They suggest, for example, that there is no case for active policy intervention in favour of the service sector, indeed such intervention appears positively undesirable in the sense of distorting an inevitable development progression. Furthermore, the higher levels of economic development achieved by the advanced nations implies a primary role for them in the supply of services and a rational international division of labour with the developing countries specialising in the export of goods. However, the most fundamental objection to these views is that they are simply not supported by empirical evidence. The stages view suggests the testable hypothesis of a systematic relationship between the importance of services in trade and GNP and the level of economic development. However, as Table 13.1 shows, there is little evidence of any consistent relationship.

It is apparent from the data above that all of the developing countries included here have a higher ratio of service exports to GDP than the most advanced nations such as Canada, the United States and Japan. The importance of services within total exports is not dissimilar for the two groups of economies. Further evidence dismissive of the stages view is provided by the complementarity of

TABLE 13.1   *Analysis of service exports for selected countries 1981*

Country	Service exports as % of GNP	Service exports as % of total exports
United States	1.3	10.9
Canada	2.7	9.2
Australia	13.3	14.7
Japan	1.9	12.1
Singapore	65.2	30.0
Taiwan	4.0	9.8
Republic of Korea	8.5	20.7
Malaysia	4.1	8.3
Philippines	4.8	23.8
Thailand	4.2	17.7

Source: Riddle and Sours (1987)

service and goods production. A number of studies conclude that only around half of all marketed service output goes to final demand; much of the other 50 per cent is intermediate demand generated by the goods-producing sector (Gershuny and Miles, 1983; Momigliano and Siniscalco, 1982; Norton, 1984). The apparent complementarity of goods and service production is not new. Riddle (1987) provides a valuable historical analogy in arguing that the Industrial Revolution was dependent on an earlier Commercial Revolution (the development of capital markets, transport systems and basic management skills). The above discussion suggests that the service sector has not been given due consideration in the development process.

Even this enabling role for services does not do justice to their importance. This is because services are typically characterised by significant economic linkages and the generation of externalities. Linkages and positive externalities are apparent in the case of infrastructure services such as transportation or the labour force benefits of improved education and health services, but are equally important in producer services such as insurance and finance. In the case of insurance the pooling of risks and premiums provides not only a widening and a deepening of financial markets but additionally a stimulus to saving, credit facilitation and the promotion of new economic activities (UNCTAD, 1985). Similar benefits accrue from the development of financial services (Boreham, 1986).

There is a potential role here for service-sector MNEs. These sectors are subject to a high degree of multinational organisation, particularly in the advanced economies (Baker, 1987; Grubel, 1988) and such firms provide one source of valuable expertise with their often superior technology, managerial expertise and quality standards. If one interprets an improvement in the quality of service provision as a valued externality then MNEs may provide both a competitive and a complementary role in stimulating, through competition, the quality of service provision and in complementing indigenous service offerings with those targeted at new market segments.

Service-based MNEs may play a role in stimulating development via the service sector in at least four other major ways. The first is where the service sector of a developing nation is grossly underdeveloped or there is an inefficient utilisation of resources.

Underdevelopment could occur because of resource scarcities, and the difficulty of trading some services suggests a role for direct investment in easing such shortages. Similarly, indigenous producers may be too small or lack particular expertise (Kaynak, 1986). Again the potential contribution of MNEs is apparent. Inefficiencies may arise perhaps because of restrictive conditions of supply which emerge under certain forms of regulation (UNCTAD, 1985) or for historical reasons certain services are absent or ineffective in their operation (Riddle, 1987). In such cases inward investment may provide a competitive stimulus to more efficient resource usage or a more balanced development of the service sector.

Second, a number of developing countries are characterised by a high degree of specialisation in their service production and face potential problems of instability not unlike those suffered by major exporters of single commodities. The extreme specialisation of island economies in insurance, shipping or tourism are examples of this. Of the developing countries only Singapore can be said to have a broadly-based traded service sector (UNCTAD, 1985). The role of MNEs as one source of diversification for service-based economies is potentially an important one. The success of such a policy depends crucially on the way in which it is operated. International investment could (and has) just as easily exacerbate problems of specialisation and instability.

Third, while many see the service sector as an attractive area for investment because of its relatively low degree of capital intensity (favouring the plentiful labour supplies of most developing countries), increasingly, the service sector spans a spectrum of capital intensity. Again, it may be attractive for a resource-scarce developing country to encourage inward investment into those service industries requiring highly scarce or specialised resources. One study for the early 1970s found that much of the service-sector investment of many developing countries went into infrastructure such as transportation, communications and storage (OECD, 1974).

Finally, the type of service-sector investment appears to be as important as the volume of such investment. There is some evidence that as development occurs the investment focus should shift from infrastructure increasingly towards business services. The importance of MNEs in these industries is well known (Enderwick, 1986b) and their role in complementing or sustaining indigenous investment may be significant.

13.3 INWARD INVESTMENT IN THE SERVICE SECTORS OF DEVELOPING COUNTRIES

As suggested in section 13.2 service industries form an important proportion of all economic activity in both the developed and developing worlds. Services account for more than 50 per cent of world GNP and even in the Pacific Rim newly industrialising countries (NICs), where there has been a rapid growth in manufacturing capability, services still comprise the single largest economic sector in terms of contribution to GNP (Riddle and Sours, 1984). The much lower proportion of world service output that is traded, 8 per cent, means that overseas markets, including those of the developing nations, hold a strong attraction for service producers.

Table 13.2 shows that for the major source nations of direct investment service industries accounted for around 30 per cent of total overseas investment in the mid-1970s.

Overseas investments in services were particularly important for countries like Italy and Japan. In the case of Japan a large proportion of investment in commerce and other services is trade-related and serves to support Japanese exports from both home and a number of NICs. Table 13.2 makes clear the concentration of service-sector investments in other advanced economies. Such countries account for an average of almost 70 per cent of the total stock of service investment. For services like retail trade or telecommunications very little investment occurs outside the most advanced economies (Blomstrom and Lipsey, 1987). In the case of telecommunications, for example, there are few grounds for believing that the position will change. In

TABLE 13.2   *Service sector direct investment abroad as a percentage of total stock of direct investment*

Country	Year	Services as a percentage of direct investment		
		All of which in:		
			Developed Countries	Developing Countries
Canada	1974	28.7	–	–
Italy	1976	38.2	89.3	10.7
Japan	1974	38.8	65.3	34.7
UK	1974	26.8	80.2	19.8
USA	1976	28.7	68.3	31.7
West Germany	1976	22.4	59.4	40.6

Source: United Nations (1978), Table III-38

1985 developing countries' share of the world-wide telecommunications equipment market was only 11 per cent. Their share of information systems such as telegraph, telex and satellite communications is expected to decline from 5 per cent to 4 per cent between 1980 and 1990 (Rada, 1987). Even for tourism services, an area where developing countries might be expected to enjoy a considerable market share, Europe and North America accounted for 80 per cent of all tourist arrivals in 1983 (Richter, 1987).

Much of the service investment in developing countries comprises banking and insurance funds which are attracted to the numerous tax haven and offshore banking centres (Grubel, 1988). In the case of insurance the developing countries constituted only 5.3 per cent of the global premium market in 1984; the large amount of funds passing through many developing countries are clearly generated elsewhere (Baker, 1987). While the share of US service multinationals, investments in Latin America amounted to around 2.5 per cent of all service output in 1982 the share of financial services was 9.5 per cent (Blomstrom and Lipsey, 1987).

Despite the relatively low level of penetration achieved in the service sectors of most developing countries, for a number of reasons they represent extremely attractive markets. The first is the increasing significance and rapid growth of developing country markets. As the figures in Table 13.3 show production of services has grown more rapidly in the developing countries than the developed world, particularly since the recession of the early 1970s.

TABLE 13.3   *Service-sector growth rates 1965–82 and level of economic development*

	Annual average growth rate:		
	1965–73	*1973–80*	*1980–82*
Developing countries	7.7	6.4	4.0
Low-income countries	7.7	6.7	4.5
Middle-income countries	7.7	6.4	3.8
Oil exporters	7.4	7.9	5.8
Oil importers	7.8	5.6	2.8
Major exporters of			
manufactures	8.5	5.7	3.0
Industrial market economies	4.6	3.3	1.5

Source: World Bank (1985)

For many services developing countries now comprise a sizeable market. In the case of insurance, for example, South Korea ranks as the eleventh largest national market in terms of premiums paid and the seventh largest when premiums are expressed as a percentage of GNP. The growth in the market has been immense: life insurance premiums increased by more than 3600 per cent between 1976 and 1984 (Cho, 1988). As the NICs have increased their manufacturing capability there has occurred a concomitant increase in the demand for business services. For Pacific Rim NICs producer services grew at an average annual rate of 23.4 per cent between 1971 and 1981 (Riddle and Sours, 1984).

The second factor attracting service-sector MNEs to developing countries is the strong competitive position these firms enjoy in developing country markets. This arises partly because of the weaknesses characteristic of many indigenous companies. An excellent example is provided by the South Korean insurance industry. Severe government regulation including restrictions on premium rates, the channelling of funds to government-nominated projects and limits on market entry have encouraged cartel practices and discouraged innovation, improvements in the quality of service and efficient resource management (Cho, 1988). US insurance companies who enjoy a degree of familiarity with the market through their servicing of resident aliens, particularly US Armed Forces personnel, now constitute a considerable competitive threat.

However, the competitiveness of service MNEs derives from considerations other than simply the weaknesses of indigenous firms.

First, the benefits of branding, which are considerable in the case of services subject to substantial quality variation (Richardson, 1987) apply increasingly to developing country markets as global media and the growth in international travel facilitate the dissemination of brand information. Second, where the competitive advantage of a service MNE is based on innovation the often incremental nature of most innovations within the service sector eases their absorption within a developing country (Enderwick, 1988a). Advantages derived from innovation may be more durable in a developing country where indigenous competitors perhaps lack the ability to replicate them in the short term. This might apply in the case of financial services where major innovations have not been generally patentable (Arndt, 1988). A similar source of continuing advantage could exist in the case of information-intensive services (banking, finance, accounting) where the poor provision of information processing and transmission technologies (see above) places developing country firms at a considerable disadvantage.

The multinational nature of leading developed country service firms also bestows upon them a source of competitive advantage often unavailable to purely national firms. This arises in services characterised by sizeable economies of agglomeration. MNEs operating in the underdeveloped markets of the developing world are less dependent on agglomeration effects than their indigenous competitors. This follows from both their larger than average size which allows the internal exploitation of economies previously consumed as externalities and their privileged access to parent services.

The third attraction of developing country markets to service MNEs is the difficulty of serving such markets by methods other than direct investment. Where it is possible to export services the considerable barriers to trade discourage this form of market servicing (Enderwick, 1988c). Licensing is discouraged by a number of features of service industries. There are likely to be problems in separating out the technology element of many services. Often successful transfer of service technologies involves close and continuing cooperation. For differentiated and branded quality services there is a danger of underperformance by licensees which imposes potential costs on licensors. For these sorts of reasons direct investment is the most widespread form of overseas market involvement as Table 13.4 shows.

Two points are apparent from Table 13.4. First, licensing income is considerably more important for manufacturing industries than it is

TABLE 13.4   *Technology receipts in relation to direct investment income from affiliates for US parents by industry 1977 ($m and %)*

		Manu-facturing	Trade	Banking	Non-Bank Finance
Developed Countries	Receipts	2 674	449	111	89
	Income	5 428	1 556	587	1 187
	Receipts as % of income	49.3	28.9	18.9	7.5
Developing Countries	Receipts	234	63	78	17
	Income	1 227	485	1 232	1 033
	Receipts as % of income	19.1	13.0	6.3	1.6

Source: United Nations (1983) p. 385 Annex Table IV.12

for trade, banking and finance. Second, for all industries licensing income is far less significant in the case of developing countries.

Offsetting these apparent attractions of developing countries are a number of disadvantages. In many cases developing country service markets are very small and are subject to extensive regulation. Often this regulation takes the form of controls over service producers, not the services themselves, and may constitute barriers to entry or restrictions on the type of business practice allowable (Hindley, 1988). The fears expressed by many developing countries about the competitive strength of service MNEs and the need to maintain some national independence over fundamental services serve to sour the investment climate (Baker, 1987). Finally, for many service MNEs there remain overwhelmingly attractive opportunities in developed world markets. For example, the creation of an integrated European market in 1992 is forcing Japanese banks to establish a presence there in the very near future as after 1992 entry of a third-country producer (that is, non-EC) will require the unanimous approval of all 12 member states.

Thus the picture regarding inward service investment is a mixed one. It is likely that in the near future, excluding any significant policy changes, the share of service investments attracted to the developing countries will remain at a similar level.

13.4 OUTWARD INVESTMENT BY DEVELOPING COUNTRY SERVICE MNEs

It is not possible accurately to quantify the significance of outward investment in service industries by developing country MNEs. Comprehensive data on international investment in services do not exist; the data for developing countries is even less systematic (Lecraw, 1988). However, the considerable degree of internationalisation achieved by developing country enterprises in a number of service industries does suggest that in comparison with their counterparts from the developed world, developing country MNEs are more active in the service industries. In the case of South Korea, for example, construction accounted for 15 per cent of total outward investment during the 1970s. Developing country MNEs play an important role in industries like construction (in 1982 South Korea was the second most important international contracting nation), shipping and banking (30 per cent of all foreign bank employees in New York are employed by banks originating in the developing world). Much of this outward service investment is destined for higher-income economies. These investments are prompted by both a desire to serve specific market segments, for instance, home country firms and nationals abroad, and in response to establishment by advanced nation MNEs in the home markets of developing world MNEs (Lecraw, 1988b).

Explanations of overseas investment by developing country MNEs have emphasised the competitive advantages available to such firms. In contrast to the technological, financial and organisational advantages generally associated with advanced nation MNEs those based in developing countries may enjoy the benefits of lower costs, particularly labour costs, familiarity with market conditions in developing countries and, in some cases, low levels of government regulation (Wells, 1983).

The availability of low-cost labour, both unskilled manuals and qualified engineers, has been a continuing source of competitive advantage for South Korean construction firms. In particular, the lower relative cost of South Korean supervisory, engineering and managerial staff has prevented contractors from the advanced nations matching labour costs by employing third-country manual workers (Kim, 1988). However, the tenuous nature of this type of advantage is illustrated by the South Korean experience in recent years. The decline in the market for labour-intensive general construction projects, particularly in the Middle East, and a rise in South Korean labour costs relative to other developing world competitors (total wages to migrant workers in the Middle East increased by 45 per cent between 1975 and 1980) meant that South Korean construction firms suffered a dramatic fall in market share (Kim, 1988). In response South Korean firms have begun to employ labour from even lower wage nations. In 1984 nearly 28 per cent of workers on South Korean overseas construction projects were non-Korean nationals (David, 1987).

Familiarity with developing nation conditions is reflected in both the product and process technology of developing nation MNEs. Their adoption of smaller-scale and often labour-favouring methods of production as well as specialisation in services for lower-income markets (generally of lower price and quality with low levels of promotion) favour their concentration in other developing countries. Often the source of this expertise is unique. The experience gained by South Korean construction firms in the completion of US military projects was applicable to the US military build-up in Vietnam in the mid-1960s. Further internationalisation occurred in the 1970s as these firms undertook similar work in US bases in Guam, Okinawa and Alaska (Kim, 1988). A similar source of advantage is provided by the experience of Brazilian contractors in undertaking large-scale infrastructure projects in geographically remote and difficult terrains (Enderwick, 1988d).

Differences in the pattern and degree of government regulation of national markets provides a further source of competitive advantage. The low level of regulation found in service industries like shipping, banking and insurance in many developing countries provides a powerful stimulus to investment and expansion in these industries. The disproportionate number of banks present in countries like Hong Kong and Singapore is partly the result of a deliberate policy of favourable regulation with low levels of taxation and liberal minimum reserve requirements (Grubel, 1988).

Criticism of the extent to which the idea of natural comparative advantage is applicable in the case of services has focused on the creation of such conditions and particularly the role of government policy. International competitiveness in financial services for example, depends more on the maintenance of economic and political stability and the creation of sound infrastructural services (telecommunications, accounting, legal) than it does on the abundance of capital (Arndt, 1988). The position of developing country service MNEs depends crucially, in many cases, on supportive government policy. The particular success of the South Korean construction industry, as opposed to another developing country, is not unconnected with the extensive provisions made by the government in providing funding (in many cases to South Korean banks), guaranteeing loans, acquiring technology, and in gathering market intelligence. The less effective measures provided by the Indian government to its construction industry have been cited as a contributory factor in that country's low level of success overseas (David, 1987).

A second criticism is the static nature of interpretations of comparative advantage. There are numerous important linkages between success in producer services and enhanced competitiveness in other services (and goods). Linkages between services both further up the value added chain (design, market research), lower down (distribution, servicing) and at the production stage (quality control, information management) are crucial to continued international success (Gibbs and Mashayekhi, 1988).

A third point of interest is the importance of recognising that the competitive assets of developing country MNEs may not be as effectively deployed in some markets. A good example is provided by the difficulties and expense of operating in the Japanese market. At the end of 1986 foreign securities companies had established 36 branches and 124 representative offices in Japan. Of these, eight representative offices belonged to MNEs originating in the developing world (Singapore, Hong Kong and South Korea). The labour cost advantages enjoyed by these companies were largely neutralised in Japan where firms have to meet expatriate cost of living expenses which are usually more than three times the level of home salary. Since most of this is accounted for by rents (average monthly rent for foreigners in Tokyo in 1987 was US $4350 per month) differences in total labour costs are virtually eliminated. These sorts of factors help to explain why much of the developing nations, investment is in countries of a similar level of development.

The nature of the competitive advantages possessed by developing country MNEs means that these firms are vulnerable to market changes. The South Korean construction industry suffered a 50 per cent decline in market share between 1981 and 1985. Its extreme specialisation, with about 85 per cent of contracts in general construction and over 90 per cent of work in the Middle East, meant that when oil revenues declined and infrastructure investment slowed, its revenues dipped dramatically (Kim, 1988). In addition their competitive base makes it difficult for firms to move quickly or easily into new market segments. Attempts to move into more technology-intensive areas of construction have been frustrated by South Korea's weakness in design and engineering functions.

There were only four South Korean firms in the top 200 international design firms in 1985 and their total market share was only 1.3 per cent. While the government has introduced several measures to upgrade capability in these areas the results to date have not been significant. These weaknesses have impeded entry into the markets of the advanced nations. In 1985 South Korea's share of revenues going to foreign constructors in the USA was only 0.4 per cent. Because of the protectionist nature of the Japanese construction industry firms have not achieved any penetration of this important market (Kim, 1988).

This discussion serves to highlight two important points. The first is the extent of linkages between service activities and between services and goods. The narrow skills basis of many developing world service MNEs means that their position is often tenuous and attempts to broaden their operating base frustrated by the absence of complementary services. The Korean construction industry was impeded in its early years by the underdevelopment of international banking experience in South Korea; in more recent years weaknesses in design and engineering services have impeded market and technological diversification.

Second, as the discussion would lead us to expect there are those service industries where developing country MNEs simply do not exist. Examples are stockbroking services, the media, health care, travel and tourism and communications (Lecraw, 1988). In these industries developing country firms do not appear to have been able to create the necessary competitive abilities. The entrenched position in these industries of major MNEs from the leading nations means that barriers to late entrants are considerable and in some cases probably insurmountable.

13.5 POLICY ISSUES

The relationships between services, multinational enterprises and developing countries raise a number of important policy issues. We discuss these under four major groupings: policy issues for developing countries as host nations; policy questions for developing economies as source nations; the policy position of major service MNEs; and the international negotiating stance of developing countries with regard to services and areas of contention.

For a developing country hosting service MNEs it is important to identify the benefits which inward investment could bring. Our discussion has highlighted three principal areas. The first is in providing resources for the establishment or expansion of crucial producer and infrastructure services. The role that MNEs might play in complementing indigenous investment in the service sector is illustrated by the example of the Korean construction industry discussed above. The significant linkages which exist between services means that uneven development could result in bottlenecks and constraints on development. The second area of benefit is where inward investors improve the efficiency with which service-sector resources are utilised. Establishment could provide a general competitive stimulus to efficiency, particularly if indigenous firms are operating cartel-type practices, and more specific benefits in upgrading human capital, improving organisational and management practices and in fostering a greater recognition of the value of the concept of marketing (Kaynak, 1986). Third, the careful attraction of particular service firms and industries could reduce the extreme specialisation and vulnerability of many developing host nations. The best example of successful diversification is probably Singapore but complementarity is also apparent in the case of St Lucia, where assembly stage electronics and tourism coexist, or Bermuda with tourism and financial services.

The second policy issue facing a host government concerns the type of service industry to encourage. For those service industries where a separation of functions or stages is possible, for example, computer services, a developing country may find itself relegated to accepting the least skill-intensive stages (UNCTAD, 1985). The problems with such investments are very similar to those associated with branch plant manufacturing; namely a low level of technology and skill transfer and a high level of investment instability. Certain service industries are more important in the development process than others. Current thinking stresses the contribution made by producer service industries. These are crucial in providing an important interface between infrastructure and the production process, facilitating innovation and providing high quality employment opportunities

(Gibbs and Mashayekhi, 1988). To encourage such investments host governments may need substantially to rethink their incentive packages, paying much greater attention to the specific economic characteristics of service production (Arndt, 1988; Enderwick, 1987).

A third policy issue concerns the degree of regulation and protection afforded the host service sector and, increasingly, the degree of liberalisation adopted. Protection of the service sector is defended on a number of grounds including the infant industry argument that indigenous suppliers could not survive foreign competition, the threat to national sovereignty created by foreign ownership of strategic services, for example, banking and the possibility of negative externalities and problems of market failure. Regardless of the wisdom or otherwise of these arguments (Enderwick, 1988c) protectionism does lead to welfare losses where prices are increased or quality impaired. Quantification of these losses is particularly difficult since the characteristics of services encourage the use of non-tariff barriers. Some work has been undertaken on the ranking of methods of protection by degree of desirability (undesirability). Where the policy objective is to encourage output of the indigenous industry a subsidy is generally superior to a tariff which in turn is more desirable than a quota (Hindley, 1988).

The welfare cost issue is not unrelated to the considerable pressures for liberalisation of the service sectors of many developing countries. Where host governments operating a policy of protectionism are forced to permit the entry of foreign suppliers welfare losses could actually increase if foreign suppliers repatriate their share of rents. If the host government chooses to couple foreign entry with deregulation then welfare losses could be reduced (as competition dissipates rents to consumers in the form of lower prices). In addition, if foreign participation stimulates innovation and a downward shift on the supply side then the welfare gain could be increased by the entry of foreign firms (Cho, 1988).

The major policy question for developing country source economies is how to nurture and sustain the competitive position of their enterprises. The earlier discussion recognised the crucial role that government policy can play in 'creating' competitive advantage. More specifically, the service MNEs of developing countries face barriers to entry stemming from their often small size and late entry to world markets. There may be a case for government investigation of the possibility of tie-ups with major service MNEs, perhaps in the form of joint ventures or links in the branding and marketing of services. Because of the high and variable information content of many services branding represents a dynamic and continuing barrier to entry which may be difficult to overcome in isolation (Richardson, 1987).

The policy position of service MNEs is essentially a desire to operate in overseas markets on an equal footing with indigenous suppliers. In the case of services this raises major issues regarding the right to establishment in an overseas market; unrestricted access to parent company data sources and processing facilities and the protection of proprietary technologies. Many of these issues cannot be tackled by individual host nations and are currently under consideration in a number of international organisations (GATT, UNCTAD, WIPO). National governments do have some influence over other areas of concern to service MNEs, particularly demands for national treatment, neutral procurement policies and restrictions on the monopoly power of national suppliers (Gibbs and Mashayekhi, 1988).

A number of other important issues have been raised by the international policy position of developing countries with regard to services. The difficulties experienced in the current round of GATT have arisen in part from differences over the type of service industry which should be included in the negotiations (with the developing countries arguing for the inclusion of labour-intensive services such as construction where they are likely to enjoy a strong competitive position) and demands for the linking of negotiations over services to concessions on goods markets and the cross-border movement of labour. More fundamentally there is the implicit assumption prevalent within OECD member nations that any liberalisation of services will be trade-creating and will encourage economic growth. While this is probably true for OECD members, it is far from clear that it applies to developing nations facing considerable barriers in entering overseas markets. However, the South Korean insurance case does provide an example of where relaxation of restrictions can be trade-inducing (Cho, 1988).

A final area of contention is the opposing positions of service MNEs and developing countries with regard to the starting point for any negotiations. While major source governments and service MNEs have been quick to point out the restrictions imposed on the service sector by many developing countries (US Office of the US Trade Representative, 1983) these countries have referred to the various restrictive business practices operated by dominant service MNEs. The development of an appropriate framework to define and handle such practices may be a necessary condition for any substantial progress in the international arena.

13.6 CONCLUSIONS

This chapter has surveyed the major issues that arise in the relationships between service industries, multinational enterprises and developing countries. The discussion suggests a number of conclusions.

The first concerns the need for a comprehensive re-evaluation of the role of services in the development process. As section 13.2 revealed, there is little evidence to support the traditional view that growth of the tertiary sector is an outcome of, rather than a determinant of, economic development. Recognition of the linkages which exist between service industries and between services and goods production also suggests a potential role for overseas-based MNEs in contributing to the growth of developing countries. There is a need for more work on understanding the contribution of service industries, and foreign MNEs, to the development process.

Second, for most service industries overseas market servicing implies direct investment; there are considerable difficulties in exporting a number of services. This means that the internationalisation of most service industries raises unavoidable issues concerning the right to establishment or a commercial presence, national treatment and neutrality in government procurement practices. The successful expansion of many service industries will necessitate more than a reduction in barriers to trade in services, the current focus of policy interest.

A third conclusion concerns the limited role that developing countries currently play as host and source nations for service-sector MNEs. There are few grounds for believing that their share of inward investment in services will increase markedly in the near future. Developing country MNEs suffer a number of weaknesses including, in many cases, extreme specialisation, below average size and non-sustainable competitive advantages. They are also disadvantaged by the very powerful competitive positions established by leading service MNEs in many industries.

Fourth, this is an area which raises a large number of complex policy issues. In the international arena there are several areas of contention between service MNEs and developing countries. A number of these issues are currently under consideration in organisations like GATT, UNCTAD and UNCTC. Further work is also needed on the relationships between domestic policy, particularly deregulation, and the attraction of foreign investment.

Finally, more work is required on a disaggregated basis to examine more fully differences by industry and by nation in the behaviour of service MNEs. Of particular importance are producer services, the current driving force in the development of the tertiary sector.

Part VI
Summary and Conclusion

14 Some Concluding Remarks

John H. Dunning

14.1 INTRODUCTION

In this review I will make no attempt to undertake any comprehensive summary of, or to present any definitive conclusions on the very varied and interesting selection of papers contained in this volume. Instead I propose to look a little at some of the more important developments in the world economy over the past few years, and the role multinationals have played in fashioning these developments; and then relate these happenings to some of the papers which have been presented here. Perhaps I should apologise in advance if I do not afford equal weight to each contribution in the course of a very personal view of some of the highlights of the previous chapters.

14.2 SOME REASONS FOR THE CHANGING ORIENTATION OF STUDIES ON THE MULTINATIONAL ENTERPRISE

If we had held this kind of meeting 15 years ago, the sort of papers which would have been offered and, indeed, the focus of the issues which we would have addressed, would have been very different. At almost every academic and other kind of gathering I attend these days to do with multinationals, I observe a fairly dramatic shift in the perceptions of the nature of the impact between these institutions and the countries in which they operate. Let me give you two very recent examples. A fortnight before this conference I was in Scotland ‐ attending a one-day colloquium on Japanese direct investment in that country. Almost without exception the Japanese were lauding the British, and particularly the Scots, for what they were doing to attract foreign direct investment and for the management of their economic affairs. And the Scots, for their part, were unqualified in their acknowledgment of the beneficial effects of the Japanese presence. If

313

there was a word of criticism about the less welcome consequences of inward investment I, for one, did not hear it.

Just ten days later I was at a conference on multinationals in Hungary where, as I am sure many of you will know, most of the activity by foreign firms takes the form of joint ventures. Most of the papers were given by Hungarian officials and by researchers from a new centre on multinationals, recently established in Budapest. The Minister of Trade started the ball rolling by describing the transformation of the Hungarian attitude towards inward investment over the past five years or so, and of how the current government recognises the enormous benefits such investment can bring to the Hungarian economy. He ended his speech with the words 'You may be sure that we shall do all we can to make our country attractive to investment by Western firms'. The Minister's speech was followed by a no less enthusiastic eulogy by the spokesman of some foreign-owned companies, who were already producing in Hungary, on the measures taken by the Hungarian government to open up their economy to market forces. Apart, rather strangely I thought, from one Japanese executive whose firm had just concluded two joint ventures with Hungarian partners and who was highly critical of the ability of the Hungarian economic machine to give the right kind of incentives to foreign investors to come into the country, everything in the garden was sweetness and light, or appeared to be so!

I imagine most of you probably would re-echo my own experiences in conferences and seminars which you have recently attended, insofar as multinational activity in both developed and developing countries is concerned. Don Lecraw and I were in Southern Africa recently, at a meeting in Lesotho. The meeting was attended by Deans of Economics, Law and Business School Faculties. The idea was that – acting on behalf of the United Nations Centre on Transnational Corporations (UNCTC) – we should try to set up a series of intensive training courses for teachers of Economics, Business Policy and Law in African universities to help them introduce material about foreign direct investment and multinational companies into their graduate courses. Again, almost without exception, the Deans seemed to applaud this idea because in their words 'our countries want to know more about how to attract inward investment'. This is in stark contrast to the situation of ten years ago when, at any conference you would go to in the developing world, you would find the main emphasis directed towards the costs and benefits of multinational activity, with particular emphasis on identifying the ways in which the governments of developing countries, through a variety of measures, could minimise the economic rent extracted by multinationals.

I do not wish to rehearse in any detail the changes which have taken place in the world economy over the last decade or more, or the reactions of multinationals to these changes. However, I would like to make just one or two general observations. The first is that I perceive that at least some of these changes are irreversible. This applies particularly to those which are the result of technological advances. On the other hand, one of the factors which has altered the views of many host developing countries about the role of the multinationals has been the deterioration in their economic prospects, as, for example, witnessed by their slower growth rates and rising unemployment. This has occurred at the same time that the investment options open to foreign investors have been widening. Data from the United Nations Centre on Transnational Corporations quite clearly show a falling percentage of investment by multinationals going to developing countries. This is partly a reflection of the resurgence in economic growth in many of the advanced countries, and the entry of Japanese multinationals as significant foreign investors, especially in Western Europe and the USA. We also see, of course, the opening up of new territories to foreign firms in both Asia and Eastern Europe. I was told, for example, that one of the main items on the agenda of Gorbachev's visit to the UK, and one of the things which he emphasised in a speech (7 April 1989) was that he wanted to encourage more joint ventures between United Kingdom and Soviet Union firms. How far these words will be translated into actions remains to be seen, but I do not think there is any doubt that the world is continually throwing up new challenges and openings for multinational companies; and because of this, countries that wish to attract such institutions into their midst will have to abide by the rules of the game and provide them with the right kind of investment climate.

At the same time, we see that the multinationals are themselves becoming more pluralistic – for example, in terms of their size and experience, and their organisational form. Strategic investments, notably those by medium-size firms and those of Asian origin, are likely to increase the most dramatically in the 1990s. There is also likely to be more outward investment by newly industrialising countries such as South Korea and Taiwan; and this may have especially interesting implications for developing countries, as one suspects that such multinationals may have certain advantages over their First World counterparts, which are particularly sought by other developing countries. I think John Cantwell told us something very interesting about his perception of the future of foreign direct investment in Africa, and it may well be that some developing country multinationals could be in a favoured position to assist some of the poorer African economies to achieve some of their goals and aspirations. Developments in organisational technology are also encouraging investments by a new generation of medium-size firms in developing countries.

Of course, there has been also a tremendous learning process which has been going on over the last 20 years. Certainly, in the 1960s most developing countries, and for that matter many developed countries did not know what to expect from inward direct investment or, if they did, they were usually quite disappointed with the results. Similarly, foreign investors did not really appreciate what was required of them by developing countries. There has also been a tremendous advance in understanding by governments of the need for the right kind of macroeconomic policies if inward investment is to be optimally beneficial. This I also find very refreshing. Increasingly, in my conversations with representatives from governments of both developed and developing countries I detect a growing sense of economic realism in their appreciation of the contributions which foreign investment can and cannot make to development. True, some emphasis continues to be given to performance requirements, and some complaints about the restrictive business practices of multinationals continue to abound. At the same time, many developing countries are making a conscious effort to put their own economic houses in order and to reduce the kind of market distortions which reduce, rather than enhance, the benefits of inward investment. Moreover, an increasing number of developing country governments are evolving a more holistic approach towards inward investment and are viewing incentives and obstacles to such investment as part of an overall package. I believe that international business scholars working in the policy advisory area, like Lou Wells, John Stopford and Don Lecraw, are doing much to guide authorities in developing countries and to persuade them of the need to take an integrated economic and political approach towards inward investment. This means not just looking at their foreign investment policies *per se*, but also at other policies relating to fiscal, trade, education, technology and transport matters which affect the production and marketing decisions of foreign-owned firms. Moreover, as Lecraw has pointed out in an unpublished paper for the UNCTC, policy-makers should not be primarily concerned with the effectiveness of different kinds of incentives in attracting inward investment, but rather with how best to encourage the kind of investment which most contributes to national developmental goals.

Now all this seems to me that we, as teachers and researchers, have to modify our research agenda insofar as it is directed to understanding developments in the world economy, the strategies and organisational forms of the multinationals, and policies towards inward direct investment. In turn, these changes have dramatically affected the nature and scope of international business activity. The papers offered here have not talked too much about non-equity participation – although it has been touched upon from time to time – nor of strategic alliances. We have focused rather more on foreign direct investment, but we all know today that this particular form of involvement is best considered as part of a package of activities by these companies in the developing as well as in the developed world.

The next point I wish to make is that I think we need to be aware that it is no longer appropriate to look at the role of multinationals in developing countries in isolation to their involvement in the rest of the world. Let me explain what I mean.

Although there is quite a lot of scholarly work currently being done on the role of multinationals in fashioning the international division of labour, for the most part the impact of foreign direct investment on a particular developing country is normally viewed from the perspective of that country as if it was quite separate from the investments made by the same firms elsewhere in the world. True, within developing countries we have always accepted, particularly in the export processing type of investment, that there may be competition between developing countries for inward investment, but we have not often brought into consideration how the operations of multinationals in developed countries affect what they do or do not do in developing countries. Admittedly, at first sight the competition between investment in the United Kingdom by Japanese companies and investment in Thailand might seem to be rather distant. But think for a moment of some of the possibilities which may follow from the completion of the internal market in 1992. These will undoubtedly affect the propensity of Japanese firms to invest in the EEC which, in turn, could well rebound on some of their activities in some developing countries. For example, depending on the level of the external tariff imposed by the EEC on imports from Japan and from developing countries in Asia, it is possible to envisage scenarios which might lead to an increase or decrease in economic activity in developing countries. But the point I am really trying to make is that, increasingly, when examining the impact of multinationals on developing countries, we must take a global perspective; and when we look at multinational investment in developing countries and particularly export-oriented investment it is necessary to consider their policies in the light of multinationals' activities in the developed world as well. To a growing extent countries like South Korea and Taiwan are now competing with developing countries in many areas of their industries.

14.3   THE CONTRIBUTIONS OF THE PRESENT VOLUME

With these thoughts in mind, how can one view the kind of contributions made here? What do you and I expect when we are presented with a collection of this kind? Clearly, we want to be stimulated with new ideas, however way-out or controversial they might be. They might go outside our own particular existing frame of reference – I am thinking in this connection of the papers by Peter Buckley and Mark Casson, and by Klaus Weiermair, which I will come back to in a moment. Secondly, I think there is always room for papers which update and extend our existing knowledge by offering new theoretical insights or by empirical testing. Often this requires us to re-think some of our previous predilections and preconceptions. I think there were a number of papers like that, including those by Rhys Jenkins and Don Lecraw. I judge each of these papers as being extremely valuable in taking us a little further in our thinking along a particular line or set of lines. And each of these papers produced their own particular nuggets of gold, which we shall all take away and ponder on.

Then there were the papers which move our knowledge into new areas. Sometimes they are rather more inductive than deductive in their methodology, and take our existing understanding about multinationals and foreign direct investment into uncharted territories. One example is the paper by John Cantwell, which has forced us to reappraise our understanding of the role of direct investment in Africa. The paper by Artisien, Svetlicic and Rojec on Yugoslavian investment in developing countries has thrown up some very

interesting ideas, particularly on the determinants of minority investments and the problems faced by firms from one institutional and
legal environment investing in another. I refer you particularly to the
extremely interesting data in their Table 10.7 (p. 243). The paper by
Jim Hamill also uses familiar techniques to chart new territories,
while the contribution by Raj Aggarwal and Pervez Ghauri has given
us a novel insight into the application of the product-cycle model of
foreign direct investment to Swedish investment in Asia. Again, I
think this is all grist to the researcher's mill.

There is another group of contributions which I would commend
for offering us some new theoretical perspectives or the empirical
testing of such perspectives; or, indeed, new testing on existing
theoretical concepts. The paper by Mark Casson and Francis Chukujama, for example, was very rich, I think, in helping us to understand
the nature, characteristics, determinants and effects of countertrade,
and some of the implications of such trade for policy-makers. I would
also put the papers by Edward Graham and Homi Katrak into this
category. I think both offer us some novel analytical insights into
important problems and their implications for government policies.

I think then you will agree with me that we have had a balanced
menu of presentations. But let me return for a moment to the papers
by Weiermair and by Buckley and Casson, because I think that, as far
as most of us were concerned, they did raise a lot of unfamiliar issues,
issues which somehow or other may well have been at the back of our
minds as business researchers but which have not been brought to the
fore, and certainly have not previously been articulated in such a
logical and persuasive way. Both papers really set out analytical
frameworks and produce agendas for further research and essentially
approach their subject from an interdisciplinary perspective. Elsewhere (Dunning, 1988, 1989) I have written on the need for scholars
to take an interdisciplinary approach to teaching and research in
international business. At the same time, I am wary of advising
scholars, and particularly younger scholars, to trespass far beyond
the boundaries of the disciplines in which they have been trained.
And yet in our study of foreign direct investment and multinationals,
we cannot escape the fact that it is often some of the non-economic
variables which are among the most relevant in explaining both the
determinants and impact of multinational activity. If I had to single
out what was distinctive about international compared with domestic
business, I would have to say that in some of the more technical areas
– for example, finance and accounting – there is very little indeed,

and that our concepts, theories and modes of thinking need little modification to account for cross-border operations. On the other hand, I would suggest that as one moves away from the more technically-oriented to the more human-oriented areas of study, so the internationalisation of business imposes new elements on our thinking.

In the Buckley and Casson paper a distinction was made between Social Anthropology and Economics. But taking the spectrum of disciplines taught in business schools it is perhaps in the area of organisation and industry that we notice the biggest differences in our theorising about businesses within national boundaries compared with those operating internationally. Why is that? Because, I believe, we are immediately introduced to differing aspects of the human dimension and particularly in terms of what I think Buckley and Casson (rather generically) refer to as 'cultural factors'. If we could take culture as a generic term, then we raise all sorts of matters which affect the way in which individuals and institutions relate to one another, both within particular firms and between firms. Because people think, react and behave differently across national boundaries, one naturally studies these hypotheses much more carefully than in the case of domestic business; and immediately one is outside the purely technical areas of economics and finance these other variables have to be introduced.

In recent times, as the Weiermair paper demonstrates, it is the Japanese who have caused us to think very carefully about the country-specific differences in the behaviour of multinationals; this is because we are confronted with differences in perceptions, mentality, thought forms and so on. Indeed, what has been missing from the past literature on multinationals in developing countries has been the *explicit* recognition of the relevance of some of these factors. Admittedly, the Political Economy literature has begun to recognise that sovereignty-related perceptions and goals are very different between developing countries and developed countries, and that the multinationals may be a creature of international capitalism which may not necessarily be welcomed by some of the developing countries in which they operate. We could trace much of this concern to the writings of Stephen Hymer, but I think the contribution of Buckley and Casson, and others which are now coming to the fore, are recognising some of these political-type aspects of multinational behaviour; these are very generally 'cultural factors', which need to be embodied in our understanding of multinationals in developing hosts and which indeed may find application in the developed countries as well. It may be that the next generation of research has to take such considerations much more explicitly into account.

As I have said, I believe that each of the papers, in their own particular way, has made a distinct contribution to our understanding. All of us will go away feeling richer for having attended this conference, and I congratulate the editors, who have good reason to be pleased.

Bibliography

ABEGGLEN, J.C. and STALK, G. Jr. (1985) *Kaisha: The Japanese Corporation*, New York: Basic Books.

ABO, T. (1987) *Japanese Local Production Systems in the USA* (in Japanese), Tokyo: Toyo Kezei Shimbosha.

ACOCELLA, N. *et al.* (1985) *Le Multinazionali Italiane*, Bologna: Il Mulino.

AGARWAL, J.P. (1976) 'Factor Proportions of Foreign and Domestic Firms in Indian Manufacturing', *Economic Journal*, 86, no. 3, pp. 589–94.

AGGARWAL, R. (1980) 'Investment Performance of US Based Multinational Companies', *Journal of International Business Studies*, 11, no. 1, pp. 98–104.

AGGARWAL, R. (1984) 'The Strategic Challenge of Third World Multinationals: A New Stage of the Product Life Cycle of Multinationals', in Farmer, R.N. (ed.), *Advances in International Comparative Management*, Greenwich, CT: JAI Press.

AGGARWAL, R. (1985) 'Third World Multinationals: A Case Study of the Foreign Operations of Singapore Firms', *Contemporary South East Asia*, 7, no. 3, pp. 193–209.

AGGARWAL, R. (1987) 'The Strategic Challenge of the Evolving Global Economy', *Business Horizons*, 30, no. 4, pp. 38–44.

AGGARWAL, R. (1988) 'Multinationals of the South', *Journal of International Business Studies*, 19, no. 1, pp. 140–43.

AGGARWAL, R. AND WEEKLY, J.K. (1982) 'Foreign Operations of Third World Multinationals: A Literature Review and Analysis of Indian Companies', *Journal of Developing Areas*, 17, no. 1, pp. 13–30.

AGMON, T. and KINDLEBERGER, C.P. (eds) (1977) *Multinationals from Small Countries*, Cambridge, MA: The MIT Press.

AGMON, T. and LESSARD, D.R. (1977) 'Investor Recognition of Corporate International Diversification', *Journal of Finance*, 32, no. 4, pp. 1049–55.

AHIAKPOR, J. (1986) 'The Capital Intensity of Foreign, Private Local and State Owned Firms in a Less Developed Country: Ghana', *Journal of Development Economics*, 20, no. 1, pp. 145–62.

AHIAKPOR, J. (1989) 'Do Firms Choose Inappropriate Technology in LDCs?', *Economic Development and Cultural Change*, 30, no. 2, pp. 557–71.

AKERLOF, G.A. (1970) 'The Market for Lemons; Qualitative Uncertainty and the Market Mechanism', *Quarterly Journal of Economics*, 84, pp. 488–500.

ALIBER, R.Z. (1971) 'The Multinational Enterprise in a Multiple Currency World', in Dunning, J.H. (ed.), *The Multinational Enterprise*, New York: Praeger.

AMANO, M.M. (1982) 'Motivational Orientation Differences between

Japan and the United States: The Key to Worker Productivity Successes and Problems', in, Lee, S.M. and Schwendiman, G. (eds.) *Management by Japanese Systems*, New York: Praeger.

AOKI, M. (ed.) (1984) *The Economic Analysis of the Japanese Firm*, Rotterdam: North Holland.

AOKI, M. (1986) 'Horizontal Versus Vertical Information Structure of the Firm', *American Economic Review*, 76, no. 5, pp. 971–83.

ARNDT, M. (1988) 'Comparative Advantage in Trade in Financial Services', *Banco Nazionale del Lavoro Quarterly Review*, 41, no. 164, pp. 61–78.

ARRIGHI, G. (1970) 'International Corporations, Labour Aristocracies and Economic Development in Africa', reprinted in Arrighi, G. and Saul, J.S. *Essays on the Political Economy of Africa*, New York: Monthly Review Press, 1973.

ARROW, K.J. (1975) 'Vertical Integration and Communication', *Bell Journal of Economics*, 6, no. 1, pp. 173–83.

ARTISIEN, P.F.R. (1985) *Joint Ventures in Yugoslav Industry*, Aldershot: Gower.

ARTISIEN, P.F.R. and BUCKLEY, P.J. (1985) 'Joint Ventures in Yugoslavia: Opportunities and Constraints', *Journal of International Business Studies*, 16, no. 1, pp. 111–35.

ASTLEY, G.W. (1985) 'The Two Ecologies: Population and Community Perspectives on Organizational Evolution', *Administrative Science Quarterly*, 30, pp. 224–41.

BAKER, A.M. (1987) 'Liberalisation of the Trade in Services – The World Insurance Industry', in Giarini, O. (ed.), *The Emerging Service Economy*, Oxford: Pergamon Press.

BALASSA, B. (1965) 'Trade Liberalisation and "Revealed Comparative Advantage"', *The Manchester School*, 33, no. 2, pp. 99–123.

BALASUBRAMANYAM, V.N. (1984) 'Factor Proportions and Productive Efficiency of Foreign Owned Firms in the Indonesian Manufacturing Sector', *Bulletin of Indonesian Economic Studies*, XX, no. 3, pp. 70–94.

BARRO, R.J. and GROSSMAN, H.I. (1976) *Money, Employment and Inflation*, Cambridge: Cambridge University Press.

BEAMISH, P.W. (1984) *Joint Venture Performance in Developing Countries*, unpublished doctoral dissertation, University of Western Ontario, London, Ontario.

BENEDICT, R. (1946) *The Chrysanthemum and the Sword*, Boston: Houghton, Mifflin.

BENNETT, D. and SHARPE, K. (1985) *Transnational Corporations Versus the State*, Princeton: Princeton University Press.

BERGER, S. and PIORE, M.J. (1980) *Dualism and Discontinuity in Industrial Societies*, Cambridge: Cambridge University Press.

BERNAL, V. (1976) 'The Impact of Multinational Corporations on Employment and Income: The Case of Mexico', *International Labour Office World Employment Programme 2–28*, Working Paper 13, Geneva.

BIERSTEKER, T. (1978) *Distortion or Development? Contending Perspectives on the Multinational Corporation*, Cambridge, MA: The MIT Press.

BILLERBECK, K. and YASUGI, Y. (1979) 'Private Direct Foreign Investment in Developing Countries', *World Bank Staff Working Paper*. Washington, DC, July.

BLOMSTROM, M. and LIPSEY, R.E. (1987) 'US Firms in Latin American Service Industries', *NBER Working Paper No. 2307*, Cambridge, MA: National Bureau of Economic Research.

BOREHAM, G.F. (1986) 'The Financial Markets Approach to Economic Development in LDCs', in Kaynak, E. (ed.), *Service Industries in Developing Countries*, London: Frank Cass.

BOWMAN, J.S. (1986) 'The Rising Sun in America – Japanese Management in the United States', *Personnel Administrator*, 31, no. 10, pp. 81–9.

BRANDER, J.A. and SPENCER, B. (1981) 'Tariffs and the Extraction of Foreign Monopoly Rents under Potential Entry', *Canadian Journal of Economics*, 14, pp. 371–89.

BUCKLEY, P.J. (1985) 'New Forms of International Industrial Cooperation', in Buckley, P.J. and Casson, M.C. (eds.), *The Economic Theory of the Multinational Enterprise*, London: Macmillan.

BUCKLEY, P.J. and CASSON, M.C. (1976) *The Future of the Multinational Enterprise*, London: Macmillan.

BUCKLEY, P.J. and CASSON, M.C. (1985) *The Economic Theory of the Multinational Enterprise*, London: Macmillan.

BUCKLEY, P.J. and CASSON, M.C. (1988) 'A Theory of Cooperation in International Business', in Contractor, F.J. and Lorange, P. (eds.), *Cooperative Strategies in International Business*, Lexington, MA: Lexington Books.

BUCKLEY, P.J., DUNNING, J.H. and PEARCE, R.D. (1978) 'The Influence of Firm Size, Industry, Nationality, and Degree of Multinationality on the Growth and Profitability of the World's Largest Firms, 1962–72', *Weltwirtschaftliches Archiv*, 114, no. 2, pp. 243–55.

BUCKLEY, P.J. and MIRZA, H. (1985) 'The Wit and Wisdom of Japanese Management: An Iconoclastic Analysis', *Management International Review*, 25, no. 3, pp. 16–32.

Business International (1984) *Threats and Opportunities of Global Countertrade: Marketing, Financing and Organisational Implications*, Geneva: Business International.

CALVET, A.L. and NAIM, M. (1981) 'The Multinational Firm in Less Developed Countries: A Markets and Hierarchies Approach', paper presented at AIB/EIBA Conference, Barcelona, Spain.

CANTWELL, J.A. (1986) 'Recent Trends in Direct Investment in Africa', in Cable, V. (ed.), *Foreign Investment: Policies and Prospects*, London: Commonwealth Secretariat.

CANTWELL, J.A. (1988) 'The Contribution of Recent Foreign Direct Investment in Services to a Changing International Division of Labour', *University of Reading Discussion Paper in International Investment and Business Studies, No. 117*, May.

CANTWELL, J.A. and DUNNING, J.H. (1985) *The New Forms of International Involvement of British Firms in the Third World*, Report submitted to the OECD, January.

CARVALHO, L. (1977) *Comparative Performance of Domestic and Foreign*

Firms in Latin America, PhD Thesis, Cornell University.

CASSON, M.C. (1979) *Alternatives to the Multinational Enterprise*, London: Macmillan.

CASSON, M.C. (1987) *The Firm and the Market*, Oxford: Blackwell.

CASSON, M.C. (1987a) 'The Economic Theory of the Multinational Enterprise: Its Contribution to the Theory of the Firm', in Casson, M.C. (1987).

CASSON, M.C. (1987b) 'Foreign Investment and Economic Warfare: Internalizing the Implementation of Threats', in Casson, M.C. (1987).

CASSON, M.C. (1988a) 'The Theory of International Business as a Unified Social Science', *University of Reading Discussion Paper in International Investment and Business Studies*, Series B, no. 123.

CASSON, M.C. (1988b) 'Entrepreneurial Culture as a Competitive Advantage', *University of Reading Discussion Paper in International Investment and Business Studies*, Series B, no. 124.

CASSON, M.C. and PEARCE, R.D. (1987) 'Multinational Enterprises in LDCs', in Gemmell, N. (ed.), *Surveys in Development Economics*, Oxford: Basil Blackwell.

CAVES, R.E. (1971) 'International Corporations: The Industrial Economics of Foreign Investment', *Economica*, 38, pp. 1–27.

CAVES, R.E. (1974) 'Industrial Organization', in Dunning, J. (ed.), *Economic Analysis and the Multinational Corporation*, London: George Allen and Unwin.

CAVES, R.E. (1982) *Multinational Enterprise and Economic Analysis*, Cambridge: Cambridge University Press.

Central Bank of Nigeria (1981) *Economic and Financial Review*, December.

Centre for International Co-operation and Development (1984a) *Potential for Trade with Developing Countries*, Fourth Yugoslav Conference on Yugoslav Economic Co-operation with Developing Countries, Ljubljana.

Centre for International Co-operation and Development (1984b) *The European Community and Yugoslavia: Conference on Economic Co-operation with Developing Countries*, Conference Proceedings, Ljubljana.

CHEN, E.K.Y. (1983a) *Multinational Corporations, Technology and Employment*, London: Macmillan.

CHEN, E.K.Y. (1983b) 'Multinationals from Hong Kong', in Lall, S. et al, *The New Multinationals: The Spread of Third World Enterprises*, Chichester: John Wiley and Sons.

CHILD, J. (1981) 'Culture, Contingency and Capitalism in the Cross-National Study of Organizations', in Cummings, L.L. and Staw, B.M. (eds.), *Research in Organizational Behaviour*, Vol 3, Greenwich, CT: JAI Press.

CHO, Y.J. (1988) 'Some Policy Lessons from the Opening of the Korean Insurance Market', *The World Bank Economic Review*, 2, no. 2, pp. 239–54.

CHUDNOVSKY, D. (1979) 'The Challenge by Domestic Enterprises to the Transnational Corporations' Domination: A Case Study of the Argentine Pharmaceutical Industry', *World Development*, 7, no. 1, pp. 45–58.

CHUNG, B. and LEE, C. (1980) 'The Choice of Production Techniques by Foreign and Local Firms in Korea', *Economic Development and Cultural Change*, 29, no. 1, pp. 135–40.

CLARK, R. (1979) *The Japanese Company*, New Haven: Yale University Press.

CLARKE, D. (1980) *Foreign Companies and International Investment in Zimbabwe*, Gwelo: Mambo Press.

CLEGG, J. (1987) *Multinational Enterprise and World Competition: A Comparative Study of the USA, Japan, the UK, Sweden and West Germany*, New York: St Martin's Press.

COHEN, B.I. (1973) 'Comparative Behaviour of Foreign and Domestic Export Firms in a Developing Economy', *Review of Economics and Statistics*, LV, no. 2, pp. 190–97.

COHEN, B.I. (1975) *Multinational Firms and Asian Exports*, New Haven: Yale University Press.

COLE, R.E. (1979) *Work, Mobility and Participation: A Comparative Study of American and Japanese Industry*, Berkeley, CA: University of California Press.

COOK, P. and KIRKPATRICK, C.H. (eds.) (1988) *Privatisation in Less Developed Countries*, Brighton: Wheatsheaf.

CUDDINGTON, J.T., JOHANSSON, P-O. and LOFGREN, K-G. (1985) *Disequilibrium Macroeconomics in Open Economies*, Oxford: Blackwell.

CURRIE, J. (1986) 'Export Oriented Investment in Senegal, Ghana and Mauritius', in Cable, V. (ed.), *Foreign Investment: Policies and Prospects*, London: Commonwealth Secretariat.

DAVID, K. (1987) 'International Competitiveness in Construction and Computer Software: The Case of South Korea and India', in Kim, W.C. and Young, P.K.Y. (eds.), *The Pacific Challenge in International Business*, Ann Arbor, MI: University of Michigan Research Press.

DAVIS, S.M. (1971) *Comparative Management: Cultural and Organizational Perspectives*, Englewood Cliffs, NJ: Prentice Hall.

DAVIS, S.M. (1984) *Managing Corporate Culture*, Cambridge, MA: Ballinger.

DEAL, T.E. and KENNEDY, A.A. (1982) *Corporate Cultures*, Reading, MA: Addison-Wesley.

DE LA TORRE, J. (1972) 'Marketing Factors in Manufactured Exports from Developing Countries', in Wells, L.T. (ed.), *The Product Life Cycle and International Trade*, Cambridge: Harvard University Press.

DICK, A.R. (1988) 'Imperfect International Competition in Innovation and Product Markets: Some Theoretical Implications and Empirical Results', mimeo, University of Chicago Department of Economics.

DICKEN, P. (1986) *Global Shift: Industrial Change in a Turbulent World*, London: Harper and Row.

DIGMAN, A.L. (1982) 'Strategic Management in US Versus Japanese Firms', in Lee, S.M. and Schwendiman, G. (eds.), *Management by Japanese Systems*, New York: Praeger.

DIXIT, A.K. (1979) 'A Model of Duopoly Suggesting a Theory of Entry Barriers', *Bell Journal of Economics*, 10, no. 1, pp. 20–32.

DORE, R. (1973) *British Factory – Japanese Factory*, Berkeley, CA: University of California Press.

DORE, R. (1986) *Flexible Rigidities – Industrial Policy and Structural Adjustment in the Japanese Economy*, London: The Athlone Press.

DUNNING, J.H. (1973) 'The Determinants of International Production' *Oxford Economic Papers*, 25, no. 3, pp. 289–336.

DUNNING, J.H. (1980) 'Toward an Eclectic Theory of International Production: Some Empirical Tests', *Journal of International Business Studies*, XI, no. 1, pp. 9–31.

DUNNING, J.H. (1981) *International Production and the Multinational Enterprise*, London: George Allen & Unwin.

DUNNING, J.H. (1981a) 'Explaining the International Direct Investment Position of Countries: Towards a Dynamic or Developmental Approach', in Dunning, J.H. (1981).

DUNNING, J.H. (1983) 'Changes in the Level and Structure of International Production: The Last One Hundred Years', in Casson, M.C. (ed.), *The Growth of International Business*, London: George Allen and Unwin.

DUNNING, J.H. (ed.) (1985a) *Multinational Enterprises, Economic Structure and International Competitiveness*, New York: John Wiley and Sons.

DUNNING, J.H. (1985b) 'US and Japanese Manufacturing Affiliates in the UK: Some Similarities and Contrasts', *University of Reading Discussion Papers in International Investment and Business Studies*, No. 90, October.

DUNNING, J.H. (1986) *Japanese Participation in the UK Industry*, London: Croom Helm.

DUNNING, J.H. (1988a) *Explaining International Production*, London: Unwin Hyman.

DUNNING, J.H. (1988b) 'The Eclectic Paradigm of International Production: A Restatement and Some Possible Extensions', *Journal of International Business Studies*, XIX, no. 1, pp. 1–31.

DUNNING, J.H. (1989) 'The Study of International Business: A Plea for an Interdisciplinary Approach', *Journal of International Business Studies*, XX, no. 3.

DUNNING, J.H. and CANTWELL, J.A. (1987) *The Directory of Statistics of International Investment and Production*, London: Macmillan.

DUTT, A.K. (1988) 'Monopoly Power and Uneven Development: Baran Revisited', *Journal of Development Studies*, 24, no. 2, pp. 161–76.

ECLA (1983) *Dos Estudios Sobre Empresas Transnacionales en Brasil*, Estudios e Informes de la CEPAL 31, Santiago, Naciones Unidas.

EISENSTADT, S.N. (1973) *Tradition, Change, Modernity*, New York: Wiley.

ELISSON, G. (1984) *De utlandsetablerade foretagen och den svenska ekonomin* (Swedish Firms Established Abroad and the Swedish Economy), Forkningsrapport nr. 26, Industriens Utredningsinstitut, Stockholm: Almqvist and Wicksell.

EMMANUEL, A. (1980) 'The Multinational Corporation and the Inequality of Development', in Kumar, K. (ed.), *Transnational Enterprises: Their Impact on Third World Societies and Cultures*, Boulder: Westview Press.

ENCARNATION, D. and WELLS, L.T. Jr. (1985) 'Sovereignty En-Garde – Negotiating with Foreign Investors', *International Organization*, 39, no. 1, pp. 47–78.

ENDERWICK, P. (1987) 'The Strategy and Structure of Service Sector Multinationals: Implications for Potential Host Regions', *Regional Studies*, 3, no. 21, pp. 215–23.

ENDERWICK, P. (1988a) 'Some Economics of Service-Sector Multinational Enterprises', in Enderwick, P. (ed.), *Multinational Service Firms*, London: Routledge.

ENDERWICK, P. (ed.) (1988b) *Multinational Service Firms*, London: Routledge.

ENDERWICK, P. (1988c) 'Policy Issues in International Trade and Investment in Services', in Enderwick, P. (ed.), *Multinational Service Firms*, London: Routledge.

ENDERWICK, P. (1988d) 'Multinational Contracting', in Enderwick, P. (ed.), *Multinational Service Firms*, London: Routledge.

EVANS, P. (1979) *Dependent Development: The Alliance of Multinational, State and Local Capital in Brazil*, Princeton: Princeton University Press.

FAIRCHILD, L. (1977) 'Performance and Technology of United States and National Firms in Mexico', *Journal of Development Studies, 14*, no. 1, pp. 14–34.

FAIRCHILD, L. and SOSIN, K. (1986) 'Evaluating Differences in Technological Activity between Transnational and Domestic Firms in Latin America', *Journal of Development Studies*, 22, no. 4, pp. 697–708.

FAJNZYLBER, F. and MARTINEZ TARRAGE, T. (1975) *Las Empresas Transnacionales, Expansion a Nivel Mundial y Proyeccion en la Industria Mexicana (Version Preliminar)*, Mexico City: CIDE/CONACYT.

FARMER, R. (ed.) (1986) *Advances in International Comparative Management 2*, Greenwich, CT: JAI Press.

Financial Times, (1987) 'Special Report: Morocco', July 13, Section II, pp. 1–8.

FORSGREN, M. (1988) *Managing the Internationalization Process: The Swedish Case*, London: Routledge.

FORSYTH, D. and SOLOMON, R. (1977) 'Choice of Technology and Nationality of Ownership in Manufacturing in a Developing Country', *Oxford Economic Papers*, 29, no. 2, pp. 258–82.

FRANKO, L.G. (1978) 'Multinationals: The End of US Dominance', *Harvard Business Review*, November/December, pp. 93–101.

FROBEL, F., HEINRICHS, J. and KREYE, O. (1980) *The New Division of Labour: Structural Unemployment in Industrialised Countries and Industrialisation in Developing Countries*, Cambridge: Cambridge University Press.

GARVIN, D.A. (1986) 'Quality Problems, Policies, and Attitudes in the United States and Japan: An Exploratory Study', *Academy of Management Journal*, 29, no. 4, pp. 653–73.

GEREFFI, G. and NEWFARMER, R. (1985) 'International Oligopoly and Uneven Development: Some Lessons from Industrial Case Studies', in Newfarmer, R. (ed.), *Profits, Progress and Poverty: Case Studies of International Industries in Latin America*, Notre Dame, IN: University of Notre Dame Press.

GERSHENBERG, I. and RYAN, T. (1978) 'Does Parentage Matter? An Analysis of Transnational and Other Firms: An East African Case', *Journal of Developing Areas*, 13, no. 1, pp. 3–10.

GERSHUNY, J. and MILES, I. (1983) *The New Service Economy: The Transformation of Employment in Industrial Societies*, London: Frances Pinter.

GHAURI, P.N. (1983) *Negotiating International Package Deals – Swedish Firms and Developing Countries*, Uppsala: Almqvist and Wicksell.
GIBBS, M. and MASHAYEKHI M. (1988) 'Services: Cooperation for Development', *Journal of World Trade*, 20, no. 9, pp. 81–107.
GOODMAN, L.W. (1987) *Small Nations, Giant Firms*, New York: Holmes and Meier.
GRAHAM, E.M. (1978) 'Transnational Investment by Multinational Firms: A Rivalistic Phenomenon', *Journal of Post Keynesian Economics*, 1, no. 1, pp. 82–99.
GRIECO, J. (1986) 'Foreign Investment and Development', in Moran, T. (ed.), *Investing in Development: New Roles for Private Capital*, New Brunswick: Transaction Books.
GROSHER, E.L. (1987) 'Can Services be a Source of Export-Led Growth?', *Federal Reserve Bank of Cleveland Review*, no. 3, pp. 2–15.
GRUBEL, H.G. (1988) 'Multinational Banking', in Enderwick, P. (ed.), *Multinational Service Firms*, London: Routledge.
GUISINGER, S. (1986) 'Do Investment Incentives Work?', *World Economy*, 9, no. 1, pp. 79–96.
GUISINGER, S. and Associates, (1985) *Investment Incentives and Performance Requirements*, New York: Praeger.
GUISINGER, S. and FARRELL, T. (1985) 'Dialogue on Investment Incentives', *The CTC Reporter*, 20, pp. 38–42. Autumn.
HACKMAN, J.R. and OLDHAM, G.R. (1980) *Work Redesign*, Reading, MA: Addison-Wesley.
HAGEN, E.E. (1962) *On the Theory of Social Change: How Economic Growth Begins*, Homewood, ILL: Dorsey Press.
HAKANSSON, H. (ed.), (1982) *Industrial Marketing and Purchasing in Europe*, Chichester: Wiley.
HAMILL, J. (1989) *Mediterranean Rim Textiles and Clothing: Competitive Threat or Investment Opportunity*, London: Economist Intelligence Unit.
HANNIGAN, J.B. and MCMILLAN, C.H. (1981) 'The Soviet Union in World Trade in Oil and Gas', in Kostecki, M. (ed.), *The Soviet Impact on Commodity Markets*, London: Macmillan.
HAYASHI, K. (1988) 'On Internationalizing Japanese Style Decision Making', paper presented at the Academy of International Business Japan Symposium, Waseda University, Tokyo.
HAYEK, F.A. von (1937) 'Economics and Knowledge', *Economica* (New Series), 4, pp. 33–54. Reprinted in Hayek, F.A. von, *Individualism and Economic Order*, London: Routledge and Kegan Paul, 1949.
HAZAMA, H. (1963) *Nihontekikeiri no Keifu* (The Origins of Japanese Management), Tokyo: Nihon Noritsu Kyokai.
HELLEINER, G. (1989) 'Transnational Corporations, Direct Foreign Investment, and Economic Development', in Chenery, H. and Srinivasan, T.N. (eds.), *Handbook of Development Economics*, Elsevier: North-Holland.
HENNART, J-F. (1982) *A Theory of the Multinational Enterprise*, Ann Arbor, MI: University of Michigan Press.
HERSKOVITS, M.J. (1961) 'Economic Change and Cultural Dynamics', in Braibanti, R. and Spengler, R.R. (eds.), *Tradition, Values, and Socio-Economic Development*, Durham, NC: Duke University Press.

HINDLEY, B. (1988) 'Service Sector Protection: Considerations for Developing Countries', *The World Bank Economic Review*, 2, no. 2, pp. 205–24.

HIRSCH, F. (1977) *Social Limits to Growth*, London: Routledge and Kegan Paul.

HODGES, R. (1988) *Primitive and Peasant Markets*, Oxford: Blackwell.

HORNELL, E. and VAHLNE, J.E. (1986) *Multinationals: The Swedish Case*, London: Croom Helm.

HORST, T. (1972) 'Firm and Industry Determinants of the Decision to Invest Abroad: An Empirical Study', *Review of Economics and Statistics*, 54, pp. 266–85.

HOSELITZ, B.F. (1961) 'Tradition and Economic Growth', in Braibanti, R. and Spengler, J.J. (eds.), *Tradition, Values, and Socio-Economic Development*, Durham, NC: Duke University Press.

HOWARD, N. AND TERAMOTO, Y. (1981) 'Japanese Versus Western Management', *Management International Review*, 21, no. 3, pp. 653–73.

HUMPHREY, J. (1982) *Capitalist Control and Workers' Struggle in the Brazilian Auto Industry*, Princeton, NJ: Princeton University Press.

HYMER, S. (1960) *The International Operations of National Firms: A Study of Direct Foreign Investment*, PhD Thesis, MIT. (Cambridge, MA: The MIT Press, 1976)

ILO (1972) *Employment, Incomes and Inequality*, Geneva: ILO.

IMAI, K-I. (1980) 'Japan's Industrial Organization', in Satoku (ed.), *Industry and Business In Japan*, New York: M.E. Sharpe.

IMAI, K-I. (1988) 'Patterns of Innovation and Entrepreneurship in Japan', paper presented at the 2nd Congress of the International Schumpeter Society, Siena.

IMAI, K-I. and ITAMI, H. (1981) 'Mutual Penetration of the Market Principle and Organization Principle', Discussion Paper No. 104, Hitotsubashi University.

INGLES, J. and FAIRCHILD, L. (1977) 'Evaluating the Impact of Foreign Investment: Methodology and Evidence from Mexico, Colombia and Brazil', *Latin American Research Review*, 12, no. 3, pp. 57–70.

INKELES, A. and SMITH, D.H. (1974) *Becoming Modern: Individual Change in Six Developing Countries*, London: Heinemann.

International Monetary Fund (1977) *Balance of Payments Manual*, 4th edition, Washington, DC: IMF.

IRABE, K. and OHMURA, K. (1983) *Nihonteki Koshikanke: no Tankyu* (Explorations of Japanese Management and Labour Relations), Tokyo: Chuokeizaisha.

ISHIDA, H. (1985) *Nihon Kigyo no Kokusai Jinji Kanri* (International Personnel Administration of Japanese Enterprises), Tokyo: Nihon Rodo Kyokai.

ISHIMURA, S. and YOSHIHARA, K. (eds.), (1985) 'Japanese Management in Southeast Asia', (Special Issue of *Southeast Asian Studies*, 22, no. 4, pp. 18–41).

ITAMI, H. (1985) 'The Firm and the Market in Japan', in Thurow, L. (ed.), *The Management Challenge*, Cambridge, MA: The MIT Press.

IVANSON, C. (1953) *Aspects of the Theory of International Capital Move-*

ments, London: Oxford University Press.

IWATA, R. (1977) *Nihontekikeiei no Hansei Genri* (The Organizing Principles of Japanese Management), Tokyo: Bunshindo.

JACOBS, W.G. (1982) 'Quality Circles and Japanese Management: Participation or Paternalism', in Lee, S.M. and Schwendiman, G. (eds.), *Management by Japanese Systems*, New York: Praeger.

JAGREN, L. (1981) 'Verkstadsindustrins produktions for utsattningar och konkurrenskraft – en intervjuundersokning', in Carlsson, B. et al, *Industrin infor 80-talet*, Stockholm: Industriens Utredningsinstitut.

JAGREN, L. and HORWITZ, E.C. (1984) *Svensk marknadsandelar* (Swedish Market Shares), Industriens Utredningsinstitut Working Paper, Stockholm.

JANSSON, H. (1982) *Interfirm Linkages in a Developing Economy – The Case of Swedish Firms in India*, Uppsala: Almqvist and Wicksell.

JENKINS, R. (1979a) 'The Export Performance of Multinational Corporations in Mexican Industry', *Journal of Development Studies*, 15, no. 3, pp. 89–105.

JENKINS, R. (1979b) *Foreign Firms, Exports of Manufactures and the Mexican Economy*, Monograph in Development Studies No. 7, Norwich: University of East Anglia.

JENKINS, R. (1987) *Transnational Corporations and Uneven Development: The Internationalization of Capital and the Third World*, New York: Methuen.

JENKINS, R. (1988a) 'Comparing Foreign Subsidiaries and Local Firms in LDCs: Theoretical Issues and Empirical Evidence'. Paper prepared for the ESRC Development Economics Study Group Annual Conference on *International Investment and Technology Transfer in Developing Countries*, University of Leicester.

JENKINS, R. (1988b) 'Transnational Corporations and Third World Consumption: Implications of Competitive Strategies', *World Development*, 16, no. 11, pp. 1363–70.

JO, S. (1976) 'The Impact of Multinational Firms on Employment and Incomes: The Case of South Korea', *World Employment Programme Research, Working Papers, World Employment Programme 2–28, Working Paper 12*, Geneva: ILO.

JOUET, J. (1984) 'Advertising and Transnational Corporations in Kenya', *Development and Change*, 15, no. 3, pp. 435–56.

JOHANSON, J. and WIEDERSHEIM-PAUL, F. (1975) 'The Internationalization of the Firm – Four Swedish Case Studies', *The Journal of Management Studies*, 12, no. 3, pp. 305–22.

KAGONO, T., NONAKA, I., SAKAKIBARA, K. and OKIMURA, A. (1983) 'An Evolutionary View of Organizational Adaptation: United States vs Japanese Firms', Discussion Paper No. 117, Institute of Business Research, Hitotsubashi University, Kunitachi, Tokyo.

KAPLINSKI, R. (1979) *Employment Effects of MNEs: A Case Study of Kenya*, Geneva: ILO.

KARSH, B. (1983) 'Managerial Ideology vs Worker Co-optations: The US and Japan', papers presented at the 6th World Congress of the International Industrial Relations Association, Kyoto, Japan.

KATRAK, H. (1985) 'Imported Technology, Enterprise Size and R&D in a Newly Industrialising Country: The Indian Experience', *Oxford Bulletin of Economics and Statistics*, 47, no. 3, pp. 213–29.

KATRAK, H. (1989) 'Payments for Imported Technologies, Market-rivalry and Adaptive Activity in the Newly Industrialising Countries', *Journal of Development Studies*, 25, no. 1, pp. 43–54.

KAYNAK, E. (1986) 'Service Industries in Developing Countries: A Conceptual Framework and Analytical Insights', in Kaynak, E. (ed.), *Service Industries in Developing Countries*, London: Frank Cass.

KAYNAK, E., GHAURI, P.N. and OLOFSSON, B. (1987) 'Export Behavior of Small Swedish Firms', *Journal of Small Business Management*, 25, no. 2, pp. 26–32.

KILBY, P. (1971) 'Hunting the Heffalump', in Kilby, P. (ed.), *Entrepreneurship and Economic Development*, New York: Free Press.

KIM, S. (1988) 'The Korean Construction Industry as an Exporter of Services', *The World Bank Economic Review*, 2, no. 2, pp. 225–38.

KINDLEBERGER, C.P. (1969) *American Business Abroad*, New Haven: Yale University Press.

KINDLEBERGER, C.P. (ed.), (1970) *The International Corporation*, Cambridge, MA: The MIT Press.

KIRIM, A. (1986) 'Transnational Corporations and Local Capital: Comparative Conduct and Performance in the Turkish Pharmaceutical Industry', *World Development*, 14, no. 4, pp. 503–21.

KIRZNER, I.M. (1973) *Competition and Entrepreneurship*, Chicago: University of Chicago Press.

KNICKERBOCKER, F.T. (1973) *Oligopolistic Reaction and the Multinational Enterprise*, Boston: Harvard University Press.

KNIGHT, F.H. (1921) *Risk Uncertainty and Profit*, (ed. Stigler, G.J., 1985) Chicago: University of Chicago Press.

KOGUT, B. (1986) 'On Designing Contracts to Guarantee Enforceability: Theory and Evidence from East-West Trade', *Journal of International Business Studies*, 17, no. 1, pp. 47–61.

KOJIMA, K. (1978) *Direct Foreign Investment: A Japanese Model of Multinational Business Operations*, London: Croom Helm.

KOJIMA, K. and OZAWA, T. (1984) *Japan's General Trading Companies – Merchants of Economic Development*, Paris: OECD.

KONO, T. (1988) 'Factors Affecting the Creativity of Organizations – An Approach from the Analysis of New Product Development', in Urabe, K., Child, J. and Kagono, T. (eds.), *Innovation and Management – International Comparisons*, Berlin: de Gruyter.

KOO, B-Y. (1985) 'Korea', in Dunning, J.H. (ed.), *Multinational Enterprises, Economic Structure and International Competitiveness*, Chichester: Wiley.

KRUGMAN, P.R. (1983) 'The New Theories of International Trade and the Multinational Corporation in the 1980s', in Kindleberger, C.P. and Audretsch, D.B. (eds.), *The Multinational Corporation in the 1980s*, Cambridge, MA: The MIT Press.

KRUGMAN, P.R. (1984) 'Import Protection as Export Promotion', in Kierzkowski, H. (ed.), *Monopolistic Competition and International Trade*, Oxford: Oxford University Press.

KUJAWA, D. (1986) *Japanese Multinationals in the United States: Case Studies*, New York: Praeger.

KUMAR, N. (1987) 'Technology Imports and Local Research and Development in Indian Manufacturing', *The Developing Economies*, XXV-3, pp. 220–33.

KUMAR, K. and KIM, K.Y. (1984) 'The Korean Manufacturing Multinationals', *Journal of International Business Studies*, xv, no. 1, pp. 45–61.

LALL, S. (1978) 'Transnationals, Domestic Enterprises and Industrial Structure in Host LDCs', *Oxford Economic Papers*, 30, no. 2, pp. 217–48.

LALL, S. (1979) 'Monopolistic Advantages and Foreign Involvement by US Multinational Industry', *Oxford Economic Papers*, 32, no. 1, pp. 105–22.

LALL, S. (1980) *The Multinational Corporation: Nine Essays*, London: Macmillan.

LALL, S. (1980) 'Vertical Inter-Firm Linkages in LDCs: An Empirical Study', *Oxford Bulletin of Economics and Statistics*, 42, no. 3, pp. 203–26.

LALL, S. (1983) *The New Multinationals: The Spread of Third World Enterprises*, Chichester: Wiley.

LALL, S. (1983a) 'The Theoretical Background', in Lall S. (1983).

LALL, S. (1983b) 'Multinationals from India', in Lall, S. (1983).

LALL, S. (1985a) *Multinationals, Technology and Exports*, London: Macmillan.

LALL, S. (1985b) 'India', in Dunning, J.H. (ed.), *Multinational Enterprises, Economic Structure and International Competitiveness*, Chichester: Wiley.

LALL, S. and STREETEN, P. (1977) *Foreign Investment, Transnationals and Developing Countries*, London: Macmillan.

LANDI, J.H. (1986) 'Vertical Corporate Linkages', *University of Reading Discussion Papers in International Investment and Business Studies*, No. 94, April.

LANGDON, S. (1981) *Multinational Corporations in the Political Economy of Kenya*, London: Macmillan.

LECRAW, D.J. (1977) 'Direct Investment by Firms from Less Developed Countries', *Oxford Economic Papers*, 29, no. 3, pp. 442–57.

LECRAW, D.J. (1985a) 'Hymer and Public Policy in LDCs', *American Economic Review*, papers and proceedings, 75, no. 2, pp. 239–44.

LECRAW, D.J. (1985b) 'Singapore', in Dunning, J.H. (ed.), *Multinational Enterprises, Economic Structure and International Competitiveness*, Chichester: Wiley.

LECRAW, D.J. (1988) 'Countertrade: A Form of Cooperative International Business Agreement', in Contractor, F.J. and Lorange, P. (eds.), *Cooperative Strategies in International Business*, Lexington, MA: Lexington Books.

LECRAW, D.J. (1988) 'Third World Multinationals in the Service Industries', in Enderwick, P. (ed.), *Multinational Service Firms*, London: Routledge.

LECRAW, D.J., with GROSSE, R. and CANTWELL, J. (1990) *A Foreign Direct Investment and Technology Transfer Policy, Incentives Systems: A*

Framework, Country Studies, and Principles, New York: UNCTC.

LEE, S.M. and SCHWENDIMAN, G. (eds.) (1982) *Management by Japanese Systems*, New York: Praeger.

LEFF, N.H. (1978) 'Industrial Organisation and Entrepreneurship in the Developing Countries: The Economic Groups', *Economic Development and Cultural Change*, 26, pp. 661–75.

LEIBENSTEIN, H. (1968) 'Entrepreneurship and Development', American Economic Review, 58, no. 1, pp. 72–83.

LEIBENSTEIN, H. (1984) 'On the Economics of Conventions and Institutions: An Exploratory Essay', *Zeitschrift fuer die Gesamte Staatswissenschaft*, 140, no. 1, pp. 74–86.

LEIBENSTEIN, H. (1989) *Inside the Firm*, Cambridge: Harvard University Press.

LEIBENSTEIN, H. and WEIERMAIR, K. (1988) 'X-Efficiency, Managerial Discretion and the Nature of Employment Relations: A Game-Theoretical Approach', in Dlugos, G. and Weiermair, K. (eds.), *Management Under Differing Labour Market and Employment Systems*, Berlin: de Gruyter.

LEVY, B. (1988) 'The Determinants of Manufacturing Ownership in Less Developed Countries', *Journal of Development Economics*, 28, no. 2, pp. 217–31.

LIM, D. (1976) 'Capital Utilisation of Local and Foreign Establishments in Malaysian Manufacturing', *Review of Economics and Statistics*, 58, no. 2, pp. 209–17.

LIM, D. (1977) 'Do Foreign Companies Pay Higher Wages than their Local Counterparts in Malaysian Manufacturing?', *Journal of Development Economics*, 4, no. 1, pp. 55–66.

LIN, T. and MOK, V. (1985) 'Trade, Foreign Investment and Development in Hong Kong', in Galenson, W. (ed.), *Foreign Trade and Investment: Economic Development in the Newly Industrializing Asian Countries*, Madison: University of Wisconsin Press.

LINDER, S.B. (1961) *An Essay on Trade and Transformation*, New York: Wiley.

LIPSEY, R.E. and BLOMSTRON, M. (1987) 'TNCs in United States and Swedish Trade', *The CTC Reporter*, Autumn, pp. 51–4.

LUIZ POSSAS, M. (1979) *Employment Effects of Multinational Enterprise in Brazil*, Research on Employment Effects of Multinational Enterprise, Working Paper No. 7, Geneva: International Labour Organisation.

LUNDSTROM, R. (1986) 'Banks and Early Swedish Multinationals', in Teichova, A. et al (eds.), *The Multinational Enterprise in Historical Perspective*, New York: Cambridge University Press.

MCCLELLAND, D.C. and WINTER, D.G. (1969) *Motivating Economic Achievement*, New York: Free Press.

MCMILLAN, C.H. (1979) *Soviet Investment in the Industrialised Western Economies and in the Developing Economies of the Third World*, Washington, DC: Joint Economic Committee, US Congress.

MCMILLAN, C.H. (1987) *Multinationals from the Second World*, London: Macmillan.

MAGDOFF, H. (1969) *The Age of Imperialism: The Economics of US Foreign Policy*, New York: The Monthly Review Press.

MARCH, J.G. and SIMON, H.A. (1958) *Organizations*, New York: Wiley.

MARSH, R. and MANNARI, H. (1976) *Modernization and the Japanese Factory*, Princeton, NJ: Princeton University Press.

MASON, R. (1973) 'Some Observations on the Choice of Technology by Multinational Firms in Developing Countries', *Review of Economics and Statistics*, 55, no. 3, pp. 349–55.

MAURICE, M., SORGE, A. and WARNER, M. (1980) 'Societal Differences in Organizing Manufacturing Units: A Comparison of France, West Germany and Great Britain', *Organization Studies I*, 1, pp. 59–86.

MELLER, P. and MIZALA, A. (1982) 'US Multinationals and Latin American Manufacturing Employment Absorption', *World Development*, 10, no. 2, pp. 115–26.

MEYER, J.W. and ROWAN, B. (1977) 'Institutional Organizations: Formal Structure as Myth and Ceremony', *American Journal of Sociology*, 83, pp. 340–63.

MIKDASHI, Z. (1976) *The International Politics of Natural Resources*, Ithaca, NY: Cornell University Press.

MIRUS, R. and YEUNG, B. (1986) 'Economic Incentives for Countertrade', *Journal of International Business Studies*, 17, no. 3, pp. 27–39.

MIRUS, R. and YEUNG, B. (1987) 'Countertrade and Foreign Exchange Shortages: A Preliminary Assessment', *Weltwirtschaftliches Archiv*, 123, no. 3, pp. 535–44.

MOMIGLIANO, F. and SINISCALCO, D. (1982) 'The Growth of Service Employment: A Reappraisal', *Banco Nazionale Del Lavoro Quarterly Review*, 35, no. 142, pp. 269–306.

MONTAVON, R. (1979) *The Role of Multinational Companies in Latin America: A Case Study in Mexico*, Farnborough: Saxon House.

MORGAN, G. (1988) *Riding the Cutting Edge of Change*, San Francisco: Jossey-Bass.

MORGENSTERN, R. and MULLER, R. (1976) 'Multinational Versus Local Corporations in LDCs: An Econometric Analysis of Export Performance in Latin America', *Southern Economic Journal*, 42, no. 3, pp. 339–406.

MORLEY, S. and SMITH, G. (1977) 'The Choice of Technology: Multinational Firms in Brazil', *Economic Development and Cultural Change*, 25, no. 2, pp. 239–64.

MROCZKOWSKI, T. and HANAOKA, M. (1989) 'Continuing and Change in Japanese Management', *California Management Review*, 31, no. 2, pp. 39–53.

NAKATANI, T. (1988) *The Japanese Firm in Transition*, Tokyo: Asian Productivity Organization.

NAKATANI, T. (1988) 'The Economic Role of Financial Corporate Grouping', in Aoki, M. (ed.), *The Economic Analysis of the Japanese Firm*, Rotterdam: North Holland.

NANTO, D.K. (1982) 'Management, Japanese Style', in Lee, S.M. and Schwendiman, G. (eds.), *Management by Japanese Systems*, New York: Praeger.

NEGANDHI, A.R. (1987) *International Management*, Boston: Allyn and Bacon.

NELSON, P.R. and WINTER, S.G. (1982) *An Evolutionary Theory of Economic Change*, Cambridge, MA: Harvard University Press.

NEMOTO, T. (1987) *Shinjinrui vs. Kanrisha* (New Generation and Management Control), Tokyo: Chuo Keizeisha.

NEWBERY, D.M.G. and STIGLITZ, J.E. (1981) *The Theory of Commodity Price Stabilisation*, Oxford: Oxford University Press.

NEWBOULD, G.D., BUCKLEY, P.J. and THURWELL, J. (1978) *Going International: The Experience of Smaller Companies Overseas*, London: Associated Business Press.

NEWFARMER, R. (1985) 'International Industrial Organization and Development: A Survey', in Newfarmer, R. (ed.), *Profits, Progress and Poverty: Case Studies of International Industries in Latin America*, Notre Dame, IN: University of Notre Dame Press.

NEWFARMER, R. and MARSH, L. (1981) 'Industrial Interdependence and Development: A Study of International Linkages and Industrial Performance in Brazil', University of Notre Dame, mimeo.

NICHOLAS, S. (1983) 'Agency Contracts, Institutional Modes, and the Transition to Foreign Direct Investment by British Manufacturing Multinationals before 1939', *Journal of Economic History*, 43, pp. 675–86.

NONAKA, I. (1985) *Kigyo Shinka Ron* (Evolutionary Theory of Business Enterprises), Tokyo: Nippon Keizoi Shinbun Publishing.

NONAKA, I. (1988) 'Creating Organizational Order out of Chaos: Self-Renewal in Japanese Firms', *California Management Review*, 30, pp. 57–73.

NORTON, D. (1984) 'Public Policy for Private Sector Services', *Journal of Irish Business and Administrative Research*, 6, no. 2, pp. 84–105.

OECD (1974) *Service Activities in Developing Countries*, Paris: OECD.

OECD (1981) *East-West Trade: Recent Development in Countertrade*, Paris: OECD.

OECD (various years) *Foreign Trade by Commodities*, Paris: OECD.

OUCHI, W.G. (1981) *Theory Z*, Reading, MA: Addison-Wesley.

OUCHI, W.G. (1984) *The M-Form Society*, Reading, MA: Addison-Wesley.

OZAWA, T. (1979) *Multinationalism, Japanese Style: The Political Economy of Outward Dependency*, Princeton, NJ: Princeton University Press.

OZAWA, T. (1982) 'A Newer Type of Foreign Investment in Third World Resource Development', *Rivista Internazionale di Scienze Economiche e Commerciali*, 29, no. 12, pp. 1133–51.

PASCALE, R.T. and ATHOS, A.G. (1981) *The Art of Japanese Management*, New York: Simon & Schuster.

PACK, H. (1976) 'The Substitution of Labour for Capital in Kenyan Manufacturing', *Economic Journal*, 86, no. 1, pp. 45–58.

PACK, H. (1987) *Productivity, Technology and Economic Development*, New York: Oxford University Press.

PALIWODA, S. (1981) *Joint East-West Marketing and Production Ventures*, Aldershot: Gower Press.

PARK, S.G., JUERGENS, V. and MELZ, H. (eds.) (1985) *Transfer des Japanischen Management Systems*, Berlin: Express Editions.

PARSONS, J.E. (1985) 'A Theory of Countertrade Financing of International Business', Working Paper 1632–85, Cambridge, MA: The MIT Press.

PEGELS, C. (1984) *Japan vs. the West – Implications for Management*, The Hague: Kluwer-Nijhoff Publishing.

PEMPEL, T.J. (1982) *Policy and Politics in Japan – Creative Conservatism*, Philadelphia: Temple University Press.

PETTIGREW, A. (1985) *The Awakening Giant*, Oxford: Blackwell.

RADA, J.F. (1987) 'Information Technology and Services', in Giarini, O. (ed.), *The Emerging Service Economy*, Oxford: Pergamon.

RADHU, G. (1973) 'Some Aspects of Direct Foreign Investment in Pakistan', *Pakistan Development Review*, 12, no. 1, pp. 68–80.

RANDSEPP, E. (1986) 'Japanese Managers: Are They Really Better?' *Machine Design*, October 23, pp. 95–9.

RANIS, G. and SCHIVE, C. (1985) 'Direct Foreign Investment in Taiwan's Development', in Galenson, W. (ed.), *Foreign Trade and Investment: Economic Development in the Newly Industrializing Asian Countries*, Madison: University of Wisconsin Press.

REED, H.D. (1983) 'Appraising Corporate Investment Policy: A Financial Center Theory of Foreign Direct Investment', in Kindleberger, C.P. and Audretsch, D.B. (eds.), *The Multinational Corporation in the 1980s*, Cambridge, MA: The MIT Press.

REHDER, R.R. (1981) 'Japan's Synergistic Society: How it Works and its Implications for the US', *Management Review*, 170, no. 10, pp. 64–8.

Republic of Liberia (1980) Project Ministry, Division of Finance, unpublished data.

REUBER, G. et al (1973) *Private Foreign Investment in Development*, Oxford: Clarendon Press.

RICHARDSON, J.B. (1987) 'A Sub-sectoral Approach to Services Trade Theory', in Giarini, O. (ed.), *The Emerging Service Economy*, Oxford: Pergamon Press.

RICHARDSON, J.D. (1971) 'On Going Abroad: The Firm's Initial Foreign Investment Decision', *Quarterly Review of Economics and Statistics*, 11, pp. 7–22.

RICHTER, C. (1987) 'Tourism Services', in Giarini, O. (ed.), *The Emerging Service Economy*, Oxford: Pergamon Press.

RIDDELL, R.C. (1986) 'Zimbabwe's Experience of Foreign Investment Policy', in Cable, V. (ed.), *Foreign Investment: Policies and Prospects*, London: Commonwealth Secretariat.

RIDDLE, D.I. (1987) 'The Role of the Service Sector in Economic Development: Similarities and Differences by Development Category', in Giarini, O., *The Emerging Service Economy*, Oxford: Pergamon Press.

RIDDLE, D.I. and SOURS, M.H. (1984) 'Service Industries as Growth Leaders on the Pacific Rim', *Asia-Pacific Journal of Management*, 1, no. 3, pp. 190–99.

RIDDLE, D.I. and SOURS, M.H. (1987) 'Service-Led Growth in the Pacific Basin', in Kim, W.C. and Young, P.K.Y. (eds.), *The Pacific Challenge in International Business*, Ann Arbor, MI: University of Michigan Research Press.

RIEDEL, J. (1975) 'The Nature and Determinants of Export-Oriented Direct Foreign Investment in a Developing Country: A Case Study of Taiwan', *Weltwirtschaftliches Archiv*, 111, no. 3. pp. 505–28.

RIEDEL, J. (1984) 'Attitudes in the Federal Republic of Germany to the Policies of Developing Countries Regarding Foreign Investors', *Industry and Development*, no. 13, pp. 1–38.

RONTANEN, P. (1983) 'The Development of the System of Bilateral Agreements between Finland and the Soviet Union', in Motlola, K., Bykov, O.K. and Korolev, I.S. (eds.), *Finnish-Soviet Economic Relations*, London: Macmillan.

ROYAMA, S. (1985) 'The Japanese Financial System: Past, Present and Future', in Thurow, L. (ed.), *The Management Challenge: Japanese Views*, Cambridge, MA: The MIT Press.

RUCH, V.W. (1982) 'Techniques of Communication in US and Japanese Corporations: Are they Interchangeable?' in Lee, S.M. and Schwendiman, G. (eds.), *Management by Japanese Systems*, New York: Praeger.

RUGMAN, A.M. (1980) 'Internalization as a General Theory of Foreign Direct Investment: Re-appraisal of the Literature', *Weltwirtschaftliches Archiv*, 116, no. 2, pp. 365–79.

RUGMAN, A.M. (ed.) (1981) *Inside the Multinationals: The Economics of Internal Markets*, New York: Columbia University Press.

RUGMAN, A.M. (1982) *New Theories of the Multinational Enterprise*, New York: St Martins Press.

SALTER, W.E.G. (1960) *Productivity and Technical Change*, Cambridge: Cambridge University Press.

SAVARY, J. (1984) *French Multinationals*, London: Frances Pinter.

SCHONBERGER, R. (1986) *World Class Manufacturing*, New York: The Free Press.

SCHOTTER, A. (1981) *Economic Theory of Social Institutions*, Cambridge: Cambridge University Press.

SCHUMPETER, J.A. (1934) *The Theory of Economic Development* (trans. R. Opie), Cambridge, MA: Harvard University Press.

SETHI, S.P. (1975) *Japanese Business and Social Conflict: A Comparative Analysis of Response Pattern with American Business*, Cambridge, MA: Ballinger.

SHAPIRO, D.M. (1983) 'Entry, Exit and the Theory of the Multinational Corporation', in Kindleberger, C.P. and Audretsch, D.B. (eds.), *The Multinational Corporation in the 1980s*, Cambridge, MA: The MIT Press.

SHEPHERD, P. (1985) 'Transnational Corporations and the International Cigarette Industry', in Newfarmer, R. (ed.), *Profits, Progress and Poverty: Case Studies of International Industries in Latin America*, Notre Dame, IN: University of Notre Dame Press.

SHIMADA, H. and MACDUFFIE, J.P. (1987) 'Industrial Relations and "Humanware" Japanese Investments in Automobile Manufacturing in the United States', *International Motor Vehicle Program, MIT*, Cambridge, MA: The MIT Press.

SIMOES, V.C. (1985) 'Portugal', in Dunning, J.H. (ed.), *Multinational Enterprises, Economic Structure and International Competitiveness*, Chichester: Wiley.

Socialist Party of Morocco (1974) National Congress documents.

SOSIN, K. and FAIRCHILD, L. (1984) 'Non-Homotheticity and Technological Bias in Production', *Review of Economics and Statistics*, KXVI, no. 1, pp. 44–50.

SPENCE, A.M. (1981) 'The Learning Curve and Competition', *Bell Journal of Economics and Management Science*, 12, no. 1, pp. 49–70.

SVETLICIC, M. and ROJEC, M. (1985) *New Forms of Equity Investment by Yugoslav Firms in Developing Countries*, Paris: OECD.

SVETLICIC, M. and ROJEC, M. (1986) *Investment among Developing Countries and Transnational Corporations*, Centre for International Co-operation and Development, Ljubljana, and Zimbabwe Institute of Development Studies, Harare.

SVETLICIC, M. and ROJEC, M. (1988) *Technological Transformation of the Third World: Progress Achieved and Problems Faced – Case Study of Yugoslavia*, United Nations University/World Institute for Development, Economics and Research, Centre for International Cooperation and Development, Ljubljana.

SWAINSON, N. (1980) *The Development of Corporate Capitalism in Kenya, 1918–1977*, London: Heinemann Educational Books.

SWEDENBORG, B. (1979) *The Multinational Operations of Swedish Firms: An Analysis of Determinants and Effects*, Stockholm: Almqvist and Wicksell.

SWEDENBORG, B. (1982) *Svensk industri i utlandet* (Swedish Industry Abroad), Stockholm: Industriens Utredningstitut.

SWEDENBORG, B. (1985) 'Sweden', in Dunning, J.H. (ed.), *Multinational Enterprises, Economic Structure and International Competitiveness*, New York: John Wiley and Sons.

TAIRA, K. and STANDING, C. (1973) 'Labor Market Effects of Multinational Enterprise in Latin .America', *Nebraska Journal of Economics and Business*, 12, no. 3, pp. 103–17.

TAKAGI, H. (1985) *The Flaws in Japanese Management*, Ann Arbor, MI: University of Michigan Press.

TAKAHASHI, Y. 'Zur Transferierbarkeit des Management Stils', in *Enzyklopaedie der Betreibswirtschaft Bd. II Export und International Management*, Stuttgart: Poeschl, forthcoming.

TEECE, D.J. (1977) 'Technology Transfer by Multinational Firms: The Resource Cost of Transferring Technological Know-how', *Economic Journal*, 87, no. 346, pp. 242–61.

TEECE, D. (1981) 'The Multinational Enterprise: Market Failure and Market Power Considerations', *Sloan Management Review*, 22, pp. 3–17.

TEECE, D. (1985) 'Multinational Enterprise, Internal Governance and Industrial Organization', *American Economic Review*, Papers and Proceedings, 75, no. 2, pp. 233–8.

TEECE, D. (1986) 'Transaction Cost Economics and the Multinational Enterprise', *Journal of Economic Behavior and Organization*, 7, no. 1, pp. 21–45.

THURLEY, K. (1983) 'How Transferable is the Japanese Industrial Relations Systems?' Paper presented at The International Industrial Relations Congress, International Industrial Relations Society, Kyoto.

THURLEY, K., TREVOR, M. and WORM, P. (1983) 'Japanese Management in Western Europe', Discussion Paper, London School of Economics.

TOKUNAGA, S. (1983) 'A Marxist Interpretation of Japanese Industrial Relations, with Special Reference to Large Private Enterprises', in Shirai, T. (ed.), *Contemporary Industrial Relations in Japan*, Madison, WI: Wisconsin University Press.

TOMER, J.F. (1987) *Organizational Capital: The Path to Higher Productivity and Well Being*, New York: Praeger.

TOSHIMASU, T. (1985) 'Japan's Industrial Policy', in Thurow, L. (ed.), *The Management Challenge*, Cambridge, MA: The MIT Press.

TREVOR, M. (1983) *Japan's Reluctant Multinationals*, London: Frances Pinter.

TREVOR, M. (1987) *The Internationalization of Japanese Business*, Frankfurt: Campus.

TREVOR, M., SCHEND, J. and WILPERT, B. (1986) *The Japanese Management Development System*, London: Frances Pinter.

UK Department of Industry (1974) *Business Monitor M4 Supplement: Census of Overseas Assets*, London: HMSO.

UK Department of Industry (1981) *Business Monitor M4 Supplement: Census of Overseas Assets*, London: HMSO.

UNCTC (1983) *Transnational Corporations in World Development: Third Survey*, New York: United Nations.

UNCTC (1985) *Transnational Corporations and International Trade: Selected Issues*, New York: United Nations.

UNCTC (1988) *Transnational Corporations in World Development: Trends and Prospects*, New York: United Nations.

United Nations, Department of Economics and Social Affairs (1973) *Multinational Corporations in World Development*, New York: United Nations.

United Nations Economic and Social Council (1978) *Transnational Corporations in World Development: A Re-Examination*, New York: United Nations.

UN Economic Commission for Africa (1981) 'L'Industrie Africaine en 1979', Report of the UNECA Mission on the Evaluation of UDEAC and the Feasibility of Enlarging Economic Cooperation in Central Africa, presented at the UDEAC Council of Heads of State, December.

UNCTAD (1985) *Services and the Development Process*, UN/TD/1008/Rev 1, New York: UN Publications.

URABE, K. (1988) 'Innovation and the Japanese Management System', in: Urabe, *et al.* (1988).

URABE, K., CHILD, J. and KAGONO, T. (1988) *Innovation and Management – International Comparisons*, Berlin: de Gruyter.

URABE, K. and OHMURA, K. (1983) *Nihonteki Roshikankei no Tankyu* (Explorations of Japanese Management and Labour Relations), Tokyo: Chuokeizaisha.

US Department of Commerce (1983) *Investment Climate in Foreign Countries*, Washington, DC: US Government Printing Office.

US Department of Commerce (1984) 'US Direct Investment Abroad in 1983', *Survey of Current Business*, 64, no. 8, pp. 18–40.

US office of the US Trade Representative (1983) *US National Study on Trade in Services: A Submission by the United States Government to the General Agreement on Tariffs and Trade*, US Government Printing Office, Washington, DC.

VAITSOS, C. (1981) 'Los Problemas del Empleo y las Empresas Transnacionales en los Paises en Desarrollo: Distorsiones y Desigualdad', in Fajnzylber, F. (ed.), *Industrializacion e Internacionalizacion en America Latina*, Vol. II, Mexico City: Fondo de Cultura Economica.

VENABLES, A.J. (1984) 'International Trade in Identical Commodities: Cournot Equilibrium with Free Entry', London: Centre for Economic Policy Research, Discussion Paper No. 9.

VERNON, R. (1966) 'International Investment and International Trade in the Product Life Cycle', *Quarterly Journal of Economics*, 80, pp. 190–207.

VERNON, R. (1971) *Sovereignty at Bay*, Harmondsworth: Penguin.

VERNON, R. (1979) 'The Product Cycle Hypothesis in a New International Environment', *Oxford Bulletin of Economics and Statistics*, 41, no. 4, pp. 255–67.

WAKASUGI, R. (1988) 'Characteristics of Japanese Corporate Behaviour: An Assessment of the Adjustment Process to the Yen Appreciation', Faculty of Economics, Shinshu University, Staff Paper Series.

WALLERSTEIN, I. (1979) *The Capitalist World-Economy*, Cambridge: Cambridge University Press.

WEEKLY, J.K. and AGGARWAL, R. (1987) *International Business: Operating in the Global Economy*, Hinsdale, ILL: The Dryden Press.

WEICK, K.E. (1979) *The Social Psychology of Organizing*, Reading, MA: Addison-Wesley.

WEIERMAIR, K. (1986) 'On the Economics of Institutional Change: An Institutional Change in Economics', *Journal of Economic Issues*, XX, no. 2, pp. 571–82.

WELLS, L.T. (1977) 'The Internationalisation of Firms from the Developing Countries', in Agmon, T. and Kindleberger, C.P. (eds.), *Multinationals from Small Countries*, Cambridge, MA: The MIT Press.

WELLS, L.T. (1972) 'International Trade: The Product Life Cycle Approach', in Wells, L.T. (ed.), *The Product Life Cycle and International Trade*, Boston: Division of Research, Harvard Business School.

WELLS, L.T. (1981) 'Foreign Investors from the Third World', in Kumar, K. and McLeod, M. (eds.), *Multinationals from Developing Countries*, Lexington, MA: Lexington Books.

WELLS, L.T. (1983) *Third World Multinationals*, Cambridge, MA: The MIT Press.

WELLS, L.T. (1986) 'Investment Incentives: An Unnecessary Debate', *The CTC Reporter*, 22, pp. 58–60.

WELLS, L.T. and ENCARNATION, D. (1986) 'Evaluating Foreign Investment', in Moran, T.H. (ed.) *Investing in Development: New Roles for Private Capital*, Washington, DC: Transaction Books, for the Overseas Development Council.

WEST, P. (1985) 'International Expansion and Concentration of Tire Industry and Implications for Latin America', in Newfarmer, R. (ed.), *Profits, Progress and Poverty: Case Studies of International Industries in Latin America*, Notre Dame, IN: University of Notre Dame Press.

WESTPHAL, L., RHEE, Y.W. and PURSELL, G. (1979) 'Foreign Influences on Korean Industrial Development', *Bulletin of the Oxford University Institute of Economics and Statistics*, 41, no. 4, pp. 359–88.

WHITE, M. and TREVOR, M. (1983) *Under Japanese Management*, London: Heinemann.

WIENER, M.J. (1981) *English Culture and the Decline of the Industrial Spirit*, Cambridge: Cambridge University Press.

WILLIAMSON, O. (1975) *Markets and Hierarchies: Analysis and Antitrust Implications*, New York: The Free Press.

WILLMORE, L. (1976) 'Direct Foreign Investment in Central American Manufacturing', *World Development*, 4, no. 6, pp. 499–517.

WILLMORE, L. (1986) 'The Comparative Performance of Foreign and Domestic Firms in Brazil', *World Development*, 14, no. 4, pp. 489–502.

World Bank (1985) *World Bank Development Report*, Oxford: Oxford University Press.

YACHIR, F. (1988) *Mining in Africa Today: Strategies and Prospects*, London: Zed Books.

YAMAMURA, K.Y. (1975) 'A Compromise with Culture: The Historical Evolution of the Managerial Structure of Large Japanese Firms', in Williamson, H.F. (ed.), *Evolution of International Management Structures*, Newark: University of Delaware Press.

YASUMURO, K. (1988) 'The Logic of Globalization in Japanese Enterprise', paper presented for the 4th International Conference on Multinational Enterprises, Taipei, Taiwan.

YAVAS, B.F. and VARDIABASIS, D. (1988) 'Countertrade: An Exploratory Assessment', *Yapi Kredi Economic Review*, 24, no. 4, pp. 37–48.

YOSHIDA, M. (1987) *Japanese Direct Manufacturing Investment in the United States*, New York: Praeger.

YOSHIHARA, H. and BARTLETT, CH. (1987) 'A New Paradigm for Thinking About Japanese Multinational Management: Can Japanese Firms Internationalize Using Local Management?' *Sekai Keizasi Hyoron*, 20, no. 3, pp. 48–54 (in Japanese).

YOSHINO, M.Y. (1968) *Japan's Managerial System: Tradition and Innovation*, Cambridge, MA: The MIT Press.

Index

Abegglen, J.C., 66
Abo, T., 70, 72
Acocella, N., 193, 221
advertising: in cross-sector studies of
    foreign investment and, 118
Africa: foreign direct investment in,
    16–17
  future of, 209–18
  resource-based, promotion of, 218–24
  sectoral comparison, 194–209
  sectoral distribution, 183–94
  by Yugoslavia, 229
Agarwal, J.P., 17, 130n
Aggarwal, R., 248–67, 319
Agmon, T., 267n, 268n
Ahiakpor, J., 116, 122
Akerlof, G.A., 146
Algeria
  foreign direct investment in, 200
  textiles industry, 270–3; exports,
      276–7; growth, 274; industry
      structure, 278–9; restructuring,
      290
Aliber, R.Z., 268n
Amano, M.M., 57
Angola: foreign direct investment in,
    200, 207
Aoki, M., 63
Archer, H., 207
Argentina
  foreign direct investment in, 187–90,
      215
  foreign investment, research on, 118,
      125, 127
Arndt, M., 299, 303, 306
Arrighi, G., 128
Arrow, K.J., 145
Artisien, P.F.R., 17, 225–47, 318
Asia: Swedish multinational enterprises
    in, 248–69
Astley, G.W., 58
Athos, A.G., 63
Australia: service exports, 294

backward linkages, failure to develop,
    30–1

Baker, A.M., 295, 297, 300
Balassa, B., 211
Balasubramanyam, V.N., 130n
Barbados: foreign direct investment in,
    189–90
Barro, R.J., 142
barter, 133–4, 139, 141
  in counterpurchase, 151
Bartlett, C.H., 70, 72
Beamish, P.W., 238
behavioural influences on foreign
    investment, 252–3
Belgium: foreign direct investment in
    Africa, 207
Benedict, R., 62
Benin: foreign direct investment in, 200
Bennet, D., 127
Berger, S., 28
Bernal, V., 118
Biersteker, T., 116, 122, 126, 127
Billerbeck, K., 15
Blomstrom, 296, 297
Boreham, G.F., 294
Botswana: foreign direct investment in,
    185–6, 188, 190, 200, 205
Bowman, J.S., 57
Brander, J.A., 82
Brazil
  foreign direct investment in, 187–90,
      215
  foreign investment, research on,
      119–22, 124–7
Britain
  foreign direct investment; in Africa,
      183–4, 191, 193, 199, 206–7;
      decline, 15
  and Maltese textiles, 282
  service-sector direct investment, 297
Buckley, P.J., 3–23, 27–55, 73, 134,
    147, 233, 237, 250, 267n, 268n, 318,
    319, 320
Burkina Faso: foreign direct investment
    in, 185, 188, 190–1, 201, 208
Burundi: foreign direct investment in,
    200
Business International, 149

343

buy-back arrangements, 134
and production sharing, 145–8

Calvet, A.L., 53
Cameroon: foreign direct investment in, 185, 188, 190–1, 194, 200, 208
Canada
and foreign direct investment in Africa, 220
service exports, 294
service-sector direct investment, 297
Cantwell, J.A., 16, 164, 183–223, 316, 318
capital
domestic and foreign direct investment, 172, 176
intensity of, 11–12
capital-intensive techniques, 92–103
and barriers to entry, 101–2
and market rivalry, 98–101
cartel cheating
in counterpurchase, 150–1
and discounting, 142–3
Carvalho, L., 117, 119, 121, 122, 124
Casson, M.C., 6–7, 11–13, 16, 19–20, 27–55, 73, 81, 129n, 133–59, 179n, 211, 250, 268n, 318–19, 320
Caves, R.E., 129, 180n, 268n
Central African Republic: foreign direct investment in, 185, 188, 190–1
by Yugoslavia, 229
centrally planned socialist economies, 133, 142
buy-back arrangements, 156–7
trade policy in, 143–5
Chen, E.K.Y., 115, 116, 117, 119, 121, 124, 220
Child, J., 62
Chile: foreign direct investment in, 187–90
China: foreign direct investment in, 189–90
Cho, Y.J., 298, 306, 307
Chudnovsky, D., 118, 125
Chukujama, F., 12, 133–62, 319
Chung, B., 117
Clark, R., 64
Clarke, D., 186, 193, 198, 207, 222
Clegg, J., 3–23, 248, 267n, 268n
clothing see textiles
Cohen, B.I., 115, 121, 122, 127
Cole, R.E., 62, 63
Colombia

foreign direct investment in, 187–90
foreign investment, research on, 119–22, 124, 127
communications
in less developed countries, 19
and process of development, 35
competitive individualism *vs* voluntary association, 33, 41–4
competitive strategy: cross-sector studies of foreign direct investment, 118
competitors in less developed countries, 11
Congo: foreign direct investment in, 185, 188, 190, 194, 200, 206–7
consensus in Japanese management systems, 63–4
contract, respect for, 41–2
Cook, P., 4
Costa Rica: foreign investment, research on, 119–22, 124
counterpurchase, 133
empirical study of, 149–56
as issue of commodity money, 138–9
policy implications of, 157–9
countertrade, 133–62
arrangements, 12–13
and export promotion, 148–9
policy implications for, 157–9
Cournot price equilibrium, 81
cross-sector studies of foreign direct investment, 113–24
advertising and competitive strategy, 118
research and development, 114–18
techniques, 113–14
trade strategy, 118–20
wages, 120–3
Cuddington, J.T., 143
culture
aspects of; in global trading systems, 44–9; in multinational enterprises operations, 50–3
entrepreneurial, 33–4
factors of and Japanese management systems, 61–2
influences on foreign direct investment, 252–3
currency
in counterpurchase, 150
preference and foreign direct investment, 252
Currie, J., 197, 220

David, K., 302, 303
de la Torre, J., 118
development, process, of 5–8, 32–5
and services, 292–6
Dick, A.R., 82
Dicken, P., 215
Digman, A.L., 57
discounting in countertrade, 141–3
disintegration of traditional social
groups and industrialisation, 31
divestment
foreign, 30
Yugoslav, reasons for, 242–6
Dixit, A.K., 93, 101
Djibouti: foreign direct investment in,
200
Dominican Republic: foreign direct
investment in, 189–90
Dore, R., 59, 63, 67
Dunning, J.H., 70, 75n, 123, 164–5,
168–73, 179n, 180n, 185, 187–9,
191–2, 194–8, 209, 222–3, 251,
268n, 313–21
Dutt, A.K., 179n
dynamic scale economies *see* scale
economies

ECLA, 121, 122
economic performance and
import-substituting investments, 29
Ecuador: foreign direct investment in,
189–90
by Yugoslavia, 239
Eden, L., 162n
education and Japanese management
systems, 61–2, 68–9
Egypt
foreign direct investment in, 185–6,
188, 190, 195–6, 201, 208
by Yugoslavia, 239
textiles industry, 270–3; exports,
276–7; growth, 274; industry
structure, 279–80; restructuring,
290
Eisenstadt, S.N., 27
Elisson, G., 263
Emmanuel, A., 111
employment and capital-intensive
techniques in less developed
countries, 103
Encarnation, D., 79
enclaves, confinement to, 30–1
Enderwick, P., 18, 19, 292–309

entrepôt potential, geographical
determinants of, 33, 35–9
entrepreneurial culture
moral aspects of, 33–4
technical aspects of, 33
entrepreneurship, 7
entry, barriers to, 101–2
environmental change and Japanese
management systems, 66–9
Ethiopia: foreign direct investment in,
201
Evans, P., 125, 126
exchange rates
and foreign direct investment, 173
overvalued, and technology transfer,
95–8
exports
earnings, stabilisation of, 140
of Mediterranean textiles, 276–7
promotion, 12; and countertrade,
148–9

Fagerstrom, C., 268n
Fairchild, L., 115, 119, 121, 127, 129n
Fajnzylber, F., 129n
Farrell, T., 179n
Fiji: foreign direct investment in, 189,
191
financial markets and foreign
investment, 251–2
firms: internationalisation, evolution of,
253–6
foreign direct investment, 3, 10–11
in Africa; future of, 209–18;
resource-based, promotion of,
218–24; sectoral comparison,
194–209; sectoral distribution,
183–94
distribution of, 15–19
factors influencing, 163–80, 250;
methodology, 170–5; results,
176–8
impact on less developed countries,
111–30; cross-sector studies,
113–24; industry studies, 125–8;
methodology, 112–13
instability of, 177–8
as modern imperialism, 252–3
process of, 250–3
resource-oriented, 14–15
theory of, 165–70
foreign divestments, 30
foreign exchange, scarcity of, 12

Forsgren, M., 261
Forsyth, D., 116, 124
forward selling in counterpurchase, 150
France: foreign direct investment in
    Africa, 183–4, 191, 193, 199, 206–7
Franko, L.G., 207, 268n
freedom of entry/exit, 41
Frisch, W., 162n
Frobel, F., 193, 221

Gabon: foreign direct investment in
    185–6, 189–90, 195, 201, 205, 208,
    219
Gambia: foreign direct investment in,
    201
Garvin, D.A., 57
General Tire, 127
geographical aspects of global trading
    systems, 44–9
geographical determinants of entrepôt
    potential, 33, 35–9
geographical distribution of Swedish
    firms, 257–9
Gereffi, G., 111
Gershenberg, I., 116, 121, 124
Gershuny, J., 294
Ghana: foreign direct investment in,
    201, 205, 207
        by Yugoslavia, 239
    foreign investment, research on, 122,
    124
Ghauri, P.N., 17, 248–67, 319
Gibbs, M., 303, 306, 307
global trading systems, geographical and
    cultural aspects of, 44–9
Goodman, L.W., 268n
Gorbachev, M., 315
government
    -business relations and Japanese
        management systems, 60–2
    policies; and capital-intensive
        techniques, 104; and foreign
        direct investment, 172
Graham, E.M., 10, 79–90, 268n, 319
Greece: textiles industry, 270–1, 273
    exports, 276–7
    growth, 274
    industry structure, 280–1
    restructuring, 290
Grieco, J., 129n
Grosher, E.L., 293
Grosse, R., 164
Grossman, H.I., 142
Grubel, H.G., 295, 297, 302

Guinea: foreign direct investment in,
    186, 191, 201, 216, 219
        by Yugoslavia, 239
Guisinger, S., 164, 179n
Guyana: foreign direct investment in,
    191

Hagen, E.E., 28
Hakansson, H. 268n
Hamill, J., 18, 270–91, 319
Hanaoka, M., 69
Hannigan, J.B., 149
Hayashi, K., 57
Hayek, F.A., 27
Hazama, H., 63
Heckscher-Ohlin-Samuelson model, 6
Heinrichs, J., 193, 221
Helleiner, G., 129n, 162n
Hennart, J.F., 179n
Herskovits, M.J., 27
Hindley, B., 300, 306
Hirsch, F., 34
Hodges, R., 36
Hong Kong
    foreign direct investment in, 189–90,
        197, 220
    foreign investment, research on, 119,
        121
Hornell, E., 249, 268n
Horst, T., 268n
Horwitz, E.C., 262
Hoselitz, B.F., 28
Humphrey, J., 128
Hymer, S., 3, 179n, 268n, 320

ILO, 130n
Imai, K.I., 62, 63, 66, 69
import restriction and capital-intensive
    techniques, 104–5
India
    foreign direct investment in, 187–8
        Swedish, 248, 263; by
        Yugoslavia, 226, 239
    foreign investment, research on, 119
individualism
    aspects of, 41–4
    and groups, 42–3
    lack of, 42
Indonesia: foreign direct investment in,
    187–8, 189–90
    Swedish, 249, 266
industrialisation and disintegration of
    traditional social groups, 31
industry, structure and socially

sub-optimal behåviour, 80–2
infrastructure, development of and foreign investment, 172
Ingles, J., 129n
Inkeles, A., 27
interest rates, differences in and foreign investment, 251
inter-firm relations and Japanese management systems, 60–2
internal relations in foreign subsidiaries, 31
international debt crisis, 4
international trade
  development of, 45–9
  in less developed countries, 47–9
investment
  import-substituting, economic performance and scale, 29
  resource-based; performance, 30
  in service sector of less developed countries, 296–300; outward, 301–4
Iran: foreign direct investment by Yugoslavia, 240
Ishida, H., 75
Ishimura, S., 75
Italy:
  and foreign direct investment in Africa, 183–4, 193
  in Maltese textiles, 282
  service-sector direct investment, 297
Itami, H., 62
Ivanson, C., 268n
Iwata, R., 63

Jacobs, W.G., 57
Jagren, L., 260, 262
Jamaica: foreign direct investment in, 189–91
Jansson, H., 268n
Japan
  foreign direct investment; in Africa, 184, 216; decline, 15
  foreign security companies in, 303
  management practices, 7–8
  management systems, 56–76; change and adaptations, 66–9; and multinational enterprises, 73–5; organisational factors; 58–66; strategies and style, 57–8; transferability, 69–73
  service exports, 294
  service-sector direct investment, 297

Jenkins, R., 11, 92, 107, 111–29, 179n, 318
Jo, S., 130n
Johansson, P.O., 143
joint ventures, with Yugoslavia, 231, 237–42
Jordan: foreign direct investment by Yugoslavia, 240
Jouet, J., 118
Juergens, V., 70

Kagono, T., 66
Kaplinski, R., 196
Karsh, B., 65
Katrak, H., 10–11, 92–107, 319
Kaynak, E., 268n, 295, 305
Kenya
  foreign direct investment in, 185–6, 189–91, 196, 201, 206–9, 219
    by Yugoslavia, 229–30, 240
  foreign investment, research on, 118, 125
Kilby, P., 28
Kim, S., 228, 246, 301–2, 304
Kindleberger, C.P., 267n, 268n
Kirim, A., 118
Kirkpatrick, C.H., 4
Kirzner, I.M., 27
Knickerbocker, F.T., 268n
Kogut, B., 146
Kojima, K., 74
Kono, T., 58
Koo, B.Y., 115, 124, 180n, 217–18
Korea, Republic of: service exports, 294
Kreye, O., 193, 221
Krugman, P.R., 82, 83, 268n
Kujawa, D., 70
Kumar, N., 119, 228, 246

labour
  divisions of in entrepôt centre, 36
  force and foreign direct investment, 172
  markets and Japanese management systems, 63–4, 67–8
  productivity gap, 96–7
labour-intensive techniques in less developed countries, 92–103
  and barriers to entry, 101–2
  and market rivalry, 98–101
lag structure and foreign direct investment, 176

Lall, S., 53, 92, 112, 114, 119, 120, 179n, 180n, 220, 222, 224n, 232, 237, 246, 268n
Landi, J.H., 222
Langdon, S., 118, 125
learning, economies of, 9–10, 82–4
Lebanon: foreign direct investment in by Yugoslavia, 226
Lecraw, D.J., 116, 121–2, 133, 149, 162n, 163–80, 228, 231–2, 236–7, 246, 301, 304, 313–14, 316, 318
Lee, C., 117
Lee, S.M., 64
Leibenstein, H., 32, 58, 59, 76n
Lesotho: foreign direct investment in, 202
less developed countries
  buy-back arrangements, 156–7
  capital-intensive *vs* labour-intensive techniques, 92–7; and market rivalry, 98–101
  concept of, 5–6
  counterpurchase in, 149–56
  countertrade in, 133–62
  foreign direct investment; impact of, 111–30; theory of, 165–70; by Yugoslavia, 225–47
  foreign regional centres in, 263–5
  and Japanese multinational enterprises, 73–5
  and multinational enterprises; interactions, 27–55; in service sector, 292–309
  and newly industrialised countries, 4
  policies of, 21–2
  trade policies, 3–4
Lessard, D.R., 268n
Levy, B., 130n
Liberia: foreign direct investment in, 184–6, 187, 189–90, 196, 201, 206, 219
Libya:
  foreign direct investment in, 185–6, 189–90, 196, 202
  by Yugoslavia, 240
  in Maltese textiles, 282
Lim, D., 115, 122, 124
Lin, T., 130n
Linder, S.B., 6
Lipsey, R.E., 269n
loans, in counterpurchase, 150–1
Lofgren, K.G., 143
Lundstrom, R., 268n

McClelland, D.C., 28
Macduffie, J.P., 66, 71
McMillan, C.H., 149, 225–6, 247n
Madagascar: foreign direct investment in, 202
Magdoff, H., 268n
Malawi: foreign direct investment in, 185–6, 189–91, 197, 202
Malaysia
  foreign direct investment in, 189–90
    Swedish, 266
  foreign investment, research on, 121–2, 124
  service exports, 294
Mali: foreign direct investment in, 202
Malta: textiles industry, 270–1
  exports, 276–7
  growth, 274
  industry structure, 281–2
  restructuring, 290
management systems in Japan, 56–76
Mannari, H., 63
March, J.G., 64
market
  domestic growth and foreign direct investment, 173
  export for Mediterranean textiles, 273–7
  forward in countertrade, 139–41
  imperfect and foreign direct investment, 250–1
  protection of and foreign direct investment, 251
  rivalry in less developed countries, 98–101
  structure; in countertrade, 134–5; and foreign direct investment, 251
Marsh, L., 114, 115, 121, 122
Marsh, R., 63
Martinez Tarrage, T., 129n
Mashayekhi, M., 303, 306, 307
Mason, R., 117, 122, 124
Maurice, M., 62
Mauritania: foreign direct investment in, 187, 197, 202
Mauritius: foreign direct investment in, 185, 202, 219–20
Mediterranean textiles
  future prospects, 288–91
  industry; restructuring, 290–1; structure, 277–86
  international competition, 286–8
  overview of, 272–7

Meller, P., 130n
Melz, H., 70
Mexico:
  foreign direct investment in, 187–90,
    215
    by Yugoslavia, 228, 240
  foreign investment, research on,
    118–22, 124–5, 127
Michaely, M., 160
Mikdashi, Z., 217
Miles, I., 294
minimum wage *see* wages
mining and foreign investment in
  Africa, 186–7, 191, 194–5, 209
Mirus, R., 138, 146, 162n
Mirza, H., 75n, 24n
Mizala, A., 130n
models in international economics, 6
Mok, V., 130n
Momigliano, F., 294
money
  commodity, counterpurchase as issue
    of, 138–9
  role of in international trade, 135–7
  theory of in countertrade, 134
monopoly, advantage of and
  internationalisation, 250–1
Montavon, R., 126
Morgan, G., 73
Morgenstern, R., 121
Morley, S., 114, 115, 117
Morocco
  foreign direct investment in, 185,
    189–91, 197, 202, 208, 283
    by Yugoslavia, 241
  textiles industry, 270–3; exports,
    276–7; growth, 275; industry
    structure, 282–4; restructuring,
    290–1
Mozambique: foreign direct investment
  in, 202
Mroczowski, T., 69
Muller, R., 121
multinational enterprises
  dynamic scale economies, 82–9
  and foreign direct investment; factors
    influencing, 163–80; by
    Yugoslavia, 225–47
  and industrial development in Africa,
    183–224
  and less developed countries;
    interactions, 27–55; and Japanese
    management systems, 73–5

and Mediterranean textiles, 277–86
operations, cultural aspects of, 50–3
in service sector, 292–309
smaller-country, 256
socially sub-optimal behaviour, 80–2
and strategic trade policy, 79–91
studies of, changes in, 313–18
Swedish, evolution of, 248–69
multilateralism, 135–6

Naim, M., 53
Nakatani, T., 67, 68, 69
Namibia: foreign direct investment in,
  186, 203, 219
Nanto, D.K., 57
Negandhi, A.R., 269n
Nelson, P.R., 58, 59, 65, 76n
Nemoto, T., 68
Netherlands, 282
Newbery, D.M.G., 170
Newbould, G.D., 233
Newfarmer, R., 111, 114, 115, 120, 121,
  122, 129n
newly industrialised countries
  and foreign direct investment, 216,
    221–2
  and less developed countries, 4
Nicholas, S., 149
Niger: foreign direct investment in, 186,
  203
Nigeria
  foreign direct investment in, 184–7,
    191, 197–8, 203, 207–8, 219
    by Yugoslavia, 241
  foreign investment, research on, 122
Nonaka, I., 58, 63, 66, 69, 73
Norton, D., 294

OECD, 296
Ohmura, K., 63
oil
  and foreign direct investment in
    Africa, 195, 208
  price shock; and foreign divestments,
    30; and Japanese management
    systems, 66–7
Okimura, A., 66
Olofsson, B., 268n
options in forward markets, 139–40
Ouchi, W.G., 57, 63, 64
ownership
  in Japanese corporations, 63
  patterns in Yugoslav foreign
    investment, 235–42

Ozawa, T., 70, 74, 216, 217, 221

Pack, H., 32, 114
Pakistan: foreign direct investment in,
    189–90
  Swedish, 248–9, 263
Paliwoda, S., 149
Panama: foreign direct investment in,
    189–90
Papua New Guinea: foreign direct
    investment in, 187–8
Paraguay: foreign direct investment in,
    189–90
Park, S.G., 70
Parsons, J.E., 139
Pascale, R.T., 63
pay systems in Japanese corporations,
    63–4
Pearce, R.D., 11, 13, 20, 29, 129n, 211
Pegels, C., 59, 60
Peron, J., 127
Peru
  foreign direct investment in, 187–90
  foreign investment, research on, 124
Philippines
  foreign direct investment in, 187–8,
    189–90
    Swedish, 249, 258, 264–6
  foreign investment, research on, 122,
    124
  service exports, 294
Piore, M.J., 28
portfolio theory and foreign direct
    investment, 252
ports as entrepôt centres, 36–8
Possas, L., 129n
price: in countertrade, 134
product life-cycle and foreign direct
    investment, 17–18
product life-cycle
  theory of; and firm
    internationalisation, 253–6;
    phases of, 254–5; and
    smaller-country multinational
    enterprises, 256
product market and Japanese
    management systems, 59
production sharing, 134
  and buy-back arrangements, 145–8
production and Japanese management,
    70–2
property, alienability of, 41, 43
Pursell, G., 127

Rada, J.F, 293, 297
Radhu, G., 130n
Rampersad, E.G., 268n
Randsepp, E., 57
Ranis, G., 116
Reed, H.D., 268n
Rehder, R.R., 62
resale in forward markets, 139
research and development, cross-sector
    studies of foreign direct investment
    on, 114–18
resources
  for development, 7
  and foreign direct investment, 173
Reuber, G., 164
Rhee, Y.W., 127
Richardson, J.B., 299, 307
Richardson, J.D., 268n
Richter, C., 297
Riddell, R.C., 198
Riddle, D.I., 294, 295, 296, 298
Riedel, J., 115, 121, 122, 123
risk in foreign direct investment
    strategy, 171
Rojec, M., 17, 225–47, 318
Rontanen, P., 149
Rowe, N., 162n
Royama, S., 63
Ruch, V.W., 57
Rugman, A.M., 179n
Rwanda: foreign direct investment in,
    203
Ryan, T., 116, 121, 124

Sakakibara, K., 66
Salter, W.E.G., 93, 94
Sans, A., 268n
Saudi Arabia: foreign direct investment
    in, 184, 189, 191
Savary, J., 193
scale
  economies, dynamic, 82–9
  and import-substituting investments,
    29
Schive, C., 116
Schonberger, R., 70
Schotter, A., 76n
Schumpeter, J.A., 27, 34
Schwendiman, G., 64
scientific outlook, 33, 39–40
Senegal: foreign direct investment in,
    185, 203, 208

service sector
  growth of; in less developed
    countries, 19; rates, 298
  investment in less developed
    countries, 296–300
  multinational enterprises in less
    developed countries, 292–309
  policy issues, 304–8
Sethi, S.P., 63
Seychelles: foreign direct investment in,
  185, 203
Shapiro, D.M., 268n
Sharpe, K., 127
Shepherd, P., 125
Shimada, H., 66, 70, 71
Shimazu, 74
Sierra Leone: foreign direct investment
  in, 185, 198, 203
Simoẽs, V.C., 180n
Simon, H.A., 64
Singapore
  foreign direct investment in, 187–8,
    189–90
  foreign investment, research on,
    121–2
  service exports, 294
Siniscalco, D., 294
Smith, D.H., 27
Smith, G., 114, 115, 117
social factors in Japanese management
  systems, 61–2
socially sub-optimal behaviour, 80–2
Solomon, R., 116, 124
Somalia: foreign direct investment in,
  203
Sosin, K., 115, 127
Sours, M.H., 294, 295, 296, 298
South Korea
  foreign direct investment in, 187–90
  foreign investment, research on,
    121–2, 124, 127
  outward investment, 301–2
Spence, A.M., 84–6, 88
Spencer, B., 82
Sri Lanka: foreign direct investment in,
  189–90
Stackelberg price leader, 81
Stalk, G., 66
Standing, C., 113, 124
status equalisation in Japanese
  corporations, 63
Stiglitz, J.E., 170
Stopford, J.M., 204, 316

Streeten, P., 53, 120, 179n
subcontracting, 145
subsidiaries
  foreign, internal relations in, 31
  and scale economies, 83–4, 89–90
  of Swedish firms, 257–9, 263–5
  of Yugoslav corporations, 231
Sudan: foreign direct investment in, 203
Svetlicic, M., 17, 225–47, 318
Swainson, N., 191, 193, 196, 207, 222
Swaziland: foreign direct investment in,
  203
Sweden
  firms in Asia, 248–69
  foreign direct investment; in Africa,
    220; international growth of
    firms, 248–9, 257–67; nature and
    growth of, 257–62; recent
    developments, 263–7
Swedenborg, B., 248, 259, 261, 268n
systems thinking, 33, 39–40

Taira, K., 113, 124
Taiwan
  foreign direct investment in, 189–90
  foreign investment, research on,
    121–2
  service exports, 294
Tanzania: foreign direct investment in,
  185, 189–91, 198, 204, 206
taxation, 172–3
techniques of cross-sector studies of
  foreign direct investment, 113–14
technology
  capital-intensive, use of, 30
  receipts from affiliated companies
    (US), 300
  transfer, 19–21; failure of, 30; and
    minimum wage, 94–8
Teece, D.J., 97–8, 179n
textiles
  and clothing, foreign direct
    investment for, 18
  Mediterranean *see* Mediterranean
    textiles
Thailand
  foreign direct investment in, 187–8,
    189–90
    Swedish, 248–9, 263, 265–6
  foreign investment, research on,
    121–2
  service exports, 294
Thurley, K., 70

Thurwell, J., 233
Togo: foreign direct investment in, 185, 204
Tokunaga, S., 65
Tolentino, P., 224n
Tomer, J.F., 66
Toshimasu, T., 60
trade
  international and role of money, 135–7
  multilateral, 42
  policies, 3–4; in centrally planned socialist economies, 143–5; strategic, 79–91
  strategy of in cross-sector studies of foreign direct investment, 118–20
transaction costs in countertrade, 134–5
transferability of Japanese management systems, 69–73
transnational corporations *see* multinational enterprises
transport
  and communications in less developed countries, 19
  systems and process of development, 35–7
Trevor, M., 69, 70
Trinidad and Tobago: foreign direct investment in, 189–90
Tunisia:
  foreign direct investment in, 204, 207–8
    by Yugoslavia, 241
  textiles industry, 270–3; exports, 276–7; growth, 275; industry structure, 284–5; restructuring, 291
Turkey
  foreign direct investment in, 285
    by Yugoslavia, 227
  foreign investment, research on, 118
  textiles industry, 270–1, 273; exports, 276–7; growth, 275; industry structure, 285–6; restructuring, 291

Uganda
  foreign direct investment in, 204
    by Yugoslavia, 241
  foreign investment, research on, 121, 124
UNCTAD, 294, 295, 305, 307
United States
  foreign direct investment; in Africa,

184, 206–7; decline, 15, 256
  in Maltese textiles, 282
  service exports, 294
  service-sector direct investment, 297
  technology receipts from affiliated companies, 300
Urabe, K., 63

Vahlne, J.E., 249, 268n
Vaitsos, C., 124, 130n
value-added local maximisation of, 9
van den Bulcke, D., 162n
Vardiabasis, D., 146
Varvias, C., 224n
Venables, A.J., 82
Venezuela: foreign direct investment in, 187–9, 191
Vernon, R., 6, 118, 253, 268n
voluntary association *vs* competitive individualism, 33, 41–4

wages
  cross-sector studies of foreign direct investment, 120–3
  and foreign direct investment, 173–4
  minimum in less developed countries, 94–8
Wakasugi, R., 67
Wallerstein, I., 28
Weick, K.E., 58
Weiermair, K., 7, 12, 20, 56–75, 76n, 318, 319, 320
welfare, and capital-intensive techniques, 103–4
Wells, L.T., 79, 179n, 228, 229, 232, 236, 246, 253, 256, 267n, 268n, 301, 316
West Germany
  foreign direct investment; in Africa, 183–4, 193, 216; decline, 15
  in Maltese textiles, 282
  service sector direct investment, 297
West, P., 127
Westphal, L., 127
White, M., 70
Wiener, M.J., 45
Wilkins, M., 207
Williamson, O., 58
Willmore, L., 113, 114, 117, 118, 121, 122, 124
Winter, D.G., 28
Winter, S.G., 58, 59, 65, 76n
World Bank, 164
Worm, P., 70

Yachir, F., 187, 191, 209, 216
Yamamura, K.Y., 59, 73
Yasugi, Y., 15
Yavas, B.F., 146
Yeung, B., 138, 146, 162n
Yoshida, M., 72
Yoshihara, H., 70, 72
Yoshihara, K., 75
Yoshino, M.Y., 62, 63
Yugoslavia: foreign direct investment,
  17, 225–47
  background to, 225–9
  divestment, 242–6

motivation for, 231–5
ownership patterns, 235–42
profile of, 229–31

Zaire: foreign direct investment in,
  184–5, 187, 204, 208–9, 216, 219
Zambia
  foreign direct investment in, 184–5,
  187, 189–91, 198, 204, 219
  by Yugoslavia, 241
Zimbabwe: foreign direct investment in,
  184–7, 189–91, 198–9, 204, 206–8,
  219